praise for *Wild Flavors*

"With brilliance, love, and a sense of humor, Didi Emmons captures the wild and wacky spirit of Eva Sommaripa and her world of herbs. She walks you through Eva's garden and into her kitchen where you'll want to dive in, roll up your sleeves and start cooking with lovage, purslane, and all kinds of plants you may never have heard of before, but probably could find in your own backyard."

—JODY ADAMS, chef, Rialto Restaurant

"If you are a city person, like me, with a secret yen to forage for wild greens, *Wild Flavors* is an inspiration. Read it, and you will want to harvest, share, and eat everything you find. Emmons's friend Eva, a committed and skilled forager and grower, not only creates delicious meals from home-grown foods, but also creates a community built around wild foods as a way of life. Best, Emmons's recipes are lovely and easy to follow."

—MARION NESTLE, professor of nutrition, food studies, and public health, NYU, and author of *Food Politics* and *What to Eat*

"*Wild Flavors* is a down-to-earth book rich in ideas and inspiration for people seeking to eat from their gardens and local areas. It's filled with mouth-watering recipes and valuable cultivation, shopping, and storage tips. But more than anything, this book is a celebration of the ethics and wisdom of Eva Sommaripa, the farmer whose herbs and outlook transformed Didi Emmons and prompted her to write this book. Eva has manifested throughout her life the kind of aspirations many are just now coming to hold. May this sharing of Eva's story help empower more people to realize their dreams of becoming more connected to the land and other creatures."

—SANDOR ELLIX KATZ, author of *Wild Fermentation* and *The Revolution Will Not Be Microwaved*

"Didi Emmons, a local rock star of vegetarian cuisine, has written a lovely and unique cookbook, jam-packed with yummy recipes for using every-thing a plant has to offer—the bulbs, stalks, leaves, flowers, and fruits. This book fills an important niche in the cookbook world."

—MELISSA KOGUT, executive director, Chefs Collaborative

"Didi Emmons has long been a hero to me. She teaches, tempts, and trans-forms all of our senses, even our common sense. Let her artistry open our eyes and taste buds to the wild flavors all around us. Enjoy!"

—FRANCES MOORE LAPPÉ, author of *Diet for a Small Planet* and *EcoMind*

wild flavors

One Chef's Transformative Year
Cooking from Eva's Farm

DIDI EMMONS

Chelsea Green Publishing
White River Junction, Vermont

All photographs are by Didi Emmons, unless
otherwise credited.
Photos on pages 7, 15, 34 (skillets), 51, 57, 71, 123,
161, 164, 173, 231, 249, 275, and 286
are by Lolita Parker, Jr.

Project Manager: Patricia Stone
Developmental Editor: Ben Watson
Copy Editor: Nancy Ringer
Proofreader: Susan Barnett
Indexer: Linda Hallinger
Designer: Sterling Hill Productions
Printed in the United States of America
First printing September, 2011
10 9 8 7 6 5 4 3 2 1   11 12 13 14 15

green press INITIATIVE

Chelsea Green Publishing is committed to preserving
ancient forests and natural resources. We elected to print
this title on FSC®-certified paper containing at least 10%
postconsumer recycled paper, processed chlorine-free.
As a result, for this printing, we have saved:

19 Trees (40' tall and 6-8" diameter)
8,904 Gallons of Wastewater
8 million BTUs Total Energy
564 Pounds of Solid Waste
1,975 Pounds of Greenhouse Gases

Chelsea Green Publishing made this paper choice
because we are a member of the Green Press Initiative,
a nonprofit program dedicated to supporting authors,
publishers, and suppliers in their efforts to reduce their
use of fiber obtained from endangered forests. For more
information, visit www.greenpressinitiative.org.

Environmental impact estimates were made using the Environmental Defense Paper Calculator. For more information visit: www
.papercalculator.org.

Our Commitment to Green Publishing

Chelsea Green sees publishing as a tool for cultural change and ecological stewardship. We strive to align our
book manufacturing practices with our editorial mission and to reduce the impact of our business enterprise
in the environment. We print our books and catalogs on chlorine-free recycled paper, using vegetable-based
inks whenever possible. This book may cost slightly more because we use recycled paper, and we hope you'll
agree that it's worth it. Chelsea Green is a member of the Green Press Initiative (www.greenpressinitiative.
org), a nonprofit coalition of publishers, manufacturers, and authors working to protect the world's endangered forests and conserve natural resources. *Wild Flavors* was printed on FSC®-certified paper supplied by RR
Donnelley that contains at least 10-percent postconsumer recycled fiber.

Library of Congress Cataloging-in-Publication Data

Emmons, Didi, 1963-
Wild flavors : one chef's transformative year cooking from Eva's farm / Didi Emmons.
    p. cm.
Includes index.
ISBN 978-1-60358-285-8
1. Cooking (Herbs) 2. Cooking (Vegetables) 3. Herb gardens--Anecdotes. I. Title.

TX819.H4E52 2011
641.6'57--dc23

2011024501

Chelsea Green Publishing Company
Post Office Box 428
White River Junction, VT 05001
(802) 295-6300
www.chelseagreen.com

CONTENTS

ACKNOWLEDGMENTS

Thanks to:

Marjorie Williams, my heroine. I could not fathom a better book coach.

Polly, my older sister, for her love and impeccably sage guidance over the many years.

Kelly Lake, who did much heavy lifting as an editor, writer, and researcher of this book. You are a machine.

Henry MacLean, who supported and loved me through my crazy deadlines and helped me editorially wherever and whenever needed.

Ann Gallager, with an artful eye, an expansive brain, and a big heart, for designing and developing my website.

Beverly Ducat, who deftly put out countless crises.

Laura Zientek, my cool-headed recipe coordinator and recipe editor.

Tim Towner, Mary Broderick, Ruth Reynolds, and others who came to my aid through Recovery International.

Sally Cheek, for her steadfast pragmatic wisdom and insights.

Lisa Thoren, my oldest sister, for guidance of the heart.

Lolita Parker, Jr., for her brilliant photographs and good times.

My backyard boys Charlie and Flynn, for their furry faithfulness and unfading love.

The good people at Chelsea Green: Joni Praded, my bright and level-headed editor; Ben Watson, my developmental editor, for preserving my voice; Pati Stone, a most-kind project manager; and Nancy Ringer, whose eagle eyes caught every possible glitch (I think). And thanks to Margo Baldwin, Susan Warner, and everyone else at Chelsea Green for a fantastically positive publishing experience.

Jack MacDonald and Thomas MacLean, for their talented word spinning.

Foragers David Craft and Russ Cohen for their editorial help and appreciation of wild plants.

Khris Flack and Kerry Jordan for their upbeat trusty editorial help.

Kathryn Deputat, who plowed my emotive fields guiding me toward this book via Dublin, Ireland.

Courtney Hester and Sage Cohen, for warm companionship and editorial support.

Darry Madden, for engineering the organization of the book.

Jon and David Strymish, who inspired me to write books in the first place.

All those at the farm and nearby who helped in the process, especially Alan Poole and farmhands Peter Levasseur, Bill Braun, and Ed Bakke.

Barbi Sanderson, for her feedback, support, and sprout expertise, as well as for being an excellent recipe tester.

Amy Bradford for being the most avid tester in the midst of her three young children. And to all my other diligent and devoted testers: Sharla Haperin, Brian Barnes, Rosemary Melli, Melissa Witcher, Marla Felcher, Roz Emmons, Robin Heyden, Carol Staszewski, Maryann Francis, Chris Laing, Arthur Lizzie, Lori Galvin, Roz Cummins, and last but not least, Diana Limbach.

My nieces Lee Tilghman, who taught me that butter tastes better than oil when making granola, and Lindsay Thoren, the ultimate cheerleader.

Andy and Amy Burnes, as well as their regal cows.

Leo and Niko Sommaripa, as well as Christina Erikson, thanks for being so kind and caring.

The chefs who gave me their time: Jamie Bissonette, Tony Maws, Chuck Draghi, Jim Mercer, Seth Morrison, Jason Bond, Patrick Campbell, Jim Stringer, Adam Halberg, Maura Kilpatrick, Paul King, Jay Murray, Peter McCarthy, Keith Pooler, Mike Pagliarini, Greg Reeves, and Patrick Connolly.

Trevor Corson, for sharing his photo of Eva's garden in the Introduction.

Jessica Gath, for her miniature cake baking and photographs.

Neil Young and Bob Dylan for their music.

Daniel Glazer and Jamie Class for their dutiful taste testing.

Herbalist Brittany Nickerson.

Roz and Harry Emmons, my parents and venerable foodies.

Terri at Blissful Monkey Yoga, for keeping my spirit intact, and those who work at making my Americanos at JP Licks.

My first coach, Becky Tuch; Bing Broderick, Kathe McKenna, Beth Ingham, Carol Steinfeld, and Sam Tan for their solid support; Lynette Ng and Barbara Harris for their editing help; Lesli Turock; Fulani Haynes; and my best friend, Germana; as well as anyone I may have forgotten. This book could not have been written save for many voices cheering me on.

Jamie Oliver and Michelle Obama, for spearheading the shift to healthy eating that will help heal many problems.

And finally, to Eva Sommaripa, who has inspired me, along with a sea of other chefs and cooks, with her generosity and garden genius.

INTRODUCTION

It was September 2001. My business partner and I had just opened a restaurant
in Cambridge, Massachusetts, the same
week as 9/11—clearly not the most auspi-
cious time for launching a new venture.

Despite the somber mood, a farmer
named Eva Sommaripa sent us a fax, offering us her herbs and including a friendly
note in the margin wishing us good luck.
I got a little overly excited about the fax, as
she was a bit of a legend. I had been hearing
about Eva for years, and the food writers
at the *Boston Globe* relied on her for articu-
late and outspoken quotes in many a food
article. Eva was a household name in the
most discriminating restaurants in the
Boston area—I know, because by that time I
had worked in many of them.

So I gave her a ring. We had a lovely
conversation. But at that point I decided
that I couldn't spend the kind of money
her wares required. My food budget was
nothing like a high-end restaurant's; I was
serving affordable pizza. Nonetheless, she
extended an invitation to visit her farm.

A month or so later I drove 80 miles
southeast of Boston to see Eva's Garden.
Nearing her farm, I found myself pass-
ing miles of old stone walls meandering
through grassy pastures, with cows loung-
ing and sniffing at the air. As I came up
over the crest of a hill, there lay the Atlantic
Ocean stretched out before me, breathtaking, vast, and completely unexpected. A few
turns later and I arrived at Eva's Garden.

As I walked toward the house, a slen-
der sixty-something woman was talking to
a male farmhand picking flowers. I sensed
the woman was Eva—she looked like she
had been plucked from the earth like a
parsnip: her pants were mud-stained, her
hands and fingers encrusted with dirt, and
her black-gray hair looked blown about by
heavy gales. She was talking alternately
into a cordless phone and to the farmhand.
I finally interrupted her by introducing
myself, and her face widened into a smile.
"Oh, *Didi*! Welcome! So glad you made it.
I wish I could show you around but unfortunately I am beset with unforeseen

emergencies. We lost electricity this morning along with forty-two phone messages, the flea beetles are decimating our arugula, and I just heard that our delivery truck backed into a BMW in Boston. Please wander and make yourself at home."

So I began to explore. Herbs and flowers inundated the landscape. Wild grapes scampered along her clothesline—charged with a penetrating grape flavor alone making the trip worthwhile. In random places colossal unearthed rocks were stacked to form handsome sculptures. Walking out of a greenhouse, I caught a glimpse of some tiny neon-yellow birds I had never seen before, darting in and out of the bushes. It felt like I was in Camelot. I ate all the herbs that I could recognize; the rest I simply inhaled. There was an herb that tasted like basil crossed with mulled cider, a red hairy fern that tasted like licorice candy, and rosemary that had such a potent saplike scent that the built-up tension in my shoulders instantly melted away. After an hour, my tongue was overloaded and numb. Still, I had covered only a small percentage of the farm: this was like the botanical version of the Louvre, impossible to absorb in a single day. Everything I tasted was so insanely good that I even began to wonder if the farm were plugged into some greater life force.

Toward the end of my edible trek, I dug my sandals into the soft, black earth and I felt a yearning. It was a feeling, a sense that I wanted to be a part of whatever was going on in this Shangri-la with all its flavors, energy, and culinary possibilities.

So I started to visit Eva's farm on a regular basis, and Eva didn't seem to mind. In fact she was ecstatic. I'd pick greens and herbs, then cook in her galley kitchen, and later she'd insist that I spend the night. Soon a steady stream of Eva's friends started to filter in for dinner and we would eat, drink, and converse. Eva would inevitably entertain us by reciting Wordsworth or Dickinson or singing us a dark-humored song slightly off-key—sometimes alongside some of her other like-minded off-key friends. Eva had a seemingly endless supply of colorful friends, many of them farmers or local food producers, but also high school counselors, artists, college professors, and others. Some loom large in my memory, like Katy, the Cornell animal behaviorist who told us the story of a seven-hour life-or-death staring contest she had with a male lion through a giant hole in a fence on an African prairie.

Eva's became my weekend getaway. It was like home to me, only better. The garden and surrounding area provided beauty and food unmatched by what the city offered, and once I returned home, I'd mope and drag myself around for a day or two. Then after a week I'd feel the undertow of Eva's garden pulling me back. Over the course of ten years, Eva and her garden transformed not only my cooking but also how I live.

I have to attribute most of my cooking transformation to Eva's peerless quality—the power of food grown extremely well, freshly severed from its life source. But Eva's creativity and the unusual herbs and foraged foods she cultivated were a continuous revelation to me as well. Every month I made new discoveries: African basil, calaminth, East Indian lemongrass, lovage, sunchokes. And I would cook up a storm in Eva's tiny, jam-packed galley kitchen. Her fridge always held an army of jars filled with recent infusions, captured from food scraps I would have discarded: stems of herbs, parsnip peels, onion tops, bruised tomatoes, the liquid from beans or any number of vegetables cooked in the pressure cooker. The nearest supermarket was a thirty-minute drive away, and I never missed it. I became dependent not just on local food, but like extreme-skiing, this was extreme-local—food that was grown or killed within a stone's throw of the farm. And because of Eva's savvy, even in the winter there was always enough food in her freezer, her in-ground barrels, or her greenhouses, no matter how many friends came to eat. Her food reflected her deep devotion to sustainability. Chef Jason Bond from Bondir restaurant in Cambridge, Massachusetts, once said "It's hard to find people who care as deeply as Eva does about the results of their actions. Eva does what she thinks is right and that is about her only deciding factor."

I'll never forget when Jason came to visit in the dank of winter and picked a salad in Eva's stark greenhouse, he found a dizzying array of greens, flowers, and weeds but to do so he had to snip away on his knees with tiny scissors in 30-degree weather for an hour. The plants were an inch tall, but the salad was so flavorful it needed no dressing.

I evolved as a cook. No longer did I need to seek inspiration from a cookbook; I let the garden speak to me directly. If the rhubarb was plump and luscious, my eyes would tell my mind to braise it with butter for fish, or cook it down into a chutney for venison, or puree it for a rose and rhubarb sorbet. And when the purslane was sprawling a mile a minute, it would leap into the evening's menu, maybe as a salad to cushion a piece of fish along with some bronze fennel, fresh cranberries, bulgur, olive oil, and good balsamic vinegar. What a rush, to have a garden inform me in every part of the meal.

Eva's intense herbs and vegetables became the building blocks I used in designing meals. And they carried so much flavor that they needed little help from common crutches like cheese, cream, pasta, meat, and spices. This was convenient, because these were the very ingredients Eva had little of. Her spices were ancient. She had no white flour, white sugar, white rice, heavy cream, or tomato paste. The complexity of her herbs and the powerful sweet flavor of her vegetables made for most of the flavor I needed. Whether I'd decide to make a teacake from parsnips, a pesto from goosefoot, or a salad from weeds, there seemed to be no end to new combinations and treatments. And Eva always applauded creativity, thank God.

I became healthier for eating such fresh flavorful food. Over a weekend, I'd find that I had more energy and I'd lose a tummy roll if I stayed a week. Things flowed better—internally, that is. None of us would ever need to diet if we could all eat as much plant food as Eva does; we'd all be eating more food, though, and it would taste so much better and more satisfying, more alive.

Eva has been a role model for me in so many ways. For instance, I have always had a strong distaste for consumerism. Eva showed me how to refrain from judging others, but at the same time to revel in and celebrate my own values. Why replace my rusty stove just because a friend recommends I buy one when it works fine? Why go clothes shopping when I already own too many clothes? Also, I admire Eva's ability to ask for what she wants or needs, without apology. She's carved out a unique and successful business of her own in a very tough line of work, through her passion, personality, and a slew of growing knowledge. "Eva holds the vast majority of the farm's intellectual property between her ears," remarks Jim Stringer, the Northeast specialty foods buyer for Costa Foods.

When she's making sales calls, Eva has the quickest recovery rate from rejection I've ever seen. Her joy in connecting with people is unstoppable, and the constant ringing of her phone is one measure of this joy. If I ran a bustling farm, working seventeen hours a day, sleeping five hours a night, could I amass the large number of friends that Eva has? Definitely not, but I like to think her gracious and bold personality has rubbed off some after enjoying her all these years.

To help organize the book, I have chosen to highlight four of Eva's core principles: salvaging, community, bartering, and preserving. While I have linked each of them to a certain season, these principles (and practices) really happen throughout the year.

WINTER: SALVAGING

Eva abhors waste, and the two trash bins in her house (which are roughly the size of cereal boxes) don't get much activity. Need some twisty ties? Eva will hook you up. Looking for thermal underwear for toddlers? Eva has a half dozen to spare. Got moldy lemons? Eva will take them. If she attends a fancy benefit, she will hang until the bitter end to make sure the leftovers have a good home. She has outfitted her highly efficient kitchen with salvaged restaurant equipment. Her composting toilet turns human waste into enriched soil. Overall, Eva's farm is the most waste-free environment I've ever hung my hat in. She has taught me to take care of what I have, and even to throw out (or rather, recycle) my trash bins!

SPRING: COMMUNITY

A number of Eva's skills come together to create a farm that has a bustle akin to that of a commuter rail station. Eva is always connecting one person to another, whether it is a chef client, a volunteer, or a plumber. Her steel-trap memory for names and details helps, as does her humor and wit, but it is her genuine interest in people and creating community that creates a sense of warmth and inclusiveness at the farm.

SUMMER: BARTERING

Bartering is Eva's favorite sport. When someone has something she really wants, bartering is her first line of attack. She has become so good at it that she never steps foot in her car to shop for food. Yet we don't all need a commercial herb garden to begin to barter. In Boston, where I live, there are trade circles. People exchange one of their skills in return for another—you might give writing lessons in exchange for a bike tune-up. And some people have clothes-swapping parties where everyone brings clothes they no longer wear and they trade.

FALL: PRESERVING AND CONSERVING

There isn't much that hasn't been preserved in one way or another at Eva's. She'll preserve venison by marinating it in a wine for up to two months. She often preserves vegetables by making fermented kimchi, and she also cans, pickles, and freezes. But then there is her obsession with conserving energy. Having passed many a winter's night in Eva's unheated upstairs, I feel that I could now change into my jammies at the summit of Mount Everest. Throughout this section of the book I share some of Eva's inspirational energy-saving tips. Though I may never adopt all of them myself, I have endless respect for her unswerving self-discipline.

A guiding tenet of this book is Eva's philosophy of eating a plant through its entire life cycle. Eva teaches us to not be afraid to try eating a plant in a new way, and to use every part of the plant. This is far more cost-efficient than harvesting the plant just once. At industrial farms, the seeds, flowers, roots, buds, and stems of vegetables and leafy greens are left by the wayside. It would be hard to use the whole plant on an industrial level—for example, the arugula flower is extremely succulent, but it would wither and die if it were transported any distance. Eva shows us that there are many stages of a plant's life that we can enjoy if we grow food ourselves.

Eating herbs when they are just plucked from nutrient-rich soil can make you reconsider their prominence in your cooking and your diet. I am thrilled to be calling attention to many lesser-known herbs. Many of the plants in this book may be a bit unfamiliar to you as well, but I hope my words, photos, and recipes arouse your curiosity and prod you to seek out these plants, whether you find them at a farmers' market, in the woods or fields, or in the pages of a seed catalog. And then I hope you cook these plants, perhaps using a recipe or two from this book. My hope is that you'll grow more familiar and confident and eventually fly out of this nest, to follow merrily wherever the plants lead you, down your own lovely herb- and weed-strewn path.

GADGETS EVA WON'T DO WITHOUT

Even if you can't have a farm like Eva's, you can still make some of the amazing food the farm generates. You can grow food yourself, or you can support farms and farmers' markets by buying their food. And then there is foraging—the most cost-effective and titillating kind of food sourcing! But you may need the right equipment to prepare some of this food. Here are the essentials. (Note: The pizza oven might be on your ten-year plan, unless you have a lot of time on your hands.)

Pressure Cooker

Eva convinced me after many years to buy a pressure cooker. Using a pressure cooker takes less time, less fuel, and less water than conventional cooking methods. If everyone in America cooked with a pressure cooker, Eva once said, we might put an end to global warming. Plus a pressure cooker yields the same texture as conventional cooking methods and preserves more nutrients. There is a learning curve, but you need to work with it for only a few weeks or months (depending how often you use it) so that you can get a feel for cooking times. Once I discovered that you can bring a pressure cooker to the sink, run cold water over it, then open it and check to see if the food is done, it didn't seem so intimidating. If the food's not ready, you can just continue the cooking. Eva says, "Once I gave in and trusted my pressure cooker, I couldn't imagine how I had lived without it." (FYI, Eva and I like the Kuhn Rikon pressure cookers.)

What are the other advantages of using a pressure cooker?

- Pressure cookers make wonderful broths. Foods cooked in just a bit of liquid yield concentrated broth or soup bases.
- A pressure cooker is a big time-saver. Dried beans take just ten minutes to cook—and the beans

don't need to be soaked beforehand. It cooks foods like stew meats, wheat berries, artichokes, and beets in a fraction of the regular cooking time.

- Using a pressure cooker can improve your diet. Because it takes so little time to cook them, foods like beans and grains retain more of their nutrients.
- A pressure cooker can be a money-saver. You may find that you eat less meat and processed foods because beans and grains are relatively cheap, and a pressure cooker makes it so easy to prepare them.

Vitamix

This is a blender with a super-strong motor—it could puree your shoe! The Vitamix machine ruptures food cells down to a microscopic level, making more of the health-giving nutrients locked inside readily available for digestion.

If you decide to take the plunge and buy a Vitamix (about $400), you will want to put your food processor in a cupboard, because this machine does everything better (except pie dough and pesto). Basically, the Vitamix transforms almost anything fibrous into a silky puree or a fine powder. So your parsnip soup will be velvety smooth, a scallion basil oil will be a silky verdant green, and your almonds or oats will turn easily into flour. Raw foodies love the Vitamix because they can put a whole fruit or veggie in, skin, seeds, and all, and presto, it becomes juice. Eva primarily uses her Vitamix to make sorbet. She throws in some chunks of frozen autumn olive puree, a few rose petals, a spoonful of honey, maybe a few frozen raspberries, and voilà! Unlike a food processor, the Vitamix will not turn the mixture into a liquid; it becomes a rich, over-the-top-delicious sorbet. You won't even crave ice cream once you start making sorbet like this (see the sorbet recipe on page 85). The blender comes with a black plastic pounder that helps you integrate large frozen chunks into the mash; the pounder is designed never to hit the blade. I bought a Vitamix for my last restaurant (from a friend, for only $200), and I use Eva's all the time. When I finish this book, as a gift to myself, I'm planning to buy one just for me!

Squeezo Strainer

Never heard of the Squeezo strainer? Well, it is a phenomenal contraption that I knew nothing about before I met Eva. When Eva pulled hers out of storage, it looked to me like it had to be at least a hundred years old. But in fact the Squeezo first came out in the 1970s. It separates the seed and skin from the pulp of fruit better than any other method I know. Eva uses it mainly to extract the pulp from autumn olives, but it's great for blackberries, elderberries, and such to make jellies, it can turn almost anything into baby food, and it purees apples (for applesauce) and tomatoes (for tomato sauce). It can also puree fibrous vegetables, grate hard cheese, and juice fruits and veggies. You just wind a crank. It spits the seeds out one end while the pulp oozes out through a conical strainer. Part of the charm is that the design has remained relatively the same for forty years. There are some newer countertop electric machines that do the job just as well; a few of Eva's friends use these more powerful machines, but they cost a lot more and aren't as much fun to use.

Putting the Squeezo together is a bit like assembling an airplane, in that all the screws and pieces must be right and tight before the machine takes off. But it's not hard—believe me, I'm dyslexic and I can do it. Squeezo's illustrated mascot, found on the box and in the product manual, will graciously guide you through the assembly instructions. Eva absolutely adores her. She has an oversized tomato head, a tiny black top hat, and skinny dancer legs with stiletto heels evoking Liza Minnelli.

The Squeezo is made by Best Products Inc., and I recommend acquiring one if you get into autumn olive sorbets, fruit leather, and the like. People find them at yard sales for cheap, but you can also get them online for around $150.

Short of that, a food mill will work just fine.

Asian Mandoline

If you are into kimchi, sauerkraut, or just slaws, don't hesitate to get this fantastic Asian vegetable slicer—you won't regret it. You'll never slice your veggies this consistently thin, even if you are Martin Yan. The Benriner brand, which I use, allows for varying thicknesses.

Dehydrator

Eva relies on her food dehydrator in the fall during autumn olive season. She takes the thick autumn olive puree (see the autumn olive puree recipe on page 217) and spreads it out very thinly on the trays of the dehydrator. It takes a good day to produce fruit leather, although the dehydrator does the work. Equally delicious are her dried Asian pears. The pears, grown by a friend of hers in the neighborhood, are super-juicy when fresh and divinely sweet when dried. Of course any fruit can be dehydrated, as can tomatoes (yes, well, some people don't consider them fruits), sweet potatoes and zucchini (made into chips), and many more foods, I'm sure. I bought myself a dehydrator for a whopping $10 at a thrift shop (new models cost $100 or more).

Pizza Oven

Here you'll need a willing and able person who will make it his or her mission to build an Italian outdoor pizza oven. Lucky for Eva, her head farmer, Peter, is a food fanatic. He knew that cooking with wood achieves a depth of flavor you normally can't get with any other cooking method. On a trip to Naples, Italy, he saw masonry pizza ovens that just blew him away. The ovens were so intensely hot that the pizzas cooked in under a minute, and he had never seen anything like them in our country. And the idea of outdoor cooking appealed to him as well. So he decided to build one for Eva with no masonry experience. He read a copy of Daniel Wing and Alan Scott's book *The Bread Builders*, then got to work.

Peter's oven is in fact an amazing machine—the pizzas that come out of it are the best I've ever had, and I owned my own pizzeria in Cambridge for nine years. It doesn't hurt that the oven is stoked all day while Peter is working in the fields, so that the residual heat climbs upward of 1,000 degrees Fahrenheit, and the oregano and basil grow just ten yards away.

So there you go, a do-it-yourself oven. It took Peter four years to build it amid his busy job of farming and some procrastination. But it was worth it. If you have some time and money up front you could get yours built over a long weekend—especially if you can find someone who knows about laying bricks and using plumb lines.

STORING, WASHING, AND CHOPPING HERBS AND GREENS

Storage

The cardinal rule for storing is: Once you wash herbs or greens, eat them. If you're going to store them, don't wash them first. Both Eva and I feel it's best to keep your herbs and greens stored in a plastic bag. But sealed or unsealed? I paraphrase Eva (because she has more to say than space allows): "We really don't know. There are too many conditions. How long will it sit in the fridge?" Then she rewinds: "What really determines freshness more than anything is the condition of your produce. You can only control so much—you don't know what it's undergone or its age when you buy it at the supermarket. Constant refrigeration once the plant is picked is key. Whether or not you seal the bag is mostly an issue of freshness and water content. If the plant is wilted or damp, the bag should not be sealed. But there are many variables that can change."

In general, if my herbs and greens are dry, I store them in a large plastic bag with the top knotted loosely. If the herbs and greens are wet, I leave the bag open or sometimes wrap them in a cloth instead. If they are dripping wet, I spin them dry before storing them; otherwise they lose flavor and deteriorate quickly. Many chefs store fresh herbs on top of a slightly damp towel in a closed plastic bin.

Eva, like many farmers, does not approve of the supermarket practice of misting greens, as it shortens their life. Unfortunately it is not cosmetically advantageous to keep everything in bags, and misting helps keep cut greens and herbs looking fresh if they are exposed to air.

Considering that I can't know the state of your herbs and greens, I do not specify storage in anything more definitive than "a plastic bag." Whether that's a bag—sealed or unsealed—or a sealed container, I'll let you make the call.

Washing

Avoid washing your herbs and greens if possible. For good reason: When herbs and greens get wet, they break down, lose flavor and can become slimy, even if they're spun dry. With lettuces, the dressing doesn't cling and gets diluted. With herbs, contact with water releases the volatile oils that give flavor and aroma. On top of that, when herbs are wet, they are harder to chop—pieces tend to clump together. If you know that the herbs you're using were not grown with chemicals, then you might want to consider not washing them. The French simply brush their herbs clean with a mushroom brush.

I almost never wash herbs and greens from Eva's garden. They are rarely dirty or gritty, and they have not been chemically treated. I do inspect them for droppings and bugs, and I eat a leaf or two to check for grittiness. If I obtain herbs or greens from someone I don't know, such as at a market, then I wash them, but only just before using them.

If you must wash, here's how: Right before you plan to use your herbs or greens, fill a large basin or sink with cold water and plunge the loose herbs into the water (remove any rubber bands or twisty ties that hold the bunch together). Let the plants sit in the water for a few minutes, agitating and shaking them a few times. Then pull the mess out with your hands and take a look at the rinse water. If there's a lot of sand or grit, you'll want to rinse them again. When the plants are clean, give them a shake to throw off excess moisture, and then place them on a clean kitchen towel and pat dry. If you have a lot of greens, you might use a salad spinner instead. But whatever you do, handle the plants gently. Pull them out of the water the way you would pull a baby out of a bath; don't just dump the greens and water into a colander. And if you're soaking the plants in a sink, don't drain the water before removing the greens, because the leaves will simply re-collect the grit.

Chopping

The most important thing to know about chopping herbs is that you should avoid chopping them if possible, or at least avoid chopping them too fine. When you chop an herb, you cut through cell walls. Volatile oils live in these cell walls and evaporate when the walls are broken, so the flavor loses its potency. This isn't so important with greens, which don't have as great a quantity of volatile oils. But either way, don't chop herbs and greens until you need them—they deteriorate much faster once chopped.

I don't normally use a food processor to cut herbs—it's too easy to turn them into a paste rather than tiny pieces, and this will hurt their flavor. Unless you're making pesto, use a good 8-inch chef's knife and chop them, but not too fine. I like Global knives, but many brands are good.

In terms of whether or not to include the stems when you're chopping:

- *Herbs with tender stems.* On some herbs, such as cilantro, the entire stem is tender and can be chopped up. For other herbs, like basil, chervil, dill, mint, and parsley, generally only that small bit of stem connecting the leaf to the main stalk is tender enough to chop. Of course, these are only general guidelines. At Eva's farm, Bill, a farmhand, loves parsley, from leaf to stem to stalk, and chops up the whole plant. And tenderness varies depending on when herbs have been pulled from the earth:

freshness equals tenderness and juiciness.

- *Herbs with woodier stems.* For herbs with woodier stems, such as oregano, rosemary, and thyme, strip off the leaves by pulling your fingers down the stem from top to bottom. The very tip of the stem is usually soft, so I pull it off with the leaves. Early in the season the entire stem may be tender so you can chop and eat all that you clip.

- *Greens.* Eva is always chopping greens. Usually she chops her broccoli, kale, or chard and adds them raw to a salad or a hot soup. But the stems to her are the best part of the plant, and I have to agree if the green is fresh. She chops the stem thinly, usually more thinly than the leaves. It is not necessary to remove the stems before chopping greens (except for broccoli); I just roll the greens up like a cigar and slice all of it at one time. If the plants are freshly harvested, there's no need to peel broccoli stems or parboil any of the stems ahead of time.

FREEZING AND DRYING HERBS

Freezing Herbs

How you freeze herbs depends in part on their consititution. In general, only thicker-skinned herbs should be frozen whole; thinner-skinned herbs should be made into a paste before being frozen. *Cook's Illustrated* staff, the kitchen testing masters of the universe, froze five different herbs in whole form for three months to see how they fared: thyme, oregano, sage, tarragon, and parsley. All retained their flavor, but tarragon and parsley became a bit discolored. Tarragon and parsley are the two most thin-skinned and delicate of the five, so the fact that they didn't freeze as well is no surprise. The heartier, woodier-stemmed herbs fared better.

You can prepare any herb as a paste and freeze it, but since thicker-skinned herbs will hold up fine when left whole, it's best to use this method for more delicate herbs such as basil, chervil, dill, lemon balm, mint, and parsley. Simply combine the herb with a bit of water or oil in a food processor or blender and pulse to puree. It's important to pulse, rather than simply running the motor, because the more the herb is pureed, the more flavor it loses. Spoon the puree into ice cube trays and freeze, then remove the cubes and store in the freezer in ziplock bags.

Sturdier, woodier-stemmed herbs such as lemon verbena, lemongrass, oregano, rosemary, and thyme can be frozen whole. When freezing herbs you can wash them first, but be sure to let them dry completely. I like to double-wrap the herbs—first in plastic wrap, then in a ziplock bag—before storing them in the freezer.

Whether in a paste or whole, herbs can be frozen for up to four months. Any longer than this and flavor declines. I like to date my bags of frozen herbs with masking tape, so I know when they were put into the freezer.

Drying Herbs

I don't dry herbs. I freeze herbs whole and in pastes, pestos, butters, and purees, and I made herbal vinegars. But I also don't grow herbs in profusion, because I don't get much sun where I live. I either buy fresh herbs or visit Eva. When I have leftovers, I find some way to freeze them.

But drying certainly has its proponents. Commercial methods of drying retain much of an herb's original flavor. When I ran restaurants, I bought dried thyme and tarragon, and they were good-quality products. If you must use dried herbs, rather than fresh or frozen, buy from a quality source, and in most cases you won't be disappointed.

Eva likes to dry lemon verbena, tarragon, and sometimes sage. I'm now fully convinced that lemon verbena and tarragon are worth drying; I'm still on the fence with sage. Eva dries them in big cardboard boxes. She punches airholes all around the sides to let air circulate within and lines the box with crinkled-up newspaper. Then she fills the boxes with fresh sprigs and leaves them in a dry place for a few weeks, uncovered, until the herbs are dry. She stores the herbs in dated sealed bags in a plastic container with a tight-fitting lid, in a cool spot.

Bill Braun, one of Eva's farmhands and an herb hound, dries lemon verbena and other herbs for tea in smaller batches than Eva's industrial method. His simple method would work for other herbs besides tea herbs, of course. Hardy herbs with woody stems like lavender, marjoram, oregano, rosemary, savory, and thyme will fare the best. I consider tarragon, despite its delicate leaves, to be part of this "hardy herb" family; its potent flavor hangs in there during the drying process

Bill's Drying Method

1. Gather the herbs together in a bunch, and secure the stems with a twisty tie.
2. Perforate a paper bag (Bill uses a lunch bag) with a few small holes to ventilate, but not so much that light will pour through.
3. Place the herbs in the paper bag, with the leaves at the bottom and the twisty tie sticking out of the top. You want the herbs to dangle in the bag, not get smushed against the bottom; they can touch the sides, but if they're basically sitting at the bottom of the bag, they

When Is a Dried Herb Too Old?

I felt like drinking herbal tea. Eva had plenty of dried lemon verbena, so I grabbed a large bag stashed in one of her kitchen crevices. I noticed that the date on the bag was from ten years ago. I asked her if the date could be a mistake, knowing she's pretty fastidious about labeling. She quipped, "Oh yes, it's right, but don't worry, it will be fine." I was dubious, knowing Eva's difficulty with throwing anything out and knowing that dried herbs lose their mojo after a year or two. I put my nose to the bag and couldn't detect any verbena aroma. But just to be respectful to Eva I went ahead and made the tea. It tasted like dusty hot water (Eva agreed). So if you aren't sure whether your dried herbs (or spices) are any good, take a whiff. It is the best way to determine if they are of any use to you.

can get yucky. Secure the top of the bag by wrapping a rubber band around it or stapling it closed, leaving the stalks sticking out.

4. Find a dry, reasonably well-ventilated area for drying. Stick a tack into a bulletin board here, or, if you don't have a bulletin board and don't care much about your walls, whack a nail in. Tie the bag to the tack or nail with another twisty tie. Or you could just staple the bag to the bulletin board. Right now I have some bags of drying sage suspended by twisty ties from cup hooks beneath a shelf. Whatever works!

5. The drying time will vary based on the herb. It can take a couple of weeks or more.

And don't cheat your tea—always steep dried herbs for a full ten minutes!

KITCHEN NOTES

On Eggs and Butter

Although I can't always find them, I prefer to use pasture-raised eggs, because I know this way the hens are leading a decent life and for the flavor and nutrients.

Also, I prefer unsalted butter over salted butter. It has a better flavor and there is less water.

On Storing Grains and Flours

Eva packs her grains in used plastic bags (with a used twisty tie) and then packs those bags in plastic containers with tight-fitting lids. At first, I saw this as excessive and unnerving, opening and repacking food like we were going to the moon. But it is a foolproof method to ward off pantry moths. After ten years of watching her methodology and nearly every year having to discard my *own* moth-ridden grains and flours, I now keep them in plastic bags inside plastic containers in a cool spot in the kitchen or in the freezer.

On Following Recipes

Please follow recipes as loosely as you like. Eva would triple the quantity of all the herbs and greens in these recipes. If you don't have an ingredient that a recipe calls for, leave it out, or try to substitute it with what you like. These recipes are not sacred, and I welcome detours.

On Salt

I recommend cooking with fine sea salt. If you're using kosher salt, you will need to increase the quantity called for by about 50 percent because the big granules make it less dense. But most important, always salt to your own taste.

WINTER

salvaging

eva hates waste. "When you grow food," she says, "you realize how much work it is, how much energy and resources go into it. If you don't grow food, you have no concept." Early into a three-month stay at her cottage, adjacent to her house, I was reminded of which camp I fell in. Nightly, after her day was done, Eva would stop by, and what was masked as a friendly check-in would reveal itself as a veiled inspection. She'd ask me about my day, and I'd rattle on about some triumph or frustration in my work while slowly becoming aware of Eva's keener interest in my trash. Nervously I'd keep talking; she'd ignore me, her hands plunging into my trash can, pulling out a pizza crust and exclaiming wonder at why it was there—"This is compostable!"—or fixating on a borderline item, say a greasy paper plate—"Perfectly compostable." With my recycling bins she let me know I was an amateur: one had to think, look, evaluate whether the items—plastic utensils and containers—could be used again as they were, with a little cleaning. My blindness was her boon. She'd pile the useful plastics high and head out the door, leaving me wiser, though traumatized.

Despite the foot of snow that blankets her fields most of the winter, Eva's lively diet is not compromised while the growing season is on hold. She celebrates the weeds, herbs, and greens growing in her unheated greenhouses. Her chest freezer is crammed full of pounds and pounds of bartered fish and venison. Her pantry is stocked with bulk grains,

and she relies on the network of year-round food producers in her community to round out her diet. And then there are her underground pickle barrels filled with root vegetables.

For farmers, winter is a period to slow down and prepare for the season to come. Slowing down is not Eva's style. She works as tenaciously as ever, but she is able to carve out some time for travel in the winter — something that is simply not an option in the busy summer.

Meanwhile, the many hardy perennial plants that call Eva's Garden home rest below ground, waiting patiently for their cue that spring has come. All summer long these plants prepare for winter by creating sugars through photosynthesis and storing them as starches in their roots. By the time winter arrives, like Eva, they have a dependable food source that will sustain them until the conditions for new growth return in the spring.

Tender perennials must be brought indoors if they are to survive New England's cold winter. Every fall Eva digs up lemongrass, African basil, and lemon verbena and arranges them in front of a south-facing window in her unheated barn.

Annual plants succumb to a natural rhythm and cycle at the end of the growing season. Before breathing their last breath, they secure their place in the summer to come by producing seeds. Some of these seeds overwinter in the soil, while others must be gathered and stored indoors until spring.

RECIPES LIST

Beets

Mo's Jeweled Rutabaga-Beet
  Soup
Ginger Tofu in Beet Broth
Shredded Beet, Apple, and
  Carrot Salad
Root Vegetable Latkes

Cabbage

Warm Salad of Cabbage,
  Green Beans, Blue Cheese,
  and Bacon
Eva's Remarkable Cabbage
  Slaw No. 1
Chambrette's Cabbage
Lemon Cabbage Kimchi
Curry of Cabbage,
  Cauliflower, and Chickpeas

Juniper Berries

Juniper Berry Paste for Meat
Juniper Berry Shortbread
  Cookies

Parsnip

Caramelized Parsnip Spread
Pita Sandwich with
  Caramelized Parsnip
  Spread, Portobello, and
  Tomatoes
Parsnip-Horseradish Slaw
Vegan Parsnip and Wild
  Mushroom Pie
Roasted Parsnip Soup
Parsnip, Tomato Water, and
  Quinoa Soup
Parsnip Tea Cake

Potatoes

Home Fries with Cranberry
  Salsa
Potatoes Santa Cruz
Potage Bonne Femme

Rutabagas

Steamed Rutabaga
Rutabaga and Cranberries in
  Cream over Kasha
Rutabaga Kimchi

Sprouts

Sprouted Hummus
Summer Rolls for Winter
Sprouted Wheat Bread

Additional Winter Recipes

Give Us This Day Our Daily
  Bread
Deer Meatballs
Fried Duck Egg on Rye Berry
  Hash
Didi's Granola
Winter Squash with Greek
  Yogurt
Personal Hot Cocoa
Nina's Mulligatawny

Beets

Beets came in very handy when I dressed as a vegetarian vampire one Halloween. I slicked my hair back, made a cape from a Hefty trash bag, powdered my face white, and then painted my lips, teeth, and the bags under my eyes with fresh beet juice, which I obtained by squeezing freshly grated beets. I let the beet juice drip from the corner of my mouth down to my throat. It didn't look exactly like blood, but then again, a vegetarian vampire is only interested in sucking the life out of vegetables, not humans.

While they make good face paint, red beets make for even better eating. Beets have a striking appearance—no vegetable approaches its density of hue. When I cut a raw beet in half, I like to look at the many tints of red, ruby, and maroon, like color gradations of a cliff wall at a quarry. Nowadays beets come in almost every size, shape, and color. The cross section of the pink-and-white Chioggia beet could double as a lollipop that could be a good selling point to a child.

Beets have the highest sugar content of any root vegetable, trumping even the carrot. Their earthy flavor teams well with many foods, but any food they intersect with will be dyed a deep fuchsia. In the case of a creamy beet risotto, the dish takes on the tint of Pepto-Bismol. Red beets get their color from a pigment called betalain, which is also responsible for the beauteous magenta of those droopy love-lies-bleeding amaranth flowers. Chioggia and Touchstone Gold beets are good choices when you want to use beets in a salad because they lack this pigment.

Culinary Uses

I often eat my beets plain, with a little vinaigrette. Chef Patrick Campbell of No. 9 Park in Boston takes it further and serves a beet salad with goat cheese mousse and walnut vinaigrette. Chef Jamie Bissonnette of Coppa and Toro restaurants in Boston likes to use roasted beets to make harissa (see page 71).

In terms of cooking beets, I go for the silky-smooth texture of boiled beets. I boil them whole, skin on, stems removed. If I have a monster beet I cut it in half, and I trim off both ends of each beet before cooking to make it easier to remove the skin afterward. Once the beets are cooked, the skins slip right off under cold water.

Lately, due to some urging from Eva, I've been using a pressure cooker, which takes less time, less fuel, and less water, while yielding the same texture and preserving more nutrients. It's helpful to cut off either end of the beet before boiling or pressure-cooking to facilitate the skin removal. Eva stresses that it would be a shame not to save the pretty slightly sweet cooking liquid, whether boiling, steaming, or pressure-cooking. You can use it as a base for soup, such as Gingered Tofu in Beet Broth (see page 8).

When beets are roasted, they become even sweeter, perfect next to venison or pork, or tossed in a salad. I just scrub them with water, cut them in quarters, toss in olive oil, season, and bake until tender.

Cooked beets are excellent in salads, and this is the most common direction I take with them. I like to boil beets and toss them in a mustard vinaigrette with toasted walnuts and orange sections. Or I'll slice beets over a bed of purslane, claytonia, or arugula, then drizzle with a balsamic dressing. Beets, because of their sweetness, work especially well with greens and herbs that have a touch of bitterness, like baby mustard, arugula, and chicory. Herbs that marry well with beets include basil, chervil, chives, dill, mint, parsley, and tarragon, and you can add one of these to a dressing or to the salad itself. I also love cooked grains with beets—especially black quinoa, because you can't see the beet and its hemorrhaging. And of course classic beet borscht is soothing and welcome comfort food, equally good served hot in the winter or cold in the summer.

Beet Greens

If you buy beets with their greens intact, cook the greens first, preferably as soon as they enter your kitchen. The leaves should be perky and shiny, not wilted. Cut the greens about half an inch up from the root. I usually strip the leaves from the stem and chop the stem, leaving the leaves whole. Sauté the greens in olive oil with lots of garlic or onion and, if you want, a dash of balsamic vinegar. Eat as is or add to a frittata or pasta dish. Beet greens can also be steamed; I like them with chile paste and rice.

The Stain Factor

If we could overcome our fear of pink fingers for five minutes, then I think beets would skyrocket in popularity. It's really not a problem. I just promptly wash my hands with lots of soapy hot water after handling beets, and the dye goes away. The same is true for the cutting board. Some people rub salt into their hands first to keep the dye from setting in.

In France beets are sold fully cooked and vacuum-packed—just slice and add to your salad. I've heard that this sort of product has lately come into the more upscale supermarkets in this country.

Health Virtues

Beets are one sweet you can feel good about eating. They are loaded with phytonutrients that may help prevent cancer. They also help detoxify the body, especially the blood and the liver. Not to mention that they are exceptionally high in iron, vitamins A and C, and folic acid.

Buying, Storing, and Prepping

Cut the greens from the beets, about half an inch above the beets. Refrigerate the beets in an unsealed plastic bag, separated from the greens, for up to three weeks. Do not wash them before storing. For winter storage, Eva keeps her beets (greens removed) in a bucket of damp sand that is buried in her yard—a makeshift root cellar that is useful for urbanites and farmers alike.

You can eat beets raw if they are spanking fresh. Raw beets usually appear grated in a salad, but they also can be thinly sliced (with an Asian mandoline). They should be peeled first.

Growing Beets

The key to growing good beets is light soil. Make sure the ground is not compacted—the long taproot needs plenty of wiggle room.

Beets are easily grown from seed that is sown in early spring or late summer. Sow seeds 2 to 4 inches apart in full sun. When the leaves emerge, thin all but the most robust plants (Eva tells me you can eat the trimmings). You'll need to thin them because each beet "seed" is actually a seed cluster. Do not let the soil dry out. The time until harvest depends on the variety, the weather, and your preference, so check your seed packet for instructions to use as a rough guide.

Mo's Jeweled Rutabaga-Beet Soup

This is a beautiful and easy soup from chef Mohamed Maenaoui, my old roommate. You can improvise, but don't omit the rutabaga since it adds crucial flavor to the broth. Also, much of the success of this soup hinges on the generous use of vinegar. The unused beet broth must not be thrown out, since Eva would object. You could just drink it and be done with it, or you can use it to prepare an easy second soup, which couples the broth with ginger and tofu (see page 8).

1. Set the beets in a medium saucepan and cover with water. Bring to a boil, then reduce the heat and let simmer partly covered until they are tender, from 20-35 minutes. Drain the beets, reserving the broth for another purpose. Remove the skins from the beets, peeling them by hand while holding them under cold water. If the beets are fully cooked, the skins should be easy to remove. Chop the beets, cutting them into ½-inch cubes.

2. Combine 6 cups water and the rutabaga, the white parts of the scallions, the carrots, the garlic, and 1 teaspoon salt in a large pot. Bring to a boil, then reduce the heat to medium and let simmer until the rutabaga and carrots are tender, about 15 minutes.

3. Add the cubed beets (but not the beet broth) to the soup.

4. Add a bit more water if necessary to reach soup consistency (it should be chunky). Season to taste with salt and freshly cracked black pepper, and then with vinegar. Ladle the soup into bowls and top with yogurt and green scallions.

MAKES 8 SERVINGS

2 small beets, both ends trimmed

1 rutabaga, peeled and cut into ½-inch cubes (about 6 cups)

6 scallions, chopped, white parts separated from green parts

2 large carrots, peeled and cut into ½-inch cubes

8 garlic cloves, thinly sliced

1 teaspoon salt, plus more for seasoning

Freshly cracked black pepper

3–5 tablespoons or more cider vinegar

Whole-milk plain yogurt, for dolloping (I like to use the creamy part on top)

Gingered Tofu in Beet Broth

MAKES 4 SERVINGS

4 cups beet broth (from rutabaga-beet soup recipe on page 7)

1 tablespoon minced fresh ginger or fresh or prepared horseradish

1 cup finely chopped cubes firm tofu

1 tablespoon cider vinegar

2 scallions, green parts only, finely chopped

Salt and freshly cracked black pepper

1. Combine the beet broth, ginger, tofu, vinegar, and scallions in a saucepan. Warm over low heat until hot, about 5 minutes.
2. Season to taste with salt and pepper and serve.

Shredded Beet, Apple, and Carrot Salad

MAKES 6 TO 8 SERVINGS

2 medium or 1 large beet (about 1 pound), peeled and grated

1 large, firm, tart apple, with peel, grated

2 large carrots, peeled and grated

4 scallions, green and white parts, chopped

½ cup chopped cilantro (leaves and stems)

3 tablespoons cider vinegar

3 tablespoons good-quality extra-virgin olive oil

Salt and freshly cracked black pepper

This recipe was inspired by Bryant Terry's book *Vegan Soul Kitchen*. The orange of the carrot plays off the ruby color of the beet.

1. Combine the beets, apple, carrots, scallions, and cilantro in a bowl, and toss to mix.
2. Whisk together the vinegar and olive oil. Pour over the beet mixture and stir well. Season to taste with salt and freshly cracked black pepper. Serve immediately, or chill for up to 6 hours.

Root Vegetable Latkes

Latkes are arguably better made with root vegetables than with potatoes. Parsnips and beets are my favorites, but rutabagas and celery root run a close second. You can limit these latkes to one root vegetable, or you can combine root veggies as you see fit. If the parsnips are woody in the middle, just grate around this central core. If you'd like to keep cooked latkes warm while you make more, set them in a 250-degree oven on a baking sheet lined with paper towels.

1. Line a baking sheet with paper towels for draining the cooked latkes.

2. Whisk the eggs together in a large bowl. Add the grated root vegetables, the starch, the onion, the salt, and the freshly cracked black pepper, and mix well.

3. In a cast-iron or other heavy-bottomed skillet, heat the oil over medium-high heat. Once it is hot, using a soup spoon, spoon about 6 or 7 spoonfuls onto the skillet, pushing them down with the back of the spoon. Turn the heat to low. Let the latkes cook until dark golden on the bottom, about 5 minutes. Flip the latkes over with a spatula and cook the other side for a few minutes, until it browns also. Then remove the latkes to the paper-towel-lined pan.

4. Continue frying latkes until you've used up all the batter.

5. Serve the latkes warm, with a dollop of sour cream on each one.

MAKES 15 SMALL (3-INCH) LATKES

2 large eggs

2 generous cups loosely packed grated root vegetable(s)

3 tablespoons arrowroot, cornstarch, or potato flour

½ cup minced onion, leek, chives, or scallions

1 teaspoon salt

½ teaspoon freshly cracked black pepper

½ cup canola or vegetable oil

Sour cream for garnish (about ¼ cup)

Preserving an Era

PATINA: a film or incrustation, usually green, produced by oxidation on the surface of old bronze and often esteemed as being of ornamental value.

Eva applied the phrase "the patina of use" to describe the beauty she sees in worn but well-made objects. The first time I heard her use this expression was when she handed me a pint-sized fork that had the words "Pan Am" imprinted on it. This, she told me, was what the airlines used in the 1950s, before plastic silverware was born. Eva treasures such silverware, which she's slowly acquired from thrift shops and proudly shows off to anyone new at her kitchen table. "The design and quality," she comments, "were formidable. You are carrying on someone else's life — it's a form of connection."

And, best of all, it's not in the landfill.

Cabbage

Brassica oleracea var. *capitata* · ANNUAL

Cabbage has a reputation in mainstream America, and it's not good. Some people recoil at the mere utterance of its name. Alice Waters explains in *Chez Panisse Vegetables*, "Because cabbage can provide food in the winter when there are few other vegetables, it has a lingering reputation as a commonplace, even coarse food." Coleslaw is perhaps the only vehicle by which cabbage has worked its way into our staple diet, but too often the shreds of cabbage are drowned in mayonnaise. All of this is a terrible shame, because cabbage is versatile and inestimable dressed or cooked in ways that I am still discovering.

My personal breakthrough with cabbage came early, at around age thirteen. One day my mother made corned beef with boiled potatoes and cabbage from *The Joy of Cooking*. The cabbage was silky and soft, with a mild, creamy horseradish sauce spooned over it, and it slid down like ice cream with hot fudge sauce.

Culinary Uses

Twenty years ago Chambrette, the head chef of the cooking school I worked at in France, made a cabbage dish that is still etched in my mind. He slow-braised a few sliced heads of cabbage in a *pound* of butter for hours, stirring with a large wooden paddle now and then. As the hours went by the cabbage seemed to drink up the butter. The outcome was a gleaming velveteen vegetable, soft like overcooked egg noodles and as sweet as parsnips. Slow-cooking cabbage is a long-standing French tradition. I once made this at Eva's, and we adored it next to smashed potatoes and leftover corned beef that I panfried until crisp.

While cooking cabbage in butter is an excellent way to raise it to a sublime level, I've discovered how tasty raw cabbage can be

thanks to Eva's slaws. She doesn't grow cabbage but is often bequeathed a case of undersized or slightly older organic cabbages by her friends who distribute vegetables. Eva looks at cabbage the way most of us look at onions: when she is flush with cabbages, she adds them to everything. For Eva, it doesn't get better than eating food that would otherwise be headed off to a landfill—she once said that she sees herself as an EMT for vegetables, and I'll vouch that many a head (of cabbage) has been resuscitated by her care and attention.

There are many kinds of cabbage. I find red cabbage less watery than the green type, and slower to soften. There are many toothsome recipes for stewed red cabbage, and they often include apples and vinegar. Savoy cabbage has very crinkly leaves and thus is packed less tightly; it is excellent in salads, soups, and stews. For kimchi any cabbage is great, but I often use thinly sliced green cabbage or a thicker-cut Chinese cabbage (such as napa).

Health Virtues

You know how nutritionists tell you to eat brightly colored vegetables because they have higher levels of vitamins? Well, cabbage is an exception. Besides being high in vitamin C and beta-carotene, it is a cruciferous vegetable, and recent studies show that people who eat the greatest amount of cruciferous vegetables have a much lower risk of prostate, colorectal, and lung cancer—even when compared to those who regularly eat other vegetables.

Buying, Storing, and Prepping

A head of cabbage should be glossy (a sign of freshness) and have the heft of a honeydew melon. The more tightly balled cabbages can withstand winter storage (40 to 50 degrees

Fahrenheit, or underground in a root cellar), or they will hold in your fridge for at least a month. Once a cabbage has been cut open, it is best to put it into a tightly sealed container or bag in the fridge, where it will keep for up to two weeks.

To prepare, remove the outer leaves or wash the outside. Cut the cabbage in half and cut out the core, making two angled incisions into each half. If you're using a mandoline to slice the cabbage thinly, hold the head at an angle for better contact with the blade.

Growing Cabbages

If you decide to grow your own cabbage, take some time to explore your options. Some vari-eties are a bit peppery, others are sweeter, and some are very tender. Many people recommend the cone-shaped heirloom variety called Early Jersey Wakefield. If you prefer red cabbage, Red Acre is a variety that is easy to grow.

Cabbage is a cool-weather vegetable, but you must sow the seeds in full sun just before the summer heat sets in. Then, water often and wait. Be patient. Many varieties don't reach full maturity for months, but don't let this deter you: these stately plants will be the focal point of your garden and are worth the trouble for their looks alone. Pick the head as soon as it has matured; overmature heads will split and rot soon thereafter.

Claiming the Spares

As a prominent farmer in the Boston area, Eva is given free tickets to dozens of high-end fund-raisers. I once accompanied her to a Chefs Collaborative event that featured ten stations offering decadent food, most from highly regarded restaurants. We arrived late, and although we received a gift bag full of local goodies, I was afraid the stations would soon shut down, so I frantically darted through the crowds, popping food into my mouth. Little did I know I was acting like a salvaging amateur. My mentor Eva, on the other hand, sniffed the air and determined that there would be ample leftovers. While hobnobbing, she was able to procure a large cardboard box from a produce wholesaler she knew. As she talked with chefs, they loaded her down with an array of gourds, fresh figs, local cheeses, dried fruits, salamis, and generous take-out containers of expensively prepared food.

As we were headed out of the hall, hauling our salvaged booty, Eva spotted a waiter carrying a couple dozen unclaimed gift bags. I could tell what was on her mind. "Excuse me, are those spares?" she inquired with a smile. "No, no, they'll be put to good use," he grumbled. She didn't flinch and kept going. Her recovery time is instantaneous in everyday situations like these.

The Power of Gleaning

A boyish seventy-five-year-old man handed me his card after I gave a talk at a Unitarian church in Arlington, Massachusetts, about starting a nonprofit restaurant. When I got home, I read the card: "Boston Area Gleaners" in big green letters, with his name, "Oakes Plimpton," below.

I was curious. I had loved Agnès Varda's documentary *The Gleaners and I.* So I called him. It was November, and

he had a plan to glean apples the next day. I asked if I could join in, and when he agreed, I started visualizing apple butter production in my kitchen with jars and jars to last me all year long. We met with three of his friends at a pastoral apple orchard and began stripping a couple dozen trees. Oakes seemed very businesslike, giving us special canvas bags that wrapped around our bodies for quick picking and rattling off instructions. Once we started, I realized I couldn't possibly keep up with him; actually, none of us could. His youthful energy and spry, limber body outpaced all of us.

In contrast to the low-key lifestyle he keeps now, Oakes grew up on Manhattan's Fifth Avenue. He went to Harvard Law School and comes from a premium lineage. He's related to two former state governors, and his father was deputy ambassador to the UN during the Kennedy and Johnson administrations. Oakes's older brother was the literary legend and New York aristocrat George Plimpton.

After a few hours we had amassed thirty cases of apples. Over the next few days, Oakes took almost all of them to area soup kitchens, but I got to keep a case for my apple butter.

While our harvest was substantial, what was now dawning on me were the thousands of pounds of apples we didn't get to pick and that we left to rot on the trees. And this was at just one of over a hundred commercial apple orchards in the Boston area. Last year Boston Area Gleaners salvaged 30,000 pounds of produce and another 50,000 pounds of retail goods from stores like Trader Joe's. Meanwhile, our city could accommodate a gleaning organization twenty times its size.

Warm Salad of Cabbage, Green Beans, Blue Cheese, and Bacon

Many chefs would place this salad next to or under a braised pork shoulder or some equally rich part of the pig, but I feel that it offers enough in the way of saturated fat on its own. Add toasted walnuts if you like, try red cabbage instead of green, or use a goat's-milk feta, sheep's-milk blue, or Stilton. Also, despite the solidification of bacon fat when it's no longer hot, this salad is satisfying served cold or at room temperature the next day.

MAKES 6 SERVINGS

½ pound green beans

2 tablespoons extra-virgin olive oil

2 tablespoons white wine or red wine vinegar

1 tablespoon Dijon mustard

2 teaspoons honey

10 ounces bacon, chopped into ½-inch pieces

1 medium head green cabbage (about 2½ pounds) cored and thinly sliced

1 green apple or Bosc pear, peeled and thinly sliced

½ head radicchio, cored and thinly sliced

6 ounces blue- or green-veined cheese (your choice, but use a harder rather than a softer, creamier cheese), crumbled

Salt and freshly cracked black pepper

1. Parboil the green beans: Bring a small pot of salted water to a boil, add the green beans, and let boil for 2 minutes. Then drain in a colander, and rinse with cold water.
2. Whisk together the olive oil, vinegar, Dijon mustard, and honey in a small bowl.
3. Cook the bacon pieces in a large skillet or sauté pan over medium heat. Remove the cooked bacon with a slotted spoon, and add the cabbage and apple to the bacon fat. Cook and stir for about 5 minutes or until wilted, then add the radicchio, green beans, crumbled cheese, and mustard sauce, tossing until everything is well coated.
4. Cook until the mixture is warmed through but still crisp, about 2 minutes. Season with salt and pepper to taste and serve warm, garnished with the bacon pieces.

Eva's Remarkable Cabbage Slaw No. 1

MAKES 3 OR 4 SERVINGS

1 tablespoon chopped rosemary

2 garlic cloves, minced

2 tablespoons lemon juice (about ½ lemon) or cider vinegar

4 tablespoons sour cream or Greek yogurt

6 cups thinly sliced green cabbage (about ½ medium head)

1 small onion, thinly sliced

3 tablespoons finely chopped preserved lemons

Salt and freshly cracked black pepper

This slaw is reason enough to preserve lemons. Preserved lemons can be found at Middle Eastern markets, or you can make them yourself—see the recipe on page 126, or, if you can't stand to wait three weeks, opt for Quick and Dirty Preserved Lemons on page 250. Eva originally bound the dressing with a cultured cream that one of her ferment-crazed farmers made, but here I call for the more readily available sour cream or Greek yogurt. Feel free to add chickweed to this slaw—it builds character.

1. Combine the rosemary, garlic, lemon juice or vinegar, and sour cream in a large bowl, and whisk together with a fork.
2. Add the cabbage, onion, and lemons to the dressing. Toss well and season with salt and freshly cracked black pepper to taste. Serve at room temperature.

Salvaging the Unsustainable

One day when Eva was making some deliveries, she found herself in the kitchen of a certain restaurant, chatting with the chef as he cleaned swordfish. He was tossing large pieces of fish into the trash. When Eva asked him what was wrong with the fish, he told her, "My clientele won't eat the dark meat." Eva asked if he would set aside the "toss-able" meat whenever he was butchering a swordfish, and her regular driver would be glad to pick it up. "No problem," the chef agreed. And soon all of Eva's freezers were brimming with swordfish, and friends, including me, were besieged with it as well. After a few weeks we were dropping it off at soup kitchens, and we still are.

One night we were eating yet another swordfish dinner, this time with Eva's long-time friend and neighbor Alan Poole. He later e-mailed us: "Swordfish is at the top of the food chain, a super predator depleting the ocean of many fish, making it the ecological equivalent of eating tigers. Not only that, but the way in which swordfish are caught (long-lined) is very destructive to sea life. Now you can find harpoon-caught swordfish, which is less wasteful but probably more expensive."

So how do you gauge whether it's a good idea to salvage food that is harvested unsustainably, in a way that harms ocean life? For Eva, it's a simple matter of salvaging food waste. Her good buddy Alan, being an avid fisherman, is more sensitive to the exploitations of the sea and would rather abstain, even if it is someone else's throwaway.

Chambrette's Cabbage

This is my own rendition of a version prepared by Chambrette, head chef at the French cooking school where I once worked. Be forewarned: this cabbage has to cook for two hours. Chambrette's version had about three times the quantity of butter I call for here. Feel free to improvise—you can use olive oil instead of butter, or cut the butter to one stick. This is perfect with pasture-raised roast chicken, pork, or leftover panfried corned beef.

MAKES 6 TO 8 SERVINGS

12 tablespoons (1½ sticks) butter

1 large head green cabbage (about 4 pounds), cored and sliced into 1-inch strips

1 large onion, thinly sliced

2 large garlic cloves, minced

Salt and freshly cracked black pepper

1. In a large Dutch oven or heavy-bottomed soup pot, melt the butter over very low heat. Add the cabbage and onions and cook, partially covered, for 2 hours, stirring every 20 minutes or so. The cabbage should caramelize but should not turn completely brown.
2. Add the garlic, stir, and cook another 10 minutes. Season with salt and freshly cracked black pepper to taste and serve.

Lemon Cabbage Kimchi

MAKES ABOUT 3 QUARTS

1 medium head green cabbage (about 3 pounds), cored and thinly sliced

3 onions, thinly sliced

2 heads garlic, cloves separated and chopped

1 lemon, sliced in half lengthwise, then sliced as thinly as possible, seeds removed

5 hot chiles, thinly sliced (optional)

2 tablespoons sea salt

This is one of my favorite kimchis because the lemons add such nice flavor. I thought of it after making a lot of preserved lemons, in the Mediterranean method of salting and preserving lemons is a salt ferment like kimchi. I would be remiss not to mention that this recipe won top prize for the most creative kimchi in the very first Greater Boston Kimchi Festival! I was tickled to watch elder Koreans taste it and smile. Its refreshing flavor works well with curries and other food.

You'll need three quart jars or crocks with tightly sealing lids for storing this kimchi. You'll also want good-quality, nonwhite sea salt, which yields the best kimchi (because of its high mineral content).

1. Toss the cabbage with the onions, garlic, lemon, chiles (if using), and salt in a large bowl. Let sit for 2 to 3 hours, pressing the mixture down and mixing it intermittently to help bring out the liquid from the vegetables.
2. Pack the vegetables tightly into jars or a crock, pressing them down to expel any air. Add enough of the liquid from the bowl to cover the vegetables in each jar. (You can add filtered water if necessary, although if your cabbage is fresh it should provide you with plenty of liquid.) Leave at least ½ inch of headspace between the top of the kimchi and the rim of the jars so it will have room to bubble. Screw the lids onto the jars.
3. Let the kimchi ferment, with the lid on, at room temperature for 3 days (it should bubble), then move it to the refrigerator, where it will continue to ferment for about 2 weeks. After this, the fermentation slows down. It will keep for up to a year in the refrigerator.

Curry of Cabbage, Cauliflower, and Chickpeas

This is a good recipe in which to use cilantro stems that you may have frozen during the summer. This curry is unusually fruity and fragrant, thanks to the cardamom and lemon. Be brazen and add other vegetables that might be in need of a home. I like this on its own or served over brown rice or kasha for a meal.

1. Heat the oil in a heavy-bottomed soup pot or Dutch oven over medium heat. Add the garlic and onions and cook, stirring often, until the onions are translucent, about 7 to 9 minutes. Add the cardamom, cumin, fenugreek (if using), and cinnamon and cook, stirring, for a moment. Then add 1 cup water and the cabbage, carrots, chickpeas, tomatoes (with their juice), and lemon slices. Season with salt and freshly cracked black pepper to taste. When the mixture reaches a simmer, reduce the heat to low and let simmer, covered, until the vegetables are almost tender, about 15 minutes.

2. Stir in the cauliflower and cook another 5 minutes. If the curry is dry, add a bit more water. Stir in the cilantro stems and serve.

MAKES 4 SERVINGS

2 tablespoons extra-virgin olive oil

2 garlic cloves, minced

1 small onion or leek, chopped into ½-inch pieces

1 teaspoon ground cardamom

1 teaspoon ground cumin

1 teaspoon ground fenugreek (optional)

½ teaspoon ground cinnamon

4 cups thinly sliced cabbage (about ⅓ medium head)

2 carrots or 1 sweet potato, peeled and chopped

1 (15-ounce) can chickpeas, drained

1 (15-ounce) can chopped tomatoes or 1½ cups chopped tomato

1 fairly large lemon wedge, seeded and very thinly sliced

Salt and freshly cracked black pepper

1 small head cauliflower, cored and cut into bite-size florets

½ cup chopped cilantro (stems are fine)

Juniper Berries

Juniperus virginiana · EVERGREEN

Despite their name, juniper berries aren't really berries. They are the female seed cones (or fruits) of juniper trees, which are in the evergreen family. In other words, they are teeny pinecones, making juniper one of the only conifers we commonly use as a spice.

Where Eva lives, the local juniper trees, called Atlantic red cedar junipers, abound. Eating these berries fresh is quite a different experience from using them dried. Fresh juniper berries are soft when mature. And they literally spurt juice when you bite into them, tasting of pine with a dash of maple syrup. The first time we went picking I found their flavor so pleasing that I popped a hundred or more berries into my mouth, like they were peanuts. I read later that they can have a laxative effect, but I managed to escape the consequences.

CULINARY USES

To my palate, juniper berries have much potential, yet there are only a few popular culinary uses. Gin is made from green (under-ripe) berries. In Germany, Austria, Hungary, and the Czech Republic, the berries are used in preparations of wild birds, game meats, pork, and cabbage, in which they impart a sharp, clean flavor. Many people use juniper berries as a holiday seasoning in mulled cider or as a paste to spread on baked ham. From time spent in my culinary "laboratory," I have found that the berries, fresh or dried, can be crushed and cajoled into delightful pastes for roasting meats or game, or they can be tossed fresh into stuffing for turkey, coleslaws, or even cookie doughs and scones.

HEALTH VIRTUES

Juniper berries are high in vitamins B and C and also contain some calcium and antioxidants. While they have been used medicinally for more than three hundred years, there is great debate about whether these berries are safe to consume, as overindulging has been known to cause severe diarrhea and cramping. Pregnant women are advised to avoid them altogether, and today's herbal medicine practitioners generally caution against prolonged consumption (extending over one month) of the berries.

FORAGING AND STORING

Foraging for juniper berries is a bit complicated, since they are not easily distinguished from similar inedible evergreen berries. To further complicate things, there are approximately sixty-seven varieties of junipers, some of which are toxic, so make sure you do your research. Look for the small, dark purplish blue berries that grow on evergreen juniper plants from August to December. The berries vary in size; some are tiny, while others grow to the size of large peas. The tastiest berries are small, dark purplish blue, and the size of a peppercorn. If the berries taste overly bitter, spit them out and move on—they are most likely of the inedible variety. If the berries are sweet and palatable, you can be confident that you've stumbled upon an edible variety.

Store in the fridge in a tightly sealed container for up to two weeks. The berries also freeze well.

Juniper Berry Paste for Meat

This paste is especially good rubbed on pork, goat, venison, or leg of lamb before roasting. To use it, smear the meat thinly with the paste at least twenty-four hours prior to roasting or grilling. Delegate the task of plucking the juniper berries from their twigs to any stray children in your field of vision.

²/₃ cup fresh juniper berries

8 garlic cloves

Peel of 1 lemon

2 teaspoons salt

1 teaspoon freshly cracked black pepper

½ cup light olive or grapeseed oil

1. Combine the juniper berries, garlic, lemon peel, salt, and pepper in a food processor or blender. Pulse until the mixture is ground, but not smooth. With the machine running, stream in the oil. Don't run it too long; let the paste have some texture.

2. Store the mixture in the fridge, where it will keep for about 1 month, or the freezer, where it will keep for 6 months. Makes about 1 cup, enough for 8 to 10 pounds of meat

Juniper Berry Shortbread Cookies

MAKES 60 COOKIES

1 pound unsalted butter, at room temperature

2 large egg yolks

1½ cups sugar

1 teaspoon vanilla

½ teaspoon salt

4 cups unbleached white flour

3 tablespoons fresh juniper berries

I once added juniper berries to a shortbread recipe, and it was very good. It reminded me of my mother's Christmas butter cookies, which taste even better. This recipe is a hybrid of the two. If you can't find ripe juniper berries (they are dark blue), try substituting half as much fresh chopped rosemary, fresh thyme, fresh fennel seeds, or even fresh or dried lavender.

1. Preheat the oven to 350 degrees F.

2. Beat the butter with a steel spoon in a large bowl. Add the egg yolks, sugar, salt, and vanilla and beat again. Stir well for about 2 minutes, or until the color is uniform. Gradually mix in the white flour. (If you have trouble mixing it in with a spoon, use a clean hand instead, and it will come together quickly.) Add the juniper berries and mix again. Chill the dough in the refrigerator for 30 minutes.

3. Pinch off small bits of dough, roll them into 1-inch balls, drop them on an ungreased baking sheet, and flatten them with the palm of your hand. Bake for 9 to 11 minutes, until just golden at the edges. Let cool slightly, then remove them from the baking sheet and set on a wire rack to finish cooling. The cookies get even better if left in a sealed tin for 2 to 3 weeks before you devour them.

Parsnips

Remember some of the less popular kids in high school? The ones who were overlooked because the rest of us were busy trying to become more popular? These good-hearted folks are the parsnips among us. They go about their business not seeking attention, but contributing to the betterment of the world—and in parsnip's case, that contribution would be a rich, nutty, creamy, and sweet vegetable that is versatile, singular in flavor, and nourishing.

Many people have known all along that the parsnip is a contender. Humans have been eating it for more than four thousand years. Before sugar was widely available, parsnips were used to sweeten dishes such as cakes and jams. In Italy, pig farmers fed their animals a parsnip diet to produce the most sought-after Parma ham. Parsnip was the leader of the European root world until a tuber from the New World, the potato, displaced it.

Parsnip season in New England extends from late fall until early spring. The fact that parsnips can survive in frozen ground through the winter makes them fairly unique among root vegetables. In New England the ground is frozen solid most of the winter, so Eva will dig parsnips on the off warm day in December or January, when the ground is slightly softer. She sells some of her parsnips in the spring. "Spring-dug parsnips" are coveted by many in New England because the long, cold winter brings out their sugars.

CULINARY USES

I believe that the parsnip is on its way to stardom once again. I went to a food fund-raiser where restaurants doled out fancy food in their booths, and not only did I taste two parsnip soups, but I even sampled a fairly decent parsnip cookie!

For cooking, I far prefer the parsnip to its cousin the carrot. Mix it with any dang vegetable and it will carry its own. I enjoy parsnips in a roasted medley—just slice them and toss with sliced butternut squash, fennel, potatoes, garlic, olive oil, salt, and a big pinch of chopped fresh rosemary, then bake in a roasting pan. Eva pressure-cooks her parsnips (as she does all root vegetables), which takes only a few minutes. She drinks the nutritious cooking liquid warm or stashes it in her fridge as a base for a future soup.

The creaminess, sweetness, and nuttiness of the parsnip make it a natural for creamy soups. It is excellent in stews because it imparts a sweet flavor to the broth. Steam or boil parsnips with potatoes, rutabaga, and even cauliflower to make a creamy mash. Chef Jamie Oliver makes a parsnip and pancetta tagliatelle with Parmesan and butter that you can't shake a stick at.

And don't overlook the parsnip's potential to go raw. I enjoy it grated in slaws if the parsnip is sweet and tender.

HEALTH VIRTUES

Like carrots, parsnips are an excellent source of vitamin C. They are also high in fiber, folic acid, potassium, calcium, and vitamins B_6 and E.

BUYING, STORING, AND PREPPING

Purchase parsnips that are firm and smooth, not gnarled or bent. Store parsnips unwashed in an unsealed plastic bag in the bottom of the fridge. They can last for two or three weeks, but keep an eye on them and use them before they get soft and limp.

I don't peel my parsnips; I simply scrub them thoroughly in warm water just before I use them. If you aren't buying organic produce, though, it's best to rinse and peel.

Parsnips with woody, tough centers most likely sat in extended storage in a supermarket or warehouse. For parsnips in this state, I grate around the woody centers and use the gratings for latkes or muffins.

Growing Parsnips

Growing parsnips is easy, but it is an investment in time and space. They will be among the first crops you sow, and because they taste best when they have been exposed to cold temperatures, they will be among the last crops you harvest.

Sow seeds ½ inch deep in rows 12 inches apart as soon as you can dig in the soil in late winter or early spring. Parsnips grow well in full sun but can tolerate light shade, and you'll need good, deep soil free of stones to prevent the roots from forking or becoming knobby. Keep the soil moist during germination, and then make sure the plants get about 1 inch of water each week. Thin the seedlings to 3 or 4 inches apart after one month.

Harvest in late fall, or leave the parsnips in the ground through the winter and harvest the following spring. In cold climates it's a good idea to mulch the plants with straw or spoiled hay to protect them a bit over the winter.

Caramelized Parsnip Spread

This spread resembles hummus in both color and texture, and it can be used similarly. You can even add a spoonful of tahini to inch it closer to hummus. I've included a quick pita sandwich recipe (below) as one option for using this spread. It also works well on pizza, on crackers, or as a dip for apple slices.

1. Combine 1 tablespoon of the olive oil with the parsnips, 3 garlic cloves, and ¾ cup water in a large skillet. Bring the mixture to a boil and cook, uncovered, until the water has evaporated, about 5 to 10 minutes.
2. Once the water has evaporated, the parsnips will begin to sauté, since the oil will not have evaporated. Reduce the heat to low and let the parsnips caramelize until golden brown, stirring only when necessary to keep them from burning. If you want a sweeter hummus, let the parsnips brown quite a bit. Either way, the parsnips should be tender.
3. Transfer the mixture to a food processor or blender. Add the remaining garlic clove as well as 3 tablespoons water and the tahini (if using). Blend until it is smooth. With the machine running, add the remaining 3 tablespoons olive oil. Season with lemon juice, salt, and freshly cracked black pepper.

MAKES ABOUT 1 CUP

4 tablespoons extra-virgin olive oil

3 parsnips, peeled and chopped into ½-inch pieces (about 3 cups)

4 garlic cloves

3 tablespoons tahini (optional)

Juice of 2 lemon wedges

½ teaspoon salt

Freshly cracked black pepper to taste

Pita Sandwich with Caramelized Parsnip Spread, Portobello, and Tomatoes

1. Heat the olive oil in a skillet over medium heat. Add the portobello slices and sear them on one side for a minute or two, then turn them over and sear the other side. Don't cook more than 2 or 3 minutes or the mushroom will begin to leach out its water. Remove from the heat and season with salt and pepper.
2. Cut the pitas in half like an English muffin. Spread a spoonful or two of the parsnip puree onto each half. Fill the sandwiches with tomato slices, mushroom slices, and as much chickweed as you like.

MAKES 2 SANDWICHES

1 tablespoon extra-virgin olive oil

1 portobello mushroom, sliced

Salt and freshly cracked black pepper

2 whole wheat pitas

4 tablespoons Caramelized Parsnip Spread (see above)

1 large tomato, sliced

Few handfuls chickweed

Vegan Parsnip and Wild Mushroom Pie

SERVES 6

Vegan Piecrust:

2 cups whole wheat flour

½ teaspoon salt

10 tablespoons margarine

4 or 5 tablespoons ice-cold water

Parsnip and Mushroom Filling:

1 pound potatoes (russet, all-purpose, or any local variety), scrubbed and quartered

1 pound parsnips, scrubbed and quartered

4 tablespoons extra-virgin olive oil

1 cup soy milk or soy creamer

Salt and freshly cracked black pepper

2 large onions, thinly sliced

1 tablespoons balsamic vinegar

12 ounces wild mushrooms, shiitakes, or portobellos, cut into small cubes

6 garlic cloves, minced

1 tablespoon minced fresh thyme or sage (optional)

This recipe takes a little time but it's a festive pie that's perfect for friends who are vegan. If you want to save time, you could buy a pie shell. If you prefer butter, then go right ahead and use it in the pastry in place of the margarine and likewise, if you'd prefer cow's milk instead of soy milk, feel free to use it. Serve with some home-made cranberry salsa (page 33) if the holidays are near.

1. To make the piecrust, lightly stir together the flour and salt in a medium bowl. Cut the margarine into the flour mixture until it resembles coarse crumbs, using a pastry cutter or two knives. Sprinkle in ice-cold water, a tablespoon at a time, mixing lightly with a fork after each addition, until the pastry just holds together. (Alternatively, you could do the mixing in a food processor, pulsing the machine to cut in the butter and mix in the water.)

2. With your hands, shape the pastry into a ball and let it rest on a plate in the fridge for 30 minutes; chilling it makes it more pliable.

3. Lightly flour a work surface and rolling pin. Roll the pastry on the floured surface into a ⅛-inch-thick circle, rolling the pin straight away from you, while turning the pastry after every roll. Make it 2 inches larger all around than the pie plate you are using (I use a 9-inch pie pan).

4. Transfer the pastry to the pie plate. The easiest way to do this is to roll half of it up onto the rolling pin, drape the loose edge over one edge of the pie plate, and unroll, easing the pastry into the bottom and sides of the pie plate. With scissors or a sharp knife, trim the pastry edges, leaving a 1-inch overhang all around the pie plate rim. Fold under the overhanging dough, and pinch a high edge all around the rim of the pie plate. Then freeze for 20 minutes.

5. Preheat the oven to 400 degrees F.

6. Remove the piecrust from the freezer. Arrange strips of aluminum foil over its high edges to keep them from slumping or burning. Bake for 15 minutes, then let cool.

7. To roast the vegetables for the filling, toss the potatoes and parsnips with 1 tablespoon of the olive oil and half the garlic. Arrange in a single layer on a baking sheet and roast in the 400-degree

oven for about 30 minutes, until tender. Transfer to a large bowl and mash them with a potato masher. Stir in soy milk, and season to taste with salt and freshly cracked pepper.

8. Caramelize the onions: Heat 1 tablespoon of the olive oil in a large skillet over medium heat. Add the onions and cook, stirring every few minutes, for 10 minutes. Reduce the heat to low and continue to cook, stirring every few minutes. When the onions start sticking to the pan, let them stick a little and brown, but then stir them before they burn. The trick is to leave them alone enough to brown (if you stir them too often, they won't brown), but not so long so that they burn. Cook until the onions are quite brown, about 15 to 20 minutes, adding the vinegar a minute or two before you turn the heat off. Season with salt and freshly cracked black pepper and remove the onions to a plate.

9. In the same skillet, heat the remaining 2 tablespoons olive oil over medium-high heat. Add the mushrooms, garlic, and thyme (if using) and sauté for 5 minutes, stirring intermittently. Remove from the heat.

10. Spread the mushrooms over the bottom of the parbaked piecrust, then spoon the parsnip mixture over them, and spread the onions on top. Bake for 20 minutes, and serve garnished with thyme sprigs if desired.

Hardcore Nourishment

One day I watched Eva eating an apple, chomping and gnawing around the core the way we all do. I had this suspicion that she might eat the entire apple, core and seeds too, so I kept watching her, which isn't easy as Eva is constantly moving. And then as she was placing some scraps in the compost, I saw her pop the core in her mouth, stem and all. It took her awhile to chew it down (definitely slower than a horse or cow), but after a few moments I was confident that she got it down.

My friend Khris, who has worked on an organic farm, tells me his farmhand friends do the very same thing. As I get older (and perhaps because I have hung around Eva too much) I am opening up to parts of plants that I previously considered inedible: the stem end of the carrot, the stump of a lettuce, the rind on some cheese, the core of cabbage or fennel, the stems of kale or collards, bruised fruit, aging veggies, orange rinds, sweet potato skins, asparagus ends, and so on . . .

Perhaps one day she'll have strengthened her jaw muscles and digestive tract enough to join the cows eating clover across the street for dinner.

Parsnip-Horseradish Slaw

MAKES 4 TO 6 SERVINGS

2 tablespoons grated fresh horseradish root or 2 teaspoons creamy Dijon mustard or prepared horseradish

1½ tablespoons extra-virgin olive oil

Juice of ½ lemon or 1 table-spoon cider vinegar

1 teaspoon honey

4 parsnips, grated (about 4 cups)

4 scallions, green and white parts, finely chopped

1 tart apple, with peel, grated

Salt and freshly cracked black pepper

Parsnips are usually quite sweet and tender even when raw, and they really go well with horseradish. One friend who tried this slaw said, "I don't even eat coleslaw—go figure!" You can also try this slaw with celery root, carrots, or cabbage instead of parsnips.

1. Combine the horseradish, olive oil, lemon juice, and honey in a large bowl, and mix well.
2. Add the parsnips, scallions, and apple, and toss well. Season with salt and pepper to taste.

Note: This slaw will keep in the fridge for up to 1 month, or in the freezer for up to 6 months.

Letting Vegetables Create Their Own Stock

You may be disappointed, but you won't find me making vegetable stocks in this book or in real life. Certainly meat and fish stocks are wonderful and economical and play a vital role in the culinary world. But when it comes to vegetable soups, my strategy is to let the vegetables, herbs, and spices create their own stock while the soup is in production. I admit that I used to use a wee too much salt back in the day, but if I have fresh or frozen herbs to rely on, this seems to quell my need to oversalt.

I start with a healthy dose of a flavorful fat like olive oil or butter. Then I add a plentiful supply of onions and garlic and any spices. Then I add water. (Eva, salvager par excellence, would substitute the remaining broth from pressure-cooking vegetables and grains for plain water.) I also sometimes add the dregs of any wine bottle I have open.

Now I add chopped vegetables, usually all at the same time, unless one of them is a green like spinach or chard that needs only a minute to cook. These vegetables are chopped smallish if I'm making a minestrone-style (clear) soup, and I leave them in big chunks if I will later puree or mash the soup. The benefit of recently harvested produce is that I can use the whole veggie, including kale and broccoli stems, outer leek leaves, and fennel stalks. I save any scraps (like corn-cobs, shiitake stems, fennel fronds, or herb stems) and freeze them for use in making meat or fish stock later. The compost gets the short end of the stick here, but our bodies are better for it. After the vegetables are in, I throw in a teaspoon or so of salt, which the vegetables will absorb while cooking.

About ten to fifteen minutes before the soup is finished, I usually stir in lots of chopped thick-leaved herbs like thyme, rosemary, or oregano or some minced ginger. Sometimes I add cooked grains or beans. I often finish the soup with a soupçon of vinegar and good olive oil. I sprinkle more of the same herbs on top, or if I want to use more delicate herbs like basil, mint, cilantro, lemon balm, or parsley, I drop a spoonful or two in the bottom of the serving bowls and ladle the soup over them, then add a pinch more for the top.

Roasted Parsnip Soup

MAKES 4 TO 6 SERVINGS

1 pound parsnips (3 or 4 parsnips), peeled and chopped into 1-inch pieces

1 large russet potato, peeled and chopped into 1-inch pieces

1 onion, chopped into 1-inch pieces

6 garlic cloves

3 tablespoons extra-virgin olive oil

2 teaspoons ground coriander or ½ teaspoon freshly grated nutmeg

1 teaspoon salt, plus more for seasoning

Freshly cracked black pepper to taste

If you ever need to be coddled and no one seems to be taking care of you, make this soup. It works like a good friend, giving you comfort and nourishment. If you want to serve it at a dinner party, I recommend spooning a bit of kimchi or homegrown sprouts on top to add flair. I don't advise using an immersion blender for pureeing this soup, as it will not achieve the proper silky smoothness. A blender or food processor is the better choice.

1. Preheat the oven to 375 degrees F.
2. Toss the parsnips, potato, onion, and garlic in a bowl with the olive oil, coriander, 1 teaspoon salt, and pepper to taste. Turn the vegetables out onto a sheet pan, arranging them in a single layer, and roast for 40 to 45 minutes, until tender and somewhat browned.
3. Transfer about half of the vegetables to a blender or food processor and add 1 cup water. Puree until completely smooth, letting the machine run for a few minutes. Transfer the puree to a medium soup pot. Puree the rest of the roasted vegetables with another 1 cup water and add to the soup pot. Whisk in an additional 1 cup water or more to thin the soup to the desired consistency. Season to taste with additional salt and freshly cracked black pepper, heat to the desired temperature, and serve.

Parsnip, Tomato Water, and Quinoa Soup

This soup's base is tomato water, made by heating tomatoes and then straining out the juice through a cloth. If you don't want to bother with tomato water, you can use canned tomatoes and white wine. This was the first soup I've ever made in my thirty years of cooking where I didn't need to add salt—not one grain.

1. Heat the olive oil in a large skillet over medium heat. Add the shallots and sauté until softened, about 5 minutes. Add 3 cups water and the parsnips, lemon verbena, and tomato water. Bring to a boil, then reduce the heat and let simmer for 10 minutes. Add the quinoa and simmer for 10 minutes more.

2. Remove the lemon verbena and add the greens. Season with freshly cracked black pepper and serve right away. If you let this soup sit for a while (an hour or more), the quinoa will continue to expand. This isn't necessarily a bad thing, but the soup will not be as pretty.

MAKES 4 TO 6 SERVINGS

1 tablespoon extra-virgin olive oil

2 shallots or 2 large garlic cloves, minced

2 parsnips, chopped into ¼-inch cubes (about 3 cups)

Handful lemon verbena leaves or a few sprigs lemon thyme, tied together with kitchen twine or wrapped up in cheesecloth and tied; or 1 stalk lemongrass, cut in three pieces and pounded lightly with a hammer; or a few slices fresh ginger

3 cups tomato water (see page 230) or 1 cup white wine plus 2 cups water and 2 vine-ripe tomatoes cut into ½-inch pieces

¼ cup uncooked quinoa

3 cups or more chopped greens (spinach, kale, mustard greens, or even sprouts)

Freshly cracked black pepper

Bacon Fat for Christmas

Niko, Eva's twenty-eight-year-old son, lives in Washington, DC, where he works as a management consultant. For some years he has been collecting bacon fat for his mom for her yearly Christmas present (Eva asks her kids to refrain from spending money on presents). So every weekend he takes on the chore of eating a few rashers of bacon so he can amass the fat. Every year she is overjoyed to receive a quart or two of the fat in pretty Ball jars. Eva slathers the fat onto logs to help start fires in her woodstove. Of course Eva always gives Niko bacon for Christmas, which she conveniently purchases from her next-door neighbors, who raise pigs.

Parsnip Tea Cake

MAKES 8 TO 10 SERVINGS

2 large eggs

¾ cup extra-virgin olive oil

½ cup buttermilk or yogurt

1¾ cups sugar

1¾ cups grated parsnip (about 3 medium parsnips)

1¼ cups unbleached white flour

1¼ cups whole wheat flour

2 teaspoons baking powder

1 teaspoon baking soda

½ teaspoon salt

1 teaspoon ground cinnamon

1 teaspoon grated nutmeg (preferably freshly grated)

1 cup chopped walnuts

One year Eva grew parsnips the size of small children. I brought one back home to Boston and made this cake. Parsnips are easy to grate when they're large, and I saved the woody core and gave it back to Eva as a housewarming gift a week later, along with some of the cake; I knew she'd make good use of it. You can also make this cake with grated carrots or zucchini.

1. Preheat the oven to 350 degrees F. Oil or spray two 8-inch loaf pans.

2. Whisk together the eggs, oil, buttermilk, sugar, and parsnips in a large bowl.

3. In a separate bowl, whisk together the white flour, whole wheat flour, baking powder, baking soda, salt, cinnamon, and nutmeg. Using a large wooden spoon, mix the dry ingredients into the wet ingredients. Fold in the walnuts, mixing until just combined. Do not overstir.

4. Pour the cake batter into the greased loaf pans. Bake for about 45 minutes, or until a knife inserted in the middle of a loaf comes out clean. Let cool for 10 minutes in the pans, then remove from the pans and set on a rack to cool completely.

Potatoes

Solanum tuberosum · ANNUAL

The potato is the most beloved vegetable in our country. Maybe a little over-loved. We eat on average 170 pounds per person every year—about one potato a day. The Irish eat still more. And as much as I love the potato, I'd rather mix it up a bit.

Consider this sobering breakdown of the 1997 U.S. intake of popular roots and tubers:

99.9999789610% potato
0.0001329078% sweet potato
0.0000000036% beet
0.0000000021% turnip/rutabaga

But the potato is a machine. It yields a much higher output per square foot than any other root or tuber. The quantity of potatoes processed in the world is trumped only by that of the quantity of tomatoes (which is processed mainly as ketchup, primarily for fries!). China, of all places, is the world's largest potato-producing country, accounting for one-fourth of the world's total production. Yet annual consumption in China is a modest 53 pounds per person.

Culinary Uses

My father is one of those Americans who helped expand our potato industry. Having grown up in New England, he recoils at the idea of an Idaho potato. He likes Maine potatoes—baked, boiled, roasted, mashed, or fried—with, as he describes, "gobs of butter" and plenty of salt and pepper. He is also fond of scalloped potatoes. Once a year at Thanksgiving he makes his famous mashed potatoes and toasts himself: "As hard as it is to believe, I have outdone myself yet again!" He loves any soup that features potatoes, like

chowder. In his hands leftover potatoes end up as home fries, fried in bacon fat and butter. I remember weekend mornings, when I was little, when Dad and I made them together. He taught me to fry the potatoes and onions into oblivion so that the potatoes were sufficiently crispy and the onions turned to black "crunchies." We named them Uncle Harry's Home Fries, and he'd continually remind me that we'd be millionaires if we ever canned them.

On my own in Boston, when I had barely begun to earn my keep in restaurant kitchens, I expanded my home-fry horizons through my boss, Chef Robin Hall, who made a brunch dish called Potatoes Santa Cruz (page 34). She'd cook and chop Red Bliss potatoes, then brown them in a wok with lots of garlic until they were crusty. Then she'd add scallions or leeks, along with broccoli, peppers, and tofu, and everything would get browned to perfection after a few minutes. The plate was piled with a mountain of colorful food, and she'd top it with her own salsa and sour cream. It was spectacular.

When potatoes are local, they don't need much elaborate preparation or even seasoning. Eva cuts her potatoes in half and steams them in a pressure cooker. Then she mashes them with lots of garlic and lots more of almost any chopped herb, salt and pepper, and butter or olive oil, or both. Sometimes she includes turnips, parsnips, or sunchokes with the potatoes.

Potatoes have an affinity for a number of seasonings. They're wonderful with hearty herbs like rosemary and sage and in simple preparations such as fried eggs with home fries, potatoes au gratin, *brandade de morue* (salt cod and potato spread), *caldo verde* (Portuguese kale, chorizo, and potato soup), and much more. Olive oil is another enhancer; I sometimes eat just potatoes for dinner, dressed with a good extra-virgin oil, salt, and fresh pepper. Also, Mo's Harissa (page 71) is perfect with potatoes, galaxies better than ketchup.

HEALTH VIRTUES

There is some controversy as to how healthy our potatoes are. On the plus side, spuds contain fiber, almost half our daily requirement for vitamin C, vitamin B_6, copper, potassium, and manganese, as well as antioxidants and proteins. On the flip side, we often consume them supersized and fried, and we tend to turn to them too often, which can prevent us from diversifying and working more vegetables and whole grains into our diet.

BUYING AND STORING

Eva stores potatoes underground, in 50-gallon pickle barrels, through the winter months. For people who actually shop for food, it's best just to buy a small quantity of potatoes at a time, like 5 pounds. Good-quality potatoes will be firm. They should have few eyes, and the eyes should be shallow. Avoid potatoes that are soft, wrinkled, sprouting, cut or bruised, or green-tinted.

Do not wash potatoes before storing them; as is the case for greens, washing them speeds the development of decay. If possible, store potatoes in a cool (40 to 50 degrees F), dry, well-ventilated, dark place to inhibit sprouting. My mother keeps her potatoes in a cupboard under the kitchen sink—which is more like 60 degrees, but it's the best spot for her. If you don't have good storage available, buy in smaller quantities and more often. Do not refrigerate or freeze uncooked potatoes, as the cold temperature will convert the potatoes' starch to sugar, altering their taste and causing the flesh to darken when cooked.

If your potatoes do begin to sprout, simply cut off the sprouts. If they develop a green tint, simply trim off the green area. The green is chlorophyll, and it results from prolonged exposure to light. Although chlorophyll itself is tasteless and harmless, a potentially toxic substance called solanine develops simultaneously with chlorophyll. In rare cases, solanine can make you sick, causing symptoms such as nausea and diarrhea. However, most of the solanine is in or under the skin. So peeling the potato removes a good amount of it.

In terms of varieties, I like any potato that is fresh. I prefer the small thin-skinned potatoes over the large russets and all-purpose potatoes because they are creamier. I also prefer to buy at farmers' markets, where potatoes of all sizes are welcome (the size of supermarket potatoes is regulated).

GROWING POTATOES

To grow potatoes, dig a 6-inch-deep trench in a part of the garden that gets full sun. Plant the halved or quartered sprouting "seed potatoes" in the trench, eyes up, spaced every foot or two and cover with soil. As the potato shoots grow, "hill up" the plants by pulling soil around them with a hoe or mulching deeply around them with straw. The new potato tubers will form underneath the plants. Hilling also helps control weeds. Potatoes aren't finicky; just make sure that the ground is relatively rock-free and the soil is loose, and give them about 1 inch of water weekly.

Harvest after the plants have flowered and died back, and don't forget to save some potatoes for next year's crop.

Home Fries with Cranberry Salsa

These are a more healthful take on my Dad's less healthful home fries. I use olive oil instead of butter, and I've added carrots and cranberry salsa. This makes a great holiday brunch dish next to fried eggs. If you can't find fresh cranberries for the salsa, you can use a tart apple like a Granny Smith. The salsa recipe makes almost twice as much as you need. The remaining salsa would be great tossed in a salad or in burritos.

1. To make the potatoes, heat the olive oil in a heavy skillet over medium-low heat, then add the chopped potatoes and cook for 15 minutes, turning every 5 minutes or so with a spatula or until a golden crust develops, and seasoning generously with salt and pepper. Add the carrots, onion, and garlic, and fry another 10 minutes, stirring now and then. The potatoes should develop a nice brown crust. Remove from the heat and season with salt and freshly cracked black pepper to taste.
2. To make the salsa, combine the green pepper, cranberries, onion, cilantro, lime juice, olive oil, and chipotle in adobo sauce (if using) in a food processor. Pulse only until the ingredients are coarsely chopped.
3. Top the home fries with the salsa and serve.

MAKES 3 OR 4 SERVINGS

Home Fries:

2 tablespoons extra-virgin olive oil

2 fully baked russet or all-purpose potatoes, chopped in ½-inch pieces (about 2½ cups)

Salt and freshly cracked black pepper

2 carrots, sliced thinly on the bias

1 small onion, finely chopped

2 garlic cloves, minced

Cranberry Salsa:

1 green pepper, halved, cored, seeded, and chopped

½ cup fresh (not frozen) cranberries, chopped

½ small onion, finely chopped

2 tablespoons chopped cilantro

2 tablespoons lime juice (about 1 lime)

2 teaspoons extra-virgin olive oil

1 teaspoon chopped chipotle in adobo sauce or hot sauce (optional)

French Fried Politics

In large-scale commercial farming, potato plants are heavily sprayed with pesticides. McDonald's and Frito-Lay have considered using a GMO potato that doesn't require pesticides, but they are afraid of bad publicity. They have requested that their french-fry suppliers stop using potatoes from Monsanto, the only biotech concern to commercialize a GMO spud, according to OrganicConsumers.org. My strategy with french fries is this: don't buy them unless you find yourself hallucinating from starvation while driving on the highway.

Potatoes Santa Cruz

MAKES 4 SERVINGS

8 small Red Bliss or other small potatoes (about 1½ pounds), halved if small, or quartered if larger

3 tablespoons extra-virgin olive oil

1 large leek or 2 onions, chopped into 1-inch pieces

5 garlic cloves, minced

2 teaspoons ground cumin

1 pound firm tofu, chopped into ½-inch cubes

2–3 cups broccoli florets, thinly sliced cabbage, or sliced Brussels sprouts

1 red bell pepper, seeded and sliced

2 carrots, cut into matchstick pieces

1 teaspoon salt

Hot sauce or harissa

This is a recipe from Robin Hall, my first chef-boss, who inspired me to persevere in food service. This is a fun brunch dish but also excellent for dinner. Robin often topped it with scrambled eggs. Serve with Mo's Harissa (page 71) or your favorite salsa.

1. Bring a large pot of salted water to a boil. Add the potatoes, and when the pot returns to a boil, reduce the heat and let simmer, covered, for 15 minutes or until tender. Drain, rinse with cold water to cool, and set aside to dry for a few minutes.

2. Heat the oil in a wok or large skillet over medium-high heat. Add the cooked potatoes and do *not* stir. Reduce the heat to medium-low and let the potatoes cook until they develop a crust, about 5 minutes. When the underside is brown, turn the potatoes using a spatula, so that the crusts of the potatoes are not left behind on the pan, and cook until the other side is brown, about 5 minutes. Add the leek, garlic, and cumin, toss everything well with a spatula, and let cook a few more minutes. Add the tofu, broccoli, red pepper, and carrots and continue cooking and tossing until the vegetables become tender, another 5 minutes or so. Toss salt over all and season with freshly cracked black pepper to taste. Serve with hot sauce or harissa.

Potage Bonne Femme

Potage bonne femme translates as "housewife's soup." My mom isn't the stereotypical housewife, but after testing this soup on my father she seemed to step right into the role: "Your father didn't say boo about meat—I can't get away with that very often!" Perhaps the soup's name has that effect. The smoked Spanish paprika (sold in most gourmet markets) lends a smoky sultriness and depth to soups, stews, and sauces, all with a shake of the hand. You can substitute kale for the cabbage.

MAKES 6 TO 8 SERVINGS

- 2 tablespoons butter or extra-virgin olive oil
- 2 cups finely chopped onion (about 2 medium onions)
- 10 garlic cloves, minced
- 5 cups diced potato (about 2 potatoes)
- 1 small head cabbage (about 2 pounds), cored and thinly sliced
- 2½ cups light cream or half-and-half
- ¼ cup chopped parsley or cilantro
- 1 teaspoon smoked Spanish paprika or chipotle powder
- 1 teaspoon salt
- ½ teaspoon freshly cracked black pepper

1. Heat the butter in a large soup pot over medium-high heat. Add the onion and garlic and sauté until softened, about 5 minutes. Add 2 quarts water, the potatoes, and the cabbage. Bring to a boil, then reduce the heat and let simmer partly covered until the potatoes and cabbage are tender, about 25 minutes.
2. Add the cream, parsley, smoked paprika, salt, and pepper. Adjust the seasoning to taste and heat to the desired serving temperature.

Nothing Beats a Used Cast-Iron Skillet

Hanging at arm's reach above her forty-year-old Wolf stove is Eva's lineup of secondhand cast-iron pans. Eva's relationship with these skillets is based on utility, practicality, and thrift. She purchased them over the years at garage sales and Salvation Army stores for a dollar or so each. She owns no other skillets and uses these for everything from searing venison to reheating leftovers. (She also bought, in these same places, lighter metal lids to keep the heat in, as well as a well-used cast-iron Dutch oven with a cast-iron lid that we bake bread in.)

Through the years the skillets have developed a shiny nonstick patina that outperforms and outlasts even the fanciest, priciest, modern-day nonstick cookware, which comes with the added risk of leaching toxins into food when the high-tech coating gets scratched, at which point it will find its way to a landfill to pollute the earth. Cast iron, on the other hand, only gets better with age, and for a frugal farmer there is no greater virtue than this. It distributes and holds heat well (which is important when you are fanatical about decreasing your energy consumption) and is virtually indestructible. Eva's cast iron is seasoned so well that she unabashedly washes it with dish soap—something that would make many of our grandmothers roll over in their graves. Perhaps instead of coins and a fancy rose, Eva will be buried with one of her cast-iron skillets and a sprig of rosemary to ensure good eating in the next life.

Rutabagas

Brassica napobrassica · BIENNIAL

Until writing this book, I did not know that a rutabaga is a cross between a turnip and a cabbage, and that it's sometimes called a Swede turnip. It tastes sweeter to me than either of these vegetables, and I'm glad for that.

Thanksgiving dinner was the only time of the year I remember eating rutabaga as a kid. I never cared much for it. I would take just one of those glowing orange cubes from the porcelain serving dish, out of pity. Frankly, I was so wrapped up with the mashed potatoes that I just wasn't emotionally available. It wasn't until I began visiting Eva in the harsh cold months of winter that I began to appreciate and relish the rutabaga.

If your feelings toward rutabaga are lukewarm, it may help to witness them grow. I was gleaning food for shelters in the fields of the Food Project, an organic farm and vital nonprofit in Boston, with some buddies. It was late November, but the day was warm. Most everyone had gone home with a sore back after picking cases of beautiful produce. My friend Khris and I continued to pick, and after about twenty minutes, we reached a nearby empty field. Khris had a better eye than I: "Look, it's loaded with rutabagas." They were bursting out of the ground. To me they seemed like the earth's children coming out of its womb, coaxed out by the sun. In just ten minutes I collected more than thirty rutabagas! The one I took home was sweet and complex, with a silky-smooth nuttiness that needed only butter, salt, and pepper. It was on that day that the rutabaga entered a holy place in my heart.

Culinary Uses

I later learned through a home kitchen taste-test that there can be a big flavor difference between waxed supermarket rutabagas and local organic ones. Once you have a good rutabaga, how to prepare it becomes the big question. Fortunately I knew how to prepare the rutabaga I brought home that fateful day from the abandoned field. A year earlier, Bob Motha, Eva's ninety-eight-year-old farmer neighbor who supplied her with some of the twenty thousand Macomber turnips he grew each season, rattled, "Steam them!" Macombers are a regional root, similar to rutabagas, albeit whiter and softer. I had been roasting these root vegetables all these years in vain? In a word, yes. If the rutabaga is fresh and local, steam it; it will reveal all the sweetness and nuttiness it can possibly offer. Top it with butter, salt, and pepper and dig in. Heaven. Eva also steams her rutabagas, but in chunks in a pressure cooker. For variation, once your rutabaga is steamed, try mashing it, adding a spoonful of butter, a good dollop of Greek yogurt, salt, and freshly cracked pepper.

You can also roast rutabaga. It is perfect abutting all kinds of meat, as a topping on pizza, or tossed with pasta—even mac and cheese. Peel and chop beforehand, toss the chunks with olive oil, minced garlic, salt, pepper, and perhaps some rosemary or cumin seed, and bake them in a single layer on a baking sheet.

The rutabaga should not be underestimated for the flavor it supplies to soups and stews. And, as I found out a few years ago, it also makes a killer kimchi when sliced paper-thin and combined with cilantro and chiles. This root can also be used in Southeast Asian Nonya Achar, which is a cooked pickle laced with chiles, turmeric, and crushed peanuts.

On a more historic note, rutabagas were

a favorite food for livestock over the last few centuries, until they were replaced by (government-subsidized) corn.

Health Virtues

Rutabaga has more calcium and vitamin A than potatoes, beets, and other turnips. It is commonly eaten to treat constipation (although beware—it contains mustard oil, which can cause gas).

Buying and Storing

Rutabaga can be hard to find gracing the produce aisle, but since most shoppers don't even really know what a rutabaga is, nobody seems to complain about the spotty availability of this underappreciated root vegetable. If you do catch rutabagas in the grocery store, feel free to buy them—they store remarkably well for months if refrigerated (especially if they are kept in a plastic bag in the crisper drawer), so freshness isn't a main concern. Just make sure that their skin is firm and that they are heavy and dense.

Growing Rutabagas

If you'd like to join the effort to popularize the lowly rutabaga, try growing some in your own garden. Sow seeds ½ inch deep and 8 inches apart directly in loosened soil when temperatures are climbing—typically early summer, but for cooler regions sow in midsummer when the soil is warm. Unlike carrots and parsnips, rutabagas can be started in cells and transplanted to the field if you have trouble with pests, weeds, or diseases. They prefer moderate watering and full sun (although they will tolerate light shade). Harvest rutabagas in mid to late fall, after the first few frosts bring out their warm, full flavor.

Steamed Rutabaga

MAKES 1 RUTABAGA

1 rutabaga (about 4
   pounds), peeled and cut
   into 1-inch cubes

3 tablespoons butter

Salt and freshly cracked
   black pepper

Bob Motha was a longtime neighbor of Eva's and a legendary
turnip farmer. Bob preferred his rutabagas and turnips steamed
with butter, and now I'm a convert. Eva would add that a pressure
cooker would render the same product faster and with less fuel.
Steamed rutabagas are excellent in bean burritos, or with a bit of
kimchi and sticky rice.

1. Place a small amount of water in a pasta pot with a built-in strainer
   or in a large steamer. Set the rutabaga in the steaming insert,
   bring the water to a boil, and steam the rutabaga until tender,
   about 10 minutes.

2. Transfer the rutabaga to a colander and empty the water from the
   pot. Set the rutabaga in the dry pot and toss in the butter. Cook
   over medium-low heat, stirring well, until the butter coats the
   rutabaga. Season with salt and freshly cracked black pepper and
   serve.

Squirreling Away Even the Mundane

Eva has a deep reverence for any object headed
for the trash. In a throwaway culture where
many people shop as a recreational hobby, I
find her squirreling behavior refreshing.

Take Eva's gallon jar of twisty ties. I'd esti-
mate that she has more than five hundred
twisty ties in her collection. They are in various states of disrepair, but all are still oper-
able. A twisty tie is deemed trash by Eva only
when it can no longer perform any function
whatsoever, even one of a lesser order than
the one for which it was originally designed.
For most of us a single use is enough. For Eva a
single use is a travesty. But can she go through
her supply during her lifespan? Probably not,
which makes me wonder who will be the lucky
soul to inherit them.

Eva's fixation on in-house recycling fasci-
nates me, and I wonder what mysterious cata-
lyst is at work inside her. Perhaps it is her
benevolent nature, appreciating that which is
unwanted. Perhaps it is simply an obsessive-
compulsive disorder that meds could quell. Or
maybe it is her deep-seated fear that the world
may go wrong some day, and she could run out
of food and supplies. I surmise that all three
of these might be at play—the last one especially, since her mother's parents, Russian Jews,
were run out of the Imperial State during the
Revolution with only the clothes on their backs.

Rutabaga and Cranberries in Cream over Kasha

This recipe is an excuse to open a bottle of red wine on a cold winter's night. The red wine forms the base of the sauce, but there will be plenty left to drink with friends or family while enjoying this hearty vegetarian meal. Use only firm, hard cranberries; the best ones are sold loose, so you can pick them over carefully.

1. Bring a large pot of salted water to a boil. Add the kasha and let simmer for 9 minutes. Drain in a colander (save the cooking water to drink as a thirst quencher or for use as soup—Eva would). Do not rinse the kasha.

2. Heat 1 tablespoon of the olive oil in a large skillet over medium heat. Add the rutabaga and sauté, stirring occasionally, until it begins to brown, about 5 minutes. Add about ¼ cup water and cook until the water evaporates.

3. Add the remaining 2 tablespoons olive oil to the skillet along with the mushrooms, garlic, and ½ teaspoon salt and freshly cracked black pepper to taste. Sauté until the mushrooms and rutabaga taste done, just a few minutes longer. Add the wine, tarragon, and allspice. Simmer until the wine has almost evaporated.

4. Reduce the heat to low and stir in the cream. The cream should boil but not reduce much. Season with salt and freshly cracked black pepper. Serve the mushroom mélange over the kasha and top with the chopped cranberries.

MAKES 4 TO 6 SERVINGS

- 1½ cups uncooked kasha (buckwheat groats)
- 3 tablespoons extra-virgin olive oil
- 1 pound rutabaga or any local turnip, chopped into ½-inch pieces (about 4 cups)
- 12 ounces chopped wild mushrooms, portobellos, or shiitakes (about 4 cups)
- 4 garlic cloves, minced
- Salt and freshly cracked black pepper
- ½ cup red wine
- 1 teaspoon chopped fresh tarragon or thyme, or ½ teaspoon dried
- Pinch ground allspice
- ⅔ cup heavy cream
- ½ teaspoon salt, plus extra for seasoning
- ½ cup fresh cranberries (preferably not previously frozen), chopped

Rutabaga Kimchi

MAKES ABOUT 2 QUARTS

1 large Macomber turnip or large rutabaga (about 4 pounds), peeled

8 carrots, grated

7 red chiles, sliced

1 bunch cilantro, stems and leaves, chopped

1 bunch scallions, green and white parts, thinly sliced

2- to 3-inch piece ginger root, peeled and grated

1 head garlic, cloves separated, peeled, and smashed

2 tablespoons good sea salt or ¼ cup whey plus 1 tablespoon sea salt

For this kimchi I use Macomber turnip, which is a white rutabaga native to Massachusetts. I recommend using a regular yellow rutabaga if you can't find a Macomber. Good-quality nonwhite sea salt yields the best kimchi, because of its high mineral content. You will need a half-gallon jar with a lid or two quart jars with lids for this recipe.

1. Cut the rutabaga into 2-inch blocks and slice it extremely thin, so you can see light coming through it. A mandoline slicer does the job well.

2. Toss the rutabaga with the carrots, chiles, cilantro, scallions, ginger, garlic, and sea salt in a large bowl. Let sit for 2 to 3 hours, pressing the mixture down and mixing it intermittently to help bring out the liquid from the vegetables.

3. Pack the vegetables tightly into jars, pressing them down to expel any air. Add enough of the liquid from the bowl to cover the vegetables in each jar. (You can add filtered water if necessary, although if your vegetables are fresh they should provide you with plenty of liquid.) Leave at least ½ inch of headspace between the top of the kimchi and the rim of the jars so it will have room to bubble. Screw the lids onto the jars.

4. Let the kimchi ferment, with the lid on, at room temperature for 3 days (it should bubble), then move it to the refrigerator, where it will continue to ferment for about 2 weeks. After this, the fermentation slows down. It will keep for up to a year in the refrigerator.

Breakfast Ideas from Eva's Head Farmer

Peter Levasseur, Eva's head farmer, is thirty-three years old and packed with lean, hard muscle, like the deer and coyote that roam the area. He lives in Eva's nearby cottage with his two dogs, Dukka and Mazi.

Peter has a talent for cooking, and as he does in farming, he pays attention to details in the kitchen. His food is some of the most delicious and imaginative I've eaten. I asked Peter about breakfast—the only meal I've ever seen him consume, since he eats lunch on the run and dinner around midnight. He told me:

The thing is, breakfast is very important. I need a breakfast that will give me energy and keep me from getting hungry. I burn a lot of calories working.

First I make French-press coffee, locally roasted. I grind it with the partially shelled cacao nibs that were given to Eva by a local chocolate company. I pour the hot coffee into a mug with a vanilla bean slit in half. Then I stir in raw honey.

My breakfast changes with the seasons. I make or buy sprouted bread. I slather on raw honey, then raw almond butter; then I drizzle on unfiltered flaxseed oil or coconut oil. I then sprinkle on Himalayan sea salt and freshly grated nutmeg. Also, for a beverage, I like to juice chickweed with ginger and apples.

I asked him whether his breakfast is seasonal.

I have a huge mortar and pestle. Come July I pound basil with garlic, olive oil, and goat cheese. I eat this layered with tomatoes on sprouted English muffins.

Another favorite is mixing raw oats and local berries (wineberries, raspberries, or blueberries) with yogurt and honey.

Other times I crush garlic in olive oil and spread this on an English muffin as a base coat, then I layer on hummus, tomatoes, and fresh herbs (they grow 3 feet away).

I make oat shakes. I soak rolled oats overnight in cold water, the odd cashews or almonds, and fruit and blend it all up in a blender or Vitamix.

Also, a favorite snack of late may sound odd: chopped ripe tomatoes, chopped onion, Heritage brand cereal (which is like frosted flakes without sugar), garlic, basil, olive oil, and lemon juice. I love it!

I asked him if he has any comments about Eva and her style of living.

Eva's kitchen reminds me of a Belgian Trappist brewery where wild yeast used in fermentation grows on the walls and floors. In Belgium, you aren't allowed to clean them. I've always thought that there must be wild fermentation going on at Eva's.

Sprouts

Growing sprouts is one of the simplest things you can do to breathe life into the deprivations of winter. As an urbanite who doesn't have much space or sun to grow food, sprouts are one thing I can grow at any point in the year. Sprouts are replete with vitamins, minerals, proteins, and enzymes. Sprouting is easy, as easy a process as cooking rice. And there is a satisfaction in fostering and watching them grow and prosper. It feeds my maternal side, without the crying and diapers.

Most any edible seed can become an edible sprout, but I like to sprout wheat berries, kamut, quinoa, lentils, and chickpeas. Other possibilities include hulled sunflower seeds, buckwheat groats, spelt, soybeans, peas, brown mustard seeds, radish seeds, broccoli seeds, rye seeds, cabbage seeds, and herb seeds. You can also sprout raw peanuts, black-eyed peas, adzuki beans, green channa, and, more commonly, alfalfa, clover, and mung bean. Tomato and potato sprouts are said to be poisonous.

I learned about lentil sprouts from a customer named David at Veggie Planet, a restaurant I once owned in Cambridge. David would wait quietly in line to place his pizza order, and before he'd order he'd unzip his jacket and discreetly expose two big bags of lentil sprouts. I'd smile, take the goods, and void any transaction so he wouldn't have to pay. It wasn't exactly legal, but his sprouts were always of the highest quality and I couldn't buy them elsewhere. We'd add them to our Caesar salad, peanut noodle salad, and house salad, and it gave our salads added pleasure and an edge on the competition.

Culinary Uses

Strange as it may seem, I love lentil sprouts on my morning cereal. They are nutty and crunchy and are a perfect alternative to my stash of frozen autumn olives. How else to eat sprouts? Kamut, spelt, and wheat sprouts are terrific substitutes for bulgur in tabbouleh. Add any kind of sprouts to tacos, burritos, or sandwiches, or use them to garnish soups. Add them to kimchi, tuna salad—anywhere a bit of crunch is needed. Consider the crunchier ones (lentil, chickpea, peanut) as nuts. Add them to panfried greens. Add them to veggie-burger mixes. Or try grinding them to a paste for an ultra-healthy sprouted yeast-risen bread (see sprouted wheat bread recipe, page 47). Another way to use sprouts is to dry them in a dehydrator or oven and grind them to use instead of whole-wheat flour for muffins, cookies, coffee cakes, and so on.

Health Virtues

In nature, seeds keep their nutrients locked inside until the conditions are right for growth, and the mechanisms for locking up those nutrients are disabled during germination (sprouting). Not only are nutrients more readily absorbed by our bodies after the seed has been sprouted, but the nutritional profile of the seed actually changes during this time as it produces vitamins, phytochemicals, and enzymes to fuel the growing plant, and when eaten, protects our bodies from many chronic common diseases.

Growing Sprouts: The Eva Way

There are two main ways to grow sprouts at home: in a jar or in a bag (of any sturdy mesh fabric, whether natural or synthetic fiber). In either case, start by rinsing about 1 cup of legumes or seeds and then letting them soak overnight. Drain, rinse again, and transfer the legumes or seeds to a big glass jar or mesh bag large enough to hold five times the quantity of seeds or legumes that you have. Tie the bag closed or secure cheesecloth over the mouth of the jar to keep debris out and to facilitate easy straining. Hang the bag or store the jar in a dark, humid place if possible, and rinse morning and night. Eventually, after somewhere between two and ten days, depending on the type of seed, you will notice that the seeds have sprouted.

You may have noticed that there is a lot of rinsing involved here, and watching all of that barely used water head down the drain goes against every fiber in Eva's body. When she rinses the seeds or legumes the first time, she catches that liquid in a bowl. To rinse the seeds or legumes afterward, she simply dips her bag into the captured water, lifts it up, and shakes the liquid out. Once the seeds or legumes have sprouted and the rinsing has ended, she uses the liquid for a variety of creative uses, from cooking her morning cereal to watering (and nourishing) plants.

Eva tells me that her friends Barbi and Bob Sanderson, who run a sprout business in rural Massachusetts, release their rinsing liquid into the surrounding land. Although there was some initial concern from the town about

potential bacterial contamination, it turns out that this stream of water has actually been fortifying the soil, which is now teeming with chubby worms and all kinds of robust living organisms.

Sources

Don't buy your seeds at a garden center, there is a risk they may be contaminated with chemicals or bacteria. I get my seeds at a local natural foods store and they sprout—no problem. But if you are serious, there are plenty of websites like Sproutman.com that sell seed grown specifically for human consumption. "The Sproutman" also offers a helpful circular sprout chart for $5 that lists an array of seeds you can sprout, with the corresponding sprouting times, the suggested method, the level of difficulty, uses, flavors, and so on. It is worth getting.

Storage

After giving sprouts one final rinse, put them back in the same container you grew them in or in a plastic bag poked with a knife to ensure air circulation. Sprouts are living plants. They last about a week in the fridge in a plastic container, though legume sprouts may last longer.

Funky Foods
Create Stronger Stomachs

Eva's zeal for developing new flavors and reducing food waste has led to a tolerance for food that might otherwise be thrown out. At her home I sometimes encounter funky-tasting broths, a sourdough starter that has been souring on its own for two years, or cooked beef that is tangy. When I politely suggest that a food may have gone sour, she either disagrees or tells me that when she reheats or boils the food, the bad pathogens will be killed.

During a break when I was getting certified in food safety in Boston, I told the instructor about Eva and how she eats food that doesn't smell right to me. She smiled and said that you can't always boil the pathogens away and that she deals with a similar phenomenon. Her husband is Chinese, and his mother, like so many non-Americans, has a perennial beef-based sauce on the back burner that never gets refrigerated (nor is it always hot). Her husband and her sons can eat the sauce without getting sick, yet whenever she eats it she gets violently ill.

It seems to me that there is a correlation between a narrow diet and the "tender tummy" phenomenon. Over the past fifty years we've made tremendous advances in combating infectious diseases, parasites, and other pathogens. We've come up with hundreds of ways to prevent food from aging. But could the highly processed "safe" food we eat (as well as a timid attitude toward food) make our digestive systems (and immune systems) weaker in the long run?

Visiting other countries, I have seen people successfully digest food and pathogens that I couldn't begin to stomach. When I witness this kind of steely resistance to food on the edge, I wonder if our culture has become weakened in this way. Do Americans have weak digestive tracts because we can afford hand sanitizer? Is it because we remain in our food ruts, eating the same foods over and over? Or is because we eat processed food that doesn't change in color, odor, and texture as time goes by, so that we begin to view real food with suspicion and fear? Could it be that much of what we consider "safe" food is not the healthiest food for our bodies? Can we expand our diets to go beyond our own comfort zones?

Sprouted Hummus

I had survived another yoga session and was basking in Shivassana when the inspiration of sprouted chickpea hummus arrived into my head. I thought I had just invented a recipe, but I Googled it when I got home and realized it was a very unoriginal thought. Still, I went ahead with my own version. I like to eat the hummus with tart apple slices or fresh whole-grain (sprouted!) bread (page 47).

MAKES 1½ CUPS

3 or 4 garlic cloves

1 cup chickpea sprouts

2 tablespoons lemon juice (about ½ lemon)

¼ cup tahini

1 teaspoon ground cumin

½ teaspoon salt

½ teaspoon freshly cracked black pepper

3 tablespoons extra-virgin olive oil

1. Toss the garlic in a food processor and run the machine until it is finely chopped. Add the chickpea sprouts and pulse until they are pureed. Add the lemon juice and 2 or 3 tablespoons water and puree again until the mixture is mostly smooth.

2. Add the tahini, cumin, and salt and pepper. With the machine running, slowly add the olive oil. Taste for seasoning and serve.

Summer Rolls for Winter

MAKES 20 SUMMER ROLLS

Peanut Sauce:

1 cup coconut milk

4 tablespoons peanut butter

2 tablespoons lime juice (about 1 lime)

1 heaping tablespoon chopped ginger

1 garlic clove, chopped

1–2 teaspoons fish sauce or tamari (soy sauce)

1 teaspoon brown sugar

Summer Rolls:

1 package of 20 rice paper rounds (at least 8 inches in diameter)

1 head crunchy lettuce (romaine, iceberg, or Chinese cabbage), shredded

3–4 cups sprouts (lentil, sunflower, wheat berry, or quinoa) or 2–3 cups homemade kimchi

6 ounces thin noodles, cooked according to the package directions and rinsed well

16 ounces firm tofu, cut into matchstick pieces

¼ cup roasted peanuts, chopped

Mint or cilantro leaves (optional)

Why would you want cold summer rolls in the winter? The peanut sauce makes these rolls hearty, and they can show off your winter harvest of homegrown sprouts and kimchi. And, after all, people like to eat ice cream in the winter too. For the noodles, I like the whole-grain rice noodles found in natural foods stores or Japanese soba, but Asian rice noodles will do fine, or even whole wheat pasta.

1. To make the peanut sauce, combine the coconut milk, peanut butter, lime juice, ginger, garlic, fish sauce, and brown sugar in a food processor or blender and puree until smooth. Transfer to a dipping bowl.

2. To make the summer rolls, bring a large pot of water to a boil. Once it boils, reduce the heat to low and cover the pot to keep the water very hot until you are ready to start rolling. Transfer the pot of hot water to a trivet near a clean work surface (a kitchen counter is best). Dip a round of rice paper into the hot water, rotating it so that it gets fully wet, and then lay it on your work surface. Dip a few more rice papers, as many as will fit on your counter in a single layer.

3. Place some shredded lettuce in the middle of each rice paper. Add a couple tablespoons of sprouts, then a tablespoon or so of the noodles, top with some tofu, then sprinkle a bit of peanuts and herbs (if using) at the top.

4. Starting with the end closest to you, roll one of the papers tightly around its stuffing. When you reach the halfway point, fold the sides of the paper in toward the center, then continue rolling to the end of the paper, lifting the roll up from the table an inch or two to help you smooth out wrinkles and pull the paper more taut. You should be able to see the herbs or sprouts through the wrapper.

5. Continue in the same manner for the other rolls. If you're planning to serve them within the hour, leave them at room temperature. Otherwise, refrigerate the spring rolls, covered with plastic wrap, but do not chill for more than 3 hours, as they will harden and lose their delicate texture. Rewrap any leftover rice papers well in plastic wrap and store at room temperature.

6. To serve the rolls as an hors d'ouevre, cut them in half and serve on a platter with peanut sauce.

Sprouted Wheat Bread

This chewy, satisfying bread rewards the work of growing sprouts (which isn't really work once you get the hang of it). I consider each slice of this loaf to be the equivalent of a power bar. After eating a slice, I find myself performing rare physical feats like organizing my shoes or dusting my apartment. Start the sprouts at least three days ahead so they can germinate.

1. Combine ½ cup of the warm water and the maple syrup in a small bowl. Sprinkle in the yeast and let sit for at least 5 minutes. It should get foamy.

2. Drain the wheat berry and sunflower sprouts well and pulse them briefly in a food processor, until pretty well pulverized.

3. Combine 2 cups of the flour, the flaxseed (if using), the salt, and the anise seed in a large bowl and stir well. Make a well in the middle and add the remaining 1½ cups warm water, the butter, the sprout paste, and the yeast mixture. Stir well with a metal spoon.

4. Add the remaining 2 cups flour by the ½ cup, stirring after every addition. Once the dough stops being sticky, turn it out onto a floured surface and knead for at least 8 minutes, adding more flour when necessary. (You don't want to add any more flour than is necessary to keep it from sticking.) The dough should be smooth and nearly bounce back when the tip of a finger is pressed into it.

5. Oil a large bowl, and grease two loaf pans (for two loaves) or a baking sheet (for one round loaf). Set the dough in the bowl, drape a towel over the top, and let the bowl sit in a warm spot until the dough has doubled in size, about 45 minutes. Punch the dough down and either cut it in two and place in the two greased loaf pans or, alternatively, shape it into a round and set on the greased baking sheet. Let rise 30 minutes.

6. Preheat the oven to 400 degrees F.

7. Bake the bread, giving oblong loaves 40 minutes and round loaves 55 minutes. The bread is done when you invert it and it sounds hollow when tapped on the bottom. Remove the bread from the pans and cool at least 15 minutes before diving in.

MAKES 2 OBLONG LOAVES OR 1 LARGE ROUND LOAF

2 cups warm water

¼ cup maple syrup or honey

1 tablespoon dried yeast

2 cups sprouted wheat berries

1½ cups sunflower, quinoa, or other sprouts of your choosing

4 cups whole wheat flour, plus a little more

¾ cup ground flaxseed (optional)

1½ tablespoons kosher salt or 1 tablespoon fine sea salt

1½ teaspoons anise or fennel seed

4 tablespoons (½ stick) butter, melted

ADDITIONAL WINTER RECIPES

Give Us This Day Our Daily Bread

**MAKES 2 OBLONG LOAVES OR
1 LARGE ROUND LOAF**

1 teaspoon dry yeast

4 cups whole wheat flour

2 cups unbleached white
flour, plus extra for shaping into loaves

2½ teaspoons sea salt

1½ cups cooked chewy
grain such as brown
rice, oat groats, wheat
berries, barley, or even
millet

This is our favorite bread to make at the farm. It is a version of the popular Jim Lahey recipe that appeared in Mark Bittman's *New York Times* "The Minimalist" column in 2006, but this version is higher in fiber. Molly MacLean, a friend, who's been perfecting her own version for years, helped me work out the kinks in this recipe. It is a satisfying way to salvage leftover brown rice, oatmeal, or wheat berries, but you have to start the bread a day before you devour it.

1. Combine the yeast, 4 cups whole wheat flour, 2 cups white flour, and salt in a big bowl. Mix well. Add 3½ cups water and mix well with a big spoon.

2. Cover the bowl with plastic wrap and then cover the entirety with a down jacket or other thick insulated material. Let rest at room temperature or in a warm spot (70–80 degrees F) for 15 to 18 hours. It will be bubbly at this point.

3. Oil two loaf pans or a large Dutch oven. Stir the dough well and add the cooked grain. Add just enough flour to form sticky balls. If you're using loaf pans, cut the dough with a sharp knife into two masses, shape them into balls, and drop into the loaf pans. If you're using a Dutch oven, shape the dough into a single ball and set into the pan. Let rise until the dough has doubled in bulk, about 1 to 2 hours.

4. Preheat the oven to 450 degrees F.

5. Bake for about 45 minutes for loaves or 60 minutes for the Dutch oven. The bread is done when you invert it and it sounds hollow when tapped on the bottom. Let the loaves cool in their pans for 30 minutes.

Deer Meatballs

When I was growing up, my family always got together with another family on New Year's Eve and ate spaghetti with meat sauce. One year when I was seven or so, I loaded up my plate at the buffet, made a fast turn, and watched the food slide onto the dining room rug. My older sisters and I picked most of the spaghetti off the floor, but due to our errant personalities we began draping the noodles on the chandelier, ever so gently, where they hung, swaying—at least until our parents got to us. When I invited friends out to Eva's one New Year's, out of nostalgia I made this version. Serve with tomato sauce and pasta with a bit of Parmesan sprinkled on top.

MAKES 18 MEATBALLS, ENOUGH FOR 6 SERVINGS

3–4 slices bread

2 garlic cloves

1 tablespoon fresh rosemary

1¼ pounds venison (stew or steak), ground

3 tablespoons butter or lard

1 large egg, beaten

3 tablespoons chopped parsley

2 tablespoons chopped chives or onion

½ teaspoon salt

1 tablespoon extra-virgin olive oil

1. Break up the bread and run it through a food processor with the garlic and rosemary. You should end up with 1½ cups bread crumbs.

2. Combine the bread crumbs, venison, butter, egg, parsley, chives, and salt in a large bowl and mix well, using your hands. Form the mixture into 18 meatballs.

3. Heat the olive oil in a large, heavy-bottomed pan or cast-iron skillet over medium heat. Add the meatballs, cover the pan, and reduce the heat to low. Cook the meatballs for 10 to 15 minutes, turning them every 3 to 4 minutes. Serve the meatballs warm over your favorite pasta and favorite sauce. (To keep them warm for up to 1 hour, cover the skillet and set in a 200-degree oven.)

ADDITIONAL WINTER RECIPES

Fried Duck Egg on Rye Berry Hash

SERVES 1

1 tablespoon extra-virgin olive oil

1 large shallot, sliced

1 garlic clove, minced

1½ cups cooked rye or wheat berries

Salt and freshly cracked black pepper

1 duck egg or 2 large chicken eggs

1 ounce briny sheep's-milk or cow's-milk cheese

It was January and I was staying in Eva's cottage. I awoke with my nose ice-covered, exhaling puffs of cold air, the woodstove having relinquished its responsibility in the night. I scurried downstairs and opened my fridge, wanting to make a warm, hearty breakfast to heat my insides. There were just three ingredients: a container of rye berries, some blue sheep's-milk cheese, and one big duck egg.

I certainly didn't have the fortitude to run over to Eva's house in the cold and rummage through her fridge. Then it came to me. A fried duck egg on rye berry hash with some cheese. I started the hash. I looked at the duck egg. It was twice the size of a hen egg. I tried to crack it but the shell was rock-hard, reminding me of a lobster shell. Then it occurred to me that, although improbable, I had heard of weirder things than a duck taking a shine to a lobster, and anyhow, it would make for one mighty fine-tasting egg. I whacked it with a chef's knife and it landed on the rye berries. The yolk was huge; it made up most of the egg, and I jumped and kicked my heels together to celebrate.

You can vary this recipe in many ways. Try adding a handful or two of chopped Swiss chard to the rye berries after they begin to brown, before adding the egg. Or add diced tomato when they are local and in season. I sprinkled parsley on the whole bit at the end, but you can do that easily when you're at Eva's.

Note: Rye berries are available at many natural foods stores and from various online retailers. They are hearty, chewy, and nutty, and you can cook them like rice or pasta. Eva uses her pressure cooker to save time and energy. The raw berries keep well for at least a year in a cool space.

ADDITIONAL WINTER RECIPES

1. Heat a cast-iron skillet over medium heat. Add the olive oil, shallot, and garlic; cook for 1 to 2 minutes, until they begin to brown. Stir well to ensure they don't burn.

2. Reduce the heat to low and add the rye or wheat berries, letting them sizzle undisturbed for a few minutes. Stir once, then let them sit for a few more minutes to build a nice crust, seasoning with salt and freshly cracked black pepper to taste. You will hear popping sounds, but don't worry.

3. Make a space in the middle of the pan for the egg. Drop it in, trying not to break the yolk. Cover the pan and let cook until the egg is done how you like it; I like the yolk runny. Scoop it all up with a spatula and relocate it onto a plate; crumble the blue cheese over the top.

Marooned with Henry

A pronounced funk sometimes greeted my return to the city from Eva's in midwinter. I had been renting her cottage for three months, commuting to work in Boston while my kitchen there was getting a makeover. But this time the funk had friends: a torn-up, filthy apartment (not the contractor's fault—he was in jail) and a raging respiratory infection, which came at the heels of four long days putting what I could of the disorder to rights and shoving the rest around.

The upside of all this turmoil was prescribed narcotics and downtime with Henry, my cat, who was markedly depressed since leaving the thrills of the farm. We were now able to support each other through our reentry, So we cuddled on the couch and thrilled listlessly to bird-themed movies like *The Falcon & the Snowman* and, yes, *Birdy*. There were throw blankets, pillows, fat socks; there was cocoa and black bean soup. Henry was like a furnace of hot pudding on my chest—17 pounds of hurricane prevention so I wouldn't blow away. We lay like that for three days, tranquilly marooned at the edge of an ocean of construction dust, our wounded spirits drawing succor from a cornucopia of modern science and technology, and a growing certainty that only a return to Eva's could completely break this worrisome spell.

ADDITIONAL WINTER RECIPES

Didi's Granola

MAKES ABOUT 1 GALLON

12 cups rolled oats

1 cup sugar or ¾ cup honey or maple syrup

1 cup raw wheat germ (optional)

1 cup raw unsalted sunflower seeds

1 teaspoon ground cardamom, clove, or star anise

1 teaspoon ground cinnamon

½ teaspoon salt

1 cup (2 sticks) butter, melted, or ¾ cup canola oil

1 cup raw unsalted pumpkin seeds

1 cup unsalted walnut pieces or slivered almonds

1½ cups raisins, currants, or dried cranberries

There are infinite possibilities with granola. I add raw millet to the mix when I'm at Eva's, since that is her favorite grain, substituting 1 cup millet for 1 cup oats; you could also add kasha. Try adding sesame seeds in lieu of sunflower seeds. Try adding fresh fennel seeds to the mixture before baking. I even have added ½ cup powdered Salvadoran *horchata* (a beverage made of morro seed) to the granola, with great success! Sometimes I top a tray of granola with chopped local cranberries, before I bake the granola; they dry as it cooks. Unsweetened carob chips can be added once the granola has cooled. I sometimes make a low-budget or no-energy-to-shop granola with oats, oil, sunflower seeds, and fun spices.

You may want to halve this recipe, since it makes a lot.

1. Preheat the oven to 300 degrees F. Line two rimmed baking sheets with parchment paper.

2. Combine the oats, sugar, wheat germ (if using), sunflower seeds, cardamom, cinnamon, salt, and butter in a large bowl. Mix until evenly combined. Spread the mixture onto the baking sheets. Bake for 35 minutes.

3. Rotate the baking sheets top to bottom and front to back. Stir in the pumpkin seeds and nuts. Bake 25 minutes, or until the granola is golden brown and no longer sticky to the touch.

4. Let cool completely. Mix in the raisins. Store in a tightly sealed container for up to 2 weeks.

Chicken Takes a Bath

Eva was making a chicken soup and added a splash of cider vinegar. The soup began to foam excessively, rising above the pot's lip, resembling a soufflé. At that moment she realized she had added Dr. Bronner's liquid soap instead of vinegar. This was understandable, since the liquid soap and the cider vinegar are stored on the same shelf in identical gallon containers under the sink. Not one to be daunted, she drained the soup into a colander, rinsed off the chicken and vegetables, placed it all back in the pot, added water, and began again.

Winter Squash with Greek Yogurt

Since Greek yogurt became widely available a few years ago, we have discovered many ways to enjoy it. Here is one of mine. Butternut or any other winter squash is roasted and pureed with the yogurt. Hubbard squash has the best flavor in my opinion, and feel free to use it, but it can be cumbersome to cut up. You need a strong 10-inch knife to tackle this blue monster of a squash. You can also make this with root vegetables like sunchokes, celeriac, and rutabaga. Any of these choices makes for a wonderful bed for roast chicken as well as wild mushrooms that have been cooked in butter.

MAKES 6 TO 8 SERVINGS

1 butternut squash (about 3 pounds)

2–4 peeled garlic cloves

1 tablespoon butter

½ cup Greek yogurt

Salt and freshly cracked black pepper

1. Preheat the oven to 400 degrees F.
2. Cut the squash in half lengthwise and scoop out the seeds (do not peel the squash). Set cut side down on a baking sheet. Bake for 15 to 20 minutes, then add the whole cloves of garlic to the baking sheet and bake for another 30 minutes, until the squash is soft and the garlic browned. Remove the squash and garlic from the pan and let cool for 20 minutes.
3. Spoon the flesh into a food processor; add the butter and process until smooth. Add the yogurt, and season to taste with salt and freshly cracked black pepper. Pulse until the puree is perfectly smooth. To warm to serving temperature, transfer to a bowl and reheat in the microwave, or spoon into a heavy pan and heat on the stove.

ADDITIONAL WINTER RECIPES

Personal Hot Cocoa

MAKES 2 SERVINGS

2 cups milk, preferably whole

2 heaping tablespoons cocoa powder

2 heaping tablespoons sugar

Few drops almond extract

I had two containers of dark baking cocoa that needed to be used up before they started to grow hair. So I decided to make hot cocoa from scratch. I realized the benefits immediately:

- It tastes twice as good. With instant cocoa, you get powdered milk and a lot of sugar making up for a scant amount of cocoa, because it is expensive. When you use fresh milk (or even better, raw milk) and dark cocoa and not too much sugar, your hot cocoa is transported to a higher ground.
- I love a bittersweet hot cocoa. You can't control the sugar level in instant cocoa.
- You save money. Even though the ingredients are better than those in most instant cocoas, it's still cheaper to make it yourself.
- It's fast. From-scratch hot cocoa takes hardly any longer to make than instant hot cocoa.

1. Combine the milk, cocoa, and sugar in a small pan over medium heat. Whisk while heating. Be careful not to let it boil or it may burn.
2. Add a few drops of almond extract and taste for sweetness.
3. Pour into two mugs. Slip your toes into slippers, grab a blanket, and curl up with a good book or flick and sip away.

Juniper Fishing

I walked through the door to Eva's house, having just arrived for a weekend visit. It was near midnight, but she was up of course, listening to Diane Rehm on NPR and waving a five-foot wooden pole in the air like she was trying to yank a fish out of the water. "I'm figuring out how to capture juniper berries that grow high on a tree," she asserted. "This is an old till from a sailboat, and if only I could attach a hook at the end, I could cajole the branches down." I suggested using a hanger to form a hook. Eva went in search of a hanger and emerged ten minutes later a bit dazed, holding a box of about 1,200 hangers. I wove a hanger through the end piece of the till so that the top of the hanger served as a hook, and I used the rest of the hanger to hug the hook to the pole. The other 1,199 hangers would have to bide their time. And the juniper grabber was good to go.

Nina's Mulligatawny

Eva invited me and my boyfriend along to a "potluck movie night" at the home of Betsy and Putty Powel. Putty was an old college friend of Eva's. At the potluck I delighted in some truly rich and delicious mulligatawny made by Nina Knowlton, who is an old friend of Putty Powel's.

Because the recipe calls for many ingredients, I recommend making a double batch and freezing some, to make it worth the effort.

1. Combine the chicken, celery, carrot, onion, mushrooms, parsley, and stock in a saucepan. Bring to a boil, then reduce the heat and let simmer, covered, until the chicken is cooked through, about 15 to 20 minutes. Remove the chicken to a plate to cool. Continue simmering the stock for 45 minutes. Strain the vegetables from the stock, pressing them to extract any liquid.

2. Heat the butter in a large saucepan over medium heat. Add the onion and sauté until translucent, about 7 minutes. Stir in the flour and curry powder and cook for 1 minute. Gradually whisk in the strained stock, and bring to a light boil. Let simmer for 10 minutes.

3. Stir in the rice, cream, and chutney to taste, and return to a simmer.

4. Shred the chicken breasts with your fingers and add them to the soup. Serve hot.

MAKES 6 SERVINGS

3 boneless, skinless chicken breasts (about 1½ pounds)

2 celery ribs with leaves, roughly chopped

1 carrot, coarsely chopped

1 onion, quartered

¼ pound mushrooms

3 sprigs parsley

4 cups chicken stock

3 tablespoons butter or extra-virgin olive oil

½ cup finely chopped onion

2 tablespoons flour

1 tablespoon curry powder

½ cup cooked brown rice

½ cup heavy cream

1 (9-ounce) bottle Major Grey's mango chutney, pureed, or 1 pureed cup Rhubarb-Raisin Chutney (page 98)

Group Meal: Tenderizing an Old Hen

We attempted to eat a hen for dinner. She was a three-year-old lady and had provided many an egg to Eva's farmhand Antone, but, as hens do, she slowed down laying eggs at about the age of two. Hens can actually live up to twelve years, but farmers don't keep them nearly that long. Holding the scrawny bird in my hands, I wondered if we'd get any meat at all.

Friends of mine had come from the city and helped me prepare the dinner. Eva reminded me that older birds needed to stew, not roast, because their meat can be tough. Eva had a few carnival squash, and I cut them in half and removed the seeds and toasted them. She had also dug some baby carrots, so the carrots and toasted seeds became the appetizers. As for the hen, I quartered, seared, then stewed her. I added chopped celeriac, shallots, garlic, wine, a good pint of tomato water (see page 230), and a lot of fresh thyme. But I could only let the mixture stew for an hour and a half, as my friends had to head back to the city. I added the squash, which thickened the stew, and—ooh mamacita!—did that taste good! We served it in large, steaming bowls and bent over and ate it. There was only one problem: the meat was as tough as rubberbands. So we pretty much went meatless that night. In hindsight, the pressure cooker would have done a better job tenderizing the old hen. But I was just learning the ways of the pressure cooker, so I wasn't comfortable with it yet.

But leave it to Eva to rescue the sinking ship and set it on a better course. After I had gone to bed, in her elf-like fashion, Eva put the bird in a pot with the stew liquid, along with a couple of quarts of water, and placed it on the wood-stove. It simmered quietly all night, and in the morning (hours before I got up) she picked two pints of meat off that bony hen. The stock turned rich and sweet, and she used it to make a redolent hen and noodle soup.

community

Jordan Road, where Eva lives, serves as the foundation for what I'd call a tight-knit community. Eva usually wakes up around 6 a.m. and takes brisk walks with her buddy Betsy Powel, who lives at the tail end of the road. In 1969 five couples, including Eva and her husband, George, together bought a large parcel of land that covers almost half the road, and over the years friendships between all the neighbors have grown. Many of Eva's best friends live on this road, and their friendship is reinforced and strengthened by the many get-togethers that take place year-round. It's a stark contrast to the tempo and feel of Boston, where I live.

I jog up and down Jordan Road when I visit. Cars are a rarity and their absence makes it a bit like the way life must have been in the late 19th century, except I wouldn't have been running unless I was very late. I often stop in the middle of the street and converse with neighbors taking strolls or walking their dogs. I don't know all of them, but everyone is friendly. I find that I've done what Eva did forty years ago when she moved here: I've found an area that feels more like home than the one I grew up in. I did love my hometown, but it was a suburb. Here there are animals—cows, foxes, deer, pigs, osprey, and hummingbirds.

There is open space, well preserved. One weekend I realized how lucky Eva is when we went to a Sunday brunch at the top of the road and then a Sunday dinner at the end of the road. Everyone was warm, gentle, and sincere. Eva wouldn't think of excluding me from these gatherings, and I'm not the only one she shepherds around. This inclusiveness is in her blood, and it makes me feel like I'm home. Without fail, when I'm headed back to the city, Eva walks me to the door and asks energetically, "So *when* are you coming back?"

Eva's community extends far beyond Jordan Road. She has buckets of friends, and her chef clients are her most steadfast fans. She in turn invites all the chefs to her garden, sometimes many at the same time, to celebrate one thing or another—the christening of her outdoor pizza oven, the spring crossing of salamanders on Jordan Road, or a fresh-killed deer to butcher. And then there is the steady stream of people who traipse in and out of the house and farm all day long—office help, farmers, plumbers, computer geeks, and all sorts of friends from beyond Jordan Road who are in one way or another entwined with Eva or her farm. I have seen other farms with a community feel, but I haven't seen one quite like Eva's.

RECIPES LIST

Alliums
Four-Allium Risotto with
  Sea Scallops
Oat Groat Delight with Green
  Garlic Compote

Arugula
Wild Rice, Arugula, and
  Parsley Salad
Bolted Burger

Cilantro
Mo's Harissa
Red Cabbage and Cauliflower
  Kimchi with Cilantro
  Berries

Curly Dock
Forager's Pasta

Goosefoot
Bread Pudding with Blue
  Cheese and Goosefoot
Angel Hair, Goosefoot, and
  Goat Cheese
Goosefoot Pancakes

Japanese Knotweed
Invasive Sorbet

Lovage
Lovage Egg Salad
Lovage Butter–Olive Oil
  Compote
Lovage Fish Chowder
Potato Lovage Spring Stew

Pea Greens
Summer Rolls for Spring/
  Summer

Rhubarb
Rhubarb-Raisin Chutney
Coconut Rice Pudding with
  Rhubarb
Pasta with Rhubarb, Swiss
  Chard, and Bacon
Asparagus and Rhubarb
Goat's Milk Flan with
  Rhubarb Compote
Amy's Rhubarb-Strawberry
  Pie

Sorrel
Flash-Cooked Sorrel
Sorrel and Salt Cod Salad
Green *Gaspacho*
Sorrel and Goat Cheese Pesto

Spruce Shoots
Spruce Shoot Compote

Stinging Nettle
Stinging Nettle Soup
Smashed Potatoes with
  Stinging Nettles and Brown
  Butter

Tarragon
Tarragon Millet Tempeh
  Cakes
Tofu Ricotta
Tarragon Vinegar

Additional Spring
  Recipes
Preserved Lemons

Alliums
(Garlic, Onions, Chives, Shallots)

Allium spp. · BIENNIAL OR PERENNIAL

Note: Leeks, also in the allium family, are profiled separately (page 251).

Garlic and onions are so basic to most people's kitchens that at first it seemed unnecessary to give them their own profile. But then I awoke to the fact that Eva eats her onions and garlic differently from most of the modern world. Her approach is more sustainable, organic, and whimsical—and explaining this might inspire some of us to expand our world of alliums.

Let me preface that the food from Eva's Garden is so flavorful that it doesn't need an onion and garlic boost the way supermarket food does. Her garden, even in midwinter, is, as Eva quips, "an embarrassment of riches." However, whenever Eva does run out of her own supply of conventional garlic and onions, she doesn't even consider buying them from the store. Rather she asks herself, "What do we have that tastes garlicky?" She takes advantage of all the different stages of growth her many alliums move through, and she enjoys a steady supply of ornamental alliums that dot her farm. She tends to clip from alliums that are still in the dirt, harvesting from them without harming their ability to reach their potential and mature. Some species continue year after year.

During the late fall (outside) and winter (in hoop houses) she'll cut the green tops off cold-tolerant onions and garlic that were not dug up in summer. She uses these greens, which she aptly dubs "onion greens," in the same way most of us use scallions. Once snipped, a variety like Evergreen Hardy White will grow back thick, white, leek-like stalks.

Culinary Uses

First to appear in the spring, front and center, are Eva's chives and garlic chives. Eva sells hundreds of pounds of them each year. She'll snip what she needs and let them grow back. She'll deluge a plate of food or a bowl of soup with a fistful or two of chopped chives. When the chives flower in the spring, they produce lavender-hued pussy-willow-sized orbs filled with tiny blossoms. A seventy-foot bed of them is a captivating sight. The flower actually provides a sharper onion flavor than the hollow green stem. Separate the orb into its spearlike florets and toss them onto a salad at the last minute for a stunning taste and visual effect.

In July or August the garlic chive flowers show up. Like chive flowers, they too add a lot of zip to food. A bit later, clusters of soft green garlic chive berries appear. Eva loves the berries in mashed potatoes, pasta sauces, and ratatouille-like mixtures. One chef she sells to pickles them. Once the green berries finally dry, the small garlicky black seeds are mature and can be sprinkled on a wide variety of foods or planted to make new plants.

Chives and garlic chives usually stop producing in October. But October and November bring forth "onion greens" from several varieties of perennial scallions, onions, and garlic. Chop these and sprinkle on anything that would have welcomed chives or scallions earlier in the season. Shallots that are left in the ground are likely to produce edible green leaves in the fall and again in the very early spring.

Throughout the spring and summer, Eva grows a variety of onions. Hardy Evergreen White, mentioned earlier, is a perennial scallion, and it's one of her favorites. She also grows ornamental alliums that can extend from spring to fall, such as the Egyptian onion, a regal-looking upside-down onion whose bulb resides at the top of the stem. The flamboyant Star of Persia is another ornamental with stunning purple petals forming a delicate sphere. Its striking beauty is long-lasting, in the garden or in a vase. Eva likes to break the flower head apart and sprinkle the florets on salads, like chive blossoms.

An unheated hoop house can stretch the season for garlic. In April and May Eva eats young or green garlic from her hoop houses. Green garlic is not a particular variety of garlic but rather any garlic's green leaves and stem, usually attached to an immature bulb. Sometimes Eva chops it and adds it to her meals, including at breakfast in omelets or Chinese pancakes. It is less bitter than garlic chives, and a lot milder. Later, in June, when the garlic greenery has grown fatter and taller, like a slim leek, she'll sometimes uproot it and chop it and cook with it, using the outer leaves to flavor a stock.

Just as the garlic is coming to maturation in the summer, garlic scapes appear. These are long, snakelike shoots that grow from young garlic bulbs. They are edible, and they should be finely chopped and cooked just like cloves of garlic. Chef Patrick Campbell of No. 9 Park in Boston collects more than sixty pounds of scapes when they are growing and pickles them. The pickling tames the scapes' intensity, he chops the pickled scapes as needed over the rest of the year, using them to flavor foods. Eva loves the clusters of garlic bulblets that the scapes eventually produce on top of the plants. When young these tiny top-setting bulbs can be grilled like asparagus. Once they are a bit more mature, they are perfect for chopping and adding to foods, just like the shoots.

In the beginning of July, the heads of garlic in the ground are almost ready—and we eat them before they have a chance to cure. The skin on the cloves is moist, not papery as we may be accustomed to seeing it, but the clove is pretty much the same as conventional garlic, though a little milder-tasting.

Health Virtues

All members of the allium family are rich with sulfur compounds and have been used to prevent and treat everything from cancer and heart disease to type 2 diabetes and hypertension. Check out this hefty statement, which was published in a 1987 issue of *Prevention* magazine: "Garlic has the broadest spectrum of any antimicrobial substance that we know of—it is antibacterial, antifungal, antiparasitic, antiprotozoan and antiviral." If true, this means that eating garlic can act as preventive medicine. And in the meantime you will be vampire-proof!

Buying and Storing

During the growing season, check farmers' markets and upscale grocers for unconventional alliums. You may be able to find green garlic in the spring and garlic scapes midsummer. Garlic chives, while less common, can sometimes be found in upscale grocery stores and Asian markets. Conventional chives are usually available year-round in large supermarkets. Whatever fresh alliums you find and wherever you buy them, you should store them in a sealed bag in the refrigerator. Cured onions and garlic (curing is the process of drying the outer skins), on the other hand, can be stored at room temperature in a well-ventilated area.

Growing Alliums

Most alliums are biennial or perennial, but they are often grown as annuals and harvested at the end of the growing season. Not surprisingly, Eva favors the self-sufficient varieties that come back year after year without much effort.

You will have to do a little research as to your variety's particular needs, but generally speaking, alliums prefer full sun and grow well in cool weather (many varieties are frost-tolerant). As an added bonus, many garden pests are repelled by their strong scent and will even steer clear of neighboring crops, making alliums useful as companion plants.

Four-Allium Risotto with Sea Scallops

This is a light, breezy risotto that is colored a brilliant emerald. If you can get ahold of local bay scallops, then by all means use them, but they take only a few seconds to cook. You certainly can make fish stock and use it instead of water, but I think the alliums (scallion, chive, garlic, and onion) and a lot of anise hyssop, dill, or tarragon give plenty of flavor.

1. To prepare for the risotto, bring 5 cups water to a boil in a medium saucepan. Once the water boils, turn the heat off and cover the saucepan.

2. Combine the scallions, chives, whole clove garlic, herb of your choosing, and 3 tablespoons of the olive oil in a blender or food processor. Puree the mixture, and set aside.

3. Heat the remaining 1 tablespoon olive oil in a medium saucepan over medium heat. Add the onion and sauté until translucent, about 7 to 9 minutes, stirring intermittently with a wooden spoon. Add the minced garlic and cook for an additional 1 to 2 minutes. Then add the rice and sauté for another minute.

4. Increase the heat to medium-high and add the wine and the teaspoon of salt. Stir well. When most of the wine has been absorbed by the rice, begin to add the hot water, about ½ cup at a time, stirring between additions, adding more water every few minutes, when the previous addition has been absorbed. After 15 minutes, add the scallion puree.

5. After about 18 minutes the rice should be nearly done. Add the mascarpone or crème fraiche and stir well. Season with salt and freshly cracked black pepper to taste.

6. To cook the scallops, heat a skillet over medium-high heat, then add the oil. When the oil is hot, add the scallops. Don't disturb them. Season with salt and freshly cracked black pepper. When the scallops turn a golden brown on their underside, turn them. Cook for just a minute on the other side, or else they'll overcook. Remove the pan from the heat.

7. Line risotto bowls or plates with bronze fennel, if you have it. Spoon risotto into the bowls or plates. Top with scallops and a leaf of the herb you used.

MAKES 4 SERVINGS

Risotto:

1 bunch scallions, green and white parts, finely chopped

1 cup minced chives (or more chopped scallions, if you can't get chives)

3 garlic cloves, 1 whole and 2 minced

1 cup anise hyssop, dill, or tarragon leaves, plus a few leaves for garnish

4 tablespoons extra-virgin olive oil

1 onion or 2 shallots, minced

1½ cups Arborio rice

²/₃ cup white wine or water

Salt and freshly cracked black pepper

½ cup mascarpone or crème fraiche

1 teaspoon salt

Freshly cracked black pepper

Scallops:

1 tablespoon extra-virgin olive oil

1 pound sea scallops, patted dry

Salt and freshly cracked black pepper

2 cups shredded bronze fennel fronds (optional)

Oat Groat Delight with Green Garlic Compote

MAKES 4 SERVINGS

- 2 cups fresh delicate herbs (such as chervil, chives, cilantro, mint, parsley, or sorrel) or ¼ cup (or less) pungent herbs (such as lovage, oregano, rosemary, sage, tarragon, or thyme), with stems removed
- 4 stalks green garlic or 3 garlic cloves, coarsely chopped
- 2 tablespoons extra-virgin olive oil
- Salt and freshly cracked black pepper
- 2 tablespoons butter or extra-virgin olive oil
- 4 cups cooked oat groats or wheat berries
- 1 stalk rhubarb, thinly sliced, or 1 cup chopped cranberries (optional)
- 4 large eggs
- 4 ounces sharp cheddar cheese, grated

A one-pan breakfast or brunch dish that will impress friends or family. The herbs are pureed in the blender with a bit of olive oil and then spooned over eggs. The eggs cook amid the crispy oat groats and melted cheese. Oat groats are available at natural foods stores, or you could use rye or wheat berries, or even whole-grain barley if you like.

1. Combine the herbs and green garlic in a food processor. Process until the herbs are finely chopped. With the machine running, add the olive oil and 2 tablespoons water. Season with salt and freshly cracked black pepper to taste. Set aside.

2. Heat the butter in a cast-iron or other well-seasoned skillet over medium-high heat. Once it is quite hot, add the groats. Don't stir, letting them develop a crust; then reduce the heat to medium-low. Once they are browned and crunchy on the underside, flip with a spatula and let them brown on the other side until they have developed a nice crust, about 15 to 20 minutes.

3. Add the rhubarb (if using) and stir well. Make four holes in the cooking grains and drop an egg into each one. Top with the grated cheese. Cover the pan and cook until the eggs are done to your liking, about 3 to 7 minutes. (I like the yolks a bit runny, so I cook them for just 3 or 4 minutes.) Season with salt and freshly cracked black pepper.

4. Bring the skillet to the table on a trivet and serve by cutting out wedges with a pie cutter or spatula, making sure everyone gets an egg if they want one. Top each slice with the herb puree and serve right away.

Arugula

Eruca sativa · ANNUAL

Julie and Alan Boegehold have lived down the road from Eva for forty years. Before that they had lived in Greece, where people forage and sell arugula. The Boegeholds developed a passion for it. Upon moving into Eva's neighborhood, they naturally gravitated to Eva and her garden of greens. Soon Julie was campaigning to Eva: "You've got to grow arugula!" So Eva tried a sample. She took a bite and thought it tasted like skunk. But the skunkiness soon tamed itself and transformed into a powerful addiction.

Eva is not alone. Most Americans have learned to love arugula. Even our president has it growing in his garden.

People living along the Mediterranean have been eating arugula since Roman times. It usually was collected in the wild and was not cultivated on a large scale until the 1990s. California takes credit, and rightly so, for popularizing arugula in our country. But Eva has been growing it for as long as Californians, and I like to imagine Eva was one of the historic arugula pioneers.

The arugula from Eva's farm is delicious. In the spring it is delicate and the flavor rich. In summer arugula can bolt and flower. Eva doesn't mind, since arugula flowers are a hot commodity and it is difficult for chefs to get them. They must be picked and transported with skilled care. The flowers eventually produce miniscule seeds, and it is mind-blowing to me that a seed the size of a grain of salt can, with a little help from water and sun, grow into leaves that are so nutty, spicy, and wildly complex and delicious.

Eva likes to point out that you can never know how any leafy greens or herbs will taste or perform on any given day or in any particular season. It is up to the weather.

In the fall I dub the herb "cranky arugula" because it takes on an attitude. It gets louder in flavor, catching fire in the nose more quickly, and the leaves and stems are tougher, but we still eat it raw. Fall arugula shouldn't take up a lot of space in the salad anymore, but instead should be used more as an accent (though Eva reminds me that "some of us hardcore addicts disagree").

Arugula is in the Brassica family. Other vegetables on this health-protecting team include broccoli, radishes, turnips, watercress, and kale. What the many hundreds of plants in this family all have in common is that their flowers and seed leaf (the very first leaf to sprout out of a seed) form the shape of a cross (hence the term "cruciferous" that's used to describe the brassicas). The arugula flower is a mighty elegant example.

Eva grows a kind of wild arugula called Sylvetta. It is smaller than regular arugula, growing no higher than eight inches, and its leaves have deeper lobes. Its flavor is fiery, complex, and well balanced, and many people, myself included, prefer it.

Culinary Uses

Arugula shines best when used in salads or as a bed for hot foods like steamed fish. Don't muddy its complex flavor with a heavy dressing (stay away from creamy blue or ranch dressing!). Instead, try tearing arugula and mixing it with mild herbs, such as parsley, lemon balm, basil, chervil, and maybe pea greens, and dress it with a touch of vinaigrette. This kind of dainty salad is perfect as a garnish for grilled meat or fish or atop homemade pizza. Because arugula is a little bitter, it does well with a sweet vinaigrette. Adding honey or using a sweet-tinged vinegar like balsamic or sherry is a good idea. A good olive oil is essential—single-estate if your budget can manage it.

And then there is cheese. Cheese is a great ally of arugula because its high fat content cuts the peppery quality, whether you use a creamy young goat cheese or a hard grating cheese like Pecorino. Arugula also pairs well with fruits, such as fresh or roasted apples, pears, or figs, as well as roasted onions or root vegetables, such as beets. It is also worthy in a potato or pasta salad. Chef Jason Bond of Bondir in Cambridge, Massachusetts, tosses arugula with roasted walnuts, fingerling potatoes, green beans, and walnut oil. And, on a simpler note, I recommend arugula in a sandwich in lieu of a lighter lettuce.

I do not, however, recommend that you cook arugula. You will find recipes in books and magazines that have you sauté it or wilt it. Turn the page. The heat just drowns out arugula's flavor, even if it's simply tossed with hot pasta at the very last moment. You are better off with spinach, chard, or kale for these uses.

Death by Pesto

A quick search on the Internet reveals that "arugula pesto" is the fourth most popular search term after "arugula salad," "arugula recipes," and "arugula salad recipes"! People gush over this newfangled concoction. But crushing and eviscerating the leaves in this manner destroys much of arugula's flavor, and I fear that arugula pesto is just one way that the typically bland American palate bypasses the green's peppery heat. In my mind, you might as well make iceberg or romaine lettuce pesto. Better yet, stick to basil, or try another herb, but keep arugula in its lovely whole state.

Health Virtues

Like many of the plants growing in Eva's garden, arugula is packed with cancer-fighting phytochemicals. It is especially high in vitamins A, C, and K as well as iron, potassium, fiber, and bioflavonoids.

Buying and Storing

Try to buy arugula with its roots intact. Store arugula, unwashed, in a plastic bag in the fridge.

Growing Arugula

If you are on the fence about growing this peppery green, consider the fact that its nickname, "rocket," refers to its speedy growth habit as well as its flavor. Especially during cool seasons, arugula will produce loads of leaves for a month or more before producing hundreds of dainty edible flowers followed by crisp, edible seedpods.

As soon as the ground has thawed, sow seeds outdoors in a sunny spot by gently raking them into fertilized soil. Keep the soil moderately moist, and thin the plants to 2 inches apart once they are established. Begin harvesting about one month after you sow the seeds, and continue to harvest until the leaves are too large and tough for your liking. If allowed to go to seed, new plants will undoubtedly spring up, or you can mow the whole crop down and allow it to regrow for a second (and possibly third) harvest.

Wild Rice, Arugula, and Parsley Salad

This recipe celebrates the bounty of late spring. Instead of arugula and parsley, you could use tarragon and sorrel, dill and pea greens, lemon balm and claytonia or watercress, chervil and baby spinach, or any other combination that appeals. If wild rice is beyond your budget, I recommend brown rice or wheat berries.

MAKES 4 SERVINGS

1 cup wild rice
⅓ cup raisins
4 cups arugula leaves
1 cup sliced strawberries
¼ red onion, minced
½ cup chopped mint or parsley
3 tablespoons extra-virgin olive oil
⅛ cup lemon juice (about ½ lemon)
Salt and freshly cracked black pepper

1. Bring a large pot of at least 8 cups water to a boil. Add the wild rice, cover, and let simmer until it is almost tender, about 45 minutes. Stir in the raisins, cover, and let simmer for 5 minutes, until the raisins rehydrate and plump up. Rinse the rice, draining it under cold running water until it is cold. Let drip-dry in the strainer for 5 minutes.

2. While the rice is cooking, combine the arugula, strawberries, onion, mint, olive oil, and lemon juice in a large bowl. Add the wild rice and raisins, stir well, and season with salt and freshly cracked black pepper to taste. Serve cold or at room temperature.

Bolted Burger

MAKES 6 BURGERS

1 teaspoon salt

¾ cup brown rice

½ cup lentils

3 cups mix of chopped bolted cilantro and bolted arugula (including flowers)

1 garlic clove

1-inch piece ginger root, peeled and sliced

1 carrot, peeled and grated

1 small red bell pepper, finely chopped

2 whole wheat hamburger buns or 3 slices whole wheat bread, broken into bits

Salt and freshly cracked black pepper

2 tablespoons extra-virgin olive oil

This is a worthwhile burger even if you don't grow your own arugula or cilantro. Just use equal portions of conventional spinach and cilantro from the store or farmers' market.

1. Bring 2 cups water to a boil in a medium saucepan. Add the salt and rice, reduce the heat, and let simmer, covered, for 20 minutes. Add the lentils and let simmer, covered, for another 20 minutes. The rice and lentils should be done when they have absorbed all the water. Uncover the pan and let them cool a bit.

2. Meanwhile, combine the cilantro and arugula, garlic, and ginger in a food processor, and pulse until the mixture is finely chopped. Transfer to a large bowl, and mix in the carrot and pepper.

3. Transfer the rice and lentils to the food processor, and pulse until the rice becomes sticky but not pureed. Add this to the bowl, scraping out the all the rice from the food processor with a rubber spatula.

4. Pulse the hamburger buns in the processor to make bread crumbs. Add the bread crumbs to the large bowl and stir well with a spoon. Season the mixture with salt and freshly cracked black pepper.

5. Using your hands, form six cakes from the burger mixture.

6. Heat the olive oil in a large skillet over medium heat. Place the burgers in the skillet (if you can't fit them in, then you'll need to cook them in batches). Cook until they brown on the underside, about 4 minutes. Flip them and cook until the other side browns as well.

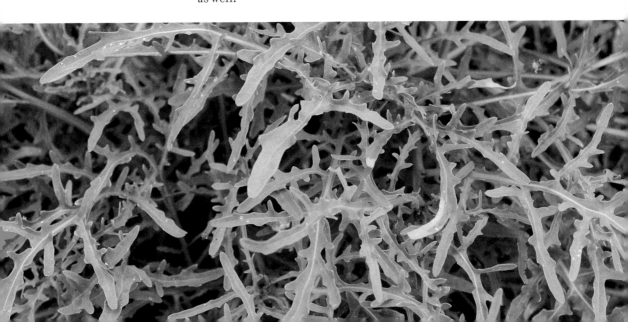

Cilantro

Coriandrum sativum · ANNUAL

Brace yourself. I feel strongly about cilantro. My central nervous system depends on it. My own dear father, the poor man, cannot handle the herb, and if I add a few measly leaves to a meat loaf he'll smell it, or worse, when he is already chewing the meat loaf, he'll taste the herb and melodramatically fake a gag so that we turn our complete attention toward him, at which point he'll drop the whole mouthful into his napkin and then look at us with disbelief, as if we just tried to poison him. I have yet to make any headway on this front.

I most often hear the complaint that cilantro tastes "soapy." But I confess that, whenever I hear it disparaged, I indulge myself in a fantasy. I think of taking half a dozen cilantro-haters hostage in my basement, just for a couple of weeks—long enough to eradicate their phobia. I'd feed them foods so luscious they wouldn't be cognizant of the subtle presence of cilantro. Every day I'd increase the cilantro quotient incrementally. For breakfast their omelets would be filled with a mélange of herbs stirred into local farmer's cheese. For lunch, they'd get grass-fed cheeseburgers with an oh-so-special sauce, and for dinner they'd start off with a mojito pounded with mint and a few leaves of cilantro; then they'd be served a Thai green curry made from cilantro roots. By the end of my carefully controlled experiment, they would be unknowingly converted. Because it truly has been my experience that people's tastes can change if they are consistently exposed to something over the course of weeks or months, and I've seen success stories from the most entrenched of cases.

In cultures where cilantro is pervasive, for example Mexico, Guatemala, Morocco, India, China, and Vietnam, it has loads of loyalty and few phobes. It also has one of the longest recorded culinary histories of any herb (five thousand years or so). Rightly so, since it has a unique, highly pleasant citric flavor. Cilantro acts like the tambourine in a band, giving a dish some much-needed pep and pizzazz, much like lemon or lime can.

CULINARY USES

The cuisine of many countries would be crippled without cilantro, and no doubt cilantro has flavored some of our most delicious dishes. It elevates raitas, chutneys, soups, salads, larb, peanut sauces, salsas, sofrito, tacos, mole, fish stew, and much more. These recipes would all be underachievers without our dear cilantro. It also can be a "good chum and not just the leader of the pack," writes Diana Henry in her exquisite book *Crazy Water Pickled Lemons*. It merges especially well with chiles, lemon, lime, garlic, olive oil, cumin, mint, parsley, and saffron.

Like a luxury car, cilantro offers features that your average herb simply doesn't have. For starters, you can eat the whole plant: the root, stems, flowers, berries, seeds, and leaves. The root is traditionally ground into Thai and Indonesian curries. Never throw out cilantro stems—they are tender and can be used in anything the leaves are meant for, with the same (albeit slightly stronger) flavor. In fact, many Mexican cooks use *only* the stems for making guacamole. Try adding the chopped stems to black beans, salsas, or Mo's harissa (page 71). I love big sprigs of cilantro in *banh mi* (a Vietnamese baguette sandwich) that includes matchsticks of pickled daikon and carrots, pork pate, and a rich chili-shrimp paste. Another Vietnamese favorite of mine is

Binh Duong's coriander chile sauce from his *Simple Art of Vietnamese Cooking*; it's great as a dip for spring rolls, tossed with noodles, or used as a salad dressing. Steven Raichlen's recipe for South African Piri-Piri Chicken Wings, found in his book *Planet Barbecue!*, features cilantro in both the marinade and the glaze.

In the summer a few cilantro sprigs elevate even the simplest of salads. Or chop the leaves and stems and toss with pasta or spaghetti squash and a dressing of lime juice, olive oil, garlic, and chiles. If you have too much cilantro, you can make a paste (I would puree cilantro, olive oil, garlic, ground cumin, lime juice, and a jalapeno) and freeze it for later use when grilling chicken, chops, or vegetables.

Cilantro Berries

If a cilantro plant is left to mature, delicate white clusters of flowers emerge; this usually doesn't occur until summertime at Eva's. These edible flowers are elegant in salads and as a garnish. If left on the plant, the fragrant flowers attract bees, and as they pollinate, cilantro berries are born. Eva's chef clients get excited about the berries, and so do I. They are juicy and pop with cilantro's sassiness, with just a hint of dried coriander coming in. These berries are spectacular in pickles and preserved vegetables, including my Red Cabbage and Cauliflower Kimchi (page 72), as well as in salsas, mayonnaise, and vinaigrettes. Dan George's Smoky Pickled Corn Circles with Coriander Seeds, in the book he coauthored, *Quick Pickles*, is one example of where the berry can shine.

After a week or two the berries dry up, turn brown, and become coriander seeds. The flavor of the dried seed is different from that of the fresh berry, with sultry undertones of lemon. Coriander seed is an essential spice in a wide array of curry powders (particularly those from India) and other spice mixes, but it's also terrific on its own, with chicken, in stews, or added to roasted vegetables before they hit the oven.

Health Virtues

Cilantro has so many health virtues that there very well may be a book out there dedicated to the subject, but to give you the abridged version, let's start with the fact that cilantro contains chemical compounds that detoxify the body of heavy metals, including mercury. Cilantro also works wonders in the digestive tract, boosting the immune system and calming indigestion. It's also been known to cleanse the liver, cure bad breath, and clear up conjunctivitis. Perhaps I can get a doctor to prescribe it for my father.

Buying, Storing, and Prepping

At the market, cilantro should be buoyant and filled with life, not limp. Its leaves should radiate a luster. Store the herb along with a moist paper towel in a plastic bag, unsealed, in the fridge. If the cilantro is fresh, it will last two weeks. Mature coriander seeds can be left to fully dry on a baking sheet at room temperature for two dry days (high humidity can cause mold). Once they're dry, place in a sealed bottle, jar, or ziplock bag.

Growing Cilantro

Cilantro, an annual herb, is remarkably easy to grow. Scatter seeds directly into your garden and lightly rake into the soil. When the seedlings reach 2 inches in height, thin any overcrowded plants to 3 to 6 inches apart. You can harvest cilantro for use as a fresh herb in about eight weeks; for berries or coriander seed, allow the plant to go to seed. Cilantro is easily grown in pots as well; just keep in mind that the soil in pots will get hotter faster than in the open garden.

Like many commercial New England farmers, Eva plants cilantro every week from spring through fall for a steady supply. High heat and long days in midsummer will cause the plants to bolt faster, and once temperatures dip in the fall your plants may develop a red tinge on their leaves. (Eva calls this her "fall foliage" cilantro.)

Mo's Harissa

This is a life-changing sauce that my Moroccan roommate Mo taught me to make. It is thicker than other harissas I've known, and it's silky, like a mayonnaise. It can be served with roasted vegetables, chicken, rice, or couscous, but it makes pretty much anything—lamb, fish, tofu, probably even old sneakers—taste crazy good. It is worth making double the recipe and freezing what you can't manage to eat. Jamie Bissonnette of Coppa restaurant in Boston makes his harissa with roasted beets. If you want to try that I would use one or two beets instead of the tomatoes.

1. Preheat the oven to 275 degrees F. Oil a large sheet pan.
2. Arrange the red and green bell peppers, tomatoes, and garlic on the oiled sheet pan in a single layer. Bake them for 1 hour to dry them out.
3. Heat a dry skillet over medium-high heat. Add the chiles and cook until they are smoky and brittle, about 5 minutes. (Alternatively, you could put them in the oven with the peppers and tomatoes for the last 10 minutes of cooking time.)
4. Combine the roasted vegetables, chiles, cilantro, cumin, salt, cinnamon, and honey in a food processor or blender. Pulse until the ingredients are finely chopped.
5. With the machine running, slowly pour in the vinegar and then the oil, followed by ¼ cup water, and process until the mixture is fairly smooth. Season the harissa with salt and freshly cracked black pepper to taste. Store in a container with a tight sealing lid. It will keep for up to one month.

MAKES 3–4 CUPS

2 red bell peppers, chopped into 1-inch pieces

1 green bell pepper, chopped into 1-inch pieces, or 1 small bunch arugula (added when pureeing)

6 plum or vine-ripened tomatoes, chopped into 1-inch pieces, or about 25 cherry tomatoes, halved

7 garlic cloves, thinly sliced

1 handful dried red chiles, 1 large ancho chile, or 1–2 tablespoons chile flakes

1 small bunch cilantro leaves and stems, chopped (about 2 cups)

2 teaspoons ground cumin

1 teaspoon salt

Pinch ground cinnamon

1 tablespoon honey

⅓ cup red wine or cider vinegar

½ cup extra-virgin olive oil

Salt and freshly cracked black pepper

Red Cabbage and Cauliflower Kimchi with Cilantro Berries

MAKES 2 QUARTS

1 head cauliflower, cut into bite-size pieces

1 medium head red cabbage, cored and thinly sliced

1 bunch scallions or 1 large leek, white and green parts, thinly sliced

½ cup freshly grated ginger

6 large garlic cloves, minced

½ lemon, quartered, then thinly sliced and seeded

1–2 tablespoons cilantro berries

1 jalapeño (or more to taste), chopped

approximately 2½ tablespoons sea salt

This kimchi has a delicious Indian flavor, which I hadn't expected when I first made it. Cilantro berries normally taste a lot like cilantro, but when pickled in this kimchi they render the flavor of dried coriander seed, which is used heavily in Indian curries. The only prerequisite for the recipe is that you need to grow cilantro, or know someone who does; chances are, you won't get the berries until the summer. Good-quality nonwhite sea salt yields the best kimchi, because of its high mineral content. As I do with all kimchis, I tend to add this one to stir-fries, pasta dishes, and soups.

It was with this kimchi that I stopped following recipes and began creating my own. I give you the pound to teaspoon ratio of veggies to salt, so you can go off on your own and choose the veggies you like with your kimchis.

1. Weigh your vegetables, or check your receipt for the weight of your veggies. This will determine how much salt to use.
2. Combine the cauliflower, cabbage, scallions, ginger, garlic, lemon, cilantro berries, and jalapeño in a bowl and toss well. Add 2 teaspoons sea salt to the bowl for every pound of vegetables you've used. Add the salt and let the mixture sit and sweat liquid for 2 to 3 hours, stirring and pressing down occasionally to help the contents release more liquid.
3. Pack the mixture tightly into jars or crocks, pressing down on it to expel any air. The liquid should cover the contents of each jar. If it does not, you should place something on the contents to press them down so that the liquid does cover. Leave at least 1 inch of headspace between the top of the kimchi and the rim of the jars to allow for bubbling during fermentation. Screw the lids on the jars.
4. Let the kimchi ferment, with the lid on, at room temperature for 3 days (it should bubble), then move it to the refrigerator, where it will continue to ferment for about 2 weeks. After this, the fermentation slows down. It will keep for up to a year in the refrigerator.

Curly Dock

Rumex crispus · PERENNIAL

About forty of us were eating at a long table at a class I was teaching when I overheard the word "foraging" three or four seats downwind from me. My attention was completely stolen and as it turned out that the man was an avid forager. He told us that he'd even written a small guidebook to urban foraging. I asked if I could join him foraging, and all I can say is, this young man, David Craft is the guy to have by your side in the woods. He is a passionate forager; there was almost no plant we passed that he didn't identify and weigh in on.

Now whenever he's biking by my neighborhood, David will leave greens on my front landing. His first delivery was a big sack of curly dock, and now it's one of my favorite plants to forage and eat.

Culinary Uses

The younger unfurled leaves in the center of the curly dock plant are the most succulent, but all the leaves are quite good. Curly dock's appealingly lemony, slightly sour flavor is reminiscent of that of sorrel. Though it doesn't cook down as much as spinach or sorrel, curly dock, like sorrel, turns an olive green color when cooked. If you undercook the leaves to retain their color, they may be hairy and a bit tough, so I usually opt for the yummy mud-colored route.

I've used curly dock with great success in stews and coconut milk curries, adding it at the last minute. I also love it in an omelet. Russ Cohen, another foraging expert, turns spanikopita into a wild delicacy by using curly dock (and/or stinging nettle) instead of spinach. Eating it raw can irritate and numb your tongue, although some do eat it raw. I think it tastes much better cooked.

Health Virtues

Curly dock leaves are high in fiber and have more vitamin A than an equal amount of carrots. The roots provide potassium, manganese, and a lot of iron. Curly dock also boasts 30 percent more protein, iron, calcium, potassium, beta-carotene, and phosphorus than spinach, and more than twice the vitamin C.

Foraging and Storing

Curly dock can be found from coast to coast in North America. The plant looks similar to sorrel, although the leaves are darker in color and coarser in texture, and they have a wavy lasagna-like edge to them. The stalk, which grows from 2 to 6 inches long, has shallow grooves running its length. The time to eat the plant is in the spring and fall, when the leaves are 6 or so inches long. It is a perennial, so, once you find it, you know it will be there year after year. Try looking in areas with disturbed soil—in fields, on fallow or abandoned land, and along riverbanks. Once you find curly dock, harvest the inner, most tender leaves by simply cutting them at the base. Make sure you respectfully leave behind about one-third of the plant so that it can regenerate (always a good foraging practice). Store curly dock in a plastic bag in the refrigerator for up to one week.

Forager's Pasta

MAKES 1 OR 2 SERVINGS

3 tablespoons extra-virgin olive oil

2 large garlic cloves, minced

3 cups cooked whole-grain pasta (a small pasta like penne will do)

Big handful curly dock or sorrel (about 1 cup)

Handful stinging nettle, stems removed, or another handful curly dock (about 1 cup)

2 medium stalks Japanese knotweed or ½ stalk rhubarb, finely chopped, or 2 tablespoons chopped kimchi

2 tablespoons chopped kimchi or 1 tablespoon capers

2–3 tablespoons good grating cheese

Rarely is a recipe so good that I begin typing it up as I'm eating it. I had been foraging one afternoon with David Craft, a spry young man who collects much of his food through foraging. We picked knotweed, curly dock, and stinging nettle, practically in my Boston backyard. The cooking takes all of five minutes, and besides garlic, pasta, and olive oil, all it needed to achieve greatness was a little kimchi du jour and some good grating cheese. I use an organic sheep's-milk cheese from Northland Sheep Dairy in New York State called Tomme Berère, but a good Pecorino or Parmesan will do. Remember to wear gloves when handling raw stinging nettle.

1. Heat the olive oil in a skillet over medium heat, then add the garlic. Once the garlic is sizzling, after just a few seconds, stir in the pasta, followed by the curly dock, stinging nettle, and knotweed. Cook and stir for a couple of minutes, until everything wilts and gets quite hot.

2. Turn off the heat, add the kimchi, and stir. Pour the pasta into bowls. Top with grated cheese and eat right away.

Feeding the Soil: Nutrient Density

Eva of late likes to talk about nutrient density like it is the cure for cancer or the solution to world hunger—and she may be on to something, at least with the hunger piece. Supermarket produce has shown a sizable decline in nutritional quality since the 1940s: from apples to zucchinis, bite for bite we are consuming fewer vitamins, minerals, and other nutrients than our grandparents did. For years we have been abusing our soil and selectively breeding vegetables to look perfect under fluorescent lighting after traveling hundreds or thousands of miles (those pyramids of tomatoes do look nice), without considering the effect this system may have on plant and human health, not to mention flavor.

As our industrialized food system continues to oversimplify the complex world of soil and plant health, plenty of farmers have opted to grow food in a way that is beneficial to environmental and human health. Eva's pal and neighboring farmer Derek Christianson has focused his energies (and his big brain) on studying nutrient density—the relative vitamin and mineral density of a crop. Nutrient density isn't just about getting more available nutrients into each bite of broccoli. It is highly scientific, seeking to understand soil and plant health on a molecular level, and it has the potential to cause a paradigm shift in our food system. Nutrient-dense crops grown on nutrient-dense soils are less susceptible to diseases and pests, they taste better, and they are healthier for us, making the concept an attractive one for producers and consumers alike. If you want to learn more, Derek's farm has a website that explores the topic: www.brixbounty.com.

GROWING YOUR OWN HERBS

(from farmhand Kelly Lake)

Unfamiliar herbs can be intimidating in the kitchen, and even more so in the garden. The first thing to keep in mind is that all herbs need the same things as any other plant: good soil, sun, water, and air. The second thing to keep in mind is that they all need those things in varying amounts; there is no one-size-fits-all approach to growing. Because I am no gardening expert, my friend and former farmer at Eva's Garden, Kelly Lake, wrote the following steps and charts to growing herbs and lettuce greens.

Step 1: Location
Because most herbs are relatively small (compared to fruit and vegetable plants), they make great candidates for container growing, especially if their roots are shallow. Basil, dill, chives, lemon verbena, anything in the mint family, oregano, rosemary, sage, tarragon, and thyme—along with almost any salad green—grow well in containers as long as the soil-to-plant ratio is good and drainage is adequate. Herbs that grow exceptionally tall and send down a deep taproot, like fennel and lovage, are happiest when planted in the open ground. Keep in mind that you may opt for growing in a container even if you have a lot of land, for example if you want to keep an ambitious herb (like mint) contained or if you are growing a tender perennial (like lemongrass) that you will be moving indoors over the winter.

Step 2: Resource Assessment
Don't set yourself up for failure by trying to grow basil (because you really love basil) if your only growing area is a fire escape that is in shade most of the day. The three most important questions to ask yourself are: How much sun will my plant get? Does the soil drain well, or does it hold water? How much space do I have? Once you have the answers, you can select plants appropriately.

Step 3: Starting from Seed vs. Transplanting
Some quick-growing herbs and salad greens will do best if sowed from seed directly into the soil. Keep the soil as moist as a wet sponge until you spot little plants poking their heads up. Some herbs can take a really long time to start growing, or are finicky at first, and so it is best to buy them as seedlings from a nursery. Give each seedling and its destination soil a good watering before transplanting, and massage the root-ball to loosen the roots just a bit before burying it in its new home.

Step 4: Herbal Adolescence
Once your plant is well established, you may be tempted to forget about it for a while and let it do its own thing. Stay strong! At this stage it is important to follow the care instructions in regard to watering, fertilizing, or thinning to keep your crop on the path to a good harvest. If weeds are left unchecked, you will fight them for the rest of the season. Some plants are more fragile than others; if you anticipate a few vaca-

tions or lots of family gatherings that will keep you away from your garden, choose a hardy perennial that can withstand slight drought (like thyme) or bounce back quickly (like mint).

Step 5: Harvesting and Maintenance

Herbs vary greatly in their harvests. Some do best when they are harvested all at once and resown (like cilantro) or left to regenerate (like loose-leaf greens). Others can be harvested on an ongoing basis until they are killed off by frost (like basil, parsley, and sage).

Step 6: Thinking Ahead

Once the temperatures begin to drop, don't forget to start moving tender perennials (like lemon verbena and African basil) indoors. Hardy perennials that will be left outdoors will benefit from a layer of mulch if you live in an extreme climate (try hay, chaff, grass clippings, or chopped leaves). And don't forget to preserve some of your herbs for next season (see page xx).

Need some inspiration? Here are some growing plans to get you started. I recommend growing your own salad mix, some perennial herbs, and some annual herbs that you can switch up from year to year.

Herb Mix: If you grow the following herbs yourself you benefit from their flavor as well as their edible flowers, which make unique and delicious garnishes if you like to entertain or if you just love functional aesthetics.

Herb	Container?	Light	Water	Perennial?
Arugula	yes	full sun	moderate	no
Bronze fennel	no	full sun	can withstand periods of drought	self-seeding
Chervil	yes	full sun	moderate	no
Cilantro	yes	full sun to light shade	moderate	no
Sage	yes	full sun	semi-arid	yes

Salad Mix: The seeds of these greens can be scattered together and raked into the soil. When you are ready to harvest, cut the greens 1 inch above the soil level. The plants will regrow, at which point you can harvest again. Repeat until the greens look unhealthy, then dig them up and put them in the compost, fertilize the soil, and sow the next batch.

Green	Container?	Light	Water	Perennial?
Arugula	yes	full sun to light shade	moderate	no
Chickweed	yes	full sun to light shade	moderate	no
Dandelion greens	yes	full sun to light shade	moderate	no
Mizuna	yes	full sun to light shade	moderate	no
Sylvetta arugula	yes	full sun to light shade	moderate	no

Goosefoot

Chenopodium album · ANNUAL

I consider "weed" to be a politically incorrect term—there is no biological definition of the term weed. It's really a value judgment.

—Peter Del Tredici, author of
Wild Urban Plants of the Northeast

There are endless statistics about food waste, but to my knowledge, no one has kept track of how much food people unknowingly obliterate whenever they mow their front lawns. Goosefoot is certainly one of the most frequent casualties, along with dandelion greens and wood sorrel. I always notice it in my neighbors' yards. I want to pick it right then and there. Instead, I'll wait until someone is home and knock on the door. If they answer, I'll compliment them first on their robust weeds, then I'll ask them if I can pick some. I usually ask if they use chemical fertilizers. I'm still new to this kind of foraging, but I haven't been turned down yet. One time I tried to excite a homeowner with his own natural edible bounty, and I'm pretty sure I went into his kook category. But there are many who have put Eva in the kook category, too, and she doesn't seem to mind.

This plant has many names, but is best known as goosefoot, lamb's-quarter, or pigweed. It is called pigweed because pigs like to eat it. Once you start cooking and eating it, you will realize the pigs were onto something.

It is sad that people want to eradicate goosefoot, especially once you start enjoying it. Forager Russ Cohen offers an upbeat suggestion: "If you can't beat it, eat it!"

CULINARY USES

It's surprising to me that goosefoot isn't better known among foodies, except as quinoa, which is not actually a grain but the seed of a species of goosefoot that has been grown in South America since the time of the Incan empire. The goosefoot that grows here in the States is typically harvested for its leaves, though the stem directly attached to the leaf is tender enough to eat also. Goosefoot tastes like really fresh, silky baby spinach when cooked, though it's actually higher in vitamins and protein than spinach, and it has an earthy, mineral-rich taste. If you enjoy leafy greens such as kale, collards, and spinach, you'll love goosefoot and will enjoy its delicate nature.

I like to sauté goosefoot with olive oil, garlic, salt, and pepper over high heat for thirty seconds or so until it is wilted. If the leaves are more mature or larger than 2 inches in diameter, I'll add a few spoonfuls of water so they steam a little before they're fried. Goosefoot also mingles well in a sauté with other wild greens like curly dock or stinging nettle. Add a spoonful of kimchi once it's been seared to give it some zip!

Although I've never tried it, Eva loves magenta goosefoot. It is green as well, but there is a splash of fuchsia toward the base of each leaf. After growing to full size (3 to 4 feet), it again puts out nice little tender leaves almost as tender as baby growth. It can be cooked in the same way as regular goosefoot.

HEALTH VIRTUES

Goosefoot is high in vitamins A and C, calcium, manganese, potassium, and iron.

FORAGING AND STORING

When you're on the prowl for goosefoot, its name provides a helpful hint: the leaf has the shape of a webbed foot. You can also look for a white powder on the newest leaves close to the stem. To harvest, just cut or snap off the youngest and best-looking branches from the top and sides of the plant. It's best to pick them in the spring when the plant is young, about 8 inches tall. You can find goosefoot in open areas where the soil was recently disturbed, such as in agricultural fields, gardens, yards, roadsides, construction sites, urban lots, and beaches.

Goosefoot holds up well in the fridge in a plastic bag. I once forgot about it for ten days and found it to be of nearly the same quality as it was on day one.

Bread Pudding with Blue Cheese and Goosefoot

MAKES 8 TO 10 SERVINGS

4 tablespoons butter

6 slices whole wheat bread

1 tablespoon extra-virgin olive oil

2 garlic cloves

6 cups goosefoot or curly dock leaves or coarsely chopped dandelion or chard leaves

½–1 teaspoon salt plus more for seasoning

Freshly cracked black pepper

6 large eggs

3 cups half-and-half or whole milk

1 cup crumbled blue cheese

Think of this as a quiche with an easy fiber-filled crust (made of whole wheat toast) instead of the predictable fatty piecrust. This is an outstanding brunch dish, perfect for a party. I prefer a U.S.-made Gorgonzola or any fairly inexpensive blue cheese, since the subtleties of more expensive blue would get lost amid all the other flavors. If you want a milder bread pudding, you could use creamy goat cheese instead of the blue.

1. Preheat the oven to 350 degrees F.
2. Drop the butter into a 9 by 13-inch brownie pan and put the pan in the oven for a few minutes, until the butter melts. Remove from the oven and add the bread to form a single layer, trimming the bread where necessary, and aiming to have all the bread evenly buttered. Place the pan back in the oven and bake for 10 minutes, or until the bread is toasted. Remove and set aside.
3. Heat the olive oil in a skillet over medium heat. Add the garlic. When it is sizzling, after just a few seconds, add the goosefoot and sauté for a minute. (If you are using chard, sauté for about for 5 to 7 minutes, adding a spoonful or two of water if the leaves are not already wet from washing; if you are using dandelion or spinach, sauté for 3 minutes.) Season with salt and freshly cracked black pepper to taste.
4. Reduce the oven temperature to 325 degrees F.
5. Whisk together the eggs, half-and-half, and salt.
6. Spread the cooked greens over the toast, then distribute the cheese evenly over the greens. Pour the egg mixture over the cheese. Bake for 50 to 60 minutes, or until a knife inserted halfway into the custard comes out clean. Let the custard cool for 10 minutes before serving and eating.

Angel Hair, Goosefoot, and Goat Cheese

This recipe is a tasty and easy meal, toothsome enough to share with friends. Start to finish, it takes twenty minutes. I'll admit that I use nonlocal cherry tomatoes for this sort of recipe, as local ones aren't around in the spring. I find that as nonlocal tomatoes go, cherry tomatoes have the most flavor. If you can't find goosefoot, then spinach or chard is a good alternative.

1. Preheat the oven to 350 degrees F.
2. Pour the walnuts onto a rimmed baking sheet. Toast the nuts in the oven about 5 minutes, until they are golden brown.
3. Bring a large pot of salted water to a boil. Add the pasta and cook until al dente. Drain the pasta, reserving ¼ cup of the cooking water.
4. Return the pasta to the pot. Place the pot over medium heat and add the reserved ¼ cup pasta water, goosefoot, tomatoes, garlic, and olive oil. Cook and stir for 3 minutes, turning the pasta over to heat the goosefoot.
5. Remove the pasta from the heat and toss with the toasted walnuts, goat cheese, lemon juice, and Parmesan. Season with the salt and freshly cracked black pepper to taste and serve.

MAKES 6 SERVINGS

½ cup chopped walnuts

1 pound whole-grain angel hair pasta or spaghettini

3–4 cups loosely packed goosefoot leaves (woody stems removed)

1 pint cherry tomatoes, halved

3 garlic cloves, smashed or minced

⅓ cup extra-virgin olive oil

½ cup crumbled goat cheese

Squeeze lemon juice

½ cup grated Parmesan cheese, plus more for sprinkling

½ teaspoon salt

Freshly cracked black pepper

Keeping Community Order

Eva's farm has a massive inventory of equipment. Countless pairs of scissors used to cut herbs, farm tools, and even kitchen utensils are liable to grow feet and walk away. Eva gets frazzled when something has disappeared or is not where it should be. Her strategy is to mark anything and everything with a permanent marker, labeled loud and clear: "BELONGS TO EVA." No object is too small to receive Eva's attention; even pencils get tagged for fear they stray from their home. But while she assiduously attempts order in her life, it seems to elude her.

Furthermore, you need to watch what you leave at the farm. A friend of mine once left behind a relatively cheap coffeemaker at the cottage, and within a few weeks it was branded: "BELONGS TO EVA."

Goosefoot Pancakes

MAKES 20–25 SMALL PANCAKES

2½ cups unbleached all-purpose flour

1 cup finely chopped chives, scallions, or leeks

Leaves from 20 parsley sprigs (or another mild herb)

1 small onion, coarsely chopped

2 garlic cloves, coarsely chopped

1 teaspoon salt, plus more for seasoning

2 cups whole milk

3 large eggs

Freshly cracked black pepper

8 cups coarsely chopped greens (goosefoot, chard, sorrel, chickweed, curly dock, or a combination)

About ½ cup grapeseed, peanut, or vegetable oil

This is an adaptation of *farçous*, a French pancake, based on Dorie Greenspan's recipe in *From Around My French Table.* I've added some goosefoot and tripled the quantity of greens, and it's sublime! This is a recipe where you can easily improvise; use another herb instead of parsley, or switch up the greens. Dorie says extra pancakes can be frozen—this probably won't be necessary. She recommends serving these pancakes on a lightly dressed salad with a dollop of crème fraîche on top. We ate them out of hand, like crackers, all day long.

1. Preheat the oven to 250 degrees F. Line a baking sheet with foil, and line a plate with paper towels.

2. Combine the flour, chives, parsley, garlic, salt, milk, and eggs in a blender or food processor, and season with freshly cracked black pepper. Process until the mixture forms a smooth batter. If your machine won't handle this quantity, work in batches.

3. Little by little add the greens to the mix, pulsing to incorporate them. There's no need to pulverize the greens—having some strands is nice.

4. Pour ¼ to ½ inch of oil into a large skillet over medium-high heat. When the oil is hot (a drop of batter should seize immediately), spoon in a scant ¼ cup batter for each pancake. Be careful not to crowd the skillet, so the pancakes cook properly.

5. Cook the pancakes for about 3 minutes, until the undersides are nicely browned and the edges are browned and curled. Flip the pancakes over and cook for another 2 minutes or so, until the other side is browned.

6. Transfer the pancakes to the paper-towel-lined plate, cover with more towels, and blot the excess oil. Place the pancakes on the foil-lined baking sheet and keep warm in the oven while you continue to make pancakes, adding more oil to the pan as needed.

Japanese Knotweed

Polygonum cuspidatum · PERENNIAL

In the spring, free food begins to appear if you know where to look throughout the city and countryside. Knotweed is easy to spot and fairly common, so it's one of the great starter plants for beginning foragers. In fact it may very well be already under your nose, because it is pervasive and invasive. I first came across knotweed at a party thrown by Boston's most famous forager, Russ Cohen. It was a wild-foods party, where he and his wife made a dizzying array of dishes, all crafted from their outings. Among the treats was a strawberry knotweed pie—the knotweed here replacing rhubarb, with its similarly sour, slightly lemony flavor.

Considering knotweed's insistence on spreading aggressively, it is understandably despised by gardeners and ecologists alike. It is also perennial, meaning that although the aboveground plant dies back after just one season, the roots remain and send up more plants year after year. Like many wild foods, knotweed is edible only in early spring, when its foot-high shoots are most tender. So tender, in fact, that it's tasty raw. Eva calls knotweed one of her "spring blinks," as the edible window is only a few weeks long. As it grows, the plant quickly begins to morph and harden into what looks like a small bamboo tree, eventually rising as high as 8 feet. At that point there's not much left worth eating. But you could build a lovely knotweed dining room set!

Culinary Uses

Some people, like my friend Russ Cohen, like to peel knotweed. This takes time. David Craft, my other forager friend, doesn't peel his knotweed, nor does Eva. So I take the route of least resistance. Chopped knotweed cooks in just a few minutes and has a crunchy texture. If you cook it longer, like rhubarb, it turns into mush.

Knotweed is commonly sweetened and, like rhubarb, used in pies, jams, sauces, compotes, cakes, and so on. Eva pressure-cooks it for a few minutes and then buzzes it in her Vitamix. She freezes the puree to form the base of sorbets. You can also make a jam or "butter" from this puree by cooking it down further and adding sugar. I think it's smart to introduce herbs or spices to knotweed, because its flavor is not as sour and beguiling as rhubarb's. Add a spice like cardamom, clove, or nutmeg when baking with knotweed, and use fresh mint or lemon verbena after cooking and pureeing knotweed for sorbets, compotes, and jams. I've found that I like knotweed best in savory dishes like pasta, gnocchi, and risotto because the slight sourness complements many popular ingredients such as garlic, caramelized onions, cheese, butter, and wild greens. It also works well raw in salads, thinly sliced.

Health Virtues

Knotweed is high in vitamins A and C and contains antioxidants. Like some plants (rhubarb, curly dock, goosefoot, and even spinach) it is high in oxalic acid, which can be harmful in really huge quantities. The acid breaks down when heated so I recommend eating knotweed cooked. Besides, it tastes better this way.

Foraging and Storing

Knotweed is easy to spot in the fall, especially along roads, when the chartreuse stalks and magenta-accented leaves stand over 5 feet tall. However, it is best eaten in the spring, when the young shoots are tender. It typically grows in dense patches, so foraging is quick and easy and you will inevitably pick much more than you could eat. The stalk is hollow, except at the bamboolike knots spaced along its length. Look for knotweed anywhere with disturbed soil, but make sure you put some distance between your foraging spot and any pollutants (cars, old buildings, and so on).

Store knotweed in plastic bags in the fridge for up to one week.

Invasive Sorbet

One night after dinner Eva embarked on what she dubbed her "invasive" sorbet, which is composed of three fairly invasive plants: knotweed, autumn olive, and beach rose. I call for a few teaspoons of sugar here, which is necessary for most people partaking of this sorbet, though not for Eva.

MAKES 8 SERVINGS

8 cups chopped knotweed

1 cup frozen autumn olive puree (page 217)

1 cup loosely packed rugosa rose petals

⅛ cup lemon juice (about ½ lemon)

1 tablespoon honey, or more to taste

Few teaspoons of sugar (optional)

1. Puree the knotweed 4 cups at a time, with ½ cup water in each batch, in a blender. Transfer the puree to a shallow pan or ice cube trays and freeze for at least 24 hours.

2. Right before serving, combine the frozen knotweed puree in a blender or Vitamix with the autumn olive puree, rose petals, lemon juice, and honey. Puree the mixture.

3. Spoon the pureed sorbet into small cups, and sprinkle with sugar if desired.

When to Add Herbs

Ever wonder when you should add herbs to soups, stews, pasta dishes, gravies, pilafs, or tagines? A lot of people think herbs are best added early on. But really it depends on which herb you're using and who you are talking to. Some herbs diminish in flavor the minute you add them to a boiling liquid, and all herbs lose their mojo after an hour or so of simmering. Our herb diva, Eva, doesn't cook herbs much at all. Mostly she chops and sprinkles herbs on top of the cooked food, or she adds herbs in the last five minutes of a soup or stew's cooking time. She feels, and I'm beginning to agree, that this is plenty long enough for herbs to mingle and infuse flavor. And Eva often uses the double-whammy method—she'll add herbs during the cooking process and then shower them onto the plated food. Eva does this even with strong herbs like rosemary. She is hard-core.

I think I agree with her on this because, like Eva, I've built up a resistance to the pungency of herbs. But also the herbs are at their truest, their most authentic, when raw. You can always regulate the amount you use.

Certain herbs fare better in cooking than others. Herbs that are rich in fragrant volatile oils will nosedive quickly when added to a simmering liquid. Examples would be basil, chervil, chives, dill, lemon balm, and lemon verbena. Parsley, mint, and cilantro are slightly hardier, but not by much. All these herbs can be classified as "thin-skinned" herbs. These thin-skinned herbs can be used in cooking, but you have to be careful. They can be infused, that is, added to a just-boiled liquid and allowed to steeped—as in cream for desserts, or water for broths or tea. If the liquid is thick, like a cream sauce, chutney, or jam, or if the herb is baked in food, like a cookie, there is an "insulating" factor that protects thin-skinned herbs from losing their flavor as quickly. For instance, the French add chervil to cream sauces and bake it with fish. However, the chervil is very subdued as a result.

If you toss these herbs into hot pasta and remove it from the heat, they usually hold onto their flavor. Basil is the quickest to lose its essence (though African blue basil has some staying power). But I mash basil into tofu and bake it in lasagna with success. Similarly, thin-skinned herbs can be added to meatballs, breads, or stuffings and then cooked, imparting good flavor; again, there is the insulation factor.

The stems in these herbs hold onto their flavor better than the leaves. Many chefs cook parsley or cilantro stems for hours in stocks. I would cook them for ten or fifteen minutes. But again, the thickness of the liquid matters: chopped cilantro stems can cook for half an hour in a pot of thickened black beans.

In general, I recommend chopping thin-skinned herbs at the last moment and adding them to the finished dish, or of course using them raw in salads or compotes.

So, which herbs can stand the heat? The woody-stemmed herbs: oregano, rosemary, thyme, marjoram, savory, tarragon, lovage, and sage, in descending order from the hardiest to the most sensitive to heat (in my opinion!). Still, most woody herbs are best cooked no longer than ten or fifteen minutes in a soup, sauce, or stock. A slow simmer will coax the flavor out of them more effectively than a hard boil.

In general, the edible flowers of herbs are best left uncooked. However, they can retain their flavor when used to make syrups and jams, such as rose petal jam.

Raw Milk for the Community

Can milk be a delicacy? This is a concept I didn't give much thought to until I drank raw milk. I've never been a big milk drinker, but now I look forward to my morning cereal with raw milk. Clean, rich, honeyed—raw milk gives me delight. I pick it up at Paskamansett Farms near Eva's. At night, I drink it warm with cinnamon. It's gotten to the point that I avoid pasteurized milk, even organic, at the market, because when the milk from hundreds or thousands of cows gets mixed and then heated to 145 degrees F, it doesn't taste like anything to me. I resort to soy milk instead.

Tom Coutu, who runs Paskamansett Farms dairy in Dartmouth, Massachusetts, grew up milking cows on his family farm, but that was just for the family to drink. When Tom was just twenty-two years old, he decided to sell raw milk.

Not pasteurizing milk demands that the milk be healthy, which means you have to raise healthy cows. Tom says, "My cows aren't depressed because they aren't crowded, they're not in a feedlot. It's quality versus quantity."

The really great news is that this milk is nutritionally rich. These cows eat grass and hay, which imbues their milk with many of the dietary building blocks that are lacking in the modern American diet. The biggest problem with store-bought milk that comes from grain-fed animals is its lopsided ratio of omega-6 to omega-3 fatty acids. This imbalance (which permeates the American diet in general) has been linked to a slew of health problems.

The only drawback is that there is a smaller window before raw milk turns—only about eight days. But when pasteurized milk goes bad, it turns rotten. Raw milk is full of living microorganisms and therefore does not become rotten. Instead, the tiny microorganisms in milk consume the milk sugars and produce lactic acid, which gives aged raw milk its "sour" flavor. At this point it can be used in pancakes, in sourdough breads, or, after a couple of weeks, to make fresh cheese. And it actually becomes healthier for us as it sours, because it becomes highly probiotic.

Lovage

I was creating a tarragon egg salad for a video production. I started out on camera following my scripted recipe, adding tarragon and chives to the egg salad. But there was a big pile of super-fresh chopped lovage within reach, set aside for another recipe, and at the last minute I went for it and grabbed a handful, adding it to the bowl. This detour resulted in the best egg salad I've ever made!

I overlooked lovage for many years at Eva's; with more than a hundred other herbs growing there, the competition for attention was stiff. But one year something was different. The plant gave off an unusually strong scent. It stood there, glistening and lush, poised for adoration. I took it in, nibbling on a leaf. This was lovage in Cadillac condition. Meanwhile, Eva's friends Brandon and Laura, who were staying for the weekend, had also discovered this lovage plant—quite a coincidence, considering the immensity of her garden. Before we could exchange niceties we were discussing the lovage plant. For the next three days we lavished our food with copious amounts of lovage. We added it to roast chicken, soups, salads, tabbouleh, and even sorbets.

Before that weekend, the lovage I had known tasted slightly bitter. But as I learned, in spring, when it is young, the leaves are mild and almost juicy, tasting of celery crossed with parsley. In the summer lovage loses some of that virginal sweetness, but Eva maintains that the sweetness returns in the fall.

Culinary Uses

Think of lovage as celery with turbo power. This herb can catapult grain, egg, potato, and pasta salads into greatness. And it is indispensable in soups. Try making a cold celery soup or a hot chicken soup, fortifying it with lovage (added in the final twenty minutes of cooking).

Lovage takes well to pureeing. Some chefs blanch the lovage leaves for a few seconds before pureeing to mute its flavor slightly and to fix the color, for example if they're making lovage oil. Chef Mike Pagliarini from Boston's Via Matta adds lovage to pureed celery root to echo the celery flavor. I once made a lovage compote, mixing lovage puree with lemon juice, garlic, olive oil, and chives, and served it next to a goat-cheese-stuffed chicken breast. It is also transcendent with seared scallops.

Many chefs use lovage as a salt substitute because it adds so much flavor. People generally warn you to be sparing with it, though, because it can overwhelm the food. This is true when the plant is harvested in hot weather, as in the summertime. But in the spring and fall lovage is sweet and you can use quite a bit. Lovage leaves at this time are not overwhelming left whole in salads. They mix well with milder herbs, like chervil, or any kind of lettuce, as well as fruit such as oranges. Mike Pagliarini makes a fresh tomato salad with pine nuts, olives, parsley, and lovage. Lovage can flavor vinegar, too; just follow the tarragon vinegar recipe (page 125), subsituting lovage for the tarragon. Lovage stems are especially tender in the springtime, at which time they can be chopped and added to salads or simple vinaigrettes.

As the weather warms, the plant matures and grows stronger-tasting, so you must be sparing with it. The best way to use lovage at this point is in soups or stocks, or for flavoring vinegar. The lovage should be added whole, not chopped, to a soup or stock. This way you can easily remove it once it has imparted enough flavor.

Health Virtues

Lovage root has been used in folk medicine for hundreds of years, especially as a diuretic, but modern medicine has yet to study this plant and little is known about its nutritional profile.

Buying and Storing

If you find lovage for sale, more power to you (and the hip farmer who grew it). The leaves on top of the plant should be perky and the stem should be stiff and shiny, not dull. Store lovage in a plastic bag, unwashed and uncut, for up to one week in the fridge. The stems can be frozen whole in a sealed plastic bag.

Growing Lovage

Perennial lovage, popular in medieval times, is enjoying a revival among herb lovers. Not only is it highly productive, it is low-maintenance as well. It thrives with or without much sun, it isn't too picky about water (as long as the soil doesn't dry out), and it attracts beneficial insects to your garden.

You can lightly rake lovage seeds into the ground in early spring, or you can start seeds indoors six to eight weeks before the last frost. As is the case for celery, germination can take up to twenty days, so keep the soil moist and don't lose hope. Thin plants to 2 feet apart once they're established.

The plants will only reach 2 feet in height during their first season, but you can begin to harvest (sparingly) the outer stems once they grow to 1 foot in height. Lovage can be harvested continually in the years to follow as long as you leave the crown of the plant intact. After a few seasons, you may want to dig up the root in the spring and divide it to keep your plant happy; simply replant the divided roots or give some to a worthy neighbor.

Lovage Egg Salad

Eva likes to say that lovage is the "cello in a symphony" with its rich and powerful flavor. Although lovage transforms egg salad, it is also exceptional in other salads, including chicken salads, potato salads, tossed salads, and slaws.

1. Mash the eggs in a bowl. Add the lovage, shallots or chives, and mayonnaise, and season with salt and freshly cracked black pepper to taste.
2. Spread the egg salad over four slices of sandwich bread. Top with lettuce, if desired. Serve open-face or with a slice of bread on top.

Note: To hard-boil the eggs, place them in a pot and cover by at least 1 inch with cold water. Bring to a boil. Once the water is boiling, turn off the heat, cover the pot, and let sit for 12 minutes. Drain, then place the eggs in a bowl of ice-cold water for 5 minutes.

MAKES 4 SERVINGS

8 hard-boiled large eggs, chopped

1 cup finely chopped lovage (leaves and stems)

1 or 2 shallots or a handful of chives, chopped

4–6 tablespoons mayonnaise or Greek yogurt

Salt and freshly cracked black pepper

4–8 slices whole grain bread

Lettuce for sandwiches, such as Bibb or romaine (optional)

Lovage Butter–Olive Oil Compote

Excellent atop sea bass, in sandwiches, or with seared scallops. Or stir into rice or pasta and add vegetables.

Combine the lovage and garlic in a food processor and pulse until chopped. Add the butter and pulse again. Slowly pour in the oil, then the lemon juice, and season to taste with salt and freshly cracked pepper. Place in a crock or bowl for serving.

MAKES 1½ CUPS

6 cups loosely packed lovage leaves

4 garlic cloves

8 tablespoons (1 stick) butter, cut into pieces

1 cup extra-virgin olive oil

Juice of ½ lemon

Salt and freshly cracked black pepper

Lovage Fish Chowder

Lovage and fish are a tough pair to beat, especially in a chowder. If you can't find lovage, then the next best option would be to chop some celery leaves to replace the lovage stems and add a handful of chervil, dill, or tarragon. But you can't use the lower stems with these herbs like you can lovage, and I'd recommend using just 2 tablespoons of chopped tarragon; you can be more liberal with the chervil or dill.

MAKES 4 SERVINGS

3 cups fish stock or 1 cup clam juice plus 2 cups water

5 sprigs spring lovage, chopped, stems and leaves separated

1 cup white wine

¼ cup chopped green garlic or 3 garlic cloves, minced

3 tablespoons chopped shallots

4 cups thinly sliced red potatoes

1⅓ pounds striped bass or any sustainable type of white-fleshed fish, cut into 6 to 8 pieces

1 cup light cream

Salt and freshly cracked black pepper

½ cup chopped bronze fennel fronds (optional)

1. Bring the stock to a boil in a large soup pot over medium-high heat. Add the lovage stems, wine, green garlic, and shallots. Reduce the heat to low and let simmer for 5 minutes.
2. Add the potatoes and cook until they are tender, about 10 minutes.
3. Add the fish and cook another 2 to 3 minutes. Break the fish up a bit with the help of a long spoon. Remove the soup from the heat.
4. Stir in the light cream and the lovage leaves. Season with salt and freshly cracked black pepper to taste. Serve garnished with fennel fronds, if available.

Eva and the Greater Community

It was my very first Internet-arranged date. I had chosen the Green Street Grill in Cambridge, as I loved its Caribbean habañero-infused menu. Unfortunately I encountered a new ownership and a rather generic-sounding "New England fare" on the menu. I surveyed the stripped-down interior and the diners, who all appeared to be from the same gene pool; and then my "new friend" arrived. Right from the start we began searching laboriously, and ultimately in vain, for a common link. Thankfully dinner finally arrived to distract me from his corny jokes that ended with a wink instead of a coherent punch line. And then, out of the blue, I noticed some baby mustard and kale leaves peeking out from underneath my onion cheese tart. Oddly familiar to me, they quickly became more interesting than my date. I took a bite of the tart, which hit all the right notes: an all-butter crust, an artisan sharp cheddar custard, offset by a ridiculously delicious mix of lettuce greens. I couldn't get over it, and as I sat there with this guy, who by this time had been eclipsed by some baby mustard leaves, it struck me. *Eva!* I was eating Eva's greens! Suddenly I was transported to Eva's beautiful and wonderfully familiar farm. With great appreciation for the gastronomic prowess of the chef, I ate my meal with renewed gusto. I had been washed ashore, at least temporarily, from navigating the stormy seas of online dating!

Potato Lovage Spring Stew

Lovage works like a ray of sunshine in this stew. You can ladle it over buttery millet for a complete meal. Feel free to add spring shell peas or even chopped knotweed. Lovage carries the broth in this stew. If you can't find it, cilantro will produce a different flavor but will be equally good.

1. To make the stew, heat the oil in a large stockpot over medium heat. Add the onions and garlic. Sauté, stirring well, until the onions are translucent, about 7 to 9 minutes.

2. Add 10 cups water, along with the potatoes and carrots. Season with salt. Bring to a boil, then reduce the heat to low and let simmer uncovered until the potatoes are nearly soft, about 20 minutes.

3. Meanwhile, make the millet. Bring 4 cups water to a boil with ½ teaspoon salt in a medium saucepan over high heat. Add the millet, cover, reduce the heat to low. Let simmer until the millet is tender, about 20 minutes. Add the butter, season with freshly cracked black pepper, and stir well.

4. When the potatoes in the stew are tender, add the greens and cook another 5 minutes. Stir in the tofu, lovage, and vinegar. Season to taste with ½ teaspoon or more salt and freshly cracked black pepper to taste. Let the flavor of the lovage meld in the stew for a few minutes, then serve the stew over millet in shallow bowls.

5. If there are leftovers, combine the millet and the stew in a container with a tight lid. They will keep in the fridge for up to 1 week.

MAKES 8 SERVINGS

Spring Stew:

2 tablespoons extra-virgin olive oil

2 large onions, chopped

4 garlic cloves, chopped

6 large Red Bliss potatoes, cut into bite-size pieces

3 carrots, peeled and sliced into ¼-inch-thick coins

6 cups chopped leafy greens (beet greens, mustard greens, chard, or kale)

1 (14-ounce) package firm tofu, cut into ½-inch pieces

1 cup chopped lovage leaves, plus some for garnish

2 tablespoons vinegar (such as tarragon or sherry)

1 teaspoon salt or more

Freshly cracked black pepper

Millet:

2 cups millet

3 tablespoons butter

Freshly cracked black pepper

Building Community:
The Old-Fashioned Rolodex

Looking for neighbor Amy Burnes's phone number in Eva's Rolodex, you have to thumb past eighteen cards in the "B" section before finding Amy. And this is just Eva's personal Rolodex. There is another equally packed Rolodex for her chef contacts. She also keeps a thorough electronic address book on her computer, but her Rolodexes are the real catch-all. She must average a new card and number a day. They are usually crammed with information; for instance, Amy Burnes's card has six other numbers, including Amy's son's first girlfriend's cell.

I've surmised that Eva's info-packed Rolodex has as much to do with saving energy as anything else. But this energy is in the form of Eva's time instead of BTUs or kilowatt-hours. Eva's Rolodexes come to people's aid dozens of times a day, assisting herself, her bookkeeper, her farmers, and even me. It's a custom-made telephone directory.

I wish I could be as diligent as Eva, as I've lost or thrown away hundreds of numbers that I scrawled on a piece of paper, deeming them unimportant after I made the call. And, unlike a cell phone or computer, a Rolodex is hard to lose and can't really break. But more so, a Rolodex is valuable because it is a visual reminder of all the people in her past and present, all patiently sitting there, waiting for Eva to call.

Pea Greens

Pisum sativum • ANNUAL

I always tell my chefs "pea tendrils" is not the correct term for what I and other farmers sell. They're pea greens. The pea green includes the pea tendril, a very tiny wiry stem that helps the plant climb and support itself. It's hard to straighten out popular culture when you participate in it only peripherally.

—Eva

If they are fresh and picked at the right time, pea greens are a delicacy, sweet and universally appealing. This explains why nearly half of Eva's total sales comes from pea greens. Pea greens are the leaves and tender stems of very young pea plants, picked before the stems and branches get tough. Some sprout companies cut pea plants just five days after they've sprouted and sell them as "pea shoots" or "pea sprouts." While these are crunchy, the shoots are all stem and very little leaf. They have less flavor (although quite good!). They are grown indoors and often not in soil. Some larger farms let them get a little too big so that can get more "pea greens" out of each plant rather than harvesting them when they are shorter and tender and at their prime. This can yield stems that are thick and tough even when cooked. Eva has found a perfect medium between these two extremes. She grows the pea greens outdoors, in dirt, until they reach just 6 inches in height. Being grown in dirt gives them more flavor, and the lobe-shaped leaves make for a much prettier nest on the plate than the sprouts, dressed or undressed. And unlike the cuttings from mature plants, young pea greens are tender enough to eat in a salad. Chefs tell me that Eva's are the only pea greens in the entire market tender enough to eat raw.

Pea plants grow exceptionally fast, so they can be harvested and replanted often, and they'll grow back after one cutting. During the warm months, Eva plants fields of pea greens every seven days or so. At any point during the summer, if you drive by her farm, you will see two or three farmhands crawling slowly through one of these pea fields, snipping tiny pea greens a handful at a time until the entire field has been mowed down. When fresh, the pea greens taste like peas, and their leaves are very delicate, feltlike, and crunchy, almost like snow peas (which is what Eva's pea greens would produce if you let them grow).

CULINARY USES

Young pea greens (harvested when they reach 6 inches in height) should be eaten raw; otherwise the delicate pea flavor is lost. Bergamot restaurant in Somerville, Massachusetts, is famous for its decadent salad of pea greens with Berkshire ham, shavings of good Pecorino, and a deep-fried egg served with truffle vinaigrette made primarily from canned truffles, truffle oil, and soy sauce.

EVOO and Za, sister restaurants in Cambridge, serve three kinds of spring rolls: pea and smoked salmon, braised oxtail, and vegetable. Pea greens are wrapped around the spring rolls, along with red-leaf lettuce, Thai basil, mint, and cilantro. The chef, Peter McCarthy, also uses pea greens as a garnish on top of other salads and foods, such as a beet salad, dressed with lemon juice and olive oil. Jason Bond at Bondir in Cambridge makes a pea green mousse and serves it on tiny crisp crackers.

Pea greens are an elegant alternative to lettuce, and as is the case with lettuce, it's nice to mix them with fresh herbs such as basil, cilantro, chervil, parsley, even tarragon. And they're artful with the delicate tendril on top. If they are really fresh and tender, eat them as a salad green or on an open-face sandwich.

If you find pea greens that are larger, they can be stir-fried with garlic and olive oil like spinach along with a splash of water to tenderize the tougher stems. But the cooking must be quick, as in a minute or two. Many Chinese restaurants stir-fry pea greens in vegetable oil and garlic, then finish them off with a tiny bit of chicken broth mixed with cornstarch and soy sauce (and sometimes sesame oil). A plate of pea greens (or shoots as they are sometimes called) at a Chinese restaurant can be twice the price of an entree and is considered a delicacy.

Health Virtues

Pea greens will add a nutritive boost to any salad, sandwich, or stir-fry. One handful contains over 50 percent of the daily recommended dose of vitamin C, 25 percent of the daily recommended dose of vitamin A, and a substantial dose of folic acid.

Buying, Storing, and Prepping

Pea greens may be available in farmers' markets in the spring. If you purchase them at a larger supermarket, you should definitely wash them. Don't buy pea greens that are yellowed or withered. They won't be sweet or tender, nor will they be as nutritious. Store pea greens, unwashed, in a plastic bag in the fridge for up to one week.

Pea greens are usually grown without pesticides in the hands of small farmers and don't tote dirt, but it's always good to ask farms what their practice is if you can. If you do wash them, soak them in a bowl of cold water, then lift the greens out with your hands and spin-dry. Pea greens need no prepping, although sometimes the ends can be woody and should be trimmed off.

Growing Pea Greens

I recommend growing pea greens only if you have some space. For every 2 square feet of pea greens, you get 8 ounces of food. But the greens can be harvested within one month of planting, so they are the perfect candidate for a recently cleared spot that would otherwise lie fallow between a harvest and a fall planting (or frost).

Any variety of pea seed will produce pea shoots, but Eva recommends using snow peas. Scatter thickly, cover lightly with soil, keep the ground moist, and watch for germination. Once the pea greens are about 4 inches tall, snip them down to soil level. In cool weather you should get a second harvest, or you can allow the plants to grow into full-fledged pea vines (once they flower, the roots begin fixing nitrogen, which is great for the soil).

Summer Rolls for Spring/Summer

Summer rolls, when made at home, have the potential for greatness one usually does not experience at restaurants. Growing your own herbs will greatly increase that potential. I prefer to scoot over a few countries and use soba noodles in these rolls rather than the traditional rice noodles. If you'd like to make them heartier, serve them with the Summer Rolls for Winter Peanut Sauce (page 46) rather than the lighter but beguiling *nuoc cham*.

1. To make the *nuoc cham*, combine the garlic, lime juice, fish sauce, maple syrup, and chile sauce in a small bowl. Stir in 1 tablespoon water. Taste for seasoning, adding more lime juice, fish sauce, or chile sauce as needed.

2. To make the summer rolls, bring a large pot of water to a boil. Once it boils, reduce the heat to low and cover the pot to keep the water very hot until you are ready to start rolling. Transfer the pot of hot water to a trivet near a clean work surface (a kitchen counter is best). Dip a round of rice paper into the hot water, rotating it so that it gets fully wet, and then lay it on your work surface. Dip a few more rice papers, as many as will fit on your counter in a single layer.

3. Place some of the greens in the middle of each rice paper. Add a tablespoon or two of the noodles, and top with the herbs. Starting with the end closest to you, roll one of the papers tightly around the stuffing. When you reach the halfway point, fold the sides of the paper in toward the center, then continue rolling to the end of the paper, lifting the roll up from the work surface an inch or two to help you smooth out wrinkles and pull the paper more taut. You should be able to see the herbs or sprouts through the wrapper.

4. Continue in the same fashion for the other rolls. If you're planning to serve them within the hour, leave them at room temperature. Otherwise, refrigerate the spring rolls, covered with plastic wrap, but do not chill for more than 3 hours, or they will harden. Rewrap any leftover rice papers well in plastic wrap and store at room temperature.

5. To serve as an hors d'oeuvre, cut the rolls in half and serve on a platter with *nuoc cham*, a spoon, and small plates.

MAKES 20 SUMMER ROLLS

Nuoc Cham Dipping Sauce:

1 large garlic clove, minced

¼ cup lime juice (about 2 limes)

2 tablespoons fish sauce or ½ teaspoon salt or more to taste

1 tablespoon maple syrup

1–3 teaspoons chile sauce, according to your palate

Summer Rolls:

1 package of 20 rice paper rounds (at least 8 inches in diameter)

1 bunch greens: arugula, Bull's Blood beet greens, pea greens, or Sylvetta arugula

6 ounces dry soba noodles, cooked and chilled

1 or more bunches herbs: African basil leaves (use sparingly), bronze fennel, chervil, chives, cilantro, dill, lovage (tear into pieces, and use sparingly), mint, sweet basil leaves, or a combination

Rhubarb

Rheum rhabarbarum · PERENNIAL

From a culinary standpoint, spring wouldn't be as miraculous if rhubarb were not one of its harbingers. It is one of the very first edibles to emerge on farms and in gardens, arriving just as the earth's warmth coaxes flora to grow.

Rhubarb's inimitable sweet/sour flavor is extremely successful in desserts. Even though rhubarb is botanically a vegetable (the stem is eaten, not the plant's fruit), Eva refers to it and sells it as a fruit. Despite her notable knowledge of botany, she finds it more useful to classify it by its culinary use, not its anatomy.

Rhubarb deserves to have its classification fussed over. It is a very underrated plant. As you probably know by now, rhubarb gets along fine without strawberries. It needs only a little heat and sugar to smooth out its rough edges. Even that is negotiable, as a lot of people (especially kids) enjoy eating the stalk raw. Like its relative sorrel, rhubarb is mouth-puckering, but it tempers when cooked, yielding a smooth flavor reminiscent of pear and lemon. Adding a bit of sugar to rhubarb tempts us to employ it in a range of desserts. In compotes and pies, its effect is a bright, almost perfumed flavor, with a relentless joie de vivre.

I am enchanted by rhubarb and just don't understand why it isn't used more often. Perhaps it is because it is not really eaten out of hand. Rather, rhubarb needs special attention when preparing it. Add it raw to a hot pan and it can blacken in seconds; stew it even a minute too long and it will break down into a soggy puddle. Or maybe it's that its shelf life is too short or it isn't easily farmed or harvested on a large scale.

Jess Thomson, a Seattle-based food writer, blogger, and rhubarb devotee, has one theory: "The thing about rhubarb is that while it always tastes beautiful—bright and sunny and tart in all the right ways—it doesn't always look so great when it's cooked. . . . You might say this here is a food with a complexion problem."

Culinary Uses

Rhubarb need not become the messy gray mass that Jess Thomson writes about, although most recipes employing it will lead you in this direction. I, along with many other chefs, prefer to abbreviate the cooking time whenever possible so that rhubarb doesn't lose all of its texture and can really show off its bright flavors. Rhubarb needs only a moment (about thirty seconds) to soften and cook through, while baked goods (with the exception of pancakes) cook for much longer than this. This is why I prefer rhubarb in compotes and sauces, often to accompany baked goods.

Rhubarb can be cooked like the vegetable it is. Panfry thin coins of spring-dug parsnips in olive oil until caramelized, add chopped rhubarb and fry for a few minutes more, and season—surprisingly, this is a well-paired match. More commonly, rhubarb is paired with all things buttery and crunchy—a rhubarb crisp or cobbler, rhubarb oat bars, rhubarb-raisin pie. Rhubarb should not be heavily sweetened, as sugar can smother its flavor.

Rhubarb too often gets overshadowed by strawberries. I'm not saying that strawberry-rhubarb pie isn't delicious, because it is. But rhubarb's flavor is so good on its own, and using it in a pie calls for extended cooking. It is better cooked just briefly with a bit of sugar, so you can really enjoy its bright concert of flavors. For a Slow Food fund-raiser, I once made a rhubarb-strawberry compote over shortcake for a hundred-plus people. The compote consisted of two-thirds rhubarb and one-third straw-berries (and some sugar). I cooked the rhubarb and strawberries for just a few minutes so the rhubarb was still a touch crunchy. The minimal sugar and the short cooking time made the flavors sing, and of course a plentiful dollop of whipped cream did no harm.

I like cooking sliced rhubarb for a few minutes on the stovetop, adding sugar to taste, until the rhubarb begins to lose its shape and forms a compote or loose jam. I add a pinch of clove and store the compote in the fridge, where it keeps for weeks and weeks, if I pace myself. I add it to my daily breakfast of yogurt or raw milk and homemade granola or spread it with butter on toast. I also like to serve it warmed to friends atop a good vanilla ice cream. Rhubarb's sour, tart flavor works well against any dairy, whether it is cream, yogurt, cheese, sour cream, or butter.

Although Eva sells most of her rhubarb to chefs who use it in desserts, increasingly they are using it in savory food. Many chefs pair it with meat or sear it for pasta, gnocchi, or dumplings. Spicy rhubarb chutneys and compotes are perfect for poultry and game and will last for months in the fridge. I've also made rhubarb salsa using raw rhubarb, instead of the tomato, its mirror opposite, the fruit that thinks it's a vegetable.

I should mention to you what *not* to eat, and that's the raw leaves. They have toxic amounts of oxalic acid. The good news is that you would have to eat pounds upon pounds of the leaves to get a lethal dose.

Health Virtues
Rhubarb contains antioxidants, dietary fiber, and calcium, and 1 cup (raw) contains over 10 percent of your daily recommended dose of vitamin C.

Buying and Storing
Farmers' markets are your best bet for finding fresh, high-quality rhubarb, unless you have a plant or two in your own garden. Once you've been spoiled by working with just-picked rhubarb, it is hard to buy it at supermarkets, where it may be a week or two old. Look for shiny, stiff stalks. Unless your rhubarb is very fibrous or old, there is no need to peel the stalks. Just cut as you would celery.

Store rhubarb in an open bag in the fridge, or you can even stand it in a shallow tray of water (like asparagus) if you want to get fancy. But if you don't think you'll be using it in the near future, simply chop it and freeze it in a tightly sealed container.

Growing Rhubarb
Rhubarb is easy to grow and propagate as long as your winter temperatures dip below 40 degrees. Buy a root division or potted plant from any garden center, or take a division from a friend's rhubarb. Plant it in rich soil in full sun or light shade in early spring. Mulch well to keep the soil moist, and cut any flower stalks that shoot up from the center of the plant. It is best not to harvest any stalks during a rhubarb plant's first season, and to harvest only a few stalks during its second season. Rhubarb should be harvested by grasping from the base of the stalk, then twisting while pulling, so that the whole stalk is unearthed. By the third season your healthy, happy plant will reward you with a bountiful harvest.

Rhubarb-Raisin Chutney

MAKES ABOUT 4 CUPS

8 cups thinly sliced rhubarb

2 onions, finely chopped

1 cup raisins

2 tablespoons minced fresh ginger

1½ cups sugar or Sucanat

¼ teaspoon ground cloves

½ cup red wine or cider vinegar

Salt and freshly cracked black pepper

This is a straightforward chutney that can accompany many meals. Try a spoonful in sandwiches, alongside curries, game, poultry, lamb, or pork, or as an appetizer with some creamy goat cheese and crackers. Use the amount of sugar you desire. You can always add more sugar at the last moment while it's hot. And if you want a spicy chutney, add a chopped chile pepper at the start.

1. Combine the rhubarb, onions, raisins, ginger, sugar, cloves, and vinegar in a heavy-bottomed saucepan over medium-high heat. Bring the mixture to a boil, then immediately remove from the heat. (If the rhubarb breaks down too much, the chutney will be very thin.)

2. Season the chutney with salt and freshly cracked black pepper and perhaps more vinegar or sugar, depending on how tart or sour you would like the chutney. Let cool. Store in the refrigerator, where it will keep for up to 2 months.

Coconut Rice Pudding with Rhubarb

I was surprised at the flavor this pudding achieved without the help of dairy. I like this pudding with dairy in it, but really, the rhubarb compote that sits atop the pudding makes either version successful. Health nuts can use 100 percent brown rice.

1. To make the pudding, combine the brown rice, white rice, sugar, cardamom, salt, 2 cups soy milk, almond milk, or half-and-half, and coconut milk in a medium saucepan over medium heat. Let the mixture come to a boil, then reduce the heat to very low, cover, and let cook until thick and the rice tender, about 1½–2 hours, stirring from time to time to keep the pudding from sticking to the bottom of the saucepan. If it does stick to the saucepan, add more soy milk, almond milk, or half-and-half as needed.

2. Transfer the pudding to a container with a lid and let it come to room temperature uncovered, then chill in the refrigerator, covered.

3. Meanwhile, to make the topping, combine the rhubarb, sugar, and ¼ cup water in a small saucepan over low heat. Let the mixture come to a simmer, and let simmer until the rhubarb softens while still holding its shape, about 5 minutes. Transfer the rhubarb to a container with a lid and let it come to room temperature uncovered, then chill in the refrigerator, covered.

4. To serve, spoon the rice pudding into clear glasses, then spoon the rhubarb mixture over the rice pudding. Serve the pudding in wineglasses for a particularly nice presentation.

MAKES 6 SERVINGS

Rice Pudding:
½ cup brown rice
½ cup white rice
½ cup sugar
½ teaspoon cardamom
Pinch salt
3 cups coconut milk (two 13-ounce cans will do)
2–3 cups soy milk, almond milk, or half-and-half

Topping:
3 large stalks rhubarb (about ¾ pound), thinly sliced
3 tablespoons sugar

Pasta with Rhubarb, Swiss Chard, and Bacon

MAKES 6 SERVINGS

6 tablespoons extra-virgin olive oil

3 medium onions, thinly sliced

4 or 5 slices of good-quality bacon

3 medium stalks rhubarb, chopped into ½-inch pieces (about 3 cups), or 1 Granny Smith apple, peeled and sliced

4 garlic cloves, minced

1 bunch Swiss chard or spinach, stems thinly chopped, leaves sliced into 1-inch ribbons

1 pound penne or any other petite pasta

2 tablespoons balsamic vinegar

½ teaspoon salt or more to taste

Freshly cracked black pepper

4 ounces good-quality hard grating cheese such as Parmigiano-Reggiano

Checking out rhubarb in the garden is a better way to get inspired than reading a cookbook (even this one!) or walking by it at the supermarket. A garden provides the most direct communication, because here rhubarb's juices are flowing, its fanlike leaves are bursting forth, and it's in its full glory. Plus it's much easier to tune in without lots of people around. If you can't find rhubarb, this dish can be made with tart apples or knotweed instead.

1. Heat 1 tablespoon of the olive oil in a heavy-bottomed skillet or cast-iron pan over low heat. Add the onions and cook for 20 to 30 minutes, stirring every 5 minutes or so, until they are a dark brown. Don't stir more than that. The onions need to be left pretty much alone so they can caramelize. Transfer the onions to a plate.

2. Bring a large pot of salted water to a boil, then cover and reduce the heat to low.

3. In the same skillet in which you cooked the onions, cook the bacon over low heat until crisp on the underside, then turn with a fork and cook the other side. Transfer the bacon to a paper towel. Drain out all but a few spoonfuls of bacon fat (save the extra for later use).

4. Add the rhubarb and garlic to the skillet with the bacon fat and sauté, stirring, for 2 to 3 minutes. The rhubarb should not lose too much shape or color. Then transfer the rhubarb and garlic to a plate (the one holding the onions will do fine).

5. Add the remaining 5 tablespoons olive oil to the skillet and turn the heat to high. Add the chard and cook, stirring, until it is tender, about 5 minutes. Add a few spoonfuls of water if necessary to help tenderize the stems.

6. Bring the pot of water back to a boil. Add the pasta, boil until al dente, then drain and return to the pot. Add the chard, caramelized onions, rhubarb, and balsamic vinegar. Season with the ½ teaspoon salt (or more to taste) and lots of freshly cracked black pepper to taste. Top with crumbled bacon and cheese. Stir well to incorporate the ingredients and serve immediately.

Asparagus and Rhubarb

I was surprised after tasting these two together that I hadn't seen the combination before, since they both share a spring harvest season. The trick is not to overcook the rhubarb so that it retains its color and shape, and, of course, to use very fresh ingredients.

1. If the asparagus is not super-fresh, trim it at the point where the stalk toughens. (To find this point, hold the asparagus spear toward the stem end and bend; it will naturally break at the point where the stalk toughens.) If it is super-fresh, trim off just the last ¼ inch of the stem. Trim off the ends of the rhubarb as well.

2. Use a sharp knife to slice the asparagus and rhubarb on the bias very thinly, giving you slices about ¼ inch thick. Leave the asparagus tips whole—consider them "flowers" among the stems.

3. Heat the butter in a large skillet over medium-high heat. Add the asparagus and tips and cook, stirring or tossing, for about 3 minutes. Add the rhubarb, and continue to toss and cook for a couple more minutes. Remove from the heat when the asparagus is a bit crispy but also tender.

4. Add the minced herb, season with salt and freshly cracked black pepper to taste, and serve immediately.

MAKES 4 TO 6 SERVINGS

¾ pound asparagus

2 thin stalks or 1 thick stalk rhubarb

3 tablespoons butter

3–4 tablespoons minced parsley, chervil, or cilantro

Salt and freshly cracked black pepper

Goat's Milk Flan with Rhubarb Compote

MAKES 6 SERVINGS

The Flan:

6 cups goat's milk or cow's milk

1 teaspoon vanilla extract

¾ cup plus 6 tablespoons sugar

3 large eggs

4 large egg yolks

Pinch salt

The Rhubarb Compote:

1 pound rhubarb (about 6 stalks), cut into ½-inch pieces (about 4 cups)

½ cup sugar

I made this for author Michael Pollan, Eva, and a group of farmers after Michael spoke at a local library in Boston. Unfortunately Michael ducked out after the main course. But everyone agreed that this dessert was the smash hit of the evening. Though I made it with goat's milk, you could also make it with cow's milk. Assemble this the day before serving or early in the morning.

1. To prepare for making the flan, get out a 1½-quart baking dish and a shallow roasting pan large enough to hold the baking dish comfortably inside it. Bring several cups of water to a boil, then cover and set aside.

2. Bring the milk to a boil in a large, heavy saucepan over medium heat. Reduce the heat to medium-low, and allow the milk to simmer until it has reduced to 3 cups, about 40 minutes. Remove the pan from the heat and stir in the vanilla.

3. Preheat the oven to 325 degrees F.

4. While the milk is simmering, combine ¾ cup of the sugar and ¼ cup water in a small, nonreactive saucepan, stirring to dissolve the sugar. Bring the mixture to a boil; when it reaches a boil, stop stirring and let the syrup cook until it turns golden amber over medium heat. Remove the pan from the heat and pour the hot caramel into the 1½-quart baking dish, tilting to coat the bottom. Work fast, or the caramel will harden before it covers the dish. Place the caramel-lined baking dish inside the roasting pan, and set aside.

5. Combine the remaining 6 tablespoons sugar, whole eggs, egg yolks, and salt in a large bowl, whisking until well blended. Strain the hot milk mixture into a small bowl—there may be a skin depending on how long it has sat—then slowly pour the hot milk over the eggs, whisking constantly.

6. Pour the egg mixture into the caramel-lined baking dish. Cover the baking dish loosely with aluminum foil, and place the nested pans in the center of the oven. Pour enough hot water into the roasting pan that it comes halfway up the outside of the baking dish. Bake for about 1 hour, until the flan is set but still slightly wobbly.

7. Lift the baking dish out of the roasting pan, leaving the hot water bath in the oven to cool. Let the flan cool to room temperature, then refrigerate uncovered for at least 4 hours.

8. To make the rhubarb compote, combine the rhubarb, sugar, and ¼ cup water in a heavy, nonreactive saucepan over low heat. Bring to a simmer, and let simmer, stirring, until the rhubarb softens and the sugar melts, about 10 minutes. Transfer the compote to a bowl and chill for at least 5 hours.

9. To serve, let the flan sit at room temperature for 15 minutes, then run a knife around the edge of the baking dish to loosen the flan, and invert it onto a rimmed serving platter. Cut the flan into pieces and serve topped with rhubarb compote.

Note: The flan can be fully prepared up to 3 days ahead and stored in its baking dish, covered with plastic wrap, in the fridge, then follow directions in step 9.

Foraging Tidbit ~ Dandelion Greens

Foraging guru "Wildman" Steve Brill points out that dandelion greens "are more nutritious than anything you can buy." In other words, if you learn to love their flavor, they will love you right back. You can mitigate their bitterness by mixing them with milder greens, a cheese like feta, apples or pears or dried fruits, or a flavorful, slightly sweet dressing.

Whether you forage or cultivate them, make sure you pick them in the spring just as they emerge, before the plants become large and have a chance to flower. They are harder to spot but they're sweetest and most tender at this point; come summer, they turn very bitter. In the fall, the bitterness is subdued once again after the first frost.

Eva cultivates dandelion greens in abundance, happily nestled between rows of flashy Speckled Trout lettuce and chartreuse baby mizuna. The tooth-shaped greens are tossed into her "wild salad mix," which is one of her biggest sellers.

Amy's Rhubarb-Strawberry Pie

MAKES 1 PIE, ENOUGH FOR 8 SERVINGS

The Piecrust:

2 cups unbleached white flour

1½ teaspoons sugar

1 teaspoon salt

6 tablespoons unsalted butter

6 tablespoons solid vegetable shortening or lard

⅓ cup ice-cold water

Rhubarb-Strawberry Filling:

8–10 stalks rhubarb (or more), cut into bite-size chunks

1½–2 cups fresh-picked strawberries, quartered or sliced

½ cup brown sugar

½ cup granulated sugar

3 tablespoons cornstarch

⅓ cup lemon juice (about 2 lemons)

2 tablespoons butter

My friend Amy Cannon, a brilliant jewelry designer, makes the best strawberry-rhubarb pie. She uses lots of rhubarb, so that's why I've reversed the fruit in the pie's name. She comments, "I just improvise and throw it all together with the essential ingredients. The key to good flavor is to use fresh, homegrown or local rhubarb, cut the same day. I vary the amount of sugar depending on how tart I want my pie. I think it's best when it's on the tart side."

1. Preheat the oven to 450 degrees F.

2. To prepare the piecrust, combine the flour, sugar, and salt in a large bowl and mix well. Cut the butter and shortening into the flour mixture with a pastry cutter or two knives, until the fat breaks down into pea-size pieces. With a large spoon, add the cold water, tablespoon by tablespoon, stirring just until the dough comes together.

3. Gather the dough into a ball, adding more flour if it seems sticky. Divide the dough in half. On a floured surface, roll out each half into a circle that is about 1 inch larger in diameter than your pie plate (a 9- or 10-inch pie pan is fine). Use a little flour if necessary to prevent the dough from sticking to your rolling pin.

4. Using a small, sharp knife, cut an incision of your liking into one of the dough circles. This will be the top crust, and the incision will allow your pie to vent properly.

5. Carefully fold the dough for the bottom crust (with no incisions) in half, then in quarters. Set on the pie plate and unfold until it covers the pan. Carefully press the dough into the dish, leaving the excess crust hanging over the edges. Refrigerate the crusts

while you make the filling (the top pastry should be floured and folded in half).

6. To make the filling, combine the rhubarb, strawberries, brown sugar, and white sugar in a large bowl. Dissolve the cornstarch in the lemon juice, and add to the bowl. Stir well.

7. Fill the bottom crust of the pie with the filling. Dot the top of the filling with 6 to 8 small dabs of butter. Place the dough for the top crust on top. Pinch the edges of the top and bottom crusts together, shaping them to make a pleasing edge.

8. Bake the pie at 450 degrees F for 10 minutes, then turn the oven temperature down to 350 degrees F and bake an additional 45 minutes, or until the crust is golden brown.

Muddy Feet

Twenty years ago, Eva and her husband, George, were strolling home after inspecting a neighbor's home renovation. The visit had inspired Eva, and she said out loud: "Let's build a mudroom."

To this, George said nothing for a while. He might have been ruminating about the reality of their "home." Formerly a garage, since their purchase of the property it had been transformed into the integral, central heart of the farm and Eva's passion. Her practicality and her no-waste values dictated its decor. There were no sofas, soft chairs, TV, curtains, or—God forbid—rugs. Instead its main room was piled high with storage containers, desks cluttered with the meticulous business of her crops and customers, filing cabinets, one table for inspecting seeds that was cleared every couple of hours for meals. A never-cold potbellied stove was the only nod to human comfort. Through it all a single path meandered, a highway endlessly traipsed dawn-to-dusk by Eva and her coworkers, making their way from greenhouse to fields and the barn, rarely taking off their coats and never their boots.

This last detail is maybe what prompted George to finally speak: Let's build a mudroom? "Eva, our entire house is a mudroom!"

Sorrel

Rumex acetosa · PERENNIAL

Eva has a good friend named Debbie who used to live in the neighborhood and frequently visited the farm. One day Debbie was making a tomato and cheese sandwich for her six-year-old daughter, Mercy. Because she was at Eva's, she added some fresh sorrel from the garden instead of the usual iceberg lettuce. Mercy gobbled it up. A few days later Debbie asked her daughter, "What would you like for lunch?" Mercy replied, "I want more of that zingy lettuce!" Eva was so impressed that a six-year-old could invent such a fitting description of sorrel that, nineteen years later, she invariably tells this story to all her chef clients. Mercy, now twenty-five, periodically works as a farmhand at Eva's. She refers to sorrel as sorrel—because she's heard the story one too many times.

Having worked with many kids in the kitchen, I've noticed a similar trend: kids are into sour food, whether it's Sour Patch Kids (a sour gummy candy), raw lemons or limes (which many kids eat like oranges), or, yes, even sorrel, despite its vegetal appearance.

Culinary Uses

I can thank my mom for introducing me to sorrel. She grew it when we were kids, and she used to make a French classic creamy sorrel potato soup. However, I have learned that sorrel in its raw state is a whole other treat.

Raw sorrel, to someone who is not used to it, is mouth-puckeringly sour (imagine biting into a lime wedge), but if you eat it often enough, the puckering eventually lessens and you can appreciate sorrel's bright, tangy glory. Like lime, sorrel's flavor can enhance recipes looking for a little acidity such as soups, sauces,

potato or egg salad, fresh Indian chutneys and Mexican salsas. Try making a vinaigrette with sorrel: puree it in a blender with olive oil, a small clove of garlic, salt, and pepper, and serve with fish or scallops or in pasta salad. Herbs can be paired with sorrel in sauces, vinaigrettes and soups; some of my favorites are mint, anise hyssop, and cilantro. Or you can try simply dressing sorrel lightly with olive oil, salt, and pepper and setting a piece of grilled fish atop it. Eva likes to chop sorrel and make it into a little nest for seared scallops, her purist variation on the more common fish with sorrel sauce.

Chef Jason Bond of Bondir in Cambridge likes to puree raw sorrel and stir it into a chowder, soup, or risotto just before serving. Chef Seth Morrison of the Gallows in Boston's South End chops sorrel adding lemon zest, roasted garlic and rabbit liver, and stuffs boned rabbit loin and hind legs with this. When sorrel leaves get large in the summer and fall I make a simple hors d'oeuvre by rolling the leaf around goat cheese. You can also tuck sorrel into Vietnamese summer rolls along with fresh mint, cilantro, and other fillings (I like soba noodles).

Most often I tear sorrel leaves in half and add them to a salad with many other kinds of greens, so as not to overwhelm the tongue. Sorrel needs mild-mannered bedfellows like spinach and Bibb or red-leaf lettuce. I also love chopped sorrel stirred into potato salad, grain salads, or slaws. It's important to cut down or omit the acid in the dressing for these salads, because sorrel provides the acidity.

When cooked, sorrel loses its bright color and most of its mouth-puckering tartness and turns an olive color. A very luscious lemony flavor remains, and if well cooked, it achieves a pudding-like texture, or as food writer Richard Olney put it, sorrel "melts." Olney recommended stuffing trout with cooked sorrel and spooning heavy cream over it all. When panfried, sorrel is splendid in an omelet, with or without cheese. Try making a simple sorrel sauce (seared sorrel with garlic and cream, pureed) for soft polenta and roast game like venison, rabbit, or even chicken, perhaps with roasted mushrooms on side. Layer seared sorrel into potatoes au gratin, or try it on pizza with a creamy cheese like farmer's cheese, fresh mozzarella, or something more decadent like Nostrale di Elva from the Piedmont region of Italy.

You may be wondering by now, should sorrel be filed under Herbs or Greens? The answer is both. Even the dictionary definition allows for the split personality: "A perennial herb that is cultivated as a garden herb or leaf vegetable." Sorrel is an herb because, when eaten raw, its pungency dictates that it be used sparingly. When cooked, it collapses like spinach and the flavor mellows. Served in this way, it becomes a grand vegetable.

Health Virtues

Sorrel is rich in vitamins C and A, and it is a good source of iron. It is high in dietary fiber and high in oxalic acid, which can interfere with our digestion and the absorption of some trace minerals. It should not be rabidly consumed in its raw form. Eating 5 pounds of raw sorrel in a half hour could be a problem but would be a Herculean feat. I eat 3 or 4 ounces at a sitting. The U.S. National Institutes of Health have determined that the negative effects of oxalic acid, which is present in spinach and a few other vegetables, are generally of little or no nutritional consequence in persons who eat a variety of foods.

Buying and Storing

Your best bet for finding sorrel is a farmers' market or high-end grocery store in the summer. Buy leaves that are bright green, not wilted or dull. Store sorrel in a plastic bag in the refrigerator for up to one week.

Growing Sorrel

Sow seeds ½ inch deep in full or partial sun a few weeks before the final frost can be expected. After six to eight weeks, you can thin the seedlings to about 1 foot apart. You can start harvesting the leaves when they are 4 to 6 inches high. As the season goes on each sorrel plant will send up multiple seed stalks, which should be cut right away so that leaf production will not taper off.

After a few successive cuttings your sorrel may start to get a bit tough and raggedy. It will still be fine to eat; just remove the stems. If it is too tough, sauté it or make pesto (see the recipe, page 111). If you prefer young, tender sorrel, you may opt to sow a second planting in the summer and grow it as an annual.

Wood Sorrel

If you get right down to it, I prefer wood sorrel (*Oxalis montana*) over cultivated sorrel. The only problem is, it's a pain to pick given its size (the whole stem and leaf is the size of your pinky finger). Wood sorrel is a wild plant most common from New England to Wisconsin and Manitoba. It can be found in many wooded areas and is easily foraged. It has heart-shaped leaves and is sometimes referred to as "shamrock" because of its three-leaf clover shape. It is quite delicious, and a bit less intense than the larger-leafed conventional sorrel. Wood sorrel is filled with vitamin C; in fact, sailors traveling around Patagonia once ate it to avoid scurvy. It works beautifully in salad, as a garnish for fish, or in any of the recipes in this book that call for cultivated sorrel.

Flash-Cooked Sorrel

MAKES 2 OR 3 SERVINGS

2 tablespoons extra-virgin olive oil

2 garlic cloves, minced

4 cups loosely packed sorrel leaves

Salt and freshly cracked black pepper

This is one of my favorite ways to enjoy sorrel when it comes back fighting (tougher and rougher) for a second harvest in the fall. Cooked sorrel is intense. Temper it by using it as a nest for cooked fish or shellfish like bay or sea scallops. Or stir the panfried sorrel into lightly smashed potatoes (with milk and butter).

Heat the olive oil in a large skillet over medium-high heat. Add the garlic and stir, cooking for about 1 minute. When the garlic is really sizzling but not yet brown, add the sorrel and cook, stirring constantly, for just 1 to 2 minutes, until the leaves are only slightly wilted. Season with salt and freshly cracked black pepper to taste. Eat immediately!

Sorrel and Salt Cod Salad

This recipe derives from Ramona Bermudez, who makes a mean Puerto Rican–style *gaspacho*, with salt cod and avocado. I've added the sorrel; you can use arugula and the juice of a lime as a crude but pleasant substitute. The salt cod needs to be soaked for two days in advance.

MAKES 6 SERVINGS

1 pound boneless salt cod

4–6 cups loosely packed, destemmed, torn-up sorrel leaves

2 avocados, peeled and cut into wedges

1 small bunch cilantro, finely chopped

1 red onion, very thinly sliced

4 tablespoons extra-virgin olive oil

Freshly cracked black pepper

1. Cover the salt cod with cold water, and let soak in the refrigerator for 24 hours. Drain the water, cover the cod with fresh water, and let soak in the fridge another 24 hours. Drain, then shred the cod into 2-inch pieces.
2. Combine the cod in a large bowl with the sorrel, avocados, cilantro, onion, and olive oil. Season the mixture with freshly cracked black pepper to taste.

Cybele: From Reject to Community Leader

Andy and Amy Burnes, Eva's next-door neighbors, brought stew beef over early in the day. It was my birthday, and they came back later that evening for dinner. They raise cows for their extended family's consumption. Andy tends to them in meticulous fashion, and the cows live their whole life in pastures. One cow wears a large bell around her neck, and whenever she so much as cricks her head, it clangs. It had worried me that one cow had to put up with all that clanging. So at dinner, because it was my birthday, I got up the gumption to ask Andy, "Why does one cow have to wear the bell while the other cows get away scot-free?"

"No, it is a sign of leadership, and the cows know it," Andy said.

Amy then unfurled the story of Cybele, the proud cow who dons the bell. Her mother was one bitchy heifer. She gave birth to Cybele, but every time Cybele approached her to suckle, she violently kicked the calf away. So Amy resorted to bottle-feeding Cybele. What was worse was that the calf was always alone, rejected by the entire herd. After three months Cybele was doing fine, no thanks to the mom. (This was the second time the mom had rejected a calf, so the Burnses sold her off.) The Burneses were set to go on vacation to Cape Cod, and Amy, who was still bottle-feeding Cybele, said to Andy, "Well, we have to take you-know-who with us!" Andy said, "Not on my life!" But the next day he realized there was no other choice, so they rented a trailer and brought the calf with them to Cape Cod. As Cybele matured and become an adult cow, Andy was surprised to see the herd defer to her. They would not cross to another pasture until Cybele made a move and if she didn't, then the collective remained put. Cybele had earned the respect of her fellow cows, and Andy awarded her the bell—a reminder of how far she had come from her orphaned days.

Green *Gaspacho*

MAKES 6 SERVINGS

1 cup almonds or pumpkin seeds, toasted

4 garlic cloves

⅓ cup extra-virgin olive oil

2–3 tablespoons red wine vinegar

6 cups loosely packed chopped sorrel

1 cup loosely packed chopped dill, basil, parsley, or mint

1 cup loosely packed chopped cilantro

1 small onion, chopped, or 1 cup chopped chives

½ ripe honeydew melon, cubed

4 cups loosely packed spinach

2 slices whole-grain bread, torn into pieces

1 teaspoon salt

Freshly cracked black pepper

Hot sauce (optional)

This recipe has been approved by Massachusetts Governor Deval Patrick. He rang me on my cell phone to tell me how much he liked it (I had never met him; one of his assistants gave him my number). He asked me what the secret ingredient was, and in shock, I told him I couldn't think of one, and he asked me to rattle off the ingredients. I did, and he stopped me at honeydew melon and said, "Aha! There's your secret ingredient!" I'm glad he figured it out because I sure wasn't able to.

1. Pulverize the almonds in a blender or food processor. Add the garlic, olive oil, and vinegar and puree the mixture. Add the sorrel, dill, cilantro, and onion, along with 1 cup water. Puree the mixture until it is mostly smooth. Pour most of the soup into a large bowl, leaving a cup or so behind.

2. Add the honeydew to the blender or food processor, along with the spinach, bread, and another 1 cup water. Puree. Pour the honeydew puree into the rest of the soup and mix well.

3. If the mixture seems too thick, thin with water to the desired consistency; this is a rather thick *gaspacho*. Season with the salt, freshly cracked black pepper, and hot sauce to taste if desired. Chill in the refrigerator for at least 2 hours before serving.

Note: To toast nuts or seeds, roast in a 350-degree oven on a rimmed baking sheet for 10 minutes, until they begin to turn golden brown.

Sorrel and Goat Cheese Pesto

If you omit the cheese, this makes a great compote for broiled or grilled fish. It's delicious stirred into pasta but also tasty mixed with brown rice and other grains. If you can't find an aged goat cheese like Caprotto or Pantaleo, use a Pecorino or Parmesan.

1. Combine the almonds and garlic in a food processor and pulse until they are finely chopped. Add the sorrel and pulse until the greens are finely chopped.
2. Add the oil in three increments, pulsing the mixture for a second or two after each addition.
3. Add the grated cheese, and season the pesto with salt and freshly cracked black pepper to taste. Pulse the mixture once or twice to incorporate the seasoning. Store in a tightly sealed container in the fridge for up to a week. It also freezes well for up to 6 months.

Note: To toast nuts, roast in a 350-degree oven on a rimmed baking sheet for 10 minutes, until they begin to turn golden brown.

MAKES ABOUT 1 CUP

½ cup raw whole almonds, toasted

4 garlic cloves

4 cups loosely packed, coarsely chopped sorrel (woody stems removed) or wood sorrel

⅔ cup extra-virgin olive oil

2–3 ounces aged (hard) goat cheese such as Caprotto or Pantaleo, grated

Salt and freshly cracked black pepper

SaLaD ACCOrDInG TO Eva

Eva eats salad greens like horses eat hay. During the growing season, which is about nine months a year, Eva eats the surplus from the weekly field collection. There is usually plenty left over from her chef's wild green salad mix, which can include various baby mustards, bronze fennel, Bull's Blood beet greens, burnet, chervil, chicories, goosefoot, lemon balm, mizuna, parcel, purslane, Red Russian kale, ruby chard, sorrel, Sylvetta arugula, tatsoi, and wood sorrel. Come winter, Eva eats the greens and herbs that persistently grow on her land and in her unheated greenhouses.

To Eva, eating salad is simple: Grow the widest variety of flavor-packed organic greens and herbs you can possibly imagine, and attend to them assiduously, sleeping four to five hours a night. Combine the greens and herbs to your heart's delight, but do not dress them! A dressing or even simply oil and vinegar masks the true flavor of the greens. (Eva understands that not everyone shares her philosophy; she totes olive oil and balsamic vinegar when she brings her beautiful salads to parties, so that people can dress if they like.)

Instead of making a "salad," treat the salad greens like salt and pepper—in other words, add greens to most everything you eat. Mix them into cooked foods, such as cooked grains to soups to curries. Or put the greens in a bowl and add a few mix-ins from the fridge, such as fresh cranberries, preserved lemons, smoked fish, kimchi, fresh herbs, local cheese, chef-made sausage, nuts, or spoonfuls of leftover food from parties you've recently attended.

Basic Tips for Better Salads

Keep your greens dry. When supermarkets mist their greens, they are doing them a disservice. They look good to the prospective buyer, but wet greens lose flavor and become slimy quicker. According to Eva, salad greens should be kept dry and their best storage spot is away from light, in the fridge, in a sealed bag. Do not wash your greens until you plan to eat them. If you grew the greens yourself or know that the grower doesn't use chemicals, taste the greens and see if they're gritty. If they aren't, refrain from washing. The problem is, any residual water from washing the leaves will dilute the dressing and break down the cell walls, detracting from the texture and flavor. And edible flowers will quickly lose their life if you wash them (or dress them)—you might as well torch them.

If you must wash greens ahead of time, use a salad spinner to spin them dry and wrap them in cotton rags or brown paper bags to help absorb excess moisture. Avoid buying prewashed packaged greens; they are often washed with chemical-laced water, and because they've been prewashed, they have less flavor and break down more quickly.

See page xviii for more advice on washing (or not) greens.

Diversify. Combine lettuce with an herb or two (or three) like basil, parsley, cilantro, bronze fennel, chervil, chives, dill, lemon balm, lovage, mint, sorrel, and tarragon. Eva's motto is, you can never combine too many greens and herbs. If you feel brazen, collect wild plants in a plastic bag and keep in the fridge for daily use. Weeds like chickweed, purslane, and wood sorrel may be right outside your doorstep. The only thing is, don't overwhelm your salad—who could eat a salad of radicchio, rosemary, thyme, and purslane (besides Eva, that is)?

On the other hand, you need only one variety of greens to make a respectable salad, especially if it's fresh. Try Bibb lettuce, romaine, lamb's-quarter, mâche, pea greens, spinach, sunflower sprouts, or even claytonia, freshly picked, lightly dressed.

Dress greens sparingly, or not at all. The worst thing you can do is drown a salad in dressing. It will dominate the salad's flavors and wilt the greens. It's like a slobbery wet kiss. Go even lighter on the dressing when you've included herbs in the salad mix, because their high notes will carry the salads. Eva doesn't ever dress greens, believing that dressing—even simply oil and vinegar—masks their true flavor.

I like to use a high-end single-estate olive oil (from Tuscany) and a good vinegar. The ratio is up to you, but in general it's three or four parts oil to one part vinegar; I personally never measure. But I've been convinced that a good oil makes a big difference. It's like adding a Persian or Turkish rug to your home—it's transformational. I also often use the juice of a lemon or lime instead of vinegar, especially with herbs. Preserved lemon transforms salads as well. If you add it, slice it thinly, and dress the salad with just olive oil, not vinegar. Preserved lemon is almost sweet, and it moistens a salad.

Use your eyes (or put on your glasses) when shopping. Buy greens that look like they were just picked, that are perky, not wilted or spotted or browned at the edges. Choose greens with thicker skins or lettuces with tighter heads because they are less vulnerable to bugs and oxygen and hold their flavor better; good choices include endive, green cabbage, iceberg lettuce, kale, napa cabbage, and radicchio. If nothing looks good at the market, consider composing instead a salad of matchstick vegetables, raw or steamed.

Treat greens gently. Tear the salad green leaves with your hands to the size you like. Cutting with a knife will break cell walls and may discolor the salad greens and herbs. Use clean hands if you can, not tongs, to toss greens.

Favorite Greens for Salad	Favorite Herbs and Flowers for Salad	
Arugula	Anise hyssop flowers	Mint
Baby kale	Arugula flowers	Nasturtiums
Baby mustard greens	Basil	Parsley
Bronze fennel	Calendula	Pineapple sage flowers
Bull's Blood beet greens	Chervil	Tarragon
Chickweed	Chive flowers	Wild rose petals
Pea greens	Cilantro	
Purslane	Daylilies (chopped bud or flower)	
Sorrel	Dill	
Sylvetta arugula	Lovage	

Spruce Shoots

Picea spp. · EVERGREEN

Yes, eating a tree can be delightful! Spruce shoots are green-yellow shoots the size of grapes which sprout from the tips of the tree branches in the spring; the needles at this stage are soft, citric, and chewy. If you take a few steps back and gaze at the tree, the boughs look like a giant hand with the shoots poised as the fingernails, as if the tree were primping for a manicure. It's hard to imagine that these tender and sweet morsels harden and darken into full-fledged needles and join the adult needle community, lengthening the tree's reach another inch each year.

CULINARY USES
Pop a shoot in your mouth and you will be rewarded with a minty pinelike tartness that is as much fun to play with in the kitchen as lemon, lime, sorrel, or rhubarb. Spruce resin is used to flavor chewing gum, and on the simplest level, you can chew (and swallow) the shoots as a convenient breath freshener when hiking. However, I find the shoots invaluable for glazes, sauces, and rubs for roast game or other meat, because the pine and citric components taste best with rich food. Unlike mustard, vinegar, citrus fruits, and other citric contributors, the shoots have very little moisture, which helps with achieving a good consistency for a paste. I like to mix the shoots in a paste with garlic, shallots, sunflower or pumpkin seeds, as well as other herbs like rosemary or sage. Or it can be made into a compote, adding garlic and olive oil, to serve alongside meat or roasted vegetables. I served Michael Pollan a spruce shoot compote next to roasted mutton one night at a restaurant in Boston. I told him he was eating a tree, and he seemed pleased.

Chef Tony Maws of Craigie On Main in Cambridge, Massachusetts, smoked some pheasant, duck, and goose and from them made a rich bouillon, with bits of wild mushrooms, duck tongue confit, and spruce shoots, and served it with a sorrel mousse to eight hundred people one night. Seth Morrison of the Gallows in Boston's South End cures salmon using spruce shoots and garnishes goose and venison with pickled shoots. The bartenders at No. 9 Park in Boston make a simple syrup with the shoots and use it in cocktails. Chef Patrick Connolly at Bobo in Manhattan torches his shoots (which caramelizes them) and combines them with fluke and grapefruit sections.

Although I haven't dabbled in this, the mature needles of spruce trees are also used for culinary purposes, mainly infusions for drinks and desserts.

HEALTH VIRTUES
Eva claims that Samuel de Champlain had his troops eat spruce shoots to prevent scurvy, a dietary illness that often resulted in death in his day. I haven't found proof of that in my own research, but Eva is not one to unleash flimsy information. But it is true that spruce needles are exceptionally high in vitamin C, making spruce shoot tea a great immune system booster.

FORAGING AND STORING
It's helpful to know what a spruce tree looks like when you set out foraging. I once spontaneously picked some shoots when catering a dinner party and told the host, who is a doctor and public health teacher at Harvard, how excited I was to find spruce shoots right there in his front yard! He looked at what I

had collected and said, "But that's my hemlock tree." To dampen my enthusiasm still further he added, "And didn't Socrates die from hemlock poisoning?" I excused myself and quickly dialed the Eva hotline, and she told me, "Hemlock trees are perfectly edible. It is the herbaceous hemlock plant, not the tree, that killed Socrates."

I have since learned a few tricks to help positively identify spruce trees. Unlike pine needles, which grow in clusters, spruce needles are each singularly attached to the twig. Spruce needles are square in cross section and should roll easily between two fingers (unlike fir needles, which are too flat). And if you can find a branch that has lost a few needles, it should be rough, not smooth (a bump is left where each needle once was). If you're still in doubt, there are always the seed cones (some of which stay attached to the tree for years) to give you one last positive ID.

Gather the lime green spruce shoots as soon as they appear in the spring, and store in a sealed container in the fridge for up to 2 weeks, or in the freezer for extended storage.

Spruce Shoot Compote

MAKES 2 CUPS

2 cups spruce shoots

½ cup raw sunflower seeds

4 garlic cloves or ½ cup chopped green garlic

1 cup extra-virgin olive oil

1 teaspoon salt

Freshly cracked black pepper

This compote is perfect with pork or lamb. I served it with mutton one spring. Mutton is meat from a sheep that is two or more years old. It tends to be tough, but slow cooking renders it sweet and tender. Ask your local sheep farmer where you can find some.

Combine the spruce shoots, sunflower seeds, and garlic in a blender or food processor. With the machine running, add the oil in a thin stream. Season with the salt and freshly cracked pepper. The compote should form a semi-smooth puree. Store in a tightly sealed container in the fridge, where it will keep for about 1 week, or in the freezer, where it will keep for up to 6 months.

Stinging Nettle

Irish chef and cookbook author Denis Cotter writes about nettles and his childhood in his book *Wild Garlic, Gooseberries . . . and Me*. He muses, "The nettles would have been all over the garden but for the furious football activity. . . . One year a man came and removed the nettles, like some gardening messiah. . . . Never in our wildest dreams, not even in the event of the bomb being dropped, did we contemplate eating the nasty, stinging, space-grabbing plants. How things change."

Not surprisingly, Eva tries to grow nettles intentionally on her farm. But even though stinging nettles grow perennially all over the wild in the United States and Europe, Eva often has trouble cajoling her nettle plants to grow year in and year out. Until Eva figures out how to keep her own source flowing, she gets new plants every year from a nearby friend. Lucky for Eva, this is not her only supply. Mother Nature is a skilled farmer and happily shares a secret nettle treasure a few miles away that produce year after year.

Culinary Uses

Eva sells stinging nettles to chefs every spring. Chef Peter McCarthy of EVOO in Cambridge, Massachusetts, makes a popular stinging nettle soup that's thickened with oatmeal. Others like to add nettles to frittatas or ravioli fillings. Chef Seth Morrison of the Gallows in Boston's South End uses it for a lasagna filling.

I had never used nettles until a few years ago, when I began adding it to soups. In the spring Eva steams and purees nettles in great quantity and freezes the thick paste. So I snatched a quart of nettles from her freezer to experiment. When I experiment (which is every time I cook), I taste the main ingredient first and let the flavor brew on my tongue so I can think about what I might want to do with it. The thawed puree of stinging nettle tasted vegetal, with a vague flavor of algae. I dipped my index finger in the tub more than a few times until I conjured up a direction that felt good to me. I decided upon a lightly curried nettle–coconut milk soup. But a few hours later my lip became sore and inflated and stayed that way for a good twenty-four hours. I learned from a forager that this "contact dermitis" skin rash results from contact with the raw plant. Although Eva had steamed her nettles before pureeing, she didn't steam them enough. Better to boil the nettles for a few minutes so that they completely lose their sting. After being boiled they don't need pureeing; they almost melt into a puree on their own.

Eva likes to slather cooked nettles on good whole-grain bread and then top it with kimchi for a grab-and-go lunch. You could also add some butter, lemon, and a touch of sugar to the cooked nettles. Fish or shellfish like scallops or shad roe are supreme served on top of the nettles prepared like this.

Health Virtues

People have been drinking nettle tea for its medicinal properties for hundreds of years, and today it is still prized as an incredibly nourishing drink. Nettles are rich in calcium, magnesium, iron, phosphorus, vitamin C, beta-carotene, and B-complex vitamins (for starters!). They are also extremely high in protein for a vegetable, so drink up!

Foraging and Storing

The most important thing to remember when foraging stinging nettle is to wear gloves.

The leaves of stinging nettles are filled with formic acid, the stuff of stinging ants, which is released on anything that brushes against them. If you do happen to be stung, one antidote is to crush and rub curly dock, which tends to grow nearby, on the affected area.

The nettle leaf looks like a very large mint leaf, and plants tend to grow in patches of a hundred or more in either sun or partial shade. They like rich soil and are often found at the edges of pastures and near farm buildings.

They are tastiest and most tender when young, about 1 to 3 feet tall. Stimulate new growth by nipping at the plant regularly, harvesting individual leaves or snipping branches off and taking the leaves off at home. Use the leaves right away, or blanch and freeze for later use. I've never seen anyone wash nettles, and I wouldn't try. But that is another reason why I prefer boiling over steaming, as it bathes them as well as cooking them.

Stinging Nettle Soup

Most recipes for nettle soups are simple and thickened with white potatoes. This one is slightly more interesting, and it's thickened with sweet potato or parsnip. I made this with nettles that Eva had kept frozen for two years, and it was great. If you can't find any of this invasively delicious plant, you could make the same soup with spinach or chard.

MAKES 6 SERVINGS

- 2 tablespoons extra-virgin olive oil
- 2 medium onions, chopped
- 3 garlic cloves, chopped
- 1 tablespoon minced fresh ginger
- 2 teaspoons ground cumin
- 1 teaspoon ground coriander
- 1 large sweet potato or 6 parsnips, chopped into 1-inch pieces (about 6 cups)
- 1 pound stinging nettles, large stems removed, or 2 cups steamed and pureed stinging nettles
- 1 teaspoon salt
- 1 (13-ounce) can coconut milk
- 1 teaspoon garam masala or ½ teaspoon ground cinnamon
- 2 tablespoons cider vinegar

1. Heat the oil in a heavy-bottomed stockpot over medium heat. Add the onions, garlic, and ginger and cook for 5 minutes, stirring frequently.
2. Add the cumin and coriander and stir well. Add the sweet potato and 5 cups water. Partially cover the soup, bring to a boil, and let simmer until the sweet potato is soft, about 30 minutes.
3. Add the stinging nettles, salt, and coconut milk. Stir well, cover, and simmer for 5 minutes.
4. Puree the soup with an immersion blender or in batches in a food processor until it is very smooth. Whisk in the garam masala and vinegar. Taste and adjust seasoning if necessary.

Smashed Potatoes with
Stinging Nettles and Brown Butter

MAKES 2 SERVINGS AS A SIDE DISH

5 or 6 small potatoes, each about 1½ inches in diameter

2 tablespoons butter

1 medium onion, thinly sliced

1 large garlic clove, minced

1 cup loosely packed, destemmed young stinging nettles

⅓ cup half-and-half or light cream

¼ teaspoon salt or more to taste

Freshly cracked black pepper

Could something this simple, without any expensive ingredients, taste so good? Yes, but it's important that the potatoes be organic; as with delicate herbs, rich soil renders rich flavor. This dish could be served as a bed for broiled or panfried fish. It is a great starter recipe for first-time nettle users. You could double the quantity of stinging nettles if you want.

1. Bring a large pot of salted water to a boil. Add the potatoes and boil until they are tender, about 20 minutes. Drain, reserving 1 cup of the cooking liquid.

2. Meanwhile, melt the butter in a large skillet over medium heat. When the butter begins to brown, add the onion and garlic and cook for 4 to 5 minutes, until the onion is browning, the garlic is a bit toasty, and the butter is a deep golden brown. Watch the skillet carefully, because your browned butter can burn very easily.

3. Stir in the stinging nettles. Add 3 tablespoons of the reserved potato cooking water and continue to cook, stirring, for a few minutes, until the nettles become limp and are cooked through.

4. Mash the warm potatoes in a large pot with a potato masher. Add the half-and-half, browned butter, nettles, and salt, and season with freshly cracked black pepper. Serve warm.

Tarragon

Artemisia dracunculus · PERENNIAL

James Beard once said, "I believe that if ever I had to practice cannibalism, I might manage if there were enough tarragon around." There are plenty of other herbs and seeds tasting of licorice, but none are as forceful and ambrosial as tarragon. In France it has been called the "king of herbs" for hundreds of years.

My mom made some wise decisions when we were kids; two were that she grew tarragon and she bought pastured chickens from a local farmer. Chicken and tarragon are a real love match. From these two ingredients my mom often made Julia Child and Simone Beck's *Poulet Poele a L'Estragon*, better known to us as chicken tarragon. Part of this recipe's genius is that the tarragon sits in the chicken's cavity and you sear the chicken in butter in an earthenware casserole, then braise it in butter in the oven. This renders incredibly tender meat that is imparted with the sultry tarragon. The chicken carcass was always sparkling clean by the end of dinner.

Culinary Uses
In his information-packed *Herbs, Spices and Flavorings*, Tom Stobart advises, "Tarragon must be added with good judgment." Yes, tarragon can overwhelm if not used with discretion, and the only way to have discretion is to learn by trial and error, since recipes aren't always designed for our individual palate. Add tarragon in increments, tasting it once it's added. Eva herself has a fearless palate. She likes to deluge soups and salads with fistfuls of tarragon. She is a perfect example of how our tolerance (and love) for flavors increases with repeated exposures.

Tarragon is one of those rare herbs that is excellent used raw or cooked. For instance, it can be added raw to green goddess dressing, lobster salad, a compound butter, or to a creamy goat cheese. On the other hand, it holds up well with steamed fish, Béarnaise sauce, or chicken tarragon. Béarnaise sauce, if you aren't familiar with it, is a sinfully rich butter–egg yolk sauce that gets a little relief from vinegar and tarragon. Eat it with a good steak or as the sauce for eggs Benedict. It's hard to think of a tastier addition to omelets than freshly chopped tarragon with a bit of tomato. It's also wonderful with grains and vegetables, though it's best to add it once they've been cooked. There is a fine veggie burger recipe in my book, *Vegetarian Planet*, that consists of kasha, portobello mushrooms, and tarragon.

Tarragon is also exceptional in green salads; simply pull the leaves off the stem and toss them with milder, tender greens and herbs. Make a vinaigrette with tarragon, lemon, garlic, Dijon mustard, and olive oil and drizzle it over a salad niçoise. Chef Seth Morrison at the Gallows in Boston's South End makes a tarragon-heavy green goddess dressing and serves it with a Waldorf-style beet salad. He also likes tarragon with "anything apples" and makes a mean tarragon grape relish for seafood.

Health Virtues
Medicinal uses of tarragon go back to ancient Greece, where it was chewed to relieve pain from toothaches (thanks to its numbing effect). It is also used as a detoxifier and is a great source of iron, calcium, and manganese.

Buying and Storing
Not many supermarkets carry fresh tarragon, which is why so many people grow it. If you can find it, relatively fresh tarragon has a long

shelf life in the fridge, possibly two weeks. Stay away from leaves that are fading in color or withering. Freezing tarragon in any form is not the best idea, but it can be done and then cooked with later—just leave it on the stem and wrap it well. Tarragon vinegar (page 125) is the best way to harness the herb's gorgeous flavor and extend it beyond its season. I've tried making oils and pestos with it, but vinegar is really the way to go. You can also dry it (see page xxi).

As with any herb, don't chop tarragon until you are ready to use it; doing so breaks down the volatile oils and the flavor gets lost as time passes.

Growing Tarragon

French tarragon is what you want to grow, not the Russian type. Buy a plant in the spring and give it about 18 inches of space and full sun. Begin harvesting by clipping some of the branches six to eight weeks after it has been transplanted.

In late summer the tarragon will die back, but the roots will stay alive under the soil, so long as they do not sit in standing water, frozen or thawed, during the winter. In the spring new growth will appear. Eva calls June International Tarragon Month because of the plant's proliferation.

Eva also cultivates Mexican tarragon (sometimes called Mexican mint marigold), a perennial herb that is unrelated to French tarragon but whose leaves have an even stronger anise flavor. It has been cultivated for more than a thousand years in Central America. Aztecs used the leaves to flavor chocolate. Its edible golden flowers are yummy.

Tarragon Millet Tempeh Cakes

These are choice partly because of their crunch. They are best served on a bed of herbs and greens, with a dollop of Lemon Balm Borani (page 164) or dill-cilantro dressing. Or fry them up in the morning with eggs! You can omit the tempeh if you are not a fan; however, this is a good way to introduce yourself to it.

MAKES SIX 4-INCH CAKES

½ teaspoon salt or more to taste

1 cup uncooked millet

1 small sweet potato, cut into 1- to 2-inch pieces

4 ounces tempeh, cut into ½-inch cubes

Leaves from 2 large sprigs tarragon

2 tablespoons canola or other neutral oil

1. Bring 2½ cups water to a boil in a medium saucepan over high heat. Add the salt, millet, and sweet potato, turn the heat down to very low, cover, and let simmer for 25 minutes. Then remove from the heat.

2. Pulse the tempeh and tarragon leaves in a food processor until well combined and finely chopped. Add half of the hot millet and sweet potato, and pulse until the mixture is thick and sticky. Transfer to a bowl, and use a spoon to stir in the rest of the millet and sweet potato. Let the mixture cool, then form it into six 4-inch cakes.

3. Heat the oil in a cast-iron or other well-seasoned skillet over medium heat. When the oil is hot, panfry the millet cakes for 3 to 4 minutes, letting them cook undisturbed so that they develop a crust on the underside. When the undersides have browned, flip the cakes with a spatula, and panfry until the other side has browned. Serve warm from the pan.

Tofu Ricotta

MAKES ABOUT 2 CUPS

16 ounces firm tofu

⅓ cup loosely packed chopped basil leaves

1–2 tablespoons coarsely chopped tarragon leaves

1 or 2 garlic cloves, minced

½ teaspoon salt

½ teaspoon freshly cracked black pepper

3 tablespoons extra-virgin olive oil

This is an easy way to lure kids to tofu. I use it instead of ricotta cheese in lasagna, adding some real mozzarella to help it along. And what's better, preparing tofu this way seems to win over unyielding adults as well. You can use it as you would use ricotta; I like to stuff tomatoes with it and spoon it raw onto fresh salads. Use the amount of tarragon that tastes good to you. Try other herbs as well, like African basil, chervil, lovage, parsley, thyme, and so on.

Combine the tofu, basil, tarragon, garlic, salt, pepper, and olive oil in a large bowl, starting with a small amount of tarragon and garlic. Break the tofu down into crumbles; I like to use my clean hand to do this, but you can also use a potato masher. Taste the mixture and add more garlic or tarragon if you like.

Community: A Vision from the Alps

It was the summer of 1968. Eva was thirty-four years old and teaching and producing pottery, but she also had a garden. Eva, George, and their three-year-old son Leo were on vacation walking through the town of Chamonix, France, nestled in the French Alps. They came upon a grocer's tiny storefront, a bay window opening onto a wooden shelf that had on display its two wares: bundles of fresh tarragon not the least bit wilted and little boxes of unrefrigerated strawberries freshly picked from someone's backyard garden. For Eva, this display was an epiphany: a business with minimal packaging, so untouched, no advertising. This enchanting storefront eventually inspired her to begin selling from her garden.

Tarragon Vinegar

All you have to do is combine vinegar and tarragon and let them hang out for a couple of weeks in a bottle, and voilà, you have created tarragon vinegar. It's more like an extract, really, since it is so intense that it transforms food with a single splash. And it lasts for months. This recipe easily multiplies. Boston chef Gordon Hamersley adds some tarragon vinegar to his deviled eggs, which are wonderful. I like it in potato or chicken salad or as a universal salad dressing.

MAKES 1 QUART
1 bunch tarragon
4 garlic cloves, thinly sliced (optional)
4 cups white vinegar

Bruise the tarragon by folding it over on itself on the counter and banging your fist down on it a few times. This will help release the essential oils. Place in a quart jar and add the garlic, if using. Top up the jar with the vinegar. Screw on the lid. Let the jar sit in a cool, dark place for 2 weeks, then remove the tarragon, leaving a sprig in the jar for eye appeal. The vinegar is now ready for use.

A MEAL WITH NO PLAN: HOW TO IMPROVISE

My mom let me cook in the kitchen when I was a kid. I specialized in inedible cookies. It was a form of play. I'd make them with random ingredients—Nestlé Quik, milk, salt, flour. I never made a viable cookie but it engaged my imagination and took my time. I became comfortable in the kitchen and consequently I developed a positive relationship with cooking.

Whenever I visit Eva we almost always have her friends over for dinner (after ten years they have become my friends as well). For me, this is another opportunity to play. First I peek in her fridge and check everything out—her cheeses, her preserved foods and leftovers, her mysterious infusions. We might thaw a small piece of venison or fish to give the meal focus, or maybe I center the meal around pasta or risotto. Then I run out to the garden, grab some scissors, and pick. This is always the best part of the day and I never give myself enough time. This is when ideas for the meal are spawned.

Improvising in the kitchen isn't always easy, but a garden filled with herbs and greens really helps. It seems to grease the wheels, helping the cook move in new directions. Farmers' markets can also provide inspiration and ideas, and although I don't recommend it, a cook can be inspired in even the dullest supermarket produce section. Cooking knowledge certainly helps, whether from reading or real life. But once you get your "sea legs," so to speak, in cooking without recipes, improvising will teach you more about cooking than recipes can. And, at least for people like me, it is also the most satisfying way to cook.

The first rule is to smell everything throughout the cooking process. Sometimes I'll sniff together a dish. I'll be cooking something and I'll take in the scent, then half a second later I'll sniff a potential herb or spice; and my nose knows if they'll work together or not. Or I'll look in the fridge and be surprised at how a food jumps out and wants to be part of the action. Improvising is like climbing a tree. You start with a few ingredients, then you climb, limb by limb, not sure how you'll get to the top, but figuring it out as you go. Sure I've had meals that go bust, but they are always edible. When things coelesce, then I feel terrific.

That is why Eva's kitchen and garden are so much fun. She has so many fabulous "colors" on her palate from which to choose. Plus she is so inventive herself that it's infectious. But the same can happen with any fridge.

If all of this sounds daunting, you can start by making a small but creative substitution in a recipe you already know or find. Then you'll start to see how enjoyable it is. Building this "creative muscle" is fun for the amateur, but it is critical to every professional chef. In France, and elsewhere, creating new and inspiring dishes is the main way people distinguish a "chef" from a "sous-chef."

Be willing to err. Every time you take a risk, you are growing your cooking muscle. If you exercise this muscle enough, you will find that you can relax while cooking, and you will begin to play in the kitchen. Plus, you'll increase your understanding of food, and you'll enjoy all the more the magic that good cooking produces.

Eva's Improvisational Style

by farmhand Kelly Lake

Dinners are Eva's heartiest meal of the day, the only meal she has any time to prepare, and they showcase her finely tuned skill of making a supper out of a seemingly hopeless assortment of raw ingredients. One night I was reading a book in my room when I heard someone come into the barn through the screen door below. I waited for a moment, secretly hoping that my time alone wasn't going to be interrupted just yet. I had just picked up my reading again when I heard Eva's voice call through the ceiling: "Kelly! I've cooked up something interesting for dinner!" "Interesting" is Eva's favorite word for describing her culinary creations.

By now it was late June, well beyond asparagus season, so you can imagine my surprise when the main course was two particularly persistent stalks of pale brown asparagus that had been growing for over a month beneath a burlap bag on one of the paths in the garden, maturing to the size and texture of small saplings. Any one of Eva's farmhands might have seen the asparagus and added them to the compost pile, but it just so happened to be Eva's luck to have gotten to them first and made them our dinner. She cut them into coins, sautéed them with a few herbs, and served them over a cooked grain, along with one of her famous vegetable "stock" soups. It wasn't delicious, but I have to admit it wasn't terrible either. After a few bites we both agreed something was missing. Eva is not one to settle for mediocrity in her kitchen. She leapt up and rummaged through her shelves, quickly returning to the table with one very small bottle of Tabasco sauce. After she concluded that this was in fact the missing ingredient, I poured a generous amount onto my own plate, only to find that it tasted more like moonshine—the contents of that small bottle must have been fermenting on Eva's dusty spice shelf for years, waiting for the glorious day when it would be deemed the perfect accompaniment to Eva's tree asparagus delight.

Preserved Lemons

MAKES ABOUT 2 QUARTS

14 lemons (Meyer lemons, Key limes, or conventional organic lemons)

½ cup fine sea salt

1–3 teaspoons cayenne pepper

Eva had given her neighbor Samina Quraeshi a bucketful of aging Meyer lemons, since Eva had received a free case of them. A month later Samina brought back a jar of those lemons, preserved. Samina's Pakistani mother had taught her this recipe. She uses Meyer lemons, which are sweeter, thinner, and smoother-skinned than our conventional thick-skinned lemons. But I give you a choice, because not everyone can find Meyers.

My favorite way to eat preserved lemons is in a salad, with no dressing except just the smallest amount of good olive oil. I recommend almost any salad green, although my favorites are Bibb lettuce and arugula. You can also chop the lemons and add them to panfried vegetables or coleslaw.

1. Scrub the lemons well with a vegetable brush and let them dry.
2. Place 10 of the lemons stem side down on a cutting board and cut ¾ the way down into quarters (wedges), without cutting all the way through, so they open up like petals of a flower. (This will help the lemons hold the salt and cayenne better.) Place the cut lemons in a large bowl.
3. Juice the remaining 4 lemons and transfer the juice to a tall sterilized glass jar.
4. Toss together the salt and cayenne, mixing well.
5. Fill the cavity of each quartered lemon with a good amount of the salt mixture, using up all of the mixture. Place the salted fruits in the tall jar with the lemon juice. Press the fruits down with a mallet or your hand. The lemons should be so jam-packed that they begin to give up their juice. If the juice does not rise above the lemons (which is what happens to me), then juice a few additional lemons and pour their juice over the salted lemons. Leave ¼ inch of headspace between the juice and the top of the jar. Seal the jar.
6. Let the jar sit at room temperature for at least 3 weeks; thick lemons may need up to 4 weeks. Turn the jar upside down for a few seconds to distribute the liquid and then set it upright again every day to ensure a good distribution of the brine.
7. Chop the lemons, and, if you want a less salty flavor, rinse them. Store in the fridge, where they will keep for many months.

bartering

e va has honed a crafty style of living, one that enables her to avoid
shopping almost without exception: she grows a lot of her own food,
and she trades and shares foods with her neighbors. She hasn't
visited a supermarket for over ten years. And her diet is far tastier and
healthier for it, as you might imagine. After all, how many supermarkets sell more than 150 varieties of just-plucked herbs and greens?

One key factor that helps Eva steer clear of the supermarket is her
gift for persuasion. She persuades good friends (like me) to buy food
for her in the city and bring it back on our next visit: a pound of peppercorns, ten pounds of black quinoa, a loaf of artisan bread. She draws
upon her sales skills, sweetening you with compliments: "No one is
better qualified than you, Didi, to hunt down black quinoa!" You know
she speaks the truth, and so the momentary boost in confidence softens
you up and gets you to take on the challenge.

But the bigger reason for her disinterest in shopping is that Eva
lives in a rich agricultural community that consists of mostly organic
farmers who produce small batches of top-quality goods like pastured
meat and milk, farmstead cheese, local wine, gleaming striped bass,
and just-dug clams—and a good measure of these foods is bartered,
rather than sold.

Just as caterers need to make more than they expect will be eaten,
farmers need to grow more produce than they intend to sell just to
ensure that they will have enough. So, for Eva and her fellow farmers,
bartering or sharing this "excess capacity" is a way to distribute what
you don't need.

I'm not sure what prompted the start of Eva's shopless lifestyle
some thirty-odd years ago—perhaps her distaste for supermarkets, her
lack of time, or both. Eva works like a beaver, maybe harder, and leaving

the farm is a huge sacrifice she reserves for doctors' appointments and parties with good food (and good friends). But Eva also has a passion for knowing her producers and sources, which means that she always gets impeccable food that is equal to, or even better than, the quality of the produce sourced by the top chefs she grows for. Her passion for good food is matched only by her love and zeal for the people who produce it, which makes for a lot of amazing food flowing from her fridge and many strong friendships. Here's a sampling of what comes her way:

- Goat, lamb (including mutton), pork, hen eggs, duck eggs, goat's milk, and goat cheese, all bartered by Antone Vieira (known as T) and his wife Ellen. In exchange Eva lets T use her refrigerated truck for his meat deliveries to the city.
- Olive oil, one of my very favorite swaps, since this olive oil is so unthinkably delicious. It is a single-estate oil called Il Lago, and it's extracted from *underripe* olives. The oil is imported from Tuscany by her neighbors, Tony and Rosemary Melli. They'll drop off a case a few times a year. In return they get picking rights to her farm. Olive oil this luscious is used only for drizzling on salads, breads, or soups. It is a greenish gold color, and its flavor cannot be compared to that of supermarket extra-virgin olive oil. It doesn't come cheap—I've even dipped into my retirement money to maintain a steady supply. For a similar grade, look on the back of bottle for a harvest date or a "Grown and produced in XXX" so that you know the olives come from only one farm.
- Alan Poole deliveries. Alan is an ornithologist who divides his time between Ithaca, New York, and a house next door to

Eva, and he operates as Eva's private delivery service. On his way from Ithaca he buys her sheep's-milk yogurt and cheese from Maryrose Livingston at Northland Sheep Dairy, as well as breads and grains from a good co-op. He also brings fabulous wines when he comes for dinner. The truer barter arrangement is that Alan has access to Eva's garden and, in exchange, he often weeds and plants seeds.

- Venison. Eva allows hunters to hunt deer on her land. In exchange she often receives an entire deer, and she will then offer up her greens and herbs.
- Seafood. Local clammers and fishermen trade their wares, mainly bluefish and striped bass, for Eva's greens.
- Wine. Winemakers from a nearby vineyard have been known to give Eva a deep discount out of friendship and respect.
- Mushrooms. Hen or chicken of the woods, puffballs, and chanterelles are frequently foraged by farmhands or neighbors, who invariably find more than they can use.
- Beef and bacon. These come from Jordan Farm next door (Eva is also the lady-in-waiting for less popular cow parts like heart and tongue).
- Coffee. Eva liberates chaff and burlap bags from Equal Exchange's roasting site, and they give her lots of test batches of coffee beans as well.
- Chocolate. Taza Chocolate gives Eva cocoa chaff for mulch, and they sell their stone-ground chocolate to her at a substantial discount in exchange for being able to visit and bunk at the farm.
- Cloumage, a rich cow's-milk lactic curd that is made one town over, is similar to farmer's cheese, but creamier. Eva currently buys it, but the producers are considering a trade for herbs that they can dry for an herbed version.
- Chef offerings. Chefs bring all sorts of inspired food (like a stuffed pig's foot) on their visits to Eva's bucolic garden. Sometimes they come to cook, sometimes just to get away from the city.
- Party leftovers. Eva is in great demand on the party and fundraiser circuits. She always brings a massive and stunning salad to parties (and a piece or two of Tupperware to help lighten the load of leftovers).

RECIPES LIST

African Blue Basil
Apple Pecan Salsa with
  African Blue Basil
Couscous Salad with African
  Basil

Anise Hyssop
Currant Scones with Anise
  Hyssop

Basil
Slightly Spicy Cilantro Pesto
Goosefoot Pesto
Opal Basil Parsley Pesto
Sage Mint Pesto
Basil Lemonade
Ratatouille with Fennel and
  Tofu

Bronze Fennel
Local Seafood Throwdown
  Bouillabaise
Bronze Fennel Butter
Fennel and Almond Biscotti

Calaminth
Wild Grape Sorbet with
  Calaminth
Calaminth Sorbet
Greek Shiitake and
  Calaminth Omelet

Dill
Creamy Dilled Dressing
Dilled Summer Salad

Lemon Balm
Lemon Balm Borani
Lemon Balm–Chive
  Compote

Lemon Verbena
Lemon Verbena Sorbet
Tofu Chard and Corn
  Mélange in Verbena Broth

Lemongrass
Pears in Red Wine with
  Lemongrass and Star Anise
Butternut Squash Soup with
  Lemongrass
Lemongrass Ice Cream
Southeast Asian–Style Beef
  Stew

Mint
Garlic Chive–Mint Pesto
Minted Lemon Water
Clams over Linguine with
  Mint and Green Beans
Minty Baba
Chocolate Intensity Cake
Minted Whipped Cream
Almond Cardamom
  Meringue Cookies

Purslane
Purslane Salad

Rosemary
Rosemary-Ginger
  Minestrone

Rugosa Rose
Raspberry Rose Milkshake
Rose Strawberry Sherbet
Rose Raspberry Ice Cream
Wild Rose and Rhubarb
  Pound Cake

Summer Savory
Potato and Smoked Bluefish
  Stew with Summer Savory

Thyme
Green Eggs (and No Ham)
Homespun Boursin
Lamb with Israeli Couscous
  and Oregano Thyme

Additional Summer Recipes
Herbed Omelet
Lavender Floating Island

African Blue Basil

Ocimum kilimandscharicum x basilicum ·
TENDER PERENNIAL

Over a lifetime, our palate educates itself and grows with little help from our conscious self. So it is not that I will always hate peas if I hate peas now. If I'm willing to expose myself to them from time to time, they will begin to taste better to me. I can remember a time when a cabernet would suck the moisture out of my mouth like a vacuum. But now cabernets lap over my tongue like a midnight shoreline. And didn't we all hate onions when we were five?

For my first few years visiting Eva's garden, I didn't like the flavor of African blue basil, or African basil, as Eva calls it. It clearly had its own agenda and didn't taste like the other basils. Still, I'd randomly pop a leaf into my mouth when I passed the plant. Now, after ten years of traipsing through Eva's garden, African basil's renegade brew of tannins, bitters, and other active compounds seem to harmonize as nicely as the the Beach Boys in "Good Vibrations." It's now one of the first herbs I turn to when I set about cooking.

I passed around a sprig of African basil to some city kids I teach in Boston, hoping to stretch a few palates. The first boy to take it bellowed, "Yech! This smells like Bengay!" He wouldn't put it near his lips, and then the sprig was passed from one kid to the next as if it were radioactive. But the boy was astute. Both Bengay and African basil contain significant amounts of camphor. The camphor in African basil comes from its East African parent plant, which is 61 percent camphor. The camphor in basil is like vinegar—straight vinegar isn't so palatable, but as a flavor enhancer, it can enliven and transform a sauce, stew, or soup. Camphor is also present in sage, rosemary, and other herbs.

One reason you may not have ever heard of this herb is that African basil hit the scene only recently, compared to most herbs. I was just blossoming myself (1983) when this herb was born from two basils that accidentally crossed in Athens, Ohio.

Culinary Uses

It is best to use African basil chopped and sprinkled onto dishes at the last minute: over hot soups, on pasta, to perk up grain salads, potato salads, fruit salad, salsas, and fish dishes. Adam Halberg of Barcelona restaurants in Connecticut makes a tomato–cucumber salad with four kinds of basil, including African basil and cinnamon basil. I sometimes just tear the leaves in half and add them to an herb salad.

As the weather warms, African basil's pretty purple flowers appear. They do not produce viable seeds, but that doesn't render them useless in Eva's garden; the flowers are the most succulent part of the plant, their fruity nectar complementing the camphorous qualities of the leaves. Eva sells these flowers to discerning chefs. Tony Maws of Craigie On Main in Cambridge serves octopus with a grilled tomato and smoked cinnamon sauce, which is infused with African basil stems, garnished with grilled lemons and a flourish of African basil flowers. I like to add the flowers to salads, especially in tandem with a chopped fruit such as figs, orange sections, or pear.

Before you start to imagine making yourself African basil pesto, I'll tell you now, stick to sweet basil. The process of making pesto definitely dumbs down this plant's complex flavor.

Health Virtues

Since African blue basil didn't even exist until 1983, we don't know much about its health virtues, although we can guess that they are similar to those of other basils. Because of its high camphor content, it may be especially good for suppressing a cough. For this purpose, or just for enjoyment, try African blue basil steeped as a tea.

Buying and Storing

Don't expect to find African blue basil at the supermarket. You will probably have to grow this one yourself. You can check your local farmers' markets during the summer. If you can't find it, you can always ask a farmer and see if you get any leads.

Buy stems that have just been harvested, with leaves that are perky and fragrant. Store the leaves in a plastic bag in the refrigerator to keep the fragile oils from oxidizing quickly. African blue basil seems to stay fresh longer (about two weeks) and bruise less easily than other varieties of basil. If you have more African blue basil than you know what to do with, all right then, go ahead and make a pesto—it's a good way to preserve the herb and it is pretty tasty, though, as I said before, it will dull its complexity. I've

tried freezing the leaves, and although this method can preserve the flavor for a month or so, the leaves turn brown and wilt upon thawing.

Growing African Blue Basil

African basil is the most cold-tolerant of all basils, although it thrives in hot, sunny weather. Since it cannot be started from seed, you must buy a plant (Johnny's Selected Seeds is a good source) or take cuttings from a friend. After transplanting the basil to a sunny spot in your yard, keep the ground moist. Don't be shy when harvesting—even if you cut it way back, this variety will keep producing new leaves. If you want African basil next year (and I know you will), move your plants to a sunny spot indoors before temperatures drop below freezing. They will not grow much (if at all) during the winter, and they should be watered sparingly until temperatures have warmed in the spring. Once any threat of frost has passed, move the plants to a sunny spot outdoors and resume consistent watering.

Apple Pecan Salsa with African Blue Basil

MAKES 4 SERVINGS

⅓ cup chopped African
   basil leaves

¼ cup chopped pecans,
   toasted

1 crisp apple, such as Fuji
   or Gala, with peel, diced

½ red onion, minced

2 tablespoons lemon juice
   (about ½ lemon)

1 tablespoon extra-virgin
   olive oil

Salt and freshly cracked
   black pepper

Serve this simple salsa with game, chicken, or pork, atop a salad,
on rice, and so on. Without the nuts it would also work nicely with
fish. Like most salsas, this one tastes best when made at the last
minute.

Combine the African basil, pecans, apple, onion, lemon juice,
and olive oil in a medium-sized bowl, and mix until they are well
incorporated. Season the salsa with salt and freshly cracked black
pepper to taste.

Note: To toast the chopped pecans, roast in a 350-degree oven on
a rimmed baking sheet for about 5 minutes, until they are golden
brown.

Couscous Salad with African Basil

**MAKES 6 SERVINGS AS A SIDE
DISH**

2 cups large couscous
   (Israeli or *maftoul*)

3 tablespoons extra-virgin
   olive oil, plus more for
   coating couscous

¼ cup chopped African
   basil leaves and flowers

¼ cup chopped chervil

¼ cup chopped chives

1 small bunch claytonia or
   watercress, chopped

2 small carrots, peeled and
   finely chopped

1 large tomato, chopped,
   or 12 cherry tomatoes,
   halved

Juice of ½ lemon, or more
   to taste

⅓ cup crumbled feta (I like
   goat's-milk feta)

Salt and freshly cracked
   black pepper

I prefer the peppercorn-size Israeli couscous over the smaller
granular type; Turkish and Lebanese markets sell a similar product
called *maftoul*. This recipe can withstand a lot of improvising. If
you don't grow African basil, you could employ other herbs like
anise hyssop, basil, dill, mint, or parsley.

1. Bring a large pot of salted water to a boil. Add the couscous and
   boil for 8 to 10 minutes, until tender. Drain the couscous and rinse
   with cold water, leaving it in the colander for a couple of minutes to
   drip dry. Gently stir a teaspoon or two of olive oil into the couscous
   so that it doesn't become sticky.

2. Transfer the couscous to a large bowl. Stir in the remaining 3
   tablespoons olive oil, along with the African basil, chervil, chives,
   claytonia, carrots, tomato, and lemon juice. Gently fold in the feta.

3. Season the salad with salt and freshly cracked black pepper to
   taste. Serve immediately, as it is best eaten fresh.

Anise Hyssop

Agastache foeniculum · PERENNIAL

Anise hyssop is among the select and privileged herbs that have the distinguished flavor of anise. Bronze fennel, chervil, French tarragon, Mexican tarragon, sweet cicely, and Thai basil are a few of the other anise-tasting herbs that I've encountered. Interestingly, aside from this strong commonality, these herbs are otherwise unrelated. Anise hyssop's aroma is multidimensional, with notes of pine, mint, sage, black pepper, and even a dash of cinnamon. But its most pronounced characteristic is its sweet flavor. It has a honeyed richness that seems improbable in a single leaf. The best part of eating anise hyssop is the finish, just before you swallow—it's like downing a tiny shot of Pernod or some other anise liqueur.

Anise hyssop is a member of the mint family. It's quite attractive throughout the growing season, especially when the lavender-hued blossoms open. When it flowers, it becomes a dizzying twenty-four-hour convenience store for bees and other insects. The leaf has a rugged sheen, as if a little gnome had brushed each leaf with polyurethane.

Eva began growing this herb three years ago after Tony Maws, chef of Craigie On Main in Cambridge, requested a continuous supply. Since then, many chefs have fallen for it, and I've been relentlessly piggish myself. It is my belief that anise hyssop deserves to become as commonplace an herb in our kitchens as parsley or mint.

CULINARY USES

Some people generalize that you can use anise hyssop in the same way you use mint. This is true, although the herb is not really minty. Along these lines, employing anise hyssop in tabbouleh works well (although don't mince the herb too finely, since it will lose its flavor, like tarragon). Or you could add torn or whole leaves to a green salad that includes sectioned oranges or grapefruits, olives, and feta. Inserting anise hyssop into Vietnamese rice paper rolls is exciting.

Odessa Piper, former chef/owner of L'Etoile in Madison, Wisconsin, likes to serve an appetizer of sliced watermelon topped with an anise hyssop leaf, a bit of creamy goat cheese, and some of the tangy anise hyssop blossom. Along the same lines I like to make watermelon or honeydew fruit salad topped with a spoonful of yogurt and julienned anise hyssop.

"Anise hyssop makes a profound marriage with cream," says chef Tony Maws. He makes a popular anise hyssop ice cream, infusing the herb into hot cream, and anise hyssop also works well in creamy pastas or risotto dishes, especially with seafood. Tony was confident and brave enough to serve a simple yet heady milk-based broth of green peppercorns, fish, and anise hyssop to eight hundred people at the *Food & Wine* Best New Chefs Awards gala.

If you'd like to carry the flavors of anise hyssop into the winter, try drying the leaves and using them to make a soothing and sweet tea all year long.

HEALTH VIRTUES

Anise hyssop contains the bitter compound marrubiin, an expectorant, and so anise hyssop tea can help with respiratory problems. It also aids digestion—drink a cup with meals to prevent gas and bloating.

BUYING AND STORING

You might have the best luck finding this herb at farmers' markets if you ask around for licorice mint, a common alternative name, but even then you may come home empty-handed. Whether you find it for sale or grow it yourself, fresh sprigs can be stored in a plastic bag in the refrigerator for a few days. You can also dry the flowers and leaves for later use by simply hanging a bundle of sprigs upside down; store in a tightly sealed container once they are dried.

Growing Anise Hyssop

Anise hyssop is easily propagated from cuttings or root division in spring or fall; otherwise start seed indoors in early spring.

Transfer established seedlings or cuttings to a sunny spot with well-drained soil, spacing them 2 feet apart and keeping them well watered. Cut the plant back by one-third when it flowers in late summer to encourage fuller, more productive growth. Continue to harvest throughout the season. Successive plantings in mid- to late summer ensure a harvest through fall, or you can nurture the volunteers that will pop up as the flowers go to seed. Be sure to enjoy the pollinators that are attracted by its sweet nectar. Watch for new growth in the spring, unless very cold winter temperatures kill the plant.

Currant Scones with Anise Hyssop

Excited by the tantalizing taste of anise hyssop flowers, I tried baking them into a scone, but the flavor went poof. It was Eva's idea to sprinkle the flower petals over a sticky lemon glaze that hardens on the scone.

1. Preheat the oven to 375 degrees F.
2. To make the scones, begin by bringing 1 cup water to a boil in a small saucepan. Add the currants, remove from the heat, and let the dried fruit sit, covered, for 5 minutes to rehydrate. Strain the currants and run them under cold water to cool.
3. Mix the all-purpose flour, whole wheat flour, sugar, baking powder, baking soda, and salt in a mixer fitted with a paddle attachment (or using a hand mixer) at low speed. With the mixer running, add the butter and mix until the dough is coarse and sandy.
4. Stir in the yogurt with a large spoon, mixing the dough until it is almost combined. Add the raisins and mix just enough to distribute them. Do not overmix the dough. If some sandy mixture remains at the bottom, mix in a bit more yogurt.
5. Turn the dough out onto a lightly floured surface. Knead the dough just until it comes together. This should be quick, because too much kneading will toughen the dough.
6. Form the dough into a rectangle about 12 by 6 inches. Cut into equal squares, based on the size scone you want. Transfer to an ungreased baking sheet.
7. Bake the scones about 20 minutes, or until they begin to brown; the time will vary depending on the size. I always test one by breaking it in half and eating it! Let cool.
8. To make the glaze, combine the sugar and lemon juice in a small bowl and stir. The sugar should melt, forming a fairly thick glaze.
9. When the scones are cool, drizzle the glaze over them and sprinkle the tops with anise hyssop flowers.

MAKES 10–12 SCONES

Currant Scones:

1 cup currants or raisins

1¾ cups unbleached all-purpose flour

1½ cups whole wheat flour

¼ cup sugar

2 tablespoons baking powder

1 teaspoon baking soda

¼ teaspoon salt

8 tablespoons (1 stick) cold unsalted butter, cut into pieces

1¼ cups plain (preferably whole-milk) yogurt, or a bit more

Lemon Glaze:

1 cup confectioners' sugar

2 tablespoons lemon juice (about ½ lemon)

½ cup anise hyssop flowers, separated from their stems

PESTO PLAY

Fresh pesto makes life worth all the trouble. If you grow herbs, making it is one of the most rewarding and practical ways to celebrate the harvest. With the added fat of their nuts, seeds, olive oil, and cheese, pestos transform herbs into near entrée status.

It's important to use fresh, clean, and dry herbs, extra-virgin olive oil, and a good-quality cheese. A hard grating cheese is the norm, though sometimes I use a soft goat cheese or a sheep's-milk feta or fromage blanc. Other times I go vegan and refrain from cheese, adding just a bit more salt instead.

If you're going to freeze pesto (and it freezes well), it's best to omit the cheese, adding it only once the pesto has been thawed before serving. Otherwise the cheese can lose some flavor.

Mixing different herbs, or just choosing herbs you haven't considered using for pesto before, is a worthwhile endeavor. It's hard to go wrong, but going wrong can be a great way to learn. Try a pinch of spice such as chile powder or fennel seed in your pesto. Or add chile peppers for a fiery pesto. Try kale pestos, which are popular now, or lovage pestos, which are wonderful. To get you started, below I've given recipes for four off-the-beaten-path pestos that I like a lot.

When pureeing, pulse the food processor only until the leaves are cut and the pesto comes together. If you puree to oblivion, you'll kill the volatile oils and the flavor will recede. If you don't have a processor you can use a blender, but you may need to add a few spoonfuls of water to get it going.

Where are the pine nuts in my pestos? Pine nuts are ideal for thickening and enriching pestos, but they are exorbitant. Some alternatives, like sunflower seeds, offer a similar creamy texture; others, like pumpkin seeds, almonds, and walnuts, give more texture than pine nuts, which I really like.

You don't need to adhere to exact measurements—if you have more or less of one herb or green, that's fine.

I'd recommend any of these pestos with spaghetti (add a splash or two of pasta water to the pesto to thin it first) or spaghetti squash (for baking instructions, see page 271), topped with cheese. Pesto is also superb in pilafs, as a compote for roast meat, or in cold or grilled sandwiches.

Mortar vs. Machine

Experts claim that pesto is better in texture and flavor if made in a mortar and pestle. The word "pesto" is a derivation of the Italian word "pounded," so using a mortar and pestle is simply implied by its name. Supposedly the pestle doesn't break down the cell walls the way a processor's blade does. To this end I tried using a large mortar and pestle (because small ones can't hold enough leaves), and my arms turned to noodles after a few minutes—it is no easy task to pound basil into a paste! I'm certainly not a big fan of electrical gadgets, but this is one time where the good ol' food processor becomes my friend. I always run the machine in short bursts, using the pulse button so as to keep from getting too smooth a consistency.

A Quartet of Pestos

Slightly Spicy Cilantro Pesto

Combine the almonds, garlic, ground coriander, and chiles in a food processor. Pulse for a few seconds until the mixture is coarsely chopped. Add the cilantro and pulse again for a few seconds. Add the olive oil in three increments, pulsing the mixture for a second or two after each addition. Season with plenty of salt and freshly cracked black pepper to taste. If you are not using it right away, store in a tightly sealed container in the fridge for a week, or in the freezer for up to 6 months.

Note: To toast the almonds, roast in a 350-degree oven on a rimmed baking sheet for about 10 minutes, until golden brown.

MAKES 2 CUPS

¾ cup almonds, toasted

5 garlic cloves

1 teaspoon ground coriander seed

1 tablespoon minced chiles

3 cups packed cilantro leaves and chopped stems

⅔ cup extra-virgin olive oil

Salt and freshly cracked black pepper

Goosefoot Pesto

Combine the basil, goosefoot, pumpkin seeds, garlic, and cumin in a food processor. Pulse for a few seconds until the mixture is coarsely chopped. Add the olive oil in three increments, pulsing the mixture for a second or two after each addition. Add the Parmesan cheese and pulse the mixture several more times to incorporate. Season the pesto with salt and freshly cracked black pepper to taste. If you are not using right away, store in a tightly sealed container in the fridge for a week, or in the freezer for up to 6 months.

Note: To toast the pumpkin seeds, roast in a 350-degree oven on a rimmed baking sheet for 6 to 8 minutes, until they are crunchy and browned.

MAKES ABOUT 2 CUPS

3 cups basil leaves

2 cups packed goosefoot leaves

¾ cup pumpkin seeds, toasted

7 garlic cloves

Pinch ground cumin

⅔ cup extra-virgin olive oil

1 cup grated Parmesan cheese (2 ounces)

Salt and freshly cracked black pepper

Opal Basil–Parsley Pesto

MAKES 2 CUPS

4 cups mixture of opal basil and parsley leaves

½ cup sunflower seeds, toasted

4 garlic cloves

⅔ cup extra-virgin olive oil

1 cup grated hard sheep cheese, such as Pecorino (2 ounces)

Salt and freshly cracked black pepper

A cilantro-parsley mix will work just as well.

Combine the opal basil and parsley, sunflower seeds, and garlic in a food processor. Pulse for a few seconds until the mixture is coarsely chopped. Add the olive oil in three increments, pulsing the mixture for a second or two after each addition. Add the grated cheese and pulse the mixture several more times to incorporate. Season the pesto with salt and freshly cracked black pepper to taste. If you are not using it right away, store in a tightly sealed container in the fridge for a week, or in the freezer for up to 6 months.

Note: To toast the sunflower seeds, roast in a 350-degree oven on a rimmed baking sheet for 6 to 8 minutes, until they are crunchy and browned.

Sage-Mint Pesto

MAKES 2½ CUPS

2 cups mint leaves (any type of mint is okay)

⅔ cup sage leaves

⅔ cup walnuts or sunflower seeds, toasted

5 garlic cloves

½ cup extra-virgin olive oil

1 cup farmer's cheese or ricotta

Salt and freshly cracked black pepper

For the cheese in this pesto, Eva and I use Cloumage, which is fresh lactic curd, similar to but more decadent than a ricotta, made in Westport, Massachusetts, by Shy Brothers Farm.

Combine the mint, sage, walnuts, and garlic in a food processor. Pulse for a few seconds until the mixture is coarsely chopped. Add the oil in three increments, pulsing the mixture for a second or two after each addition. Add the cheese and pulse the mixture several more times to incorporate. Season the pesto with salt and freshly cracked black pepper to taste. If you are not using it right away, store in a tightly sealed container in the fridge for a week, or in the freezer for up to 6 months.

Note: To toast the walnuts or sunflower seeds, roast in a 350-degree oven on a rimmed baking sheet for 6 to 8 minutes, until they are crunchy and browned.

Basil

Eva grows a slew of basil, enough to keep the cities of Rome and Naples afloat for at least 24 hours. Eva's basil is especially potent, something I attributed to her habit of enriching the soil with organic cocoa and coffee chaff and other rich organic fertilizers. But when I ask Eva why her basil achieves such greatness she unapologetically responds, "The reasons can only be speculative."

Basil is sweet and spicy, pulsing with notes of mint, anise, pepper, and clove. Even after what seems like months of a streaming supply of basil, no one's interest at the farm ever wanes; good fresh basil is very difficult to tire of. Some of the farmers even tear it onto their morning cereal!

As summer intensifies, the basil grows with a vengeance, and if Eva doesn't sell it before the basil starts to flower, then the whole planting of it becomes like a used car lot, rapidly losing its value. The flavor changes as the plant's energy is redirected into creating the flowers. It's still good, but it has a bitter edge and the sweetness has waned. The leaves lose their silkiness and stiffen. You can remove the flowers to forestall the plant's reproduction mode, but given Eva's 800-square-foot thick basil jungle, she'd have to enlist an army of full-time flower pinchers. At this point Eva just sells her basil at a reduced price but usually can't dispense with all of it. Sometimes I fantasize that I will hack the remainder down in the middle of the night and jump into the pesto business, making all kinds of wildly original pestos, pairing basil with calaminth, or African basil, or goosefoot, or any other renegade flavors I deem fit, calling my outfit "Fearless Pesto Co." Then, once thousands of jars and dollars had been exchanged, I'd take a well-deserved vacation to Costa Rica.

In the home garden, this is why it is important to pinch off the flowers—so that the plant can continue to grow leaves. Or, if you feel industrious, you can sow a new crop every week or two for a continuous young and tender supply.

VARIETIES

In addition to your typical sweet Genovese basil, Eva grows large quantities of opal purple basil, Thai basil, lemon basil, and African blue basil. (African blue basil gets its own profile in this book since it has such a unique flavor and mode of propagating.)

Opal purple basil's flavor is compelling—it mimic's sweet basil's, yet the sweetness is cut and one can detect an essence of clove. Its color is forbidding yet alluring—dark as midnight. In the evening the plants resemble Cousin Itt from *The Addams Family* TV show, dark, shaggy-haired phantom creatures with sloping shoulders, and I imagine they shift and trade places when you're not looking. The deep color and slightly sharper flavor are fitting in salads like the fabulous chef/author Suzanne Goin's heirloom tomato salad with burrata (a soft cheese), torn croutons, and opal basil.

Thai basil is basil on a power trip. It has an aggressive anise flavor, with a floral perfume and some camphor as well. Camphor is a flavor that's hard to explain, but it tastes rather medicinal, like menthol and clove. It isn't as easy to munch on as sweet basil, but Thai basil is revelatory in soups and broths. Thai basil's leaves are a bit stiffer than sweet basil's, and it bears purplish flowers.

Lemon basil has smaller leaves than other varieties, and it is definitely a worthwhile diversion. Add some to tuna, egg, or potato salad, or to rice or grain salads; it is also first-rate infused to make a tea or for sorbet. Eva's neighbor Alan Poole purees fresh tomatoes, passes them through a sieve, add a little salt and pepper, chopped onion, and lemon basil, and chills it down for a super-refreshing cold soup.

CULINARY USES

Like most everyone who enjoys the flavor of basil, I revel in a good pesto. There is the straightforward and difficult-to-beat pesto Genovese, and then there are zillions of variations. I've heard of some Sicilian pestos using capers and mint, and another made with sun-dried tomatoes. But I've gone out on my own limb with pestos (see page 141), and I hope you venture out on your own limb too.

Some people think basil exists mainly for tomato salads. Diana Henry writes in her cookbook, *Crazy Water Pickled Lemons*: "We get so used to employing certain herbs in particular ways . . . like a partner in a comfortable marriage, we begin to see them only in a particular light, or even cease to notice them at all. Then, suddenly, you taste a new dish and it's like being with a different person." So how else can we celebrate basil? For starters, fruits other than tomatoes make for fun matches. Cookbook author Julie Sahni makes a basil-pineapple ice. I've made a salad of watermelon, feta, basil leaves, and Bibb lettuce with a balsamic vinaigrette. Or try adding slivers of basil to any fruit salad or fruit salsa, such as peach salsa or fresh fig salsa. In her aforementioned book, Diana Henry boasts a lemon and basil ice cream.

Black cracked pepper has an affinity for basil, and they can be used together on all savory and even sweet dishes. Basil also fuses well with other herbs, like bronze fennel, cilantro, dill, mint, and parsley. Lightly dressed herb salads with basil are excellent propped up on grilled or panfried fish—add a few leaves of watercress or arugula to round them out. Try hot corn kernels with olive oil and slivers of basil, or with fresh corn off the cob in a salad with tomatoes and a big squeeze of lime. Thai basil is traditionally used atop *pho*, the classic Vietnamese beef noodle soup, along with mung bean sprouts and scallions. But both sweet basil and Thai basil are equally great in Indian and Thai curries.

The key is to remember that basil's crucial volatile oils, which give it aroma and flavor, begin to evaporate the moment the plant has been harvested, and they give up altogether when exposed to heat. So don't add basil to a dish until the last minute, and be sure that the basil you're using is fresh.

HEALTH VIRTUES

Basil is mildly anti-inflammatory. It is especially high in vitamin K and also supplies vitamins A and C, antioxidants, and healthful flavonoids and volatile oils.

BUYING, STORING, AND PREPPING

During the warmer months, your local farmers' market will probably be bursting at the seams with basils of all sorts, and I recommend trying them all. Buy basil stems with the leaves still attached. They should look perky and vibrant, not browned or withered.

Basil is a delicate herb that bruises easily, so store it carefully. If the basil is prepackaged and has been refrigerated, put it in your refrigerator in a plastic bag. Stems from the farmers' market should be carefully transferred to a plastic bag and stored in the refrigerator as well. Better yet, buy a bunch of stems with roots still attached and store them in a glass of water on the counter, where they'll keep for about a week.

To slice basil, first make sure the leaves are dry. Stack the leaves together, roll them tightly (like a cigar), and slice through them thinly to make a chiffonade, or thin little strips.

GROWING BASIL

Basil is easy to grow as long as its needs are met. It requires fertile soil, lots of sunlight, and warm weather. If you are growing from seed, sow indoors as early as February and allow the plants to grow at least two sets of true leaves before transplanting into your garden after all danger of frost has passed. Space plants 9 to 12 inches apart and keep the soil moist, but not soaked.

The trick to ensuring that your basil plants fill out is to "pinch" or sever the main growing stem. The plant will send out two new stems from the place where the plant was pinched back, and so it will grow out rather than up. Every time you harvest basil you are essentially pinching it; just be sure not to harvest more than one-third of the plant at any given time or you may hinder new growth. As the temperatures climb, be sure to pick off most of the flowers so the plant does not go to seed. Most varieties will not survive any frost.

Basil Lemonade

MAKES 8 SERVINGS

2 cups basil leaves (about 1 bunch)

1½ cups sugar

Grated peel of 6 lemons

Juice of 6 lemons

1 lemon, thinly sliced, for garnish

This lemonade is off the hook. It has "pulp"—that is, the zest of the lemon and the pounded basil form a kind of pulp that falls to the bottom. You can enjoy this extra treat by sucking it through a straw or spooning it up from the bottom of the glass. When you are grating the lemon peel, be careful to shave off just the yellow part of the rind, as the white part is bitter.

1. Pound the basil and sugar together in a large mortar and pestle or in a pitcher with a blunt object (such as a rolling pin that has no handles), for about 2 minutes. The basil should be pounded almost to a paste.

2. Add the lemon peel and juice and 8 to 9 cups room-temperature water. Stir the mixture well until the sugar has dissolved. Serve the lemonade in ice-filled glasses with a few lemon slices for garnish.

How the Farm Changed My Cat

Henry, my tail-less cat, spent ten of his last years vacationing at Eva's. The farm to him was our equivalent of a spa resort.

At the farm, his daily agenda was packed. He'd wake up in the morning and promptly jump on vole patrol, which was his main activity. This allowed him carte blanche to roam all parts of the farm, including the greenhouses. His eyes became focused and his energy level surged. He had hundreds of plants to sniff, dozens of voles to snuff out, and acres of junglelike plants to traipse through. Once he'd rid the farm of a vole, he could choose to frolic in the woods or nap in a warm greenhouse. On the weekends he enjoyed walks with me, trailing me for more than an hour. In the city, in contrast, Henry's sense of purpose was muted—his main goal was to be adored by me. At the farm he was exhausted every evening and would generally retire at around 7 p.m. And he'd sleep through the night, whereas in Boston he'd wake me up routinely for multiple snacks. Besides the voles, he developed a love for venison. He ate it rare, stewed, fried, smoked—even curried with lemongrass.

One incident made it clear how happy he

Ratatouille with Fennel and Tofu

I've morphed this classic French recipe so that I can eat it as an entrée, not a side dish. And I've discovered that fennel bulb, basil, and tofu work well in ratatouille and don't damage its integrity. In France I was taught never ever to stir ratatouille so that the vegetables don't break down. It's good advice and something that is often left out of translation. All the vegetables must be fresh and the tomatoes local for this dish to be stellar. Serve it hot over rice or quinoa, or eat it cold, as many French do.

1. Heat the olive oil in a large earthenware casserole or heavy-bottomed saucepan over medium-high heat. Add the garlic and sauté for 1 minute, until it begins to brown, then add the zucchini, eggplant, fennel, and green pepper. Reduce the heat to medium and cook the vegetables for 5 minutes. Try not to stir.

2. Stir in the tomatoes and thyme, cover the saucepan, reduce the heat to medium-low, and let the mixture cook for 10 minutes.

3. Stir the vegetables, then gently mix in the tofu and a 1/2 teaspoon salt. Reduce the heat to low and let the mixture cook, uncovered, for 10 to 15 minutes. Refrain from stirring.

4. When the vegetables are tender, add the basil, capers, more salt if needed and freshly cracked pepper to taste, and a bit more of the capers liquid if you like the flavor. Stir well to incorporate the seasoning and serve immediately.

MAKES 4 TO 6 SERVINGS

4 tablespoons extra-virgin olive oil

3 garlic cloves, minced

2 small zucchini, cut into ½-inch cubes

1 small eggplant, cut into ½-inch cubes

1 fennel bulb, cut into ½-inch cubes

1 green pepper, chopped into ½-inch cubes

4 tomatoes, chopped (4 cups)

2 teaspoons chopped thyme

1 pound firm tofu, cut into ½-inch cubes

½–1 teaspoon salt

1 cup roughly chopped basil

1 tablespoon capers (some liquid is fine)

Freshly cracked black pepper

was at the farm. Back in the city, Henry would lick my neck once or twice as a gesture of affection with his scratchy tongue. But one day at the farm he licked my neck and chin not once or twice but for five minutes! Now, this is a long time to tolerate any animal licking you, much less one with a Velcro tongue. I had to think of it as a free neck and facial exfoliation, because there was no way I could resist or pull back—it would have been totally rude. I think it was his way of saying: "Thank you, Mom, for bringing me here. I am completely happy."

Bronze Fennel

Foeniculum vulgare · PERENNIAL

When I was a kid, our family would drive to Vermont in winter to go skiing. Across from our rented house stood a rickety old country store. It featured a penny candy section that filled an entire room—root beer barrels, string licorice by the inch, squirrel nut zippers, candy dots on paper, Swedish fish, and a hundred other choices. My heart rate would ramp up, and I'd whiz through my dollar allowance in less than two minutes. Now that I'm (much) older, I get that same rush when I walk through Eva's garden, especially if I haven't been there in a while. I skip, pick, and nibble my way through the dozens of wild flavors, savoring the herbs in much the same way I did penny candy years ago. But it is Eva's bronze fennel that makes me feel like a kid in a candy shop: it is everywhere, I snack on it incessantly, it is surprisingly sweet (a little like Good & Plenty), and I never tire of it.

Unlike conventional fennel, bronze fennel is grown for its fronds and umbels alone; the bulb is so small that it's hard to find. But it pays to consolidate energy: these fronds are more tender than the conventional green fennel fronds, and they're intensely licorice-like! When I offer tastes of bronze fennel to my teen cooking students in the city, I am always impressed by how much they like it.

Eva's bronze fennel plants look like big, soft, feathery bushes, stretching 4 or 5 feet up from the ground, buffering spaces between the earth and Eva's other plants. There are at least a hundred bronze fennel plants strewn throughout her 2-acre farm. It wasn't always like this. Winter cold at Eva's kills this perennial, but it self-seeds, so it keeps coming back and has slowly been multiplying over the years.

Eva doesn't dig up the excess plants as many a commercial farmer would do. She appreciates their delicate brindled beauty and allows them to come and go at their leisure. The fronds of a single plant flaunt hundreds of tones: purple, sepia, burnt umber, cinnamon, and army green. These subtle juxtapositions are a sight to behold, existing only in nature. (On humid days, it is uncanny how I feel like one of Eva's bronze fennel plants, because my hair turns to frizz with tones of red and sepia.)

Culinary Uses

Bronze fennel, sometimes known as sweet fennel, is one herb where the less that's done to it, the better. Like thin-skinned herbs, the fennel fronds should not be cooked or they'll lose their flavor. Pureeing also kills the personality of this delicate green. It is best eaten in salads, torn into bite-size pieces and tossed with milder greens like mizuna, Bibb lettuce, mesclun mix, and perhaps herbs like chervil and basil, and weeds like chickweed and purslane. It is nice to have some lighter-colored greens to show off the fennel fronds. But stay far away from heavy creamy or cheesy dressings—the fronds will retain the dressing and turn into little wet mops. Better to use very little vinaigrette, such as a little olive oil and lemon juice, and to tear or chop the fronds into pieces.

Fennel fronds can be chopped into grain salads, especially with minced tomatoes and a cheese like feta. The fronds also work nicely as a bed for fish or shellfish. Try garnishing a creamy pasta or risotto dish with fennel fronds. Bill Braun, one of Eva's foodie farmers, sees chopped bronze fennel as a universal garnish. His favorite: fried eggs topped with goat cheese and chopped fennel fronds. He also mixes the chopped fronds with yogurt, strawberries, and granola. Eva lays the fronds as a purple veil over a platter of bright pink cured salmon for visual and flavor magic. Chef and restaurateur Jean-Georges Vongerichten makes bruschetta slathered with aioli and topped with crabmeat and fennel fronds.

At the end of the season the plant produces sweet yellow flower heads. Chefs clamor for these tiny flowers to garnish all kinds of seafood. And then there are the fresh green seeds, called fennel berries. These fresh (not dried) seeds are otherworldly—sweet, meaty, and priceless. Use them in crackers, biscotti, breads, cookies, seafood stews, and even granola, to which they should be stirred in at the last ten minutes of baking. You can stir something as miniscule as fennel seed into granola as it cooks. You do need to pull it out of oven for a minute, but this is done routinely enough, like when nuts/seeds get added in Didi's Granola.

One small warning: the fennel fronds, once chewed and supposedly on their way down the hatch, often have a pesky way of drifting to your front teeth and staying put. If I ever meet you at the farm, you can expect that I'll greet you with some stragglers dangling from my front teeth.

HEALTH VIRTUES
In India it is customary to eat a handful of fennel seeds after each meal to freshen the breath and aid digestion (certainly a better option than a sugary mint!). Because bronze fennel is grown primarily for decoration, not much is known about the nutritional content of its fronds and flowers.

BUYING AND STORING
Whereas bulb fennel (also called anise) has secured a place as a vegetable in our marketplaces, bronze fennel might prove difficult to find; check gourmet produce shops and farmers' markets. You can recognize it by its bronze or dark green fronds. It can be stored, unwashed, in a plastic bag in the refrigerator for a few days, but it is best used right away.

GROWING BRONZE FENNEL
To start growing bronze fennel, scatter seeds in full sun in early spring. It prefers fertile, well-drained soil but will make do in less desirable circumstances, putting up with partial shade or short droughts. Plants often grow to over 5 feet in height during a growing season and can be harvested for fronds or flowers as needed. If you are trying to contain your bronze fennel to a designated area, make sure you harvest the seeds before they drop. Cut plants down in winter and watch for new growth in spring; in colder climates your bronze fennel will probably die, but don't fret—new plants will undoubtedly crop up in the spring wherever the seeds fell.

Local Seafood Throwdown Bouillabaise

MAKES 6 SERVINGS

1 whole pollock (about 5 pounds)

2 leeks, coarsely chopped

1 head garlic, cloves separated and smashed with a knife, skin still on

1 tablespoon fennel seeds

1 lemon, very thinly sliced, or 1 tablespoon chopped preserved lemons

2 pounds purple Peruvian potatoes, cut into large bite-size pieces

1 fennel bulb, thinly sliced

1 small bunch Tuscan kale, chopped

4 tomatoes, chopped

Good handful fresh basil (I used opal basil), chopped

3 tablespoons good-quality extra-virgin olive oil

3 tablespoons tarragon vinegar

½–1 teaspoon salt

freshly cracked black pepper

I was competing in a chef contest at the first Boston Local Food Festival. They handed me a large pollock on ice. I hadn't skinned and boned a fish in twenty years, and I swore the fish rolled his big eyes once he realized who was going to fillet him. I was cooking against one of Eva's more high-profile chefs. We had to run to a nearby farmers' market to fetch produce. We were each allowed two secret ingredients. We both chose ingredients from Eva's Garden. I chose tarragon vinegar and fresh bronze fennel seeds; he picked out fennel pollen and pickled garlic scapes. All eyes were on him, as his techniques were flawless and his food impressive.

The *Boston Globe* wrote about me the next day, "Her effort to fillet the rest of the fish was effective but not pretty." And then they quoted me ("I'm kind of a vegetarian but went to cooking school in France"), to help explain my sorry attempt at deboning the fish. However, the bouillabaise won the contest, and I think it was because of Eva's tarragon vinegar!

1. Fillet and debone the fish, setting aside the fish meat. Place the head and carcass in a large pot with 2 quarts water, the leeks, the smashed garlic, and the fennel seed. Bring to a boil, reduce the heat, and let simmer for 25 minutes, uncovered. Add the lemon slices, remove the broth from the heat, and let sit for 10 minutes. Strain the broth, discarding the solids.

2. Pour the broth into a soup pot and add the potatoes, fennel, and kale. Bring to a boil, then reduce the heat and let simmer until the vegetables are tender, about 10 to 15 minutes.

3. Add the boneless fish and the tomatoes. Simmer the broth until the fish is fully cooked, about 10 minutes.

4. Remove the stew from the heat and stir in the basil, olive oil, and vinegar. Add the salt and season with freshly cracked black pepper to taste.

Bronze Fennel Butter

This butter is especially fitting on panfried, roasted, or steamed fish. Some good choices include Arctic char, Pacific cod, skipjack tuna, and mahimahi.

MAKES 6 TO 8 SERVINGS

½ cup (1 stick) unsalted butter, softened

½ cup minced bronze fennel

2 teaspoons lemon juice

salt and freshly cracked pepper to taste

1. Combine the butter, bronze fennel, lemon juice, and salt and pepper in a bowl, and mix well with a spoon or your hand.

2. Transfer the butter compound to a long piece of parchment paper, waxed paper, or plastic wrap. Fold the paper or plastic over the butter, and then use the back of a long knife to press the mound of butter into the fold of the paper, forcing the butter evenly up and down the length of the paper in the shape of a log. Twist the two ends of the paper to enclose the butter log, and store it in the fridge until it has hardened (or the freezer if you're eating soon). Store in the fridge, where the butter will keep for a couple of weeks. I like to save leftover butter by slicing it into rounds and storing them in a ziplock bag in the freezer, where they'll keep for up to 3 months.

Restaurant Community Visits Eva

Reporter Alexis Hauk covered a tour of Eva's Garden with Chef Jody Adams and her Rialto restaurant staff from Cambridge in an article for *SouthCoast Today*:

"We do a lot with weeds that are really edible," [Eva] says. "It's kind of a game. Sometimes I'll just let an area just go, but then all kinds of interesting things happen here because of my neglect."

She points affectionately to a giant asparagus bush, whose prickly little stems made some people guess it was dill. Speaking of the overgrown plant, she says, "This is like when you have a horse and it can't be ridden anymore and you just keep it because you like the horse."

Fennel and Almond Biscotti

MAKES 36 BISCOTTI

2 cups unbleached white
  flour

1 cup sugar

½ teaspoon baking soda

½ teaspoon salt

3 large eggs

1 tablespoon olive oil

½ teaspoon almond extract

1¼ cups whole, sliced,
  or slivered almonds,
  toasted

1 tablespoon fennel seeds,
  preferably fresh

This is adapted from food writer Corby Kummer's "Unbeatable Biscotti," which live up to their name. I haven't found any other biscotti so good, and I've made my share. I don't bake my biscotti as long as he does because I fear my teeth would fly out if the biscotti were any crisper. You can use part whole wheat flour, but no more than ½ cup—any more will detract from the texture and flavor. I experimented with many different seeds and herbs with this recipe, trying to give it an "Eva" spin. I tried sweet cicely seeds, thyme, rosemary, tarragon, and cilantro berries, but most lost their flavor in the double baking process. I finally used the sweet seeds from Eva's bronze fennel plants. I should have trusted tradition from the beginning.

1. Preheat the oven to 300 degrees F. Line two baking sheets with parchment paper.
2. Combine the flour, sugar, baking soda, and salt in a large bowl, and mix well. In a separate bowl, beat the eggs with the olive oil and almond extract. Add the egg mixture to the flour mixture. Stir well; the dough will be heavy and sticky. Add the almonds and fennel seeds and stir the mixture to begin to incorporate them.
3. Turn out the dough onto a floured surface. Fold it over itself three or four times to distribute the nuts and seeds throughout the dough. With floured hands, divide the dough into three equal portions. Form each into a log, about 7 inches long and 3 inches wide. Transfer the logs to the parchment-lined baking sheets.
4. Bake for 35 minutes, rotating the baking sheets on the racks. Remove from the oven and let cool for 10 minutes. Then slice the logs into ½-inch-thick cookies, and set the cookies on their flat side on the baking sheets.
5. Bake the sliced cookies for 15 minutes. Let cool, then store the cookies in a tightly sealed container for up to one month.

Note: To toast the almonds, roast in a 350-degree oven on a rimmed baking sheet for 8 to 10 minutes, or until they taste toasted.

Herbal Tidbit
Herbs: A Matter of Life and Death

Why bother growing parsley, dill, and cilantro when they're always available at the supermarket? This was my thinking before I started hanging with Eva. You can compare supermarket herbs to orange juice made from frozen concentrate. Like fresh-squeezed orange juice, the kind that is handed to you the moment it is squeezed, before someone pasteurizes it, parsley, dill, and cilantro still growing in rich organic soil are far superior to the stuff sold in a big supermarket. Herbs still on the vine are juicier, sweeter, and more pungent, especially if they're organically grown. Of course fruits and vegetables taste a whole lot better like this as well. But the flavor disparity is much more pronounced in herbs than in other edibles.

Why does the flavor of grocery-store herbs decline so much? Herbs owe their explosive flavor to essential oils. These oils are also called volatile oils, because they evaporate quickly. An herb that is still growing in the ground keeps producing these oils as they evaporate. Once the herb is cut or harvested, however, all of the plant's energy is quickly diverted to whatever is most necessary so it can reproduce. Most herbs have little to no chance of going to seed once the stem has been severed, but they don't know that: they just know that things aren't going well, and they do whatever they can to conserve energy and speed up maturation. Unfortunately for consumers, the production of volatile oils doesn't make the cut of what's necessary for survival, and so the more time an herb spends out of the ground, and the more oxygen is around, the more flavor it loses (which is why Eva insists on storing freshly clipped dry herbs in sealed plastic bags in the fridge).

Most amazing to me is that her herbs don't seem to lose any life or flavor if stored in sealed plastic bags for two weeks—even if I drive them seventy miles north to Boston and throw them in my fridge! Eva coddles her herbs, and they spend only about twenty-four chilled oxygen-deprived hours between getting snipped and reaching the hands of a chef. This kind of expediency and care is highly unusual in the world of commercial produce, and it separates her business from the rest.

The moral of the story: even though supermarket herbs are available year-round, they are a poor substitute for homegrown!

Calaminth
(Lesser Calamint)

Calaminth is a brave, little-known herb from Italy that belongs to the mint family. Its flavor soars to supersonic menthol heights, with a strong oregano current, although some people taste lavender. Either way, one bite gives a raucous blast of minty flavor that ignites on your tongue. I don't know why the Altoids manufacturer hasn't taken hold of this herb and capitalized on it. For years I didn't appreciate the cross section of herbal flavors at play in calaminth, and I made sorbets with it. Which were splendid. But there is much more to this herb than just its usefulness in sweets.

Culinary Uses

Being in the mint family, calaminth is rich with volatile oils, and it's best that it not linger in simmering or boiling liquids. Rather, infuse calaminth (steeping it in a liquid, such as water or cream), add it toward the end of cooking, or use it raw.

In Tuscany calaminth is added to wild mushrooms, artichokes, zucchini, and meat-based tomato sauces. It seems that in Italy, calaminth (or *nepitella,* its Italian name) is used in dishes that might otherwise take oregano. Chef Adam Halberg of Barcelona restaurants in Connecticut uses it with fresh porcini mushrooms. He also infuses vodka with calaminth flowers for the bar. Chef Mike Pagliarini from Via Matta in Boston makes calaminth-infused gelato.

Try adding calaminth at the last minute to a lamb tagine or to rhubarb chutney. Make a red quinoa salad with calaminth, chives, and parsley. Mash it into a sheep's-milk feta and enjoy on flatbread drizzled with good olive oil. Chop it into raita instead of mint.

Eva grows calaminth in abundance. In one of my best interludes with the herb, I added a few leaves to a chocolate milkshake, and the results were scintillating.

Health Virtues

In medieval times, before it became popular for its culinary contributions, calaminth was prepared as a medicinal tea as a digestive aid, to promote sweating, and for insomnia. It is also believed to lift melancholy moods.

Buying and Storing

You probably won't find calaminth in a store, unless you happen to frequent the few high-end supermarkets in the Northeast, mostly in New York City, that Eva supplies. Store calaminth, unwashed, in a plastic bag in the fridge for up to two weeks. When you are ready to use the herb, pinch off the leaves and discard the tough stems. It also dries well (see page xxi).

Growing Calaminth

Calaminth will be a unique addition to your garden (unless, of course, you are living in Tuscany) and is easy to grow if you can find seeds or a cutting. Grow in full sun, spacing plants 18 inches apart. Calaminth is a hardy plant that prefers semiarid conditions and will grow with or without much assistance from its gardener.

A well-established plant will grow into a small shrub 18 inches high. To harvest, grab stems by the handful and cut like an unruly lock of gnarled hair. The dainty pink-and-white edible flowers will spread their seeds, so be sure to manage your volunteer population, allowing some new plants to grow every now and then to replace any older, diseased, or weary shrubs.

Wild Grape Sorbet with Calaminth

I made this sorbet twelve years ago when I first met Eva and cala-minth. If you aren't growing calaminth, I recommend infusing the grape juice with a strongly flavored herb like marjoram, mountain mint, peppermint, rosemary, or thyme. Use a food mill or Squeezo strainer to extract the juice from the grapes.

MAKES 6 SERVINGS

⅓ cup sugar

½ cup loosely packed calaminth

2½ cups fresh wild grape juice

1. Combine the sugar with ½ cup water in a saucepan. Bring to a boil, then stir in the calaminth, and remove from the heat. Cover the pot, and let the mint steep in the sugar syrup for 5 minutes.
2. Strain the calaminth from the syrup. Combine the syrup with the grape juice in a large bowl. Mix well. Freeze the mixture, in the bowl, until it begins to harden, about 3 hours.
3. Mash with a fork, then return to the freezer until the sorbet is frozen. Serve.

Herbal Tidbit
Oregano and Marjoram: Look-Alikes

I love both marjoram and oregano, but they look alike, smell alike, and taste a lot alike. And I am compelled to help others distinguish between the two because I've been confused for most of my life.

First, both oregano and marjoram are in the mint family. The two share a chemical called carvacrol, which accounts for the similar aroma and flavor. So I'm not crazy. But here is the skinny on how to distinguish between the two herbs:

Marjoram's scent is flowery, and its flavor is milder and sweeter than oregano's, and slightly minty. Some people detect a bit of citric flavor. Perhaps that is why adding some marjoram to a tangerine granita I made at a restaurant called Nosmo King in New York City sixteen years ago worked out so successfully; the granita was so memorable that it sticks in my mind, unlike most things I make. I've also added it with great success to panfried mushrooms, soups, and meat loaf. The marjoram plant is more compact and the leaves are smaller than oregano's.

Oregano smells of pine, lemon, and pepper. It is more pungent than marjoram. It is the operative herb for pizza sauce. Add it to pungent foods that include olives and ancho-vies. Its flowers are pinkish purple. And it dries better than many other herbs.

Calaminth Sorbet

MAKES 6 TO 8 SERVINGS

2 loosely packed cups calaminth leaves, plus another handful

¾ cup sugar

1 cup light white wine (such as a dry Riesling)

2 tablespoons lemon juice

This is a much more recent recipe than the Wild Grape Sorbet with Calaminth (page 155). It is worth growing calaminth just to make it! Serve it with biscotti or any good crunchy cookie. You'll need an ice cream maker; if you don't have one, you can make granita instead, which is made in the same way until step 3.

1. Combine 2 cups of the calaminth and the sugar with 2 cups water in a medium saucepan over medium heat. Bring to a boil, then cover the pan, reduce the heat slightly, and simmer the mixture until the sugar is dissolved, about 5 minutes. Remove from the heat and let cool to room temperature.

2. Stir in the white wine and lemon juice. Pour half of the mixture into a blender and add the remaining handful of calaminth. Process the mixture until the leaves are finely chopped.

3. Chill the mixture in the refrigerator for 5 minutes. Pour the mixture into your ice cream maker and process, following the manufacturer's directions. If you don't have an ice cream machine, you can make granita instead: freeze the mixture in a shallow pan for 3 hours, flaking it with a fork every hour.

4. When the sorbet or granita is completely frozen, spoon into cups or wineglasses.

Greek Shiitake and Calaminth Omelet

The profusion of herbs makes this a luscious-looking dish. My thanks to Martha Rose Shulman, who introduced me (via an article she wrote) to the concept of yogurt in omelets. If you have any stinging nettles, boil them, drain them, and distribute a cup of them onto the mushrooms.

1. Preheat the oven to 350 degrees F. Butter a very large baking dish. I use a roasting pan; you could also use a 9 by 13-inch casserole pan, though you'll need a loaf pan or other small casserole for the extra egg mixture in addition.

2. Heat the olive oil over medium heat in a large, heavy skillet. Add the onion and cook, stirring, until transparent, about 7 to 9 minutes. Add the garlic and the shiitakes, stirring them together until they are until fragrant, about 30 seconds. Cook the mixture, stirring, until the mushrooms are tender, about 5 minutes. Season the mixture with salt and freshly cracked black pepper and remove it from the heat.

3. Meanwhile, whisk the eggs in a large bowl. Season with salt and freshly cracked black pepper, then whisk in the yogurt, cream, calaminth, chives, and parsley.

4. Distribute the feta and goat cheese in the buttered pan, followed by the mushroom mixture. Pour the eggs over the mushrooms.

5. Bake for 30 minutes, or until the omelet is puffed and lightly colored. Let cool for at least 10 minutes before serving. Serve hot, warm, or at room temperature.

MAKES 8 TO 10 SERVINGS

1 tablespoon extra-virgin olive oil

1 onion or leek, thinly sliced

2 garlic cloves, minced

½ pound shiitake mushrooms, stems removed and caps thinly sliced

Salt and freshly cracked black pepper

12 large eggs

1 cup plain yogurt (whole milk, low-fat, or nonfat is fine)

½ cup heavy cream or half-and-half

2 cups chopped chives (optional), cut into 1-inch pieces (chive flowers are welcome)

¾ cup chopped fresh parsley

¼ cup chopped fresh calaminth

½ cup feta cheese

½ cup creamy goat cheese or local blue cheese, or a mixture

Herb and Flower Butters

I can't think of an herb that doesn't like butter. Like pesto, herb butters preserve herbs by replacing oxygen, which deteriorates flavor, with fat. Fat retains and transmits flavors, which is one reason we like it so much. Plus butter has a nice flavor of its own and a great mouthfeel.

Herb butter's special virtue is that when it is placed on hot food, it melts slowly, hugging the item (fish, meat, polenta, or what have you) on which it was placed—in other words, it doesn't go running off in all directions like most sauces do. Hundreds of foods can be made better with herb butter, among them steamed potatoes, corn, turnips, fish, omelets or poached eggs, and hot rice, millet, and other grains. And herb butter is resilient. It can taste good three weeks into its sojourn in the fridge, or after six months in the freezer.

The Three Categories of Herb Butter

Some herbs require more mass to make a flavorful butter than others. With this in mind, I have created a master recipe for three categories of herb butters. The first is made with a delicate or thin-skinned herb such as basil, cilantro, or dill. The second is made with a thick-skinned herb like rosemary, sage, or thyme. The thick-skinned herbs are more pungent than thin-skinned herbs, so you need less of them to achieve the same impact. The third type of butter is made with an herb flower. Flowers are terrific chopped into butters because they have the flavor of the herb plus a sweet nectar and lovely color.

One note: I often add twice as much herbs or flowers as I call for in the master recipe, so don't consider the quantities set in stone; use whatever amount you prefer.

You can combine herbs in a butter, but usually I stick to a single herb, though often I'll often add chopped chives to another herb butter for extra flavor and a striking speckled look. Sometimes I combine flowers, like nasturtium and anise hyssop. Adding orange zest, lime zest, or lemon zest to any butter can be a good idea (for example, sage-orange, cilantro-lime, or dill-lemon). Even adding a few pinches of curry powder or ground cumin can be fun. I encourage playing!

CHOOSING HERBS FOR BUTTER		
Type	Amount	Examples
Thin-skinned herbs	1½ cups chopped	Anise hyssop, basil, bronze fennel, chervil, chives, cilantro, dill, lemon balm, mint, parsley
Thick-skinned herbs	¾ cup chopped	Calaminth, lavender, lemon verbena, lovage, marjoram, oregano, rosemary, sage, summer or winter savory, tarragon, thyme
Edible flowers	1 cup chopped	African blue basil, anise hyssop, bronze fennel, calendula, chive, marjoram, nasturtium, pineapple sage

Master Recipe for Herb Butter

Butters taste best when made with the best and freshest butter you can find. Unsalted is always best. Manufacturers have a more refined process for producing unsalted butter so it tastes better and is less apt to be old or have off flavors.

Organic and/or local is good. I like to make herb butter one stick at a time because my freezer fills up quickly and I prefer variation over quantity. But making two sticks' worth saves time, and it does freeze well. Herb butters cut fairly easily when frozen, so freeze the butter in a log and you can cut rounds as needed. You'll need plastic wrap as well as parchment paper or waxed paper for wrapping the butter.

Note: You can make herb butter in a standing mixer; the butter does not need to be soft if you use the paddle attachment. When chopping thin-skinned herbs, be sure not to mince them; they should be cut into pieces that are the size of a large freckle.

2 sticks unsalted butter, softened

Appropriate quantity herbs (see chart)

Salt and freshly cracked black pepper

1 teaspoon lemon or lime juice

1. Mash together the butter and herbs by hand in a large bowl. Add salt and pepper to taste and mix well.
2. Transfer the butter to a long piece of parchment or waxed paper (you can also use plastic wrap). Fold the paper (or plastic) over the butter, and then use the back of a long knife to press the mound of butter into the fold, forcing the butter evenly up and down the length of the paper. You're aiming here for a log shape. Wrap the paper-covered log in plastic wrap. Store in the freezer, where the butter will keep for up to three months.

Dill

Dill was one of the few herbs readily available in supermarkets back in the 1970s, and it was a mainstay for me as a teenage caterer. But I must have overused it, because I avoided it for the next twenty-five years.

Recently, though, dill came into my life again. When I was the chef at the Haley House Bakery Café, a nonprofit cafe in Roxbury Massachusetts, customers began asking for it. So I began to use it.

Dill tastes like summer. After all, who would think of serving a dilled potato salad or a cold cucumber-dill yogurt soup in the chill of winter? Yet dill has also ventured into heartier territory; it's used to flavor Russian meatballs, pickled herring, and German cream sauces for fish.

Dill's flavor evokes a bouquet of parsley, mint, and a bit of the back lawn. The fact that one can detect parsley is not random—they are both in the carrot family, along with caraway, cilantro, cumin, and fennel. Dill's craggy, lace-like strands are deceiving; its robust flavor can stand up to curry, ginger, mint, horse-radish, and mustard, among many other bold ingredients. Surprisingly, dill is so popular in Southeast Asia that it is commonly referred to as Laotian cilantro. It is also used in the cuisines of the Middle East, Nordic countries, eastern and western Europe, and India.

Culinary Uses

My friend and co-teacher Fulani Haynes, who is originally from Barbados, sprinkles it into soups and salads as a salt substitute. I've added it to creamy dressings as well as vinaigrettes for potato salads, beet salads, and green bean salads. Try it in curried sweet potato soup, or add it to Greek yogurt dips for crudités. I always use a heavy hand with dill, but that's me.

Dill is native to southern and eastern Europe and central Asia. Persian fava bean pilaf is over-run with dill. Georgians add dill to a pilaf made with rice, lamb, and sour cherries. The well-known borscht, a Russian beet soup, usually includes dill. And in the United States, many mothers make chicken soup (a.k.a. "Jewish penicillin") flavored with dill. But I advise that the herb should generally be added just before serving so the heat does not kill the flavor.

The Seeds

Dill seeds are highly valued in the culinary world. Chef Tony Maws buys his from Eva—he describes them as "incredible, almost dangerous." He uses them in sauces for fish, for a quick burst of flavor, straining them out before serving. And, of course, what would life be like without dill pickles? (Though nowadays dill seed oil is used instead of the actual seed by large pickle manufacturers.) The seeds can be effective in breads and teas.

Health Virtues

The name "dill" is probably derived from the Saxon word *dilla* or *dillan*, meaning "to lull." This could refer to the herb's purported ability to pacify and calm babies with colic or flatulence. It contains iron, manganese, and calcium along with vitamins A and C, and it has antibacterial properties.

Buying and Storing

When buying dill at the store or market, avoid bunches that have rotting fronds in their middle. The green leaves should be shiny and dry to the touch. Do not wash the dill before storing it, as this speeds decomposition. Store in a partially sealed plastic bag in the fridge for up to one week.

Growing Dill

Dill is easy to grow, and it is a welcome addition from an aesthetic standpoint, with its whimsical bright yellow umbels and fernlike leaves. After all danger of frost has passed, scatter seeds and rake into the soil in a place that gets full sun, and keep the ground moist until germination, which may take as long as two weeks. Thin the plants to 12 to 18 inches apart, and harvest fronds and flowers selectively as the plants grow. Once the plant begins to flower, the quality of the leaves will deteriorate, so at this point it is best to allow the plant to mature in order to harvest the dill seeds. Garden seed companies frequently offer selected varieties of dill that are geared more toward leaf production and don't go to seed as quickly as the common herb.

Cut the flowers once most of them have gone to seed, and hang them upside down to fully dry. The seeds will fall out when they are ready to use (as the plant nears its final stage of reproduction), so make sure you've made arrangements to catch them before they scatter. The simplest method is to hang the flower heads in paper bags so that the seeds fall into the bag.

Creamy Dilled Dressing

MAKES 1½ CUPS

1 lime or lemon

½ cup chopped chives

½ cup roughly chopped
cilantro (leaves and
stems)

½ cup roughly chopped dill

1 small garlic clove

½ cup creamy goat cheese,
crème frâiche, or cream
cheese

½ cup half-and-half

½ cup extra-virgin olive oil

Salt and freshly cracked
black pepper

This dressing is great drizzled over beets or any steamed or roasted vegetable. Dill and cilantro make a great duo because neither pushes the other out of the picture. But basil could be substituted for either with good results. Your dressing will be bright green if you use a blender or Vitamix.

1. With a sharp knife, remove the skin and pith from the lime, and discard. Quarter the flesh of the lime.
2. Combine the lime quarters, chives, cilantro, dill, garlic, and goat cheese in a blender, food processor, or Vitamix, and puree.
3. With the machine running, slowly add the half-and-half and then the oil. Season the dressing with salt and freshly cracked black pepper to taste.

Dilled Summer Salad

**MAKES 8 SERVINGS
AS A SIDE DISH**

3 pounds small waxy pota-
toes, such as Red Bliss,
Yukon Gold, Yellow Finn,
or fingerlings, quartered
or cut into 1-inch pieces

½ pound green beans, tails
trimmed

1 medium zucchini or
summer squash, cut into
1-inch pieces

1 cup (or more) roughly
chopped dill

⅓ cup good (prefer-
ably local) crumbly blue
cheese or goat cheese

¼ cup lemon juice (about 1
lemon)

½ cup extra-virgin olive oil

Salt and freshly cracked
black pepper

1 cup chopped chives or
scallions

¾ cup chopped walnuts or
pecans, toasted

Many summer vegetables would work here instead of green beans and squash; try corn (parboiled), cucumber, snap peas, bell peppers, tomatoes, or thinly sliced fennel. The vegetables, dressing, and nuts can be prepared separately up to a day in advance and combined at the last minute.

1. Bring a large pot of salted water to a boil. Add the potatoes, reduce the heat, and simmer for 8 minutes. Add the green beans and squash and simmer for 1 to 2 minutes. Drain the vegetables in a colander and rinse them with cold water until they are cool. Leave them in the colander for 5 minutes so they can drip-dry.
2. Combine the dill, cheese, and lemon juice in a blender and puree. With the blender running, add the olive oil. Season the dressing to taste with salt and freshly cracked black pepper.
3. Combine the cooked vegetables, dressing, chives, and walnuts in a large bowl, and mix well. Season to taste and serve.

Note: To toast the walnuts or pecans, roast in a 350-degree oven on a rimmed baking sheet for about 5 minutes, until golden brown.

Lemon Balm

Melissa officinalis · PERENNIAL

Crinkle a leaf of lemon balm in your fingers and bring it to your nose. Breathe deep and prepare for a short but blissful olfactory vacation. Lemon balm's aroma comes from its powerful essential oils. The taste is clean and sharp, akin to that of lemongrass. But it's a heck of a lot easier to chop.

Some comment that the smell reminds them of furniture polish. Many companies use lemon balm's oil in their products. But it is not just because of its aroma; if you rub the leaves of lemon balm on wood, its surface will begin to shine.

But lemon balm is too wonderful to relegate to cleaning wood; it is a highly pleasurable edible.

CULINARY USES

Simply put, lemon balm enlivens food. I disperse the leaves in salads with greens such as Bull's Blood beet greens, chickweed, claytonia, purslane, and Treviso radicchio. Enjoy it in slaws or seafood or chicken salad (stack, roll, then slice the leaves into thin slivers) or use whole leaves in wraps or on canapes. I also pulverize the leaves into pesto or chop them up to make a compound herb butter (see page 159). It is a fitting garnish for Southeast Asian soups. Lemon balm brightens up fruit and green salads.

Eva chills water overnight with a lot of lemon balm leaves, for a quenching drink. Infuse lemon balm to make hot or iced tea, crème brûlée, ice cream, granita, or sorbet. You can use lemon balm–infused sugar syrup to make lemonade, or add it to vodka for homemade Limoncello.

HEALTH VIRTUES

The well-known English herbalist John Evelyn (1620–1706) stated, "Balm is sovereign for the brain, strengthening the memory and powerfully chasing away melancholy." The many traditional uses of lemon balm have yet to be backed up by modern science, but I can attest to the fact that a few leaves in my green salad lifts my spirit.

BUYING AND STORING

Lemon balm can be stored, on the stem, loosely packed in a plastic bag in the refrigerator for up to one week.

GROWING LEMON BALM

Lemon balm makes a low-key addition to any herb garden and is a good candidate for edible landscaping as well. Each plant will grow into a bright green lemon-scented bush approximately 2 feet in diameter.

Lemon balm is happy in full sun or light shade and grows best in loose, fertile soil. It can tolerate dry conditions and seldom needs watering (especially if you get a rain shower now and then). Sow seeds indoors in early spring. Transplant into the garden after the last frost date, spacing plants 2 feet apart. You can begin to harvest once the plant has grown to a small bush. Just clip the stems as needed, or harvest the entire plant by clipping stems a few inches above the soil. Since it is a perennial, you can clip and mulch the plant to help it overwinter.

Lemon Balm Borani

**MAKES APPROXIMATELY
1½ CUPS, ENOUGH FOR 8
SERVINGS OF CHICKEN OR
VEGETABLES**

1 bunch chives, coarsely
chopped (about 1 cup)

1 cup loosely packed dill
leaves

1 cup loosely packed lemon
balm or mint

2 cups chopped arugula or
spinach

1 clove garlic

3 tablespoons extra-virgin
olive oil

1½ cups Greek yogurt

Salt and freshly cracked
black pepper

This is a thick yogurt sauce that is teeming with herbs. You can
serve it with cold roast chicken, as a dressing for potato salad, or
as a dip for vegetables. I adapted this recipe from one given by
Sam and Sam Clark in their book *Casa Moro*. You can substitute
other herbs for the dill and lemon balm, such as chervil, lovage,
parsley, or tarragon, in any combination—though if you use tarragon, use less, because it is potent.

1. Wash the chives, dill, and lemon balm and let them drip-dry.
   Don't spin them dry because you will need some moisture to make
   the puree.
2. Combine the herbs, arugula, and garlic in a food processor and
   pulse until finely chopped. Add the olive oil and yogurt and
   process until the mixture is mostly smooth. Season with salt and
   freshly cracked black pepper.

How I Got Some Good Portuguese Recipes

It wasn't one of my better visits to the farm. The first snag was that I started a fire in Eva's two-hundred-year-old cottage. While waiting for the fire in the woodstove to take hold, with the door ajar, I turned my back for a minute. Just then a badly behaved ember leapt out and ignited a fleece blanket. I grabbed a big pillow to stamp out the fire.

The cottage filled with a black cloud of smoke, and a few moments later I began to confront the damage. I was hoping that a quick cleanup could take place, so Eva would never know. But the walls had been blackened and thousands of creepy cobwebs, even those that were upstairs or inside cupboards, were encrusted with soot. To add to the feeling of doom, a cacophony of smoke detectors sounded off, and my cat Henry began bellowing like a fog horn.

When Eva came in her eyes bulged. She ran around collecting the shrieking smoke alarms, all four of them. Clutching the still-sounding smoke alarms to her chest, she approached me and said loudly, "I take it you were never a Girl Scout!"

She was right. I'd quit the Brownies after just two weeks when I was seven, obviously a grave mistake.

Once the smoke alarms were disabled and Eva had calmed down, she called Doug, a carpenter neighbor, who arrived with his sweet old dog Mollie to replace the burned floor with soapstone. I should mention here that Henry, my sixteen-year-old cat, had taken to attacking dogs in his elder years. Not without reason: Years ago, a mean one-eyed dog had bitten him and literally ripped off his tail. The vet said Henry was lucky to have survived.

Just as we stepped back to admire Doug's fine inlay of soapstone, Mollie and Henry tumbled down the stairs in a ball, with Henry hissing and Mollie whimpering. Molly had made the mistake of lumbering upstairs to where Henry had been resting after the stress of the fire. Although arthritic, my cat was attacking Mollie like a savage. Once they were downstairs, I feared murder and reached into the fray to grab my cat. Henry promptly sank his fangs into my wrist. I knew I had to get to the hospital, and once the staff there saw the bite, they put me on antibiotics.

I woke up the next morning expecting to feel better, but instead my arm was frigid and a streak the color of rare roast beef ran up it. Henry's venom was obviously very effective, just misguided. I ended up spending four days and nights at a hospital near Eva's farm, while Henry—repentant, lonely, and probably fairly dangerous—wandered the farm. It was four days before Thanksgiving, so the promise of good food helped me to heal, but the food served at the hospital was scary at best. I complained to the food-service manager, offering many handy tips. My ideas fell on deaf ears, but the nurses were my allies. Most were Portuguese and loved to talk about food. I entertained myself by jotting down all the recipes they gave that I could remember.

I was released just three hours before Thanksgiving dinner, and I took a taxi back to the farm to check on Henry before joining Eva's friends. I found him outside, still dirty with soot from the fire, and with a wild, faraway look in his eye. He purred happily when I scratched his chin. It was time for both of us to eat well.

Nurse's Portuguese Chicken

Mash 2 tablespoons red pepper flakes, ¼ cup olive, oil, 4 cloves minced garlic, and 1 tablespoon sea salt. Rub this mixture on both the outside and inside of the chicken, and let marinate for one whole day. The next day, transfer the chicken to a heavy casserole pot, add a bottle of ale, and cook over low heat, covered, until done, about 1 hour.

Lemon Balm–Chive Compote

MAKES APPROXIMATELY 1½ CUPS

4 cups loosely packed lemon balm

3 cups finely chopped chives and/or garlic chives (flowers included)

¾ cup extra-virgin olive oil

¼ cup lemon juice (about 1 juicy lemon)

½ teaspoon salt

Freshly cracked black pepper

Make this when your lemon balm runneth over. Not a pesto, but more substantial than a puree or sauce, this ethereal compote won everyone's heart one weekend. We ate it for dinner with a roast lamb that had previously resided up the road. In the morning the compote landed on top of some sunny-side up eggs nestled in fried crunchy oat groats. For lunch we dabbed spoonfuls on lentil minestrone. The compote is also enjoyable with crackers and soft goat cheese. But Eva and I strangely enjoyed it most when we made popcorn and very pleasurably dipped the kernels into this thick bright sauce. Now Eva, months later, refers to this as "that amazing sauce." You can also make a variation of this with many herbs besides lemon balm, such as lovage.

1. Combine the lemon balm and chives in a food processor or a blender, and pulse until they are finely chopped.
2. With the machine running, add the olive oil in a thin stream. Process the mixture until it is somewhat smooth; don't puree it to a total pulp. It may appear to have a lot of stems. That's fine.
3. Season the compote with the lemon juice, salt, and freshly cracked black pepper to taste. Pulse the machine once or twice to incorporate the seasonings. Add a tablespoon or two of water if it seems too pasty.

Note: This compote will keep in a tightly sealed container in the fridge for up to 1 week. If you think you won't be finishing it after a few days, store it in the freezer, where it will keep for up to 6 months.

Lemon Verbena

Aloysia triphylla · TENDER

PERENNIAL

One fall day I came upon Eva decimating thirty large pots of lemon verbena that had been attacked by spider mites. She ruthlessly clipped them down to their bones. They stood like inch-high tree stumps. It seemed more fitting to arrange a funeral for these plants than to expect regrowth. Instead, she kept the stumpy plants in the dark, unheated barn all winter long to fend for themselves. I walked in one March day, and every plant was growing new leaves. Eva had moved them into the light, where they had regained their vigor. In the early summer they were transplanted outdoors, where they produced profusely for her until the late October frost. Her only challenge was to sell all they produced; luckily lemon verbena is popular among chefs, so she did.

CULINARY USES

Verbena's aroma is luscious and limey; just smelling it bathes your insides and relaxes your system. Despite verbena's voluptuous fragrance and good survival tactics, it is somewhat fragile in the kitchen. If you boil or cook it in a soup or stew, its flavor will eventually disappear. However, if you infuse it like a tea, steeping it in just-boiled water (or milk or cream) for ten minutes, the flavor holds up. Cooking it with fruit and sugar into jams or jellies also seems to allow it to retain its flavor. June Taylor, jam chef extraordinaire in Berkeley, California, cooks her blackberry–lemon verbena jam for some time, yet the citrus flavor comes through. As with other tender herbs, you can add a sprig or a handful of chopped verbena toward the very last minutes of cooking a dish, whether a curry, soup, or stir-fry (it takes well to tofu).

To chop verbena you need a sharp knife, because the leaves can be tough. However, it is easily ground to a paste in a processor. If it's for a sweet recipe, grind with sugar or ginger, if it's for a savory dish, grind with salt and ginger or salt and several cloves of garlic. It also makes a wonderful herb butter (see page 159); try serving lemon verbena butter atop seared scallops or cod.

I like to flavor water with lemon verbena for a refreshing drink. Crinkle a handful of verbena leaves to release the oils, then add to a quart of water. Let sit for a few hours at room temperature or overnight in the fridge.

Eva's farmhand Bill Braun introduced me to lemon verbena tea. First Bill dries the verbena (see page xxi for drying tips), and then he infuses it, letting a handful of leaves steep in just-boiled water for ten to fifteen minutes.

Many people add verbena to their flower arrangements because it imparts a lovely aroma inside the house.

HEALTH VIRTUES

Lemon verbena essential oil is often used in aromatherapy, and it is said to ease stress. Little is known about its specific nutritional profile and it has no proven health effects, although it is commonly used as an herbal remedy to treat fevers and digestive disorders.

BUYING AND STORING

Chances are you will have to grow your own lemon verbena if you want to use it in the kitchen. Store unwashed sprigs in a plastic bag in the refrigerator, where they may last up to one week.

To ensure a year-round supply, lemon verbena leaves can be dried. But they will have limited value, useful only for making teas, stocks, and perhaps a few other applications. For desserts or drinks you can preserve lemon verbena by combining fresh leaves with a healthy dose of sugar in a food processor; blend to make a thick paste, and freeze the paste in small portions.

Growing Lemon Verbena

If you are looking for a low-maintenance plant, be forewarned—growing lemon verbena outside its native climates takes some TLC. Lemon verbena can be grown from seed, but it is much easier to find a seedling or cutting. Plant it outdoors in spring once nighttime temperatures are well above freezing and any threat of frost has passed. The plant prefers full sun and fertile, well-drained soil that is kept relatively moist but never overwatered—when in doubt, keep the soil on the dry side. Harvest by trimming branches as needed, but don't harvest more than half the plant at one time. In the fall, dig the plant up and bring it indoors in a pot until the following spring (or grow lemon verbena in pots year-round to facilitate its indoor-outdoor lifestyle).

Lemon Verbena Sorbet

I adapted this recipe from *The Herbfarm Cookbook* by Jerry Traunfeld. This sorbet had Eva sighing, a reaction she saves for only the most profoundly delectable foods. Either you'll need an ice cream maker or you can make granita instead.

MAKES 1 QUART, ENOUGH FOR 8 SERVINGS

2 cups loosely packed fresh lemon verbena

⅔ cup sugar

¼ cup freshly squeezed lime juice

1. Process the lemon verbena and sugar in a food processor until the mixture forms a bright green paste, about 30 seconds; stop to scrape down the sides as necessary.

2. Add the lime juice and process the mixture for 15 seconds. Transfer to a bowl, add 3 cups of warm water, and stir. If you'd like to remove any bits of leaf, strain the resulting liquid through a fine sieve; we find the pieces are so small that they aren't noticeable.

3. Chill the mixture for 5 minutes in the fridge, then pour it into your ice cream maker, and make ice cream according to the manufacturer's directions. If you don't have an ice cream machine, you can make granita instead: Freeze the mixture in a shallow pan for 3 hours, flaking it with a fork every hour. Serve when it is completely frozen.

Deer for Kale

A few years ago Eva and I were picking autumn olives near her friend Barbara's (expansive) property. We had separated, and I was a few hundred yards from Eva. A red truck barreled down between the shrubs and pulled up beside me. A hurried and irritated driver stuck his head out the truck window. He told me he had been granted permission by the owner to hunt deer. The hunting season began the next day, and he'd asked that no humans enter that land. He was afraid of shooting someone by mistake.

I quickly assured him that we had no interest in being shot and would not return the following day. I asked him to drive a bit farther and meet Eva, since it was she who had the connection to this land. As he drove away I was guessing that Eva would charm him into a barter arrangement if she could. The very next morning, at 6 a.m., he delivered a dead deer to Eva's doorstep, and she gave him a box full of Tuscan kale, his wife's favorite vegetable.

Tofu Chard and Corn Mélange in Verbena Broth

MAKES 4 SERVINGS

2 large tomatoes

1 tablespoon canola oil

1 leek or large onion, chopped into ½-inch pieces

3 garlic cloves, minced

8 cups chopped chard of any kind (including finely chopped stems)

1 (14-ounce) can coconut milk

Kernels from 4 ears very fresh corn

1 pound box firm tofu, drained and cubed

3 or 4 fresh lemon verbena sprigs or the peel of 1 lime

2 tablespoons lime juice (about 1 lime)

1 tablespoon fish sauce or about ½ teaspoon salt

Asian chile sauce

This is a Southeast Asian–inspired dish, incorporating the citric tang of lemon verbena and the soothing richness of coconut milk with the juice of tomatoes. It is meant for the height of summer tomato and corn season.

1. Using a sharp knife, score the bottom of each tomato with an "X," and cut out the core. Fill a medium bowl with ice-cold water.

2. Heat the oil in a stockpot over medium heat. Add the leek and garlic and cook until they have softened, about 5 minutes, stirring often. Add 4 cups water and bring to a boil. Drop the tomatoes into the boiling liquid and boil about 15 seconds. Remove them with a slotted spoon to the bowl of cold water. The skins should begin to peel off. Remove the skins and chop the tomatoes.

3. Add the chard and coconut milk to the boiling water, cover, and simmer for 3 minutes. Add the tomatoes, corn, tofu, and lemon verbena. Let the stew simmer for a few more minutes, letting the corn cook, about 5 minutes.

4. Remove the stew from the heat. Stir in the lime juice, and season with fish sauce or salt and chile sauce to taste.

Bartering: The One-Way Exchange

Equal Exchange, a cooperatively owned fair-trade business in Bridgewater Massachusetts, once posted on Craigslist an ongoing giveaway offer of coffee chaff and burlap bags. When it comes to deals like this, Eva is always ahead of the pack, and she eagerly took them up on their offer. She uses the chaff as ground cover and mulch. The burlap bags make great walk-way material as well as row covers; Eva also lays them over the beds of some winter-hardy root vegetables, like parsnips, to keep the ground from freezing, which makes the roots easier to harvest. She shares the burlap bags with her farmer friend T, who uses them for animal bedding.

Lemongrass

Cymbopogon citratus and *Cymbopogon flexuosus* · TENDER PERENNIAL

Lemongrass emits one of the most pleasurable fragrances in Eva's garden. If you snap it in half, a perfume of pine resin and lemon will pour forth. Then, if you bite into it, you'll taste a wild brew of raw lemon and ginger.

In parts of Indonesia, young girls are given the privilege of harvesting lemongrass, as it's said that a virgin's pure thoughts will coax the fragrance to intensify. Though I lack these qualifications, the fragrance is always intense when I cut lemongrass at Eva's. Lemongrass originated in Asia but now grows in South, Central, and North America, as well as Africa. It's been making headway in the United States for the last half century due to an influx of Southeast Asian immigrants. The applications of lemongrass are extensive—it is used for culinary, medicinal, cosmetic, and cleansing purposes.

DISTINGUISHING CULINARY VARIETIES

Only two of the fifty-five varieties of lemongrass are employed for culinary use. There is the East Indian species (*Cymbopogon flexuosus*), which Eva grows, which has thin stalks the width of a chopstick. It is purplish red at the base and has a heady citrus perfume. It is lemongrass to the tenth power, and its essential oils, citral and geraniol, are used in many perfumes, soaps, and cleaning agents. The tubbier lemongrass is the so-called West Indian type (*Cymbopogon citratus*), which is native to Malaysia. It is much milder in flavor and usually about the width of a pudgy index finger. It's light green along most of the plant, but white toward the bulbous end.

You can buy either type from several sources, including Johnny's Selected Seeds.

CULINARY USES

Lemongrass is a fundamental ingredient in Southeast Asian cuisine. Jean-Georges Vongerichten, an inventive and accomplished French chef, was once quoted in the *Wall Street Journal* as saying, "I went to Bangkok for the first time when I was twenty-three and I stopped for street food and had the best shrimp soup in the world. I came from making formal stocks that cook for twenty hours and this woman used lemongrass, shrimp, mushrooms and chiles and it was done in three minutes. I thought, 'What have I been doing for the last eight years?'"

Lemongrass creates a smooth citrus essence without too much pungency. It melds well with many flavors, such as coconut milk, cilantro, chiles, Thai basil, fish sauce, curry, kaffir lime leaf, and ginger. Recipes most often call for the entire stalk to be added to a soup, stew, or sauce. You generally first cut the stalk into two or three pieces and then whack them with a large knife or the bottom of a heavy pan to release the oils. Some recipes call for the lower third of the stalk, finely chopped, which is added to panfried vegetables, stir-fries, meat marinades and pastes, meatballs, rice pilaf, cabbage slaws, and even baked goods like scones.

Lemongrass ice cream is insanely good. Not store-bought, but made from scratch and preferably with the recipe from this book (page 175). I once made a large quantity using Eva's East Indian lemongrass for a fund-raising dinner. The leftover ice cream suffered a thaw, and we refroze it. Still, despite millions of ice crystals, it was so good we ate every drop!

Health Virtues

From facial masks to yoga mat sprays, massage oils to kitchen floor cleaners, lemongrass is helping to make our whole world smell nice and clean. But it's not all aromatic hype, as lemongrass actually has antibacterial and antifungal properties, deriving primarily from its citral oil. It's not the only culinary flavoring that doubles as a cleaning agent: bergamot, cinnamon, lavender, lemon, and thyme are other examples. And citral also repels insects. Lemongrass developed citral, a "fighting" oil, to survive in the jungle, so that bugs wouldn't eat it. So we are free to enjoy the smell of lemongrass while the bugs stay away—a happy arrangement indeed.

Buying and Storing

West Indian lemongrass is available in Asian markets as well as many greengrocers and

natural foods stores. Many people prefer this more mellow variety. It helps to have the lemongrass sold unwrapped, so it can breathe and you can inspect it. It should not be dried out but rather, like garlic cloves, should feel quite solid and heavy, not "airy." I have never actually seen East Indian lemongrass for sale, though it's common in the kitchens of the chefs Eva sells to. If you want it, you must grow it yourself.

Store lemongrass whole in the fridge, wrapped in plastic, for up to two weeks. I sometimes freeze it whole, double-wrapped in plastic, for up to six months. Its texture softens as it thaws, which makes it easier to cut.

Growing Lemongrass

You can buy lemongrass seedlings at nurseries, or you can find healthy stalks at your grocery store and root them in a glass of water. If you want to grow the more scintillating East Indian variety, you'll probably have to buy seeds, which are available from Johnny's Selected Seeds and other sources. Sow the seeds indoors in late winter.

Transplant seedlings into your garden after any threat of frost has passed. Plant in full sun, and water regularly. Harvest by clipping stalks just above soil level as needed.

In climates that experience freezing conditions (in other words, most of North America), lemongrass must be brought indoors to overwinter. When temperatures start to drop in the fall, cut the plant down to about 8 inches, dig out, and pot up. Place in a window and water only lightly, allowing the plant to be dormant. In midwinter move the plant to a sunny windowsill and resume regular watering. Return to the garden after any threat of frost has passed in the spring.

Pears in Red Wine with Lemongrass and Star Anise

Lemongrass adds a welcome twist on the classic French recipe of pears poached in red wine. I almost always buy Bosc pears, because even if they are hard and unripe, they will still yield to the fork when cooked, and they'll have good flavor. Serve with real vanilla ice cream.

MAKES 8 SERVINGS

- 1 cup sugar
- 2 stalks lemongrass, cut and crushed, or the peel of 1 lemon
- 10 star anise
- 2 cups dry red wine such as Zinfandel, Shiraz, or Merlot
- 4 Bosc pears, peeled, halved, and cored
- 2 tablespoons lemon juice
- Vanilla ice cream, for serving

1. Combine the sugar, lemongrass, star anise, and wine in a medium saucepan and bring to a boil. Reduce the heat, add the pears, and simmer for 10 to 12 minutes. Turn each pear over and simmer for an additional 8 to 10 minutes, or until a fork or knife can be easily inserted into a pear. Remove from the heat and let cool. Remove the pears to a container with a lid.

2. Bring the wine sauce back to a boil, and boil until it is reduced by half. Remove from the heat and stir in the lemon juice. Pour the sauce over the pears, making sure the pears are fully immersed in the sauce. Chill in the refrigerator overnight.

3. Before serving, if you want to get fancy, use a sharp knife to make 6 to 8 incisions in the fat part of each pear, so that it fans out. Serve cold or lukewarm on plates with sauce spooned over pears and vanilla ice cream.

Butternut Squash Soup with Lemongrass

MAKES 6 SERVINGS AS A FIRST COURSE

1 fat stalk lemongrass or 1 tablespoon grated lemon rind

2 tablespoons extra-virgin olive oil

1 leek or large onion, chopped into ½-inch pieces

3 garlic cloves, chopped

2 rounded tablespoons finely chopped lemongrass or 1 tablespoon grated lemon peel

2 cups peeled, chopped potato (1 large potato), in ½-inch pieces

1 medium butternut squash (about 3 pounds), peeled, seeded, and chopped into ½-inch pieces

2 apples or pears, peeled and finely chopped

½ teaspoon salt

Freshly cracked pepper

Yogurt, for serving

Chopped fresh herb of your choosing (such as basil, chives, cilantro, or lemon balm), for serving

There is plenty of overlap between fall squash and summer lemongrass, and this is one of the happy results. There is not a single unhealthy ingredient in this recipe, and vegetable stock is unnecessary.

1. Cut off the bulbous bottom third of the lemongrass stalk. Remove the tough outer leaves and set them aside. With a large, sharp chef's knife, mince this lower piece; you should end up with about 2 rounded tablespoons of finely chopped lemongrass. (You can save the rest of the stalk for a stock or just freeze it for the next time you make this soup.)

2. Heat the oil in a heavy soup pot or Dutch oven over medium heat. Add the onion and sauté until it begins to soften, about 3 minutes. Add the garlic and chopped lemongrass and sauté for 5 minutes, stirring every now and then to prevent them from burning. The garlic should turn a bit brown.

3. Add the potato, squash, apples, and outer leaves of the lemongrass along with 6 cups water to the soup pot. Bring to a boil, then reduce the heat and let simmer until the vegetables are tender, about 30 minutes. Remove the lemongrass stalks.

4. Puree the soup, either in a food processor or with an immersion blender. Season well with the salt and freshly cracked black pepper. Reheat if necessary. Ladle into bowls and garnish with yogurt and chopped fresh herb.

Bolting to the Table

Bolting plants are not plants that have run away. Bolting is a phenomenon of hot weather, when the high heat flips a switch in a plant and it begins to move rapidly from the leaf stage to the flowering stage. It is trying to reproduce quickly before it kicks the bucket, and it sends up elongated stalks. Most people consider the plant at this point to be inedible, but Eva treats bolted plants with respect, not in terms of salability, but rather in terms of edibility. When a plant bolts, its energies go into producing seeds, and the leaves become a bit bitter and less tender. Still, because Eva's garden is organic and her soil so rich, her bolted spinach tastes much better than supermarket spinach. And I like the flavor of her bolted cilantro. You do have to discard what is too tough, but that hasn't stopped Eva or me from using the leaves. But substituting supermarket spinach or cilantro would be fine if you don't have your own "bolted" plants.

Lemongrass Ice Cream

Lemongrass ice cream is especially good when made with the more fragrant East Indian lemongrass. If you can't find that kind (or don't grow it yourself), you can substitute West Indian lemongrass, lemon balm, or lemon verbena. You'll need an ice cream maker for this recipe.

MAKES ABOUT 5 CUPS

8 stalks lemongrass or 4 cups loosely packed lemon balm or lemon verbena

3 cups half-and-half

½ cup sugar

2 large egg yolks

2 large eggs

1 cup sour cream

1. To prepare the lemongrass, remove the tough outer leaves and use a large, sharp chef's knife to cut each stalk into 4-inch pieces. Set the lemongrass stalks on a towel on a counter, and lightly pound with a hammer until they have flattened somewhat.

2. Bring the half-and-half to a boil in a medium saucepan over medium heat, adding the lemongrass just as it begins to rise to a boil. Cover, reduce the heat to low, and simmer for 10 minutes. Remove from the heat and let the lemongrass steep for another 10 minutes or so. Pass the half-and-half through a sieve into a bowl, straining out the herb.

3. Whisk together the sugar, egg yolks, and whole eggs in a large saucepan. Slowly whisk in the infused half-and-half. Place the mixture over low heat and cook, stirring continuously with a wooden spoon, until the mixture has thickened to the consistency of eggnog, about 10 or 15 minutes. Be careful not to let it curdle at the bottom. Remove from the heat and whisk in the sour cream. Pour this ice cream base into a container and refrigerate for at least a few hours, until cool.

4. Transfer the mixture to an ice cream maker, and make ice cream according to the manufacturer's instructions. Once the ice cream is churned, let it harden in the freezer for at least 1 hour before serving.

Southeast Asian–Style Beef Stew

MAKES 6 SERVINGS

- 2 pounds beef stew meat, cut into 1-inch pieces
- Salt and freshly cracked black pepper
- 1 tablespoon canola oil
- 3 stalks lemongrass
- 2 leeks or 1 large onion, chopped into ½-inch pieces
- 5 garlic cloves, minced
- 3 medium carrots, peeled or washed, cut into 1-inch pieces
- 1 small bunch kale, cut into small bite-size pieces
- 3 plum tomatoes or 2 large tomatoes
- 1 (14-ounce) can coconut milk
- 3 tablespoons chopped cilantro (leaves and stems) or lemon balm
- 2 tablespoons lime juice (about 1 juicy lime)
- 1–2 teaspoons chile paste (or more to taste)
- 1 teaspoon salt or 2 tablespoons fish sauce
- Up to 1 cup chopped chives (optional)

Look for grass-fed stew beef if you can. I made this stew for the birthday of Eva's next-door neighbor Andy, using meat from one of his (deceased) cows. This cow had led her life the way cows were meant to: she had plenty of land, exercise, and high-protein grass to graze. When I'm not at Eva's, I make the Tofu Chard and Corn Mélange in Verbena Broth (page 170). It's similar to this stew, except there's no beef! Either way, I prefer this stew with short-grain brown rice or quinoa.

1. Blot the beef dry on paper towels. Sprinkle the beef with salt and pepper. Heat the oil in a Dutch oven or wide soup pot over medium-high heat. Brown the beef in two batches.

2. To prepare the lemongrass, remove the tough outer leaves and use a large, sharp chef's knife to cut each stalk into 4-inch pieces. Set the lemongrass stalks on a towel on a counter, and lightly pound with a hammer until they have flattened somewhat.

3. Add 4 cups water to the Dutch oven or soup pot, along with the seared beef, lemongrass, leeks, and garlic. Bring to a simmer over low heat, and let simmer, covered, until the beef is tender, about 2 hours.

4. Remove the lemongrass with a slotted spoon. Add the carrots, kale, tomatoes, and coconut milk. Simmer, covered, until the vegetables are cooked, about 20 minutes.

5. Add the cilantro, lime juice, and chile paste to taste. Season with salt (or fish sauce) and freshly cracked black pepper, top with chives if you are using them, and serve over cooked quinoa, rice, or barley in shallow bowls.

Mint

As far as I knew when I was growing up, mint was created to doll up a glass of Nestea. Mint grew in our garden in suburban Connecticut and that's how we used it. I also experienced mint in processed forms, of course, such as chewing gum, toothpaste, mint jelly, chocolate mints, breath fresheners, and, my favorite, mint chocolate chip ice cream. But somehow I never connected the flavor of the herb in our backyard to these products. And it never occurred to me that mint had been busy flavoring thousands of traditional foods around the globe.

It was at my first cooking job that fresh mint progressed beyond iced tea. Twenty-five years ago I worked in the cramped basement of a restaurant, as the early morning baker. A handsome, bohemian man would arrive at 6 a.m. and make tabbouleh in the same hovel where I worked. He sold sandwiches out of an old postal truck called the "Blackbird." He added what seemed like a pillowcase of dried mint to his tub of hot bulgur, chopped parsley, tomatoes, lemon juice, olive oil, and onion. Despite the fact that the mint was dried and a little musty, the tabbouleh always tasted marvelous. I'd eat it warm for breakfast, and to this day I still think that tabbouleh should be eaten warm. Even though he stopped driving the truck twenty years ago, people still talk about his Blackbird sandwich—a big pita stuffed with tabbouleh, curried hummus, sprouts, tomatoes, lettuce, and a garlicky dressing made of tahini, olive oil, and lemon juice.

The mint gods must have been smiling on me, because at about this time I got to try my first taste of fresh mint ice cream (no chips needed!). Then I spent a year in France, where mint was relegated to Vietnamese restaurants

(herb authority Tom Stobart writes, "The French consider mint an English mistake!"). Then I opened a French-Vietnamese restaurant, and I used mint mercilessly. It enlivened summer rolls, *bun bo* (Chinese noodles with a tangy mint-lime dressing), and also a salad that got stuffed inside a bright yellow mung bean crepe.

Mint Varieties

The two most popular mints in America are spearmint and peppermint. Spearmint has a grassy green color, and while it does add nice flavor to iced tea it can also be chopped into many foods. Peppermint's color is darker, and it has a deeper menthol flavor and aroma.

There are dozens of other mints, each with its own alluring and unique flavor profile. Many of these Eva grows and peddles with great success. My favorites are pineapple mint, apple mint, orange mint, curly mint, and mountain mint (which is also a great insect repellent when rubbed into clothes and body). Chocolate peppermint, sometimes called just chocolate mint, has an aroma reminiscent of chocolate.

Culinary Uses

Mint's culinary range is wide: for example, consider a salad of California beets, tangerines, and orange flower water (per chef Suzanne Goin, author of *Sunday Suppers at Lucques*); a South Indian ground mint coconut and tamarind chutney; Sicilian spaghetti with mint and walnuts; Moroccan roast lamb with apricots and mint; and Mexican beef meatball soup (the mint is in the meatballs).

Like most herbs with lots of volatile oils, mint's clean flavor is best enjoyed raw. But mint is not subtle, and it may be an herb you'll want to use in small amounts at first. For diehards like Eva and me, though, a dish can hardly have too much.

When it's fresh, add mint leaves to a green salad. I like crunchy minty salads that are similar to the fresh chutneys of South India or the shrimp salads of Vietnam. I'll add lots of chopped mint to finely chopped raw vegetables (I use what's on hand, like fennel, cucumber, apple, scallion, or green beans) with toasted pumpkin seeds or peanuts, minced chile pepper, and lemon or lime juice. Sometimes I add desiccated coconut and a touch of sugar and olive oil. You can also pair mint with other herbs or spices, for example, basil, dill, fennel seed, ground cumin, oregano, or parsley, either in the aforementioned chopped salad or with couscous, bread or rice salads, or raitas. I also like to puree mint into cold cucumber or melon soups.

As food writer Diana Henry writes, "Mint is never hard to find—it grows so easily that you have trouble finding uses for it." Eva's best tactic when she has mint coming out her ears is to make iced mint tea. She fills up a gallon jar with mint sprigs, covers them with cold water, and lets them steep for twenty-four hours at room temperature or in the fridge.

Health Virtues

Many health benefits have been attributed to members of the mint family, most notably their ability to soothe and heal the digestive tract. In many countries mint products are used as remedies for indigestion, stomach cramps, flatulence, nausea, vomiting, and colic.

Buying and Storing

Popular varieties of mint can be found in supermarkets year-round, but you may have to dig a little deeper to seek out some of the underground superstars like chocolate, orange, and ginger mint. Try upscale green-grocers and farmers' markets.

Store mint in the refrigerator in a plastic bag, where it will last for about four days. You can also dry mint by hanging it upside down, transferring it to a tightly sealed container when the leaves have dried. Just don't expect the flavor of dried mint to hold a candle to its fresh counterpart.

Growing Mint

Mint grows so well that you will probably spend more time keeping the plant from invading undesignated garden space than getting it to grow in the first place. Buy seedlings from a nursery or take some rooted sprigs from a friend and plant them directly into your garden, spacing plants 1 foot apart. Water deeply, especially during the first week when the plant is adjusting to its new home. In full sun or in shade, so long as the soil is satisfactory, mint will thrive—just be sure to keep it watered, as it is a thirsty plant. Harvest the mint as needed, making sure to clip any flower buds to extend the growing season.

Garlic Chive–Mint Pesto

If you don't have garlic chives, then conventional chives will do. I love this simply with pasta. Eva ate this on top of a seared lamb chop. She spooned the pesto onto the chop in the pan just as it finished cooking, then removed the pan from the heat, put on the lid, and let it sit for a few minutes, until the pesto warmed up.

MAKES ABOUT 1½ CUPS

- 1½ cups roughly chopped garlic chives or regular garden chives
- 1½ cups loosely packed mint leaves
- ½ cup almonds, toasted
- 4 garlic cloves
- ½ cup extra-virgin olive oil
- ¼ cup grated Parmesan or Pecorino
- Salt and freshly cracked black pepper

Combine the garlic chives, mint, almonds, and garlic in a food processor. Pulse for a few seconds until the mixture is coarsely chopped. Add the olive oil in three increments, pulsing the mixture for a second or two after each addition. Add the cheese and pulse the mixture several more times to incorporate. Season the pesto with salt and freshly cracked black pepper to taste. Store in a tightly sealed container in the fridge if not using right away, or in the freezer for up to 6 months.

Note: To toast the almonds, roast in a 350-degree oven on a rimmed baking sheet for about 10 minutes, until they are golden brown.

Minted Lemon Water

In summertime, you want a refreshing beverage to cool you off. There are many ways to go, but my favorite is simply a cold-water infusion of lemon and mint that has zero sugar or caffeine. The great thing is that you can replenish the pitcher with water numerous times without losing flavor. For a twist, you can replace the lemon with slices of fresh ginger or rose petals, or you can replace the mint with lemon balm, lemon verbena, anise hyssop—even basil.

- 1 bunch spearmint (or any kind of mint)
- 1 lemon, thinly sliced

1. Place the mint in a large pitcher. Scrunch up the mint leaves with your hand a few times to release their oils. Add the lemon slices. Fill the pitcher with water.
2. Refrigerate for at least 2 hours, and preferably overnight. If you drink it in the next day or two, you can refill the pitcher with water at least once, using the same mint and lemon.

Clams over Linguine with Mint and Green Beans

MAKES 4 SERVINGS

5 pounds clams, such as quahogs, littlenecks, mahogany clams, or mussels

1 pound spaghetti, fettuccine, or linguine

½ cup extra-virgin olive oil

1 onion or leek, sliced thinly

5 garlic cloves, minced

1 cup white wine

½ pound snap peas, green beans, or haricots verts (skinny French-style green beans)

Salt and freshly cracked black pepper

½ cup chopped spearmint or calaminth

2 lemons, halved

This is a very special dinner that is also fun to prepare with kids. Older kids can wash and scrub the clams, and the younger ones can trim the green beans. Serve with garlic bread for mopping up the juices!

1. Soak the clams in a bowl of cold water for 20 minutes. Pick out the clams and set aside in a bowl or strainer.

2. Bring a large pot of salted water to a boil. Add the pasta and boil until al dente. Drain well.

3. Heat 2 tablespoons of the olive oil over medium heat in a very large skillet or any wide, heavy-bottomed pan. Add the onion and cook until browned, about 15 minutes. Stir in the garlic and cook for 2 minutes. Then add the wine, snap peas, and clams to the skillet. Season with salt and freshly cracked black pepper. Increase the heat to medium-high, cover the skillet, and let simmer until the clams open up, which should be just a few minutes. Discard any clams that do not open.

4. Place the pasta on plates using tongs. Add the remaining olive oil to the clams. Spoon the clams and vegetables over the pasta. Squeeze lemon juice over each plate of pasta and top the dish with chopped mint. Serve with more cracked black pepper.

Minty Baba

One of the champion recipes of my second cookbook, *Entertaining for a Veggie Planet*, was a smoky baba ghanoush. It is truly a foodie's baba, one that calls for slowly smoking eggplant over fire, creating an intense smokiness that might overwhelm a timid palate. This version is also smoky but includes copious amounts of mint, a pleasant twist. Try it with raw vegetables, crackers, or pita bread. You can prepare this dish up to two days ahead of time and store it in a tightly sealed container in the fridge, adding the onion right before serving.

MAKES 3 CUPS

1 (1-pound) Italian eggplant

½ cup loosely packed mint leaves (if using peppermint or calaminth, use ¼ cup)

2 garlic cloves

3 tablespoons tahini

2 tablespoons extra-virgin olive oil

2 tablespoons fresh lemon juice (about ½ lemon)

½ salt or more to taste

½ teaspoon freshly cracked black pepper

1 medium onion, finely chopped

1. Set the eggplant over a gas burner or on a grill with a low flame. Use tongs to turn and move the eggplant every few minutes, until it is blackened on all sides and quite soft; this should take about 25 to 30 minutes. Err on the side of overcharring it rather than under-charring. The eggplant should be quite limp after 25 minutes.
2. Preheat the oven to 400 degrees F.
3. Place the eggplant in a baking dish. Bake until it is soft but not mushy, about 15 to 20 minutes. Remove the pan from the oven and let cool. Remove the skin from the eggplant with your hands, over the sink. You'll see little black specks left on the eggplant. Don't rinse them—they yield much of the flavor.
4. Combine the mint and garlic in a food processor, and pulse the machine until they're finely chopped. Add the skinless eggplant along with the tahini, olive oil, lemon juice, salt, and pepper, and process the mixture until it's smooth.
5. Transfer to a serving bowl and stir in the onion. Serve warm or chilled.

Chocolate Intensity Cake

MAKES 10 TO 12 SERVINGS

1 cup milk

1 pound bittersweet or semisweet chocolate, finely chopped

1 cup unsalted butter

2 tablespoons brandy (I use kirsch)

1 tablespoon vanilla extract

8 large egg yolks (reserve the egg whites for use in the recipe for Almond Cardamom Almond Cardamom Meringue Cookies (on page 184)

Minted Whipped Cream (page 183), for serving

Pureed raspberries, for serving (optional)

This unctuous cake is better than any flourless chocolate cake I've tried. Jessica Gath, a friend of chef Brandon Hinman, wanted to bake him a cake, so she asked him what kind of cake he wanted. He replied, "The world's smallest cake, only smaller." The cake she made was remarkable in its petiteness; it was roughly the size of an eraser head! I figured Jessica had cut it out of a larger baked cake. But she told me that she had crafted a tiny springform pan out of a foil baking pan. Her boyfriend, who makes violins, made a cake stand and cover for the tiny cake. They presented the cake to Brandon at Eva's Garden, which is where he likes to spend his birthday. The recipe below is for a normal-size cake; if you want to try making the teensy cake, just use a small amount of the batter—that's what Jessica did.

1. Preheat the oven to 350 degrees F. Butter a 9-inch springform pan, or butter a 12-inch cake pan and line it with buttered and floured parchment paper.

2. Heat the milk in a large heavy saucepan over low heat until tiny bubbles form around the edges of the pan. Add the chocolate and cook, stirring occasionally, until it is melted and the mixture is smooth.

3. Stir in the butter, brandy, and vanilla. Cook, stirring, until the butter is melted. Remove the saucepan from the heat.

4. Whisk the egg yolks together in a small bowl. Whisk a small amount of the chocolate mixture into the egg yolks to temper them. Then whisk all the yolks into the chocolate mixture in the saucepan. Pour the batter into the prepared pan.

5. Bake the cake for 20 minutes, or until just set in the center. Set in its pan on a wire rack to cool completely. Cover and refrigerate the cake until you are ready to serve it.

6. To serve the cake, remove it from its pan. Serve with Minted Whipped Cream and pureed raspberries for a sauce, if desired.

Minted Whipped Cream

I like to use mountain mint or calaminth for this, but any mint will work.

1. Combine the cream and sugar in a small saucepan. Bring to a boil over medium heat. Add the mint, then turn the heat down and let the mixture simmer for 2 minutes. Remove from the heat, cover the saucepan, and let the contents steep for 15 minutes.
2. Pass the cream through a sieve into a bowl. Squeeze the mint leaves as hard as you can to extract any pent-up flavor.
3. Refrigerate the cream until it is very, very cold. Whip the cream with a whisk or electric mixer until the cream is just stiff and soft peaks hold their form.

MAKES ENOUGH FOR ONE WHOLE CAKE

2 cups heavy cream

2 tablespoons sugar

1 cup loosely packed mint (leaves and stems)

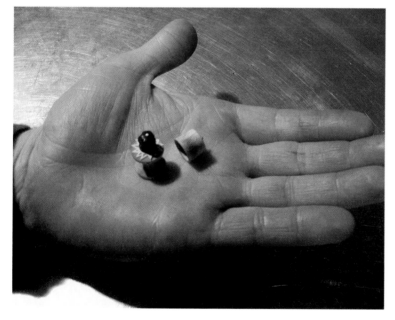

Almond Cardamom Meringue Cookies

MAKES 40 COOKIES
8 large egg whites
Pinch salt
1½ cups sugar
**½ teaspoon ground
cardamom**
1 teaspoon almond extract
**½ cup shaved almonds
(optional)**

I made these meringue cookies to decorate the top of the Chocolate Intensity Cake (page 182). The crunch of the cookie works amazingly well with the rich cake and the whipped cream. Play with the spice and extract in this cookie—for example, you might use vanilla extract and ground cloves.

1. Preheat the oven to 200 degrees F. Line a baking sheet with parchment paper.

2. In the bowl of an electric mixer, with the whisk attachment, beat the egg whites on low speed until foamy. Add a pinch of salt and increase the speed, beating the whites until they hold soft peaks. Add the sugar, a bit at a time, and continue to beat until the whites hold very stiff peaks. Beat in the cardamom and almond extract. Feel the meringue; if it feels sandy, the sugar has not dissolved. Keep beating until it feels smooth between your fingers.

3. Place a little of the meringue underneath each corner of the parchment paper on the baking sheet to help hold the paper down. Transfer the meringue to a ziplock bag that has one of its corners cut away, with the hole about the size of a quarter, and use it to pipe rounds of meringue onto the baking sheet. Alternatively, use two spoons to drop mounds of meringue to form 2-inch cookies onto the baking sheet. Sprinkle the tops of the cookies with a few shaved almonds, if desired.

4. Bake the meringues for approximately 2 hours, turning the baking sheet halfway through to ensure even baking. The meringues are done when they are pale in color and crisp. Turn off the oven, open the oven door just a crack, and leave the meringues in the oven to finish drying overnight.

Purslane

Portulaca oleracea · ANNUAL

The US Department of Agriculture was making a short film about very nutritious wild plants in 1985 at the Charles Hotel kitchens in Boston. Chefs were demonstrating how to cook them. Eva, who sold herbs to the chefs there, provided purslane for the video. Though she knew it well as a weed, this was the first time she'd considered purslane as an edible. All she remembers was that it tasted as slimy as seaweed.

But times have changed. Eva now eats pounds of purslane every summer, and she sells much more. What changed is how it's prepared: now Eva enjoys purslane in its uncooked raw state, as a salad green.

Purslane was the very first plant I foraged without anyone by my side helping me out. It met all my foraging criteria: First, it's not just easy to find, it's unavoidable. Second, it's easy to identify. Third, I can make it taste great without a lot of doctoring. And fourth, it is preposterously good for you.

Purslane is a weed, but many cultures, and more and more progressive Americans, consider it a prized edible. It is a very accessible wild food during the summer. You may not have to go any farther than your own yard to find it. It pops up in sidewalk cracks and in gardens (but you want to avoid purslane that grows next to busy roadsides, because car exhaust collects on the plant). Some varieties and plants taste better than others, so you just have to sample them until you find one that you deem good enough.

Growing purslane in your own organic soil is certainly the best option, and it can transplant well from the wild. Also, it may inspire you to know that both Henry David Thoreau and Gandhi were passionate about purslane.

CULINARY USES

Purslane stems, leaves, and flower buds are all good to eat. At its best, purslane is a bit tangy and citric, salty, and sweet—all at the same time. It should be crunchy when you bite into it. Chefs like it because it has a refreshing flavor and doesn't get tired-looking or beat up like watercress.

Though they are different in flavor, purslane can be used like celery and watercress. Like celery, it adds crunch to egg salad, potato salad, and tuna salad. Like watercress, it can become a crunchy green for salads and sandwiches. Try ham and purslane on rye. Chef Jamie Bissonnette of Coppa in Boston puts purslane on paninis (grilled sandwiches). In the Middle East, where you can buy purslane at the market, it's used in *fattoush*, a salad containing pita bread, tomatoes, olive oil, and garlic. In Greece it is often pickled.

Visiting Eva's years ago, I enjoyed purslane in a classic Turkish salad. Ihsan Gurdhal, a well-known cheese expert, originally from Turkey, had shared the recipe with Eva: chopped purslane, olive oil, yogurt, cucumber, onion, and parsley. The salad has a fun crunch and is memorable if the yogurt, olive oil, and purslane are all of good quality.

Chef and cheesemonger Matt Jennings of Farmstead cheese shop in Providence, Rhode Island, loves to fry purslane: the lightness of a tempura-style batter really complements the citrus quality of the green. Serve it with a small ramekin of spicy aioli. Matt also pickles purslane with champagne vinegar, a touch of honey, and sea salt—great for garnishing roast chicken thighs or scallops.

Health Virtues

Purslane contains more omega-3 fatty acids than any other leafy land plant. For a land vegetable, it has an extraordinary amount of eicosapentaenoic acid (EPA), an omega-3 fatty acid found mostly in fish, some algae, and flaxseed. Purslane also contains potent antioxidants, as well as vitamin A, potassium, and calcium. And it is extremely low in calories. It is also high in dietary fiber and high in oxalic acid, which can interfere with our digestion and the absorption of some trace minerals. It should not be overconsumed in its raw form, like over a pound a day. The US National Institutes of Health have determined that the negative effects of oxalic acid, which is present in spinach and a few other vegetables, are generally of little or no nutritional consequence in persons who eat a variety of foods.

Foraging, Storing, and Prepping

When foraging for purslane, look for paddle-shaped leaves and thick, gnarled, reddish stems. But beware of euphorbia or spurge (also called milk purslane), which has dull-looking smallish leaves. It is a poisonous creeping wild plant that sometimes grows near purslane. Its stem is wiry, not thick, and it exudes a white, milky sap when you break it.

Store purslane unwashed in a plastic bag in the fridge, for up to 3 days. To prepare it, just wash well and cut off any roots. Spin dry or leave it in a colander to drip dry. The stems are as edible as the leaves.

Growing Purslane

Here is some good news for anyone who wants to grow purslane: it grows like a weed. In fact, it is a weed—farmers from coast to coast rip up tons of the stuff as it invades their fields every summer. In the Northeast it starts showing up around June or July, and then it explodes in August.

Purslane likes heat, rich soil, and plenty of water and grows well when direct-sown from seed (Fedco and other seed suppliers sell the seed), although you may have an easier time plucking a young, healthy specimen out of the ground and transplanting it into your garden. You probably won't have to look far—there is a very good chance that you have purslane on your property already (the trick is getting it to grow where you want it and not everywhere else). Over time your purslane patch will thrive if left to its own devices; the plants sprawl as they grow and drop seeds to ensure successive crops.

Purslane Salad

This is a Turkish-inspired salad. If you have dried ground sumac, a pinch or two would make a nice addition. If you have your own kimchi on hand, add a handful to this salad; it is especially delicious. Any number of chopped herbs, greens, or edible flowers could be added to this salad; use your imagination or what you've got.

Combine the onion, garlic, yogurt, olive oil, and vinegar in a large bowl and stir well. Add the purslane, apple, raisins, and walnuts and stir well again. Season the salad with the lemon juice, cumin, and salt and freshly cracked black pepper to taste.

Note: To toast the walnuts, roast in a 350-degree oven on a rimmed baking sheet for about 5 minutes, until they are golden brown.

MAKES 6 SERVINGS

⅓ red onion, chopped

1 large garlic clove, minced

½ cup good-quality whole-milk yogurt

3 tablespoons extra-virgin olive oil

1 teaspoon balsamic vinegar

6 cups chopped purslane (leaves and stems)

1 tart apple (such as a Granny Smith), peeled and chopped

⅓ cup raisins, currants, or dried cranberries

⅓ cup walnuts, toasted

2 tablespoons lemon juice (about ½ lemon)

Salt and freshly cracked black pepper

2 pinches ground cumin (optional)

Rosemary

Rosmarinus officinalis · PERENNIAL

Just a few feet from Eva's house sits her oldest greenhouse, appropriately enough named Greenhouse 1. Here she grows a hodgepodge of greens and herbs through most of the year for her own personal use. It is not very well maintained, unlike her other seven greenhouses. In the cold of winter it sits like a battlefield post-siege, with just a few hardy survivors still standing—mostly sprigs of baby mustard and arugula.

But off to the side, four rosemary bushes stand strong amidst the fallout. These bushes are 3 feet high, their needles tough as leather. The base stems—now fourteen years old—are deeply scaled, and they twist and turn like ancient olive trees. Whenever I walk by the plants, I reach down and give a few stems a gentle squeeze. Then I cup my hand to my nose and inhale, and I am transported to another world. I imagine standing in the dew among a thousand young pine trees infused with a billion glowing night stars, where rain clouds of the sea shower down their essences upon the forest. The herb's Latin name, *Rosmarinus*, translates as "dew of the sea," and it's easy to see why.

Eva's older rosemary is very hardy. It can thrive in her greenhouse during the coldest months of the year, and on subzero nights that greenhouse cuts out only the wind, not the single-digit temperatures. This rosemary has an aroma so rapturous that I repeatedly have asked her to remember the variety. Eva finally answered me in an e-mail: "It's probably Salem—we selected our seeds based on maximum weight and ease of cutting: upright growth and heavy leaves. Fine needles and drooping habit are not an advantage for production." High production or low production, I advise you to seek out this variety.

CULINARY USES

Rosemary is perhaps most popular in Italy. Italian butchers will stick a bunch of rosemary into the twine when wrapping lamb, pork, or other meat. In Italy rosemary is usually left whole; a sprig or two is added to a soup or sauce and then removed before serving. There's no doubt that it has a slight camphor flavor, a medicinal quality. In his book *Herbs, Spices and Flavorings*, Tom Stobart goes so far as to say that rosemary has "a violent taste."

Rosemary is strong-willed; it can stamp out other flavors and is reluctant to share the stage. But with outspoken flavors like curry, fresh ginger, thyme, lavender, and, of course, onion and garlic, a synergy can be created. I love to stir chopped garlic and rosemary into goat cheese, adding a bit of thyme and sage as well. Rosemary, unlike many thin-skinned herbs, holds up well in a simmering liquid or when roasted with meat or vegetables. Nothing can surpass a chicken soup or roast chicken cooked with garlic and rosemary. It can also improve a winter vegetable or potato gratin. I once paired rosemary and fresh ginger in a minestrone, and as odd as that sounds, it worked. Meat is rich enough to take quite a bit of the herb. Make a paste of rosemary, oil, and garlic, and rub it on meat such as lamb, rabbit, venison, or pork.

Chef Patrick Campbell of No. 9 Park in Boston likes to deep-fry rosemary sprigs in duck fat, which makes it crunchy. He serves the fried rosemary as a garnish, and he uses the rosemary-flavored duck fat for searing meat.

There are two ways to cook with rosemary: on the stem or chopped. I use the whole stem for a more subtle effect: drop it in a simmering soup, stew, or stock and remove it before serving. However, in Eva's school of herbs (and

I agree), showering the stew or soup with additional chopped rosemary just before serving is a necessity. I also like to add chopped rosemary to shortbread. And adding a sprig to warm olive oil and letting it sit for a few days makes a great medium for bread dipping.

HEALTH VIRTUES

In the winter rosemary tea will make you feel better, and not just because it tastes good; it is purported to have strong restorative powers for chest colds and general discomfort, and its essential oil is used by aromatherapists to aid in fighting depression. Pour boiling water over a sprig in a mug, cover with a saucer, and let steep for five minutes. Add honey if you desire.

BUYING, STORING, AND PREPPING

Rosemary typically can be found in supermarkets year-round, and the quality is usually decent. Look for needles that are secured tightly to the stems; older or unhealthy rosemary easily sheds its needles. You want needles that have "meat" to them, rather than being flat and dried out. Of course, buying fresh sprigs at the farmers' market (or, better yet, nurturing your own plant) will result in superior quality.

Fresh rosemary can be stored as sprigs in a tightly sealed container or bag in the refrigerator for over a week. It also freezes well for up to six months; I like to freeze a bunch and take a sprig out whenever I need to. I don't recommend using the herb dried, because it loses a lot of its flavor. If you are using dried rosemary, introduce it to a hot liquid to release its flavor before cooking with it. Chop rosemary before adding it to food; the needles do soften after cooking, but in general they are an irritation in the mouth and throat.

GROWING ROSEMARY

You can either start rosemary from cuttings or buy a plant from a garden center and transplant it into your garden. It prefers lots of sun and warm temperatures year-round as well as semiarid growing conditions. If temperatures in your area drop below 30 degrees in the winter, it is best to keep rosemary in a pot and move it indoors to your best-lit window in the fall. Sudden change is not good, so acclimatize your plant by bringing it inside at night and leaving it outdoors during the day, gradually increasing the amount of time it spends indoors. Harvest rosemary as needed, being careful not to overdo it, especially in the beginning stages of growth. Clip back the main growing stem to encourage bushy growth.

Rosemary-Ginger Minestrone

MAKES 6 TO 8 SERVINGS

2 tablespoons extra-virgin olive oil

2 onions or 1 leek, finely chopped

3 garlic cloves, minced

2 cups chopped green cabbage (about ¼ of a small head)

1 small fennel bulb, chopped

1 small potato, peeled and chopped

1 red pepper, chopped

3-inch piece fresh ginger, unpeeled, cut into 6 thin slices

4 large sprigs rosemary

½ cup red or beige quinoa

1 (14-ounce) can unsalted white cannellini or navy beans, drained and rinsed

1 teaspoon salt

freshly cracked black pepper

Sometimes two flavors you never eat together can connect like old friends. I discovered this with rosemary and ginger years ago at a restaurant when I was making soup day after day. You can improvise with the vegetables.

1. Heat the oil in a heavy-bottomed stockpot over medium heat. Add the onions and garlic and cook about 7 minutes, stirring, until they begin to brown. Add the cabbage, fennel, potato, red pepper, ginger, and three sprigs of the rosemary. Stir well. Add 8 cups water and the quinoa. Bring the soup to a boil, then reduce the heat and let simmer until the potatoes are tender, about 20 minutes.

2. Remove the rosemary sprigs and discard them. Chop the remaining rosemary sprig (you should have at least 1 tablespoon) and add it to the soup. Add the beans and salt and season the soup with freshly cracked black pepper to taste.

Bartering with Andy's Cattle

Andy and Amy Burnes live a few houses up from Eva. They often give Eva meat in exchange for herb-picking rights. Andy breeds cows in the downtime from his other, more lucrative but less "cowboy" job. He owns fifteen Hereford cows. These regal-looking cows wear copper spots on bright white fur, and they glow in the afternoon sun. Recently I heard he was "downsizing" to an even smaller Hereford breed. Andy explained that many grass-fed beef producers are shifting to breeding smaller animals for the following reasons:

- Smaller animals convert feed to meat more efficiently. This isn't a concern for the feedlot system of industrial agriculture. Because the grain feedlot animals eat is subsidized by the federal government, it's cheap, and producers aren't much concerned about meat conversion efficiency.
- Smaller animals are easier on the land, especially in springtime mud. Lighter animals means better-quality pastures and better meat. The feedlot system doesn't have to deal with damage to the land since the cows gain most of their weight in concrete pens, so their size is not a factor.
- Smaller animals generally mean easier births. The trend of breeding bigger and bigger bulls and cows clearly makes the breeding cycle riskier. In a small operation like Andy's, any loss is too much. Breeding smaller bulls seems to be working; after switching to a smaller breed their cows had three easy births in one month.

Andy's cows (mostly heifers) graze on 50 acres of land, some of which doesn't belong to him, but he trades and barters for the use of his neighbor's land. Andy takes good care of the pastures and grows high-protein legumes like red clover and alfalfa. Some people claim that grass-fed meat is stringy, but Andy says it will be tender if the cows' diet consists of 100 percent high-protein grasses (many grass-fed animals are finished on grain).

I asked Andy how his fifteen cows would fare if they mistakenly walked across the street to Eva's garden. He said they'd eat her entire garden in a day. But I'm guessing her herbs would give their meat some very refined built-in seasoning.

Rugosa Rose

Rosa rugosa • PERENNIAL

Gather ye rosebuds while ye may,
Old Time is still a-flying;
And this same flower that smiles today,
Tomorrow will be dying.
>—"To the Virgins, to Make Much
of Time," by Robert Herrick (1648)

Eva's keen aptitude for rounding up volunteers first made itself evident to me when she needed some warm bodies to pick roses. Rugosa rose, that is, a shrublike species called *Rosa rugosa*, grows wild and in profusion come late spring and summer, often in sandy soil (which explains why it is sometimes called wild beach rose).

Eva informed me that there was to be an afternoon "adventure" by the ocean. She described fields of fragrant rosebushes that dropped off to a thrashing sea, while ospreys plucked sea bass out of the ocean. How could I say no? Off I went, with Mercy and Sarah, two teenage neighbors, as co-adventurers.

We drove down a narrow road onto a peninsula. Sarah and Mercy flitted off together, waist-high among the beach roses, chatting and coaxing the petals off their casings, dropping them into the pillowcases that Eva had provided us. They giggled like teenagers do, and they plucked as swiftly as professionals. As I grasped for the roses, the thorny underbrush clawed my legs, digging for blood. My fingers were inflamed from the prickly rose stems. A cloud of mosquitoes swarmed around my head, feasting on my face, my neck, in between my fingers, in my ears. After an hour I went to Mercy and Sarah and announced that my personal rose adventure was over. Their bags were full; mine was pathetically empty. And

I never saw a single bird of prey, let alone an osprey clutching a fish.

Kelly Lake, a farmhand, writes of rose picking with Eva:

I'm sure we confused beachgoers by our strange dress, our first line of defense against the elements. We wore two faded oversized suede jackets from the '80s. Beneath the jackets, which went to our knees, our soil-stained pants were tucked into our socks to keep ticks from latching on to our ankles. Our uniforms extended to two raggedy knapsacks that contained dozens of what used to be Ziploc bags, but by the time they were assigned to *Rosa rugosa* duty, they were brittle and opaque—their zippers had long ago ceased functioning. So instead of zippers we used those big black clips that are meant to organize stacks of paper.

As we headed down the sandy path in search of the most productive rugosa patches, Eva's eyes began to glimmer—a look that was just a little bit frightening. Some primal foraging instinct seemed to be taking over.

Culinary Uses

Place a rose petal on the tongue. If you're unaccustomed to the taste, it may seem as though you're eating some kind of cologne. Then, when you actually bite into the petal, the flavor intensifies. The flavor of roses can be too much for some, but most everyone can enjoy it in small doses.

Eva sells rugosa rose petals mainly to pastry chefs in the city. Maura Kilpatrick at Sofra bakery and Oleana restaurant makes a rose jam that is remarkable. Most chefs and cooks boil the petals to make a syrup, discarding the petals. They use the syrup to flavor a myriad of desserts and savories.

But Eva and I don't make syrup with beach roses: we have great success using the rose petals whole. Eva uses them in sorbets. She adds a handful of petals to the blender with any one of her frozen fruits (such as raspberry or autumn olive) and a bit of honey. The rose flavor doesn't overwhelm but harmonizes with the fruit. I buzz the petals into smoothies and lassis, sometimes adding fruit, sometimes with a pinch of cardamom. I also chop the petals and add them to pound cake, scones, or muffins. We also add rose petals to salads.

Whole rose petals can be added to jams, if you are industrious enough to make your own jam. Or you can infuse them, adding a handful of petals to lemonade or water and steeping overnight in the fridge. Some people like to infuse rose petals in boiling water for a tea. You can always vary the quantity, using less if you want just a hint of rose or more if you are game.

If you can't get to the fresh roses, then store-bought rose water is certainly a good substitute for the real deal, and in the winter this is what I use. Rose water is what gives many Middle Eastern pastries their character, and it is often combined with phyllo dough, cheese, yogurt, nuts (as in baklava), ice cream, doughnuts, and much more. In India it is used in desserts like rice pudding. In Europe it is sometimes used to flavor marzipan and madeleines. In Malaysia rose syrup and sassafras syrup are poured over shaved ice, then topped with gelatinous beans and corn; in fact that's the national dessert.

Rose Hips

Rose hips are the small, orange-red fruits that grow after the blossom dies back. The hips from rugosa buds are especially large and have thick, fleshy walls. They can be eaten raw or cooked. The taste is sweet and unusual, with the typical bite of foods that are rich in ascorbic acid (vitamin C). Take care to remove the irritating hairs that surround the seeds before eating or processing. Rose hip jams and jellies are probably the two most popular uses of this fruit.

Health Virtues

Rose petals contain vitamins C and K, carotene, and B-complex vitamins, and the hips are one of the best plant sources of vitamin C on the planet (step aside, oranges).

Storing/Preparing

Eva stores her rose petals in the freezer, because they will wither and discolor quickly in the fridge. She freezes them in plastic ziplock bags. But the petals need to be tossed first with lemon juice (in a big bowl or right in the ziplock bag), about 1 lemon per gallon of petals to preserve their color.

Foraging and Growing

Rosa rugosa comes in various shades of pink and white. These roses are prevalent in the northeast United States; many coastal communities have planted them near sand dunes and on beaches for erosion control. Look for large green bushes that are spotted with bright fuchsia or white petals encircling a bright yellow center in a single layer. The flowers blossom and die within a day, as Herrick's poem states. The bushes themselves can be 4 to 6 feet in height. Only a few flowers may be visible, depending on the time of year.

Rugosa rose's value as an erosion-control plant makes it desirable for roadside planting, and its use has recently been expanded to include sand dune stabilization. This makes for fun foraging, as the plants are ubiquitous and in the sand dunes there are generally no exhaust fumes or pesticides used. These roses thrive on neglect. I find them in public spaces in Boston, along roadsides and near public transportation—and I do pick them!

If you prefer, you can transplant bushes onto your own property. If you haven't mastered the technique of propagating roses from cuttings, it will probably be easier to start *Rosa rugosa* from seed. It is a popular ornamental. Eva grows the Double Hansa cultivar because it yields more petals per flower. You can buy seeds online, or, if you know of a wild patch, you can collect the ripe hips in September, allow them to dry, remove the seeds, and plant them directly in your garden. If pests are a problem, plant the seeds in a pot, and cover the pot with a screen or anything that will allow sunshine and water in but keep pests out. Bury the pot just beneath the surface of the soil in the fall, and simply leave the pot outdoors all winter. Watch for growth the following spring and then transplant the plants into your garden. The plants prefer full sun but will survive in partial shade, as long as the soil is well drained. Once established, these wild rosebushes don't need much babying (as many other varieties do). In fact, if you forgot about them altogether they would do just fine.

Raspberry Rose Milkshake

This recipe makes two shakes: one to drink now, and one to drink about twenty minutes later. It's so good you won't want to share it. Raw milk improves the shake, but if you can't find it I recommend a good organic yogurt in its place. If you haven't run into any wild roses, then rose water will work. You can use frozen raspberries instead of fresh; in that case, just omit the ice cubes.

Combine the raspberries, rose petals, sugar, ice cubes, and yogurt in a blender. Process on high speed until the shake is smooth. Taste the shake, adding more petals or rose water if you'd like more rose flavor. Pour into two glasses and serve.

MAKES 2 SERVINGS

2 cups fresh raspberries

1 small handful rugosa rose petals (about 20 petals) or 2 teaspoons or more rose water

3–4 tablespoons sugar

4–6 ice cubes, depending on size

3 cups raw milk or plain organic yogurt

Rose Strawberry Sherbet

I was so wowed by this sherbet that I spooned out some for Eva and set it down next to where she was working, then quietly slinked back to the kitchen. Like a geyser erupting, finally the sounds of euphoria burst forth as she tasted it. If you own a Vitamix or a very powerful blender, you can make this sherbert quickly by using frozen fruit. Either way, the berries must have been absolutely freshly picked. You'll need an ice cream maker.

MAKES 6 SERVINGS

1 quart fresh-picked strawberries, green tops removed

20–30 rugosa rose petals

1–2 tablespoons sugar

Pinch salt

½ cup organic whole-milk plain yogurt

1. Puree the strawberries and rose petals with the sugar, salt, and yogurt in a blender or food processor.
2. Pour the mixture into your ice cream maker and make ice cream according to the manufacturer's instructions.

Rose Raspberry Ice Cream

MAKES 6 SERVINGS

2½ cups fresh raspberries

2 cups loosely packed rugosa rose petals

2 tablespoons lemon juice (about ½ lemon)

1 cup sugar (or more to taste) or ¾ cup mild-flavored honey

Pinch salt

1 cup heavy cream

1 cup Greek yogurt

I wanted to make rose raspberry ice cream with Greek yogurt, but Eva had only plain yogurt. So I put it in a superfine strainer and left it in the sink to drain. An hour later Eva looked in the sink. "What are you doing?" she asked. "Making Greek yogurt," I replied. She scowled. "But all the whey is going down the drain!" "Yes," I said, "the recipes tell you to discard the whey." "Well, that is just sinful," Eva cried. "I drink the whey or pour it on my morning cereal—don't you know it's good for you?" So I got a bowl and collected the whey that was still draining out. A bit later I tasted the whey. This watery, milky juice was actually buttery-tasting and rich. Around Eva it seems like I'm rarely right.

You'll need an ice cream maker for this recipe.

1. Puree the raspberries, rose petals, and lemon juice in a blender or food processor. Add the sugar and process until the sugar has "melted" and the puree is no longer visibly grainy. This may take a few minutes.

2. Add the salt, cream, and yogurt, and taste the mixture for sweetness. Pour the mixture into your ice cream maker and make ice cream according to the manufacturer's instructions. Once the ice cream is churned, let it harden in the freezer for at least 1 hour before serving.

Wild Rose and Rhubarb Pound Cake

Eva's son Leo and his wife Christina were visiting from their home in the Middle East. I wanted to make a beautifully decorated pound cake for Christina, who was turning thirty-three. Lacking a mixer (which is how pound cakes leaven), I improvised and used baking soda and hoped for the best. The cake rose well enough, but I charred the bottom (Eva's oven has a few hot patches). So I scraped off the char like a giant piece of burnt toast. Happily, the topping and Eva's breathtaking edible flowers hid the imperfections. It is a heavenly tasting cake. And it's one of the many good reasons to chop up some rhubarb in the spring and freeze it for later use.

1. To make the pound cake, preheat the oven to 350 degrees F. Butter a large at least 2½-inch deep 11- or 12-inch round cake pan (it can be springform). Line the bottom of the pan with buttered parchment paper, then dust the pan(s) with flour.

2. Whisk together the sugar and eggs in a large bowl for a minute or two. Whisk in the rose petals and almond extract. Whisk in the yogurt, 1 cup of the flour, the baking powder, the baking soda, and the salt and mix until smooth. Cream the butter and gently whisk it in.

3. Fold in the remaining 1 cup flour with a spoon. Fold in the rhubarb, mixing just until it's incorporated. Spoon the batter into the cake pan(s).

4. Bake for 45 to 55 minutes, or until a knife inserted halfway into the center comes out clean. Invert the cake, removing it from the pan, then cool on a rack.

5. To make the topping, whip the cream with the sugar until stiff. Fold in the yogurt and the rose petals.

6. When the cake is cool, set it on a platter. Spread the topping over the cake with a spatula. Arrange edible flowers on the cake. Serve immediately, or refrigerate for up to 3 hours.

MAKES 10 TO 12 SERVINGS

Pound Cake:

1⅔ cups sugar

5 large eggs

Petals from 2 or 3 rugosa roses, chopped, or 2 tablespoons rose water

1 teaspoon almond extract

⅔ cup plain yogurt

2 cups all-purpose flour

1½ teaspoons baking powder

½ teaspoon baking soda

½ teaspoon salt

1 cup butter, very soft, creamed

2½ cups chopped rhubarb

Topping:

1 cup heavy cream

3 tablespoons sugar

1 cup plain or Greek yogurt

1 cup coarsely chopped rugosa rose petals

Rugosa roses and other edible flowers for garnish

Summer Savory

Satureja hortensis · ANNUAL

Summer savory tastes like thyme that's been in a car accident with oregano, mint, and dill. Its intense flavor ignites quickly on the tongue, leaving a pleasant anesthetic sting, similar to the numbing sensation you get when biting into a cinnamon stick. It is a potent herb, like lavender or rosemary, that needs to be used with a light hand.

Culinary Uses

Many chefs don't encounter and enjoy summer savory until they are at the end of their career—or, more likely, not at all. Peter McCarthy, who owns three restaurants in Cambridge, Massachusetts, including EVOO, is the chef who urged Eva to grow it. His customers love it, although they don't always know what they are eating. He sprinkles summer savory (and salt) on his French fries.

Savory is pungent, like thyme and rosemary. But savory can walk the middle way; it can be used in cooked foods as well as more delicate raw edibles, like salad. Raw savory is often paired with (local) tomatoes or potato salad. Sprinkle raw savory on top of pizza, scrambled eggs, or roasted vegetables.

The easiest way to get comfortable with cooking with summer savory is to think of it as a sister to thyme; it's just a little more demure. Soup is a natural destination, especially onion or garlic soups, or soups with dried beans, lentils, potatoes, or green beans. Just add the leaves one to ten minutes before the soup is finished. Peter McCarthy bakes summer savory into breadsticks. Chef Tony Maws, of Craigie On Main in Cambridge, likes to work with summer savory in lamb dishes. Savory is also perfect when paired with roast chicken, stewed rabbit, or venison. Eva's neighbor Alan once had a venison pie with savory, carrots, and beans and a vodka crust. Mussels and summer savory are another good match.

Savory is commonly used in herb blends, particularly the Middle Eastern blend *za'atar,* which includes savory, thyme, marjoram, dried sumac, and toasted sesame seeds. Savory produces sweet little flowers for a brief period, which are succulent. Add them to salads and use them to top creamy cheeses and the like.

Health Virtues

Summer savory has been used medicinally for centuries to treat a wide variety of ailments. It is said that savory, infused like a tea, aids in digestion and prevents flatulence. Rubbing a leaf on your skin may lessen the irritation from a bee sting, and like other members of the mint family it is an expectorant.

Buying and Storing

Fresh summer savory may be difficult to find if it isn't growing in your garden, although you may be able to find it dried in the spice section of supermarkets. Fresh summer savory should be stored on the stem in a plastic bag. It will keep for a couple of weeks in the fridge, and 4 months or so in the freezer.

Growing Savory

Summer savory is easy to grow. It likes full sun and average, well-drained soil, and it does best when started indoors in early spring. You can also sow it directly into the garden after the danger of frost has passed. Thin plants to 10 inches apart once they are established. Summer savory can be harvested lightly after only six weeks of growth, and it can be harvested as needed after another month of growth. Sow successive crops in May, June, and July to ensure a steady supply until cold temperatures kill the plants.

Potato and Smoked Bluefish Stew with Summer Savory

I often scrounge through Eva's fridge when making dinner, since it is often filled with remarkable food. One day I happened to find smoked bluefish, parsley, summer savory, and some steamed vegetables. This dish turned out especially nice, and it is worth repeating.

1. Steam the eggplant and squash whole if possible, or cut them in half so they'll fit in a steamer basket. Place in a pot or pan that is a bit bigger, add a cup of water and bring to a boil. Turn the heat to low and cover. Steam for 4–5 minutes and remove the veggies. Add the potatoes to the steamer and steam until tender, about 10 minutes. The vegetables can also be pressure-cooked in even less time. Place to cool on a cutting board. Cut the vegetables into smaller pieces (smaller than your mouth, which it must fit in).

2. Heat the olive oil in a cast-iron skillet or heavy-bottomed Dutch oven over medium heat. When it is hot, add the potatoes and carrots and let cook, undisturbed, for 4 minutes, or until the potatoes begin to brown and form a crust. Flip the vegetables over with a spatula. Season with salt and freshly cracked black pepper.

3. Add the eggplant, squash, tomatoes, garlic, and summer savory, and reduce the heat to low. Cook until the tomato breaks down and releases its juices, about 5 minutes.

4. Add the bluefish and stir well. Remove from the heat. Season with hot sauce, more salt, and freshly cracked black pepper to taste. Spoon the stew into bowls and sprinkle with parsley.

MAKES 4 SERVINGS

1 Asian eggplant

1 small yellow squash

3 Red Bliss or other creamy potatoes, skin-on, cut into 4 pieces each

3 tablespoons extra-virgin olive oil

2 carrots, peeled and thinly sliced

Salt and freshly cracked black pepper

4 tomatoes, quartered

2 garlic cloves, minced

1 tablespoon (or more) chopped summer savory

1 cup (or 6 ounces) smoked bluefish

Few dashes chipotle-based hot sauce

4 tablespoons chopped parsley

Thyme

Thymus spp. · PERENNIAL

Eva and I were hopelessly late, later than our already tarnished reputations allowed. We had been invited to an elegant fund-raising dinner at an estate by the ocean. We were, on the other hand, not elegant. We left late and drove in circles, working off Eva's memory. The relentless rain was no help.

We finally found the estate, but the tent eluded us! We splashed along a spaghetti-thin road that hugged the stormy Atlantic. It was not hard to imagine that we were driving along the coast of Scotland. The rain had morphed into hail the size of mothballs as we approached the glowing white tent. We parked and, holding our coats above our heads, scurried up the hill. Out of the blue there wafted up an overwhelming aroma of fresh thyme, and I stopped dead in my tracks. For a moment I simply inhaled and forgot all about the outside world. I looked down and gasped, "Eva, this whole hill is covered with thyme!" She was already way ahead of me, and either she couldn't hear me or she ignored me, being more concerned with our dinner obligations. Ever since that evening, though, I have dreamed of one day enjoying a backyard carpeted in wild thyme.

When I recounted this story to Eva she began to sing an old song from the 1700s:

> Will ye go, lassie, go?
> And we'll all go together
> To pluck wild mountain thyme
> All around the blooming heather
> Will ye go, lassie, go?

Thyme has been a steady and dear friend to me. About twenty-five years ago, when I was just beginning to cook on a professional level, I discovered its versatility and complexity and used it like salt. I was monogamous as far as herbs went, and we were quite happy. I saw it as the bass player in a rock band, pulling all the elements together with its deep, mellow undertones. But, like any good instrument, it has its own character. Its flavor evokes pine, mint, lemon, and the numbing bite of clove. It is a well-balanced herb that gives countless soups, stews, and many other foods their complexity and intrigue. Even history attests to its value: thyme has been cultivated for more than five thousand years.

Eva's favorite variety of thyme is oregano thyme (*Thymus vulgaris*). She loves to smell it, cook with it, walk on it. Lemon thyme (*Thymus* x *citriodorus*, specifically the 'Aureus' cultivar, known as gold lemon thyme) is my favorite variety. It has a distinct lemony undercurrent, with tinges of coconut and mint. It is so fragrant that it drove me to behave deviously one day. I saw a large patch of it growing in one of Eva's greenhouses, so I impetuously (with a paring knife!) dug a fistful of it to replant at home. Later I confessed to Eva and showed her my "fresh kill." She told me sternly to replant it *immediately* where I had found it. So I scurried back to the greenhouse.

Culinary Uses

Fresh thyme can be used on or off the stem. Sprigs of thyme on the stem can be added directly to soups or stews in the last ten to fifteen minutes of cooking; just remember to fish out the stems with a fork before serving. You could also bundle twelve or so stems together with string and add this to your simmering dish, as a simplified bouquet garni, removing it before serving. For less soupy dishes, strip the leaves from the stem and add them whole. Oregano thyme and other creeping varieties are often tender enough to chop and add to food without being stripped, stems and all.

Thyme, in my mind, is best if cooked with a food, whether a stew, pilaf, or paste on meat, for at least ten minutes. Take for example Suzanne Goin's dreamy *bagna cauda* with thyme in *Sunday Suppers at Lucques*. This is a traditional Italian "hot bath" of butter and olive oil, heavily spiked with garlic, anchovy, and thyme and used for both bread and vegetables.

Onions slowly caramelized in butter and thyme is heavenly. Cut hardy vegetables like winter squashes, root vegetables and tubers into chunks, and roast them with thyme, garlic, and olive oil. Thyme improves any kind of mushroom, whether wild or cultivated. And any kind of thyme makes a terrific paste for dry-roasting meats—it can be ground in a food processor with garlic, Dijon mustard, and other herbs or spices such as fresh juniper berries or spruce shoots, or even lavender.

Fresh thyme likes the company of other herbs, especially those that can stand up to cooking, like marjoram, rosemary, sage, and oregano. It is popular in Jamaican cuisine, balancing the allspice and Scotch bonnet peppers in jerk seasoning.

Lemon thyme is wonderful baked with chicken or fish. It makes a delicious hot or iced tea. Just a bit of it will brighten a basil pesto.

Eva likes thyme raw, sprinkled onto hot foods and soups so that it won't lose a shred of flavor. Try raw thyme in herb butter (for use on steak, pork, lamb, venison, or steamed potatoes), stirred into goat cheese, or pureed with olive oil for bread dipping or drizzling on fish (the latter works especially well with lemon thyme).

Health Virtues

Thyme is a good source of iron. On a much smaller scale, *Thymus serpyllum* (wild or creeping thyme) is an important nectar source for honeybees and insects.

Buying, Storing, and Prepping

Thyme is durable, so buying it at a supermarket (if it looks fresh) is a fine idea. Look for stiff stems and leaves. Farmers' markets are a great place to buy thyme, especially if it's a potted plant, which could supply you all summer long. As far as storage goes, any kind of tightly sealed container will do, and thyme will keep two to three weeks in the fridge. Thyme freezes well, both on and off the stem, but again, a tightly sealed container is key. Thyme also dries well (see page xxi for drying information).

To strip the leaves off the stem, I squeeze my fingers around the stem, starting at the middle, and pull down toward the root end, as the leaves fall away. The upper third of the stem is usually soft enough that it can just be chopped up and used along with the leaves.

Growing Thyme

Eva recommends that beginners buy thyme from a nursery rather than dealing with starting the slow, delicate plants from seed. Transplant into your garden in the spring, in a spot that gets full sun and good drainage. Eva likes to grow oregano thyme, golden thyme, and lemon thyme. These varieties are easy to grow from cuttings—simply clip a piece of stem with a bit of root, plant it in a pot or right in the garden, and give it some time to settle into its new home. Thyme may overwinter, depending on your climate zone and conditions; it is helped by mulch, wind protection, and a full southern exposure. You may opt to bring the plant indoors if you have a sunny window or a grow light. Eva's thyme is quite happy in her greenhouses.

Green Eggs (and No Ham)

MAKES 4 SERVINGS

- 1 handful thyme leaves (2–3 tablespoons)
- Small handful any other available herbs (e.g., basil, lovage, parsley, sage)
- 3 or 4 scallions, green and white parts, chopped
- 6 large eggs
- Few tablespoons butter
- Salt and freshly cracked black pepper

A chef and a close friend of Eva's, Brandon Hinman loves to stroll into Eva's at around 7 a.m. and make everyone breakfast. He is an outrageously adventuresome cook. Here's an unusual recipe he created one morning that I found revelatory. It reads rather loosely, because this is how he approaches recipes. I've never eaten eggs so green or good. Brandon spread some soft goat cheese on toast and we all topped it with the jade green eggs. He served it alongside some cooked oat groats mixed with cinnamon, butter, and raisins. Brilliant!

1. Whiz the thyme, herbs, scallions, and 2 eggs in a blender or Vitamix until the mixture turns jade green. Add the remaining eggs and whiz a bit more.
2. Heat the butter in a heavy skillet over low heat. Add the egg mixture and cook, stirring often, until cooked through and scrambled. Season with salt and freshly cracked pepper to taste. Serve right away.

Homespun Boursin

When I was a teenager I worked at a cheese shop that sold Boursin, a pre-packaged French cow's-milk cheese that was creamy but dry enough to form a little cake, and heavily spiked with dried herbs and garlic. Since then I have made many versions, but all are creamier and wetter than the original Boursin. I always scoop it into a funky ceramic crock or bowl that Eva crafted back in her pottery days. I could let it hang in a cheesecloth to dry so it becomes firmer to form a cake, but it's always so good that I never get that far.

Combine the cheese, herbs, garlic, pepper, and olive oil in a small bowl, mixing well. Season the mixture with salt to taste.

MAKES 1½ CUPS

10 ounces creamy goat cheese or farmer's cheese

½ cup chopped herbs (a combination of two or more: African basil, anise hyssop, basil, chives, lemon thyme, mint, oregano, parsley, rosemary, sage, tarragon, thyme)

2 garlic cloves, minced

½ teaspoon freshly cracked black pepper

3 tablespoons extra-virgin olive oil

Salt

Eva Ruminating on Supermarkets

Didi: "When was the last time you went supermarket shopping, Eva?"

Eva: "I don't even remember the last time I stepped foot in a supermarket. I find it visually stressful because of their large inventory. So much of what they sell I don't need or want. And the lights are terribly bright. Most importantly, I like to follow things back to their origins—I like to know the field the potato grew in. I can't remember when it wasn't important and fascinating to me to see how food grew.

"Thinking back on when I picked the food, perhaps with friends, makes eating a richer more gratifying experience. Like a good relationship, there needs to be intimacy with food. Shopping in most supermarkets is like consuming food blindfolded: we don't know the history or life of these foods. The supermarket is the great disconnect. And this is disturbing to me.

"But the reason I can avoid shopping in supermarkets is that I have neighbors with similar values who make cheese, raise cattle, catch fish, dig clams. And I'm lucky I have my own farm in my backyard. It makes me happy to know that farmers' markets are so popular, because now everyone can enjoy what I enjoy—fresh local food."

Lamb with Israeli Couscous and Oregano Thyme

MAKES 6 SERVINGS

2 tablespoons extra-virgin olive oil

1¼ pounds ground lamb

1 tablespoon minced oregano thyme (or any thyme)

2 cups large couscous (Israeli or *maftoul*)

2 cups chopped garlic chives or regular garden chives

2 tablespoons chopped preserved lemon (page 126)

Salt and freshly cracked black pepper

The three Rogers brothers came with their father to the farm one afternoon. The brothers were plotting to open a restaurant together. All three were as big as NFL noseguards, and I was impressed that they had such reverence for herbs, considering their low calorie count. Ken, the oldest, had been a chef client of Eva's. So I invited him to cook with me in her tiny kitchen and we created this dish. Oregano thyme is the strongest thyme Eva grows, and it must be used judiciously. Here the lamb's intensity stands up to the thyme's.

1. Heat 1 tablespoon of the olive oil in a large sauté pan over medium heat. Add the lamb and stir well. Add the thyme and continue to stir. Cook, stirring often, until the lamb is cooked, about 5 minutes. Transfer this mixture to a plate.

2. In the same pan, heat the remaining 1 tablespoon olive oil over medium-high heat. Add the couscous and cook, stirring occasionally, until slightly browned and aromatic, about 3 to 5 minutes. Add 4 cups water and bring to a boil. Simmer for 10 to 12 minutes, or until the liquid has evaporated.

3. Add the chives and preserved lemon. Stir well. Add the lamb mixture, heating it slightly and adjusting the seasoning with salt and freshly cracked black pepper. Serve.

Herbed Omelet

Making omelets requires the mind-set of a lion going in for the kill. Once you add your eggs to the hot pan, don't check your iPhone or even roll up your sleeves, because your omelet will be history if you lose focus. An omelet takes about thirty seconds once the eggs hit the pan. If they're left any longer, they will toughen and brown. I most often eat omelets for dinner. If you'd like to add cheese, I'd recommend an ounce or two of a mild cheddar, a good ricotta, or soft goat's-milk cheese.

A seasoned omelet pan is best, but a nonstick skillet work fine. A skillet that is 9 inches in diameter is best.

MAKES 1 SERVING

2 or 3 large eggs

pinch of salt

Big pinch freshly cracked black pepper

1 tablespoon butter

About ½ cup herbs, coarsely chopped, stems removed (basil, chervil, chives, dill, parsley, and/or tarragon are my favorites)

Cheese (optional)

1. Beat the eggs, salt, and pepper in a mixing bowl with a fork (*not* a whisk) until the whites and yolks are just blended; do not overmix, as this will make the omelet lose tenderness.

2. Melt the butter in a medium-sized skillet over high heat. Tilt the pan so the butter covers its base and sides. When the foam has subsided and the butter is at the point of coloring, pour in the eggs. You should hear a loud hissing sound when the eggs hit the hot pan.

3. Let the eggs set for about 5 seconds, then with a wooden spoon pull the cooked eggs to one side of the pan and let the liquid eggs run through to form the bottom layer. Do this once more if you still have more liquid eggs. Remove the pan from the heat.

4. Fill the omelet with the herbs, and any cheese you might like. Using a plastic spatula and tilting one side of the pan toward a plate, fold the omelet so that it can roll onto the plate. The omelet should be a tiny bit browned, but it should not be heavily colored. (If you are making a second omelet, you can wipe the pan with a paper towel and begin again at step 1.)

ADDITIONAL SUMMER RECIPES

Lavender Floating Island

MAKES 10 SERVINGS

The Custard:

1 cup sugar

1 tablespoon fresh lavender flowers, plus more for garnish

4 cups whole milk

10 large egg yolks

The Meringue:

6 large egg whites

1 teaspoon cream of tartar

1½ cups confectioners' sugar

½ teaspoon vanilla extract

"Ambrosia" is what my father says when I make his favorite dessert for him: Floating Island. This is an old French recipe that makes imaginative use of milk, sugar, and eggs. I served this unconventional version, using Eva's lavender, for his eightieth birthday. He and the rest of our family ate every last drop.

1. To make the custard, bring the sugar, lavender flowers, and milk to a simmer in a medium saucepan over medium heat, without stirring. Cover the pan and keep the milk at a low simmer for about 10 minutes to infuse the lavender in the milk.

2. Whisk the yolks until they are blended, then very gradually whisk in the hot milk mixture. Return the mixture to the saucepan and cook over low heat, stirring constantly, until the sauce thickens enough to coat the back of a wooden spoon. This may take 10 to 15 minutes. If you push it and cook the mixture over too high of heat, you could scramble the eggs.

3. When the custard has thickened, immediately pour it through a fine sieve into a metal bowl, and place the bowl in the fridge. Stir it occasionally until it is cool, then cover the surface with a piece of wax paper to prevent a skin from forming. Chill the custard until it is cold.

4. To make the meringue, preheat the oven to 350 degrees F, leaving just one rack on the lower third of the oven. Butter a 10-cup nonstick fluted tube pan or soufflé mold (or, alternatively, a glass 9 by 13-inch brownie pan) and nest it inside a large roasting pan. Heat several cups of water in a teakettle or saucepan, and set it aside.

5. In the mixing bowl of an electric mixer, combine the egg whites with the cream of tartar and beat at a high speed until soft peaks form. Continue beating the egg whites at a lower speed and slowly add the sugar and vanilla. Beat until the whites are very stiff, about 2 minutes.

6. Spoon the meringue mixture into the prepared pan. Smooth the top of the meringue with a spatula. Place the nested pan on the rack of the oven and pour enough hot water into the roasting pan that it comes halfway up the outside of the custard pan.

7. Bake the meringue for 15 minutes. It will rise like a soufflé above the top of the pan. Remove the custard pan from the oven, leaving the water bath behind to cool. Allow the meringue to cool in its pan for 5 minutes, then remove from the pan. At this point, the meringue can be held for up to 3 hours.

8. To serve, set the meringue on a deep platter or glass bowl. Spoon the lavender custard around it. Sprinkle the floating island with lavender flowers.

Ratatouille Rebirth

Late one summer, searching the depths of the fridge for dinner, I found myself confronted by my own leftovers, a seven-day-old fennel ratatouille in the fridge that I had forgotten about until that very moment. It smelled fine, but my reflex was to toss it, not so much because it was old, but because I hated to waste my precious calorie intake on food that I had already eaten. But things are changing; I'm now haunted by Eva's anti-waste militancy. She can't throw out any food if there might be a speck of nutritive value to reap. Yes, she's frugal, but she also has a deep respect for what Mother Earth gives us. But did I really want to eat that elderly ratatouille? Would my cat eat it?

I went to bed with this question weighing on me, and I awoke with an idea. Piperade, a Basque specialty, had been one of my favorite dishes when I lived in France. It is usually composed of slow-cooked peppers and onions, which are set in a gratin dish, with eggs cracked over the top before the dish is baked.

I ran to the kitchen and put together a completely scrumptious (and cheap) meal of baked ratatouille topped with farm-fresh eggs, served with toast. It was delicious, and I could feel Eva was smiling upon me.

Eating Flowers

Plants have two main phases in their life cycle: their vegetative or leaf stage and their reproductive or flowering stage. Gardeners like to extend the leaf stage as long as possible, because when plants flower, they focus all their energy on reproducing and the leaves decline in flavor. At this point a gardener usually lets the plant go to seed, and oftentimes the flowers are neglected.

Flowers are rich with volatile oils, which gives them a lot of flavor but also a short shelf life, making it tricky to get them to market. Eva has succeeded in this highly risky area of specialty foods because she pays attention. She knows how to get flowers into her chefs' hands before they even have time to blink. Timing and care is everything; identifying and picking newly opened flowers is key. Flowers are powerful because they draw in the flavor from nearby leaves and manufacture nectar to attract pollinating animals. This is a heady combination for herb flowers especially, as they benefit from the sweetness that nectar offers as well as the volatile aromas and flavors of the herb. In July and August, Eva's flowers seem to having daylong cocktail parties with all kinds of busy buzzing winged creatures, with hummingbirds, pudgy bumblebees, hornets, wasps, bee flies, bluebirds, swallows, chipping and song sparrows, and robins imbibing to their heart's content.

Pick flowers on a dry day, as they don't last when moist or wet. Flowers are usually added right before the plate gets whisked to the diner, with a few exceptions. If you're adding them to a salad, do so after it's been dressed, or else the flowers will collapse.

Listed below are my top choices for edible flowers. Being a foodie, I've chosen these based on flavor, not looks. Almost all these flowers are beautiful, but they really kick butt in the culinary dimension. I'm really just skimming the surface here, since all herbs and most vegetables flower, and most make for a tasty addition on any plate or in any salad. (By the way, if I were going to choose based on looks alone, I'd choose calendula, ornamental alliums, tulips, and violas.)

- African blue basil flowers. These babies are loaded with flavor. Chefs often make infusions with them. Jay Murray of Grill 23 in Boston uses them in tomato salads, and he steams stone crabs, infusing them with African basil. Crabs, like clams, leach their juices while steaming and African basil lends its complex zesty flavor.
- Anise hyssop flowers. A profundity of purple flowers on a spike; Eva likens the flowers to bristles on a round hairbrush. These flowers are magnets for bees. Perfect in green salads and fruit salads.
- Arugula flowers. A handsome and righteous-tasting flower. Scatter on salads, soups, and other savory foods.
- Chive and garlic chive flowers. Chives sport a pinkish/purplish flower head, while garlic chives can have either pink or white flowers. Chive flowers are nice in herb butters, in salads, in omelets, atop creamed soups, or with soft cheeses. Garlic chive flowers are more intense and spice up stir-fries or salads.
- Daylily flowers. Shades of orange and yellow. Unopened, the buds are similar to zucchini in flavor and can be sauteed

in olive oil and garlic. Fully opened flowers can decorate cakes. Petals can be used like crackers as a platform for herbed goat cheese, or they can be floated on soup. Dried daylily flowers are a common ingredient in Chinese moo-shu and hot-and-sour soup. It's a good idea to eat daylilies in modest amounts at first, as about 5 percent of the population experiences digestive upset upon eating them.

· Lavender flowers. Strong fragrance and flavor. I mostly like to grab a few and put them in my pocket. Chefs have many uses for them. I use lavender in cream-based desserts like ice cream and Lavender Floating Island (page 206).

· Nasturtium flowers. Ablaze in orange, yellow, and red. A relative of watercress, and delivering that peppery sting even more. Nasturtiums can be used in salads as unopened buds or opened flowers; if the flowers are a bit too open, tear off petals to toss in the salad, or mash into an herb butter. Whole flowers can be stuffed with creamy goat's-milk or farmer's cheese. Or try them chopped and mixed with ricotta for summer lasagnas. They thrive in semi-neglected spots; if you feed them too much fertilizer, the flowers will diminish and the foliage will grow in abundance. (Nasturtium leaves are practically as good as the flowers. The sharp, peppery-tasting leaves are great to insert in sandwiches, wonderful as a "spring roll" wrapper for herbed cream cheese and the like, and fitting and progressive as greens in salads.)

· Pineapple sage flowers. These aromatic flowers resemble miniature dark crimson trumpets and taste like a tropical fruit. Every day new flowers bloom on their spikes. You'll get a month of blooming if you're lucky (by the way, the leaves are not so tasty, and don't taste like sage).

· Rose petals. See the rugosa rose profile (page 192). There are many uses for wild rose petals, including sorbet, ice cream, jam, and salads.

Peter's Tips For Snips

When it comes to snipping herbs, following some simple guidelines will help keep your herbs alive and productive. Peter Levasseur, herb snipper extraordinaire and head farmer at Eva's, has been harvesting herbs for ten years. I talked with him to get some tips for snipping.

- Herbs whose stems are woody, such as African basil, anise hyssop, lavender, lemon verbena, marjoram, oregano, rosemary, sage, savory, tarragon, and thyme, need to grow a bit and establish themselves before you begin harvesting them. Try to snip only feathery, nonwoody sprigs. The less you take off the better for the overall health of the plant, especially when it's young. The more you cut into the woody stem area, the greater the likelihood that growth will be terminated, or that the plant will take a lot longer to grow back. For lavender and rosemary, cut the central leader (the middle stem that grows higher than others) so that the plant grows outward, not upward. It is wise to stop harvesting from woody-stemmed herbs about a month before the first hard frost, because snipping can encourage tender growth that cannot harden off before winter arrives, and this may stunt future growth. Two exceptions: Tarragon can be cut all the way back before a frost. And savory is an annual and thus is killed by the cold, so harvest it completely before a frost.
- Tender herbaceous plants like chervil, chives, cilantro, lemon balm, lovage, and sorrel all have the same snipping rule at Eva's garden: once a plant grows to the most desirable size, it is cut to the ground. You don't need to cut new growth that is near the base. Nor do you have to be this extreme. You can snip however you like according to your needs, in which case the plant will continue to grow and eventually go to seed. But if you completely cut these plants down (leaving an inch or two of stem above the surface of the soil), they will grow back at least once, unless there is a frost. One exception: For parsley, once the stems are covered with leaves, harvest the outside stems and leave the crown (the central growth) intact. The central stems will continue to mature and move their way to the outside, at which point they can be cut and new stems will have popped up at the crown.
- After the summer solstice you can begin to snip all herbs more heavily; otherwise they will begin to flower. When herbs flower, pinch off the flowers to prevent the leaves from declining in flavor and texture. As an added bonus, most herb flowers are edible.
- Harvest on a dry day, after the morning dew has dried. It's best if the previous day was dry, not wet. Peter likes to quickly weed with his hands around the plant when he harvests: he sees it as quick maintenance, like making your bed every day or brushing your teeth.

preserving
and conserving

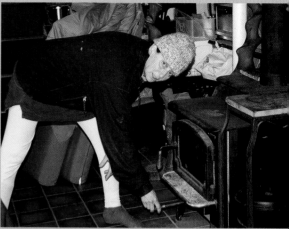

In fall food flows from Eva's garden with increasing momentum. Eva works overtime trying to harvest as much as possible before the first serious frost zaps it all. The increasingly cool weather intensifies and sharpens the flavor of many greens, and by mid-November the plant population has thinned. But there are still many treasures to be gleaned from the garden.

Some herbs, including burnet, chervil, cilantro, lovage, parcel, parsley, rosemary, sage, sorrel, and thyme, can withstand cold temperatures. It seems impossible that a lacy herb like chervil can survive even snow, and yet it does.

In the world of greens, chard, chicories, crucifers, certain lettuces, and spinach can handle the cool nights and even withstand a light frost. Look for them now at farmers' markets and take advantage of the natural sweetening that occurs in these and other crops as the chill settles in. Eva explains that many greens increase their simple sugars in cold weather, which act as a kind of antifreeze in stems and leaves, the flavor gaining in the process.

Outside the garden, there is much to forage during this season, especially autumn olives and wild grapes. And Eva puts food up between summer and winter whenever time avails her, as much for her own winter sustenance as for her dislike of food waste. Tomato water strained from bruised tomatoes, autumn olive fruit leather, sorbets and pureed fruit, stocks and soups—she preserves such foods with regularity, and they will help her get by until spring.

While the food gets preserved, energy conservation is being celebrated throughout this season. In this regard Eva surely must stand in the foremost ranks of the most devout energy-efficiency advocates on our planet. Of course she conserves energy year-round, but I have chosen to highlight some of her favorite tricks and techniques during this season,

perhaps because the fall seems so synonymous with the whole notion of preserving—including the desire to make energy last longer.

If you spend time with Eva in the fall, you'll hear her reciting an Emily Dickinson poem, one of Eva's fall favorites, again and again. The poem is about how Indian summer plays tricks on all of us, including the birds and the bees. Dickinson's knowledge of nature seems truly remarkable, because it's true—some birds actually reverse their migration if the weather is warm enough!

> These are the days when Birds come back—
> A very few—a Bird or two—
> To take a backward look.
>
> These are the days when skies resume
> The old—old sophistries of June—
> A blue and gold mistake.
>
> Oh fraud that cannot cheat the Bee—
> Almost thy plausibility
> Induces my belief.
>
> Till ranks of seeds their witness bear—
> And softly thro' the altered air
> Hurries a timid leaf.
>
> Oh Sacrament of summer days,
> Oh Last Communion in the Haze—
> Permit a child to join.
>
> Thy sacred emblems to partake—
> Thy consecrated bread to take
> And thine immortal wine!

RECIPES LIST

Autumn Olive

Autumn Olive Nectar and
  Puree
Russ Cohen's Autumn Olive
  Fruit Leather
Salad Dressing
Adult Autumn Olive Sorbet
Quick Yogurt Sorbet
Just Yogurt and Berries
Autumn Olive Jam
Crunchy Curried Millet with
  Winter Squash, Autumn
  Olives, Ghee, and Pecans
Eva's Sorbet
Autumn Olive Thumbprint
  Cookies

Cardoon

White Bean and Cardoon
  Minestrone
Cardoon and Potato Gratin

Chervil

Chervil-Almond Pesto
Bean-Vegetable Soup with
  Chervil and Tomato Water
Salad of Chervil, Apples,
  Walnuts, Quinoa, and
  Onion

Chickweed

Chickweed Cheddar Grilled
  Cheese Sandwich
Chickweed Apple Slaw with
  Ginger Dressing
Laryngitis Tea

Claytonia

End-of-Harvest Salad

Kale

Kale with Apples, Raisins,
  Feta, and Walnuts
Peter's Kale Salad
Linguine with Kale, Lemon,
  and Brown Butter
Quick-and-Dirty Preserved
  Lemons
Creamed Kale

Leeks

Cod Potato Leek Gratin
Leek Miso Soup
Leek Pie with a Millet Crust
Smashed Leeky Potatoes

Mustard Greens

Mustard Green, Potato, and
  Corn Soup
Pasta with Mustard Greens,
  Shredded Chicken, and
  Smokey Cream Sauce

Parsley

Fish with *Charmoula* Sauce
Victoria George's Tabbouleh
Preserved Lemon Tabbouleh

Sage

Spaghetti Squash with
  Lentils and Sage
Eva's Remarkable Cabbage
  Slaw No. 2
Grits with Sage and Cheddar
Café DiCocoa's Apricot Sage
  Cookies

Sunchokes

Sunchokes in Chicken Broth
Sunchoke Bisque
Sunchoke Dumplings with
  Swiss Chard and Walnuts
Roasted Sunchokes

Additional Fall
  Recipes

Lesli's Sweet Corn Pudding
Chipotle Apple Butter
Sweet Potato, Nut, and Fruit
  Biryani
Intensely Pumpkin Bread
  Pudding
Sharon Kane's Fermented
  Butternut Squash

Autumn Olive

Elaeagnus umbellata · PERENNIAL

One of the greatest gifts Eva has shared with me is her passion for autumn olives. Don't let the name mislead you. These shrubs grow berries, not olives. The name "autumn olive" was adopted because the leaves resembles olive leaves. The leaves have a silver sheen on their underside that creates a lustrous shimmer whenever the wind blows. The small red berries resemble currants but are a shade darker and not translucent. When you get really close you can observe tiny silver specks all over the berries, like they've been dusted with glitter. The berries appear in midfall and remain for six to eight weeks. Their flavor is a complex mix of tart and sweet, but it varies from bush to bush, and week to week, intensifying in sweetness steadily from October through November, and also after a few frosty nights.

Sam Thayer, one of our foremost authorities on foraging, writes on his website, Forager's Harvest (www.foragersharvest.com), "It truly baffles me how the autumn-olive remains one of the biggest wild food secrets in North America. Over vast regions of this continent, it is our most common wild fruit."

It didn't get to be so common through human effort. The shrub has the ability to "fix" nitrogen from the atmosphere—much like legumes do—nourishing both the plant and the soil it grows in. It is drought-tolerant and disease-resistant. Because of this, autumn olive shrubs have been widely planted in disturbed areas and along highways, where its spreading roots help prevent soil erosion. The shrubs also act as screens and noise barriers and provide cover and food for wildlife. What state planners did not take into account, however, was the shrubs' ability to outcompete native species and colonize infertile soils.

Nowadays it is illegal, in some states, to transplant or sell autumn olive shrubs because they are so invasive. They can threaten local ecosystems, outcompeting indigenous plants. Some localities have eradicated them, but Eva has assured me these tenacious shrubs will be impossible to obliterate completely.

Autumn olive was first cultivated in the United States in the 1800s, but it originated in China, Korea, and Japan. On the west coast of North America can be found a related species called Russian olive (*Elaeagnus angustifolia*), which produces yellow berries. My friend Russ Cohen, a well-known forager in New England, tells me that Russian olive berries are not quite as good for eating as those of the autumn olive.

CULINARY USES

In my humble opinion, the autumn olive's highest purpose is to sit atop a bowl of morning cereal. A handful of these berries boosts your nutrient intake and offers fruity enjoyment with your morning. In fact, I usually freeze a gallon or so of berries every fall for this very purpose.

Each berry contains a single seed, and for such tiny berries, the seeds are surprisingly large. Still, they almost never bother me. They are pleasantly chewy and merrily float down my digestive tract along with the fruit. But, if you prefer, you can remove the seeds by running the berries through a food mill.

The berry is tart and acidic, so it works well in both desserts and savory dishes. I can't say I've ever tasted better sorbet than Eva's made from autumn olive. To this end, cooks the berries to separate the "nectar" from the pulp. She freezes the pureed pulp in quart containers and cans the nectar in glass jars that she keeps in her pantry. To make sorbet, she combines frozen berry puree with the nectar, along with some kind of fabulous accent like frozen rose petals, raspberries, strawberries, knotweed puree, pears, or a liqueur, all of which she purees in her Vitamix blender. These sorbets can range from simply delightful to mind-blowing. It's hard to imagine a healthier dessert, and you don't leave the table feeling weighed down. There are many sorbet recipes in this book that call for the autumn olive nectar and puree.

I make a simple and tart autumn olive jam. It's an exquisite preserve that people don't forget, and it is great on toast, with venison, or added to yogurt. Then there is Russ Cohen's autumn olive fruit leather, which alone makes buying a dehydrator worth it. The chefs at No. 9 Park in Boston make jellied candy with these berries (don't ask me how), and they also make an autumn olive syrup for cocktails.

Chefs around town like to offset the berries against meat or game. Adam Halberg of Barcelona restaurants in Connecticut says that the berries' tannin structure complements meat. He serves an Umbrian duck with lentils sauced with the autumn olive juice, red wine, and verjus, garnishing it with fresh berries. Keith Pooler of Bergamot in Somerville, Massachusetts, serves autumn olives with pork shoulder. He also makes a caramel sauce from the berries, red wine vinegar, and pork jus and serves it with roasted local turnips.

Health Virtues

No wonder Eva has so much energy. These berries are crammed with nutrients. When I find a grove of autumn olive shrubs with branches so loaded with fruit that they droop,

I imagine this berry solving the world's malnutrition problem. Each glittering red fruit contains about eighteen times as much lycopene as a tomato, and the lycopene content is only increased by cooking. Yet these berries go largely uneaten, perhaps because they don't come packaged and have no marketing budget.

Foraging and Storing

Look for autumn olive shrubs along roads, in parking lots, or in fields. They are usually about 8 feet tall but can grow to almost twice that, and the thin green leaves shimmer in the breeze, like a school of silver fish swimming upstream to spawn. This treelike shrub grows wild in most states. When you see one shrub, undoubtedly others will be nearby. Luckily for me, there are thousands where I live in Massachusetts.

If you find a tree flush with berries, you can pick 3 or 4 gallons of berries in less than an hour by stroking the berries off the branches into a tub. There are probably all sorts of high-tech ways to maximize your efficiency. Eva picks by cutting off choice loaded branches with pruning shears into a bin, and she strips them at home. This method seems to benefit the shrub.

If you want to nibble on fresh berries, they store best when kept on the branch in the refrigerator or an equally cool spot. In the fall the multipurpose table in Eva's house always sports a branch or two for drive-by nibbling. As I mentioned earlier, I like to save some autumn olives for the rest of the year by taking them off the branches and freezing them in ziplock bags. I add them daily to my granola, improving its taste and hoping to increase my days on this planet.

Autumn Olive Nectar and Puree

Every fall Eva makes her sacred autumn olive nectar and puree, which she uses as a base for her sorbets and fruit leathers all year long. When the autumn olives are cooked, the berries fall to the bottom and a milky, pinkish liquid that we call "nectar" floats to the top. Eva treats this nectar like liquid gold. It is sweet, tart, and so fruity, almost like a fine *moscato* wine. She preserves the nectar in jars for use as a sweetener throughout the winter. You need a significant amount of autumn olive berries—at least a gallon (which shouldn't be difficult if you can find a single shrub)—to make this process worthwhile, but the end product is divine, healthful, and useful to have on hand for an easy, unusual dessert.

Autumn olives, rinsed well

To can the nectar, you'll need to have a supply of clean, sterilized glass canning jars with lids, and you'll process them in a boiling water bath. To puree the pulp, you'll need a Squeezo strainer, a food mill, a juicer, or a standing conical strainer (and pestle).

1. To make the nectar, place the autumn olives in a large, heavy-bottomed stockpot over low heat. Mash the berries continuously with a potato masher as they begin to cook; if you don't, they will likely burn. Keep mashing until you see the liquid start to simmer. Let simmer 2 to 3 minutes—just long enough to break the cell walls. Then turn the heat off and let the berries sit, covered, overnight.

2. Line a strainer or colander with a layer of cheesecloth or other porous cloth, and set over a large, clean bowl. Scoop the berries into the strainer and let drain; the liquid that passes through is the nectar. Press the berries to squeeze out all the nectar. Set the mashed berries aside to make the puree. (The mass of mashed berries is easier to work with if it's still warm, but it can be stored in a sealed container in the fridge for up to 2 weeks, if necessary.)

3. Ladle the nectar into clean, sterilized glass jars and seal. Following any trustworthy general directions for canning, process the jars in a boiling water bath.

4. To make the puree, pass the berry pulp through a food mill or other extractor. Freeze the resulting puree for future use in fruit leathers or sorbets.

Russ Cohen's Autumn Olive Fruit Leather

1 gallon or more autumn olives

Forager, environmentalist, and teacher Russ Cohen doles out a little fruit leather to his students before they begin a foraging tour. Everyone marvels at the sweet flavor, including me! To make this leather it's helpful to have a dehydrator, but you can also make it on top of a woodstove or in an oven warmed by the pilot light. (Traditionally, of course, fruit is dehydrated by the sun.) Russ sees this leather as the best way to use autumn olive berries, which are quite tart when fresh, because the drying process concentrates the sugars, so much so that he need not add sugar. Which is unusual, Russ says, since he's found that he generally needs to add at least a little sugar to all leathers, even wild grape leather.

1. Place the berries in a large, heavy-bottomed pot. Add water to a depth of approximately ⅛ inch in the pot, to prevent the fruit from scorching. Heat to a low simmer, and let simmer (no boiling) for 30 minutes, stirring occasionally.
2. Run the cooked fruit through a food mill. Then pass it through a sieve to get a very thick, tomato-sauce-like consistency. The pulp that's left behind in the sieve is not a waste product—save it and add it to your morning cereal!
3. Line the trays of a dehydrator with the fruit roll sheet accessory or parchment paper. Pour the fruit puree into a gravy boat or an old soy milk carton. Drizzle the puree onto the prepared trays in the thinnest layer possible.
4. Dry the fruit leather at 135 degrees F, or according to the dehydrator manufacturer's instructions, for 12 hours. Rotate the trays and dry for another 12 hours.
5. Cut the leather into strips and store in ziplock bags; they'll keep indefinitely.

Sustaining the Fish

Alan Poole, Eva's friend and neighbor and a noted ornithologist at Cornell University, enjoys fishing local waters. He kindly contributed this information on sustainable seafood.

The locavore who enjoys cooking fish and wants to eat sustainably has fewer and fewer choices these days. Fortunately, there are websites to help guide you, at least broadly; the Seafood Watch program at the Monterey Bay Aquarium in California has a particularly good one: www.montereybayaquarium.org/cr/seafoodwatch.aspx.

But nothing substitutes for local knowledge, and for some basic ecological thinking, when it comes to choosing seafood. For instance, eating low on the food chain generally makes more sense than eating high. Take swordfish—top predators in the sea, they are the ecological equivalent of tigers in the jungle; it takes hundreds of pounds of smaller fish to make a pound of swordfish. Sardines, by comparison, are "grazers" on ocean plankton, very low on the food chain. As a result sardines are "closer to the sun" (ecologically), vastly more numerous, and, not surprisingly, a lot healthier to eat. Swordfish, living off all those smaller fish, tend to accumulate heavy metals and other contaminants (for this reason pregnant women, for example, are advised *not* to eat swordfish). So the cook with health and sustainability on her mind will tend to reach for smaller fish, making those big predators an exception rather than the rule on her table.

Eating low isn't always the solution, however. Shrimp, like sardines, are small grazers, but the fisheries that target them end up catching a *lot* of other critters as well, including larval fish and shellfish. These critters get tossed, dead; the shrimp are kept for market. So, when it comes to choosing seafood, knowing how fish are harvested is as important as who they are and what they eat.

Along the coast of southern New England, where I live, some seafood stands out for sustainability and value and taste. Here are a few examples:

- Lobster tops the list; who doesn't like lobsters, and what creative cook can't find interesting things to do with them? It's a huge fishery and generally well managed, with stringent restrictions on size and numbers taken.
- Bay scallops, a true southern New England specialty, are expensive, found in just a few locales now, nutty in taste, and really the champagne of seafood (maybe more like a good sherry). Because they're taken by small boats in shallow waters, the impact of this fishery on local ecology is minimal. Small amounts cooked with other fish will flavor the whole dish—a good way to stretch your scallop dollars.
- Striped bass and bluefish are summer and fall favorites, found in markets throughout New England. Although predators and sometimes large, they're taken by rod and reel and so generally are not overharvested. Here again the big predator "rule" is worth keeping in mind: not too much. Both species harbor contaminants, especially the bigger fish, so save these for the occasional treat. And use the *whole* fish; the carcasses make wonderful soup stock.

Why does this all matter? The Seafood Watch website answers this question well: "There are only so many fish in the sea; the choices we make today will determine the fate of tomorrow's ocean wildlife."

Autumn Olive Jam

MAKES SIX 8-OUNCE JARS

9–10 cups autumn olive
  berries

3 cups sugar

1 package SureJell pectin
  or Pomona's Universal
  Pectin for low- or
  no-sugar jellies

It is hard to improve on plain autumn olive jam. I've tried adding spices and blending the autumn olives with wild grapes, but I have not been able to improve on the straight stuff. Try it on toast, on a scone, with soft goat cheese on crackers, or on grilled meats. Or just make yourself a peanut butter and autumn olive jam sandwich.

You'll need six 8-ounce jelly jars, with lids and rings, and they'll need to be sterilized before you get started. Sterilize the jars in the canning kettle. You have to bring the water to a boil beforehand anyway, and you can just drop the jars in for 5 minutes but you'll need jar or grilling tongs to pull them out. Or you can wash them by hand and then put them in a 325-degree oven for at least 25 minutes.

1. Crush the autumn olives in a food processor by pulsing it a few times.

2. Transfer the crushed berries to a heavy pot. Very slowly heat the berries, bringing them just to the boiling point, and then remove from the heat.

3. Run the berries through a food mill or conical strainer to extract the juice and pulp. You should end up with about 5 cups autumn olive puree.

4. Fill a jam kettle fit with a canning rack inside with water about half full and bring it to a boil.

5. Mix three-quarters of the pectin in a small bowl with ¼ cup of the sugar. Reserve the rest of the pectin. Place a metal spoon in a glass of ice water.

6. Transfer the autumn olive puree to a large stockpot. Sprinkle the pectin and sugar mixture over it and whisk well. Bring the puree to a boil over medium heat, while whisking constantly. You must continually stir the berries or they will burn. It should take about 5 to 10 minutes to bring the puree to a boil. Boil for 1 minute, then whisk in the remaining 2¾ cups sugar and boil hard for 1 minute, whisking constantly. Remove the jam from the heat.

7. Using the spoon that's been sitting in ice water, take half a spoonful of jam from the pot and let it cool to room temperature. If it thickens up the way you like it, then you're done. If it's too loose for your liking, mix more pectin with a bit of sugar and add to the puree, boiling the contents for 1 more minute, while constantly whisking. Continue to add pectin-sugar mix until the jam reaches the desired consistency.

8. Using a ladle, fill the jars with the jam, leaving ¼ inch of headspace at the top of each jar. Put a lid on each jar, securing it with a lid ring. Use tongs to transfer the jars to a large canning kettle. The jars should be covered by at least 1 inch of water in the kettle. Bring the canning kettle to a simmer and boil the jars for at least 5 minutes to ensure a good seal.

9. Carefully remove the jars from the water with the jar tongs, and set them on a kitchen towel to cool. Check to see if the jars have been sealed properly; the center of the lid should have been sucked down. Properly sealed jam will keep for 12 months, unrefrigerated. Once a jar has been opened, it should be refrigerated, as should any jar of jam that has not sealed properly.

Crunchy Curried Millet with Winter Squash, Autumn Olives, Ghee, and Pecans

MAKES 6 SERVINGS

2 cups millet

1 medium butternut squash (about 2½ pounds), peeled and thinly sliced

1 onion, thinly sliced

1 garlic clove, minced

1 tablespoon curry powder

1 tablespoon extra-virgin olive oil

Salt and freshly cracked pepper

8 tablespoons (1 stick) butter

⅔ cup autumn olives or chopped fresh cranberries

½ cup pecan pieces, toasted, or shaved almonds

2 tablespoons minced cilantro (leaves and stems)

Why isn't millet more popular? Do people still think of millet as bird feed? Why does it lack the cachet of quinoa? Millet is very healthy and much less expensive than quinoa. And it's Eva's favorite grain. It develops a delightfully crunchy crust when left to sit in a pan with a bit of butter or extra-virgin olive oil over steady low heat, something quinoa can't do to save itself. Look for it in the bulk food section at natural foods stores.

1. Preheat the oven to 400 degrees F.

2. Bring 4 cups salted water to a boil in a medium saucepot. Add the millet, turn the heat to the lowest setting, cover, and let simmer for 20 minutes. Remove from the heat, stir the millet, and let it cool, uncovered, for 20 minutes or so.

3. Meanwhile, toss the squash with the onion, garlic, curry powder, and olive oil, and season generously with salt and freshly cracked black pepper. Spread the mixture on a rimmed baking sheet in a single layer. Bake for about 25 minutes, until the squash is tender and darkens at its edges.

4. Clarify the butter by melting it in a small saucepan over medium-low heat. After the butter melts, skim the foam from the surface and discard, then ladle the yellow clarified butter from the pan into a bowl, leaving behind the milk solids.

5. Heat the clarified butter in a cast-iron or any well-seasoned skillet over medium heat. Add the cooked millet, patting it down, and let it cook, undisturbed, until it forms a golden brown crust, about 5 minutes. Break up the millet with a spatula. Add the roasted squash mixture and cook for 10 minutes, stirring just every 5 minutes or so to allow the millet to continue to develop a crust.

6. Stir in the berries, pecans, and cilantro. Taste and adjust for seasoning and serve.

Note: To toast the pecans, roast in a 350-degree oven on a rimmed baking sheet for about 5 minutes, until they are golden brown.

Eva's Sorbet

It takes Eva all of three minutes to whip up one of her outrageously delicious sorbets after dinner. How does she do it? Well, in the fall she makes lots of autumn olive puree, and in the spring knotweed puree, and she freezes both in quart containers. She lets one or the other sit out as we're eating dinner, a half hour perhaps, so they partially thaw; then she can pry out what she needs with a spoon, returning the rest to the freezer. She puts the scooped-out puree in her Vitamix and adds rose petals that have been tossed in lemon juice and frozen in ziplock bags. Her sorbets often also include blueberries, currants, raspberries, strawberries, and wineberries, which she grows herself and freezes. She adds a spoonful of maple syrup, honey, or a sweet liqueur to taste, and purees the mixture. No matter how harsh and cold the winter is, Eva's sorbet always does the job.

Autumn Olive Thumbprint Cookies

MAKES 32 COOKIES

12 ounces (3 sticks)
    unsalted butter

²/₃ cup sugar

2 cups flour

½ teaspoon salt

Autumn olive jam (page
    220) or your favorite jam

This cookie is ridiculously good. It comes from Maura Kilpatrick, pastry chef at Sofra bakery in Cambridge, Massachusetts, who turned a recipe for Syrian-style shortbread into a thumbprint cookie. Clarifying the butter creates an irresistible sandy texture and a nutty flavor. Autumn olive jam is the ultimate for this cookie, which is my suggestion (Maura asks for raspberry jam). You can use any good-quality jam that's not terribly sweet. This is not a quick cookie—it takes a couple of hours to make, but much of it is idle time, during which you can be doing something else.

1. Clarify the butter. You can do this in the microwave: In a microwave-safe bowl, melt the butter on high, uncovered, for about 2 minutes, or until the milk solids have separated from the butterfat. Do not stir. Skim off the white foam on top, then ladle the yellow clarified butter from the bowl, leaving the milk solids at the bottom.

    You can also clarify butter on the stovetop: Melt the butter in a medium saucepan over medium heat. After the butter melts, skim the foam off the top and discard, then ladle the yellow clarified butter from the pan to a bowl, leaving the milk solids at the bottom.

2. In the bowl of an electric mixer, whisk together the clarified butter and sugar. Refrigerate until firm, at least 45 minutes.

3. Beat the chilled butter and sugar mixture until very light and fluffy, about 4 to 5 minutes. Add the flour and salt and mix until smooth.

4. Use a rubber spatula to form the dough into a ball. Cover the dough with plastic wrap and chill for 30 minutes to firm slightly. (If chilled longer, it will need to sit at room temperature for an hour or two to soften for shaping.)

5. Preheat the oven to 300 degrees F. Line a large cookie sheet with parchment paper.

6. Once the dough is chilled, pinch off tablespoon-size pieces and roll them into 1-inch balls, placing them about 2 inches apart on the prepared sheet. Make a small but fairly deep indentation in each cookie using the rounded end of a wooden spoon or your thumb. Fill each indentation with about ½ teaspoon jam.

7. Bake the cookies for 23 minutes, or until they are just slightly golden (halfway through, you may want to rotate the baking sheet).

8. Carefully slide the parchment paper, with the cookies on it, off the cookie sheet and onto a wire rack. Cool the cookies completely before removing from the parchment paper. (Crumbs will stick to your fingers unless the cookies are thoroughly cooled.) Store the cookies, layered between sheets of waxed paper, in a tightly sealed container for up to 5 days.

Eva's Dream Wedding

Actually, it wasn't the wedding ceremony itself that was dreamy, but the wedding reception for her son and his new wife. Two-hundred-plus guests feasted on local organic foods, dining off biodegradable plates with biodegradable utensils. Leftovers were split between the pigs next door and Eva's freezer. Eva's greatest prize of the evening (second, it is assumed, to her new daughter-in-law) was a single white trash bag, which was all that was needed to hold the uncompostable, unrecyclable "waste" for the entire event.

Cardoon

Cynara cardunculus · TENDER PERENNIAL

I was in Turin, Italy, in the fall of 2002, when I ate my first cardoon. I was attending Slow Food's "Salone del Gusto," a five-day food expo that flaunts the crown jewels of the country's many artisan foods. Held in a renovated and repurposed Fiat factory that's roughly the size of a small town, the expo was a gustatory magnet, bringing together foodies from all continents. Food stalls lined both sides of makeshift aisles, and you could graze on dozens of aged cheeses, wines, piles of olives, olive oils, cured meats, and, best of all, dark chocolates. From my cheap hotel room nearby, I could see the Alps in the distance, looking like a thin streak of saber-toothed clouds nestled in valleys a hundred miles away. I imagined what life must be like for people who live in these mountains. As a small substitute for traveling there in person, I took a class offered by Slow Food about the cheeses made in the Alps.

The class cost me the equivalent of $5, so I did not expect much. But we were met by a squadron of waiters who descended on us every ten minutes, each time bearing a new Alpine cheese and an accompanying Alpine wine. One dish presented there still rests in my heart: braised cardoon with cheese fondue. The cardoon had been slow-cooked, and it tasted like sweet artichoke pudding. The fondue was drizzled on top like a wedding ribbon, and its base was a creamy Reblochon cheese, a perfect counterpoint. The class was the deal of a lifetime and had me floating on my own little Alp. It tempted me to buy property near the Alps, so that I could have easy access to cardoons, Reblochon, and those gorgeous mountains. Unfortunately, not everything in life comes as cheap as that class.

Culinary Uses

These days cardoons are beginning to appear in Italian specialty markets as well as some farmers' markets in the United States. Cardoons taste very similar to globe artichokes, and indeed they are close relatives, both being members of the thistle group in the aster family—although you eat the rib of the cardoon plant and the buds of the artichoke plant. At the market cardoons look like overweight celery, but with jagged edges and leaves running up each rib. Thankfully, there is much less labor involved in eating a cardoon than in eating an artichoke. It is worlds easier than scraping a scant amount of meat off each artichoke petal with your teeth, or excavating the hairy parts of the artichoke heart, just to get a bite or two of the tender delicacy.

Aside from melting some pricey Reblochon cheese into rich alpine cream, what's the best way to enjoy a cardoon? A simple braising is a good place to start. Braising means searing the vegetable in fat, then adding a liquid, usually water, wine, or stock, to steam it. (I don't cover the pan so I can see what's going on, but Eva would to save energy.) Cardoons can take anywhere from ten to thirty minutes to soften, depending on the size and freshness.

Once braised, the cooked cardoon is then poised for further treatment. The simplest way to enjoy it is to drizzle a little good-quality olive oil on it, a squeeze of lemon, and a bit of salt and freshly cracked pepper. But farmhand Bill Braun makes a terrific and unorthodox "pesto" in the processor with braised cardoons, lemon juice, lemon zest, parsley, fresh garlic, and olive oil. He eats this with quinoa penne, topped with Romano cheese. Braised cardoons are also wonderful in risotto.

Raw cardoons can be added to soups, or they can be blanched and added to gratins, as in the recipe for Cardoon and Potato Gratin (page 229). Try steamed cardoons with a grated hard-boiled egg and Caesar or anchovy-lemon dressing. Like any delicious vegetable, there are a thousand ways to prepare them.

Health Virtues

Cardoons have been cultivated for three thousand years for their edible ribs, but only recently have we begun to see this wild plant as a medicinal herb. Researchers recently discovered that the leaves contain a bitter compound, called cynarin, that supports liver health and lowers cholesterol. If you eat just the ribs, like me, you will be getting a healthy dose of important vitamins and minerals; they are high in vitamin B_6, folate, and calcium for starters, in addition to containing vitamin C and iron. And, as revealed by their rigid structure, the ribs are loaded with dietary fiber.

Buying, Storing, and Prepping

As mentioned earlier, cardoons can be found at some Italian markets and farmers' markets. Of course, growing them increases their availability (see below).

You can store cardoon ribs in the fridge for a few days; just trim the leaves off beforehand. When you are ready to use them, use a paring knife to remove the fibers that run lengthwise, like those in celery ribs. Hollow outer ribs should be avoided, as they are tough. If you want to preserve your cardoons, you can freeze them after they have been cooked down. If you've braised your cardoons, freeze the broth for use in enhancing an endless variety of soups during the winter months.

Growing Cardoons

You have to coax out this plant's sweet side as it grows, since its first line of defense against the natural world is to grow bitter and tough. But if you are up for the challenge, I recommend making room for this plant in your garden. If all else fails, you can spruce up your living room with the pretty purple thistles and funky leaves.

Sow seeds ¼ inch deep indoors six weeks before the last frost date, and transplant to a sunny spot in the garden about two weeks after any threat of frost, spacing plants 3 to 4 feet apart. (If your winters are mild, sow seeds directly into the ground in the fall and watch for germination the following spring.)

Once your cardoons are growing, keep the soil moist, but not soaked. Cardoons will grow 3 to 7 feet high and produce stunning purple thistles, which should be cut before the seeds have a chance to infiltrate your garden. If you plan on eating the ribs, start blanching them (protecting them from sunlight) when they are knee-high by wrapping them in newspaper or burlap and tying with twine, or by hilling up soil around them, to prevent photosynthesis and maximize sugar production. After three to four weeks of blanching, harvest the ribs by cutting the ribs just below the soil surface. If your winter is mild, the plant will survive as a perennial and will grow new leaves the following spring.

White Bean and Cardoon Minestrone

MAKES 6 SERVINGS

1 cup dried white beans, soaked in cold water overnight

2 tablespoons extra-virgin olive oil, plus more for drizzling

1 yellow onion, finely chopped

3 cloves garlic, minced

2 baby fennel or 1 medium fennel bulb, finely chopped

1 red bell pepper, finely chopped

2 or 3 cardoon stalks

1 rounded teaspoon chopped rosemary, lemon thyme, or thyme

6 cups chopped greens (one or more of arugula, chard, collards, kale, mustard greens, and spinach)

1 teaspoon salt

¼ cup lemon juice (about 1 lemon)

Salt

Freshly cracked black pepper

Grated Parmesan

There is loads of wiggle room in this soup. No cardoons? Chop up another bulb of fennel. Don't like fennel? Trade it for another vegetable like cabbage, carrots, or even chopped Brussels sprouts. Prefer leeks to onions? Fine. No fresh herbs? Dried herbs will work (just halve the amounts). When I made this soup, I simply used the vegetables and herbs Eva had on hand.

1. Drain and rinse the beans. Bring the beans and 8 cups water to a boil in a pot, then reduce the heat and let the beans simmer, partially covered, for at least 1 hour, or until soft. Then strain and rinse well.

2. Heat 2 tablespoons of the olive oil in a heavy-bottomed stockpot over medium heat. Add the onion and garlic and cook, stirring often, until the onions begin to soften, about 5 minutes. Stir in the fennel and red pepper and remove from the heat.

3. To prepare the cardoons, cut off and discard any leaves that are still attached to the cardoon stalks. Cut the stalks into thirds, so they will be easier to work with. Using a paring knife or vegetable peeler, peel the convex side of the stalks, which is stringy and slightly bitter. Thinly slice the stalks and add them to the stockpot.

4. Add 6 cups water to the stockpot, along with the rosemary. Bring the contents to a boil, then reduce the heat to medium-low and let the soup simmer until the vegetables are tender, about 30 minutes. Add the greens, salt, and the cooked beans and simmer another 3 minutes.

5. Stir the lemon juice into the soup. Season to taste with more salt if necessary and freshly cracked black pepper. Serve the soup drizzled with a good extra-virgin olive oil and topped with a bit of grated Parmesan.

Cardoon and Potato Gratin

This recipe is adapted from Jen Carlile, who lives in California and writes a sweet blog called Modern Beet. I've added garlic to her rendition, and I offer up sunchokes as an alternative for the 98 percent of us who won't be growing cardoons. Serve this with a big salad and crusty bread.

MAKES 4 TO 6 SERVINGS

2 or 3 cardoon stalks or 10 sunchokes (about 1 pound)

3 garlic cloves, finely chopped

2 cups half-and-half

2 medium-large yellow potatoes (about 1 pound)

1¼ cups loosely packed grated hard, salty cheese, divided (such as Pecorino, Manchego, Gruyère, Appenzeller, Parmesan, or Comté)

Salt and freshly cracked black pepper

1. Preheat the oven to 425 degrees F.
2. To prepare the cardoons, cut off and discard any leaves that are still attached to the cardoon stalks. Cut the stalks into thirds, so they will be easier to work with. Using a paring knife or vegetable peeler, peel the convex side of the stalks, which is stringy and slightly bitter. Cut the cardoons into ¼-inch-thick slices. You should end up with about 6 cups.
3. Blanch the cardoon stalks (if using sunchokes, omit this step) in a large pot of boiling water with a pinch of baking soda. Cook until they are tender, about 10 to 15 minutes.
4. Meanwhile, bring the half-and-half and garlic to a simmer in a small pot, and let simmer over low heat for 5 minutes. Remove from the heat.
5. To assemble the gratin, peel the potatoes and cut them into matchstick pieces, about 1 inch long and ¼ inch wide (though there's no need to be too exact). Distribute the potatoes in a casserole dish, followed by two-thirds of the cheese and the cardoons. Season with salt and a generous amount of freshly cracked black pepper.
6. Pour the half-and-half mixture over the casserole until it comes a little over halfway up the sides of the vegetables (you may not use all 2 cups of it). Sprinkle the remaining cheese over the top.
7. Bake the gratin for about 40 minutes, until the potatoes are cooked through and the top is nicely browned. Remove from the oven and allow to cool for about 5 minutes before serving.

Chervil

Anthriscus cerefolium · ANNUAL

After battling the city traffic, I like to walk through Eva's garden when I first arrive and snatch chervil from the ground. That exquisite first bite melts away all the road rage I am harboring. Perhaps Mother Nature had stress relief in mind when she created this herb. Its diminutive lacelike leaves and docile flavors of anise, citrus, and honey allow for easy eating, so you can munch to your heart's delight. Its flavor is complex and full, perfectly seasoned—no salt or pepper needed here. Unlike most herbs, you can eat a lot of chervil all by itself; it doesn't overwhelm the tongue.

Chervil is native to southern Russia. The mighty Romans helped move this dainty herb to western Europe. Like carrots and parsley, it belongs to the umbel family (named after the flower cluster of these plants, which resembles an umbrella). To my dismay, we produce very little chervil commercially in the United States, although California has recently begun cultivating it. In New England it is rarely sold in supermarkets. It is a vicious cycle: writers don't call for it in cookbooks or magazines because it is not readily available; consumers don't demand it because it's not in recipes. This is yet another case of herb stagnation without due representation!

Culinary Uses

Eva says that chervil is known as the herb for "all things fish," but she has shown me that chervil's versatility extends far beyond the sea. Both of us strongly believe in eating chervil raw, and we eat it mainly in salads, usually combined with a variety of lettuces and other herbs like mint. In general I never take a knife to chervil, mainly because it is tender and mild enough that you can eat the whole sprig. I like to add chervil to breakfast eggs, potato salads, and pasta dishes. Many chefs toss chervil in a light vinaigrette, then rest it atop a dish—for example, on a pizza with some fromage blanc or creamy goat cheese, caramelized onions, and roasted quince, or on a simply poached sea bass. Its flavor, unlike that of many herbs, can be easily drowned out, so chervil should steer clear of pungent foods like red sauces, soy sauce, bacon, pungent cheeses, and anything else that could overwhelm its delicate nature.

Chervil blends flawlessly with many herbs, including basil, cilantro, and parsley. It is one of the herbs in the French *fines herbes*, which is a combination of fresh chervil, chives, parsley, and tarragon. Try lining the inside of an omelet with *fines herbes*.

Though Eva and I prefer it raw, the French like to cook with chervil, adding it to fish, chicken, and egg dishes. To my tongue, which is decidedly not French, it is a shame to cook with chervil because the herb's sweet, vivid anise flavor gets woefully dulled.

Health Virtues

Chervil is considered a diuretic, expectorant, and stimulant. Made into a tea, it is said to aid in digestion. Folklore has it that chervil makes one merry, sharpens the wit, and bestows youth upon the aged. I agree that it can make one merry, but as for the other two claims, I myself have seen little to no improvement.

Buying, Storing, and Prepping

You can sometimes find chervil for sale at greengrocers in large cities and on the West Coast. Despite its fragile appearance, it keeps well. It has a shorter shelf life than most herbs but will hold its flavor for ten days in the

Preserving the Garden "Orphans": Tomato Water

When the weather grows cold and the tomato fields have long been harvested, there is nothing but a smattering of red orbs left to rot on the ground. These were fruits with poor timing. Not quite ripe enough for picking at the final harvest, they fell to the earth with a thud a couple of weeks later and were left behind, forlorn and neglected. I know of only one woman who will come to their rescue. Yes, Eva saves countless rotting tomatoes each fall, not only from her own garden but from others' gardens as well. At age seventy, Eva still crawls on her hands and knees among the almost forgotten tomatoes on a cold rainy Sunday, salvaging the wreckage.

Her goal is not canning whole tomatoes or making tomato sauce, both of which would be difficult with these badly bruised fruits. Instead she extracts the tomatoes' liquid essence, a sweet, clear golden juice referred to as "tomato water." Eva values tomato water the way most people cherish their high-definition TVs.

Tomato water works like an instant vegetable Prozac, making soups and stews sweeter and more enjoyable. It is far better than any stock I've ever used. And drinking the tomato water chilled and straight up is refreshing and divine.

How to Make Tomato Water

Cut eight or more round tomatoes into big chunks (they won't cook properly if you use fewer than eight). Cut out any rotted areas, then heat them in a heavy pot with *no* water. Let them cook only until they soften and their juices have been unleashed, about ten minutes. Then pass the tomatoes through a fine-meshed chinois or a strainer lined with cheesecloth, using the back of a ladle or spoon to help move things along. Eva cans her tomato water, usually in pint containers. Follow your manufacturer's directions for safely canning a liquid that is akin to water in its density. You could also freeze tomato water in plastic containers just as successfully. (I use quart-sized recycled yogurt containers.)

Finding Tomatoes for Tomato Water

Vendors at your local farmers' market are the best source for tomato-water tomatoes, unless you grow legions of tomatoes yourself. Ask them if they'd be willing to sell you a case or two of tomatoes they find bruised, imperfect, banged up or on the ground—when the season is ending. You should expect to pay much less for these tomatoes, but they do have to go to the trouble to collect them. You may have to buy a nice big stockpot, perhaps at a restaurant supply store, or perhaps you have two smaller ones.

fridge, stored unwashed in a plastic bag. If the stems are tough, you can either mince them or save them for a broth or stock.

Growing Chervil

If you grow only a handful of plants, make low-maintenance chervil one of them. If you purchase your chervil seed from Fedco, you may be planting seeds that Eva sold to the company straight from her own garden.

You can sow chervil indoors in late winter and transplant it outdoors in the spring, or sow it directly outdoors in mid- to late summer and early fall (it will likely bolt if grown during hot weather). Find a spot that gets full or partial sun and scatter the seeds thickly. Water liberally, and harvest when the leaves fill out, approximately two months after sowing. No matter when you plant chervil, it will always go to flower and then to seed in late spring. Eva collects the mature seed in July to sow again in August or September for a succession crop. Despite its dainty appearance, chervil thrives in Eva's unheated greenhouses through the cold and dreary New England winters.

Chervil-Almond Pesto

Besides the usual pasta treatment, I enjoy this pesto tossed with baked spaghetti squash (for the baking directions see the Spaghetti Squash with Lentils and Sage recipe on page 271). I also like it in a hard-boiled egg and potato salad—just thin the pesto with some vinegar and toss in some chopped cucumber and baby greens for a late lunch.

Pulverize the almonds and garlic in a food processor. Add the chervil and pulse until finely chopped. Add the oil in four increments, pulsing for a few seconds after each addition. Season the pesto with the salt and freshly cracked black pepper to taste. Store in a tightly sealed container in the fridge for up to one week, or in the freezer for up to 6 months.

MAKES APPROXIMATELY 1 CUP

¼ cup slivered almonds

5 garlic cloves

3 cups loosely packed chervil leaves

½ cup extra-virgin olive oil

½ teaspoon salt

Freshly cracked black pepper

Preserving Smoke (Tasting a Log)

I once knew a chef who added liquid smoke to her black beans. While I absolutely loved them, I felt an almost illicit thrill because I thought that "liquid smoke" was an artificial flavor, and, even if it were naturally made, the beans hadn't really been "smoked." It was so delicious, though, that I began to use liquid smoke myself, adding it to a vegetarian collard green recipe I used at a restaurant.

One winter day I cracked open the door to Eva's woodstove, to see if it needed another log. Some liquid was bubbling up on the log. Doing what any curious chef would do, I poked my finger in the woodstove, scooped up a drop or two, and tasted it. To my surprise, it tasted exactly like liquid smoke. I did a little research and found out that liquid smoke is really just that—liquid smoke! Commercially, it is most often made from mesquite or hickory wood, which is burned in a large condenser and then cooled until water forms.

Liquid smoke can be found in many supermarkets and online as well. It is great for flavoring barbecue sauces, beans, collard or mustard greens, even chickweed. If you are still not sold on the virtues of liquid smoke, some smoky substitutes include chipotle chiles, smoked paprika, and lapsang souchong tea.

Bean-Vegetable Soup with Chervil and Tomato Water

MAKES 4 SERVINGS

2 tablespoons extra-virgin olive oil

1 cup chopped celery leaves or ¼ cup finely chopped lovage

3 carrots, peeled and finely chopped

¼ cup finely chopped green garlic or 3 garlic cloves, minced

4 cups tomato water (see page 230) or 2 cups white wine plus 2 cups water and 2 vine-ripe tomatoes cut into ½-inch pieces

2 cups cooked white beans of any kind, drained

2 cups cooked quinoa, millet, or other grain

½ teaspoon salt

Freshly cracked black pepper

2 cups loosely packed chopped chervil or 1 cup chopped any other thin-skinned herb (such as basil, cilantro, dill, or parsley)

½ cup chopped chives or scallions

If you've gone to the trouble of salvaging end-of-the-season toma-toes to make tomato water, here is the soup for you! This recipe is just a guide: add pea greens or chard to the soup if you desire, or another mild herb instead of chervil, and any grain—it's really very versatile.

1. Heat the olive oil in a heavy-bottomed soup pot over medium heat. Add the celery leaves, carrots, and green garlic and cook for 3 to 5 minutes, stirring to makes sure the garlic doesn't burn. Add the tomato water. Bring the soup to a boil, reduce the heat to medium-low, and let simmer for 10 minutes.

2. Add the white beans and the quinoa. Cook another minute or two. Add more water if the soup is too thick. Season with the salt and freshly cracked black pepper to taste. To serve, ladle the soup into bowls and garnish with chopped chervil and chives.

Conserving Energy while Cooking

The pot had been boiling for what seemed like forever, and the barley still hadn't finished cooking. Suddenly there she was behind me, peering over my shoulder. "Why don't you put a lid on that?" piped a slightly vinegar-lipped Eva. "Do you have any idea how much energy you waste by doing that?" She subtly but definitively elbowed me out of the way so she could turn down the flame and drop on a lid. "It boils just as hard on a lower flame once the lid is on." In defiance, I suggested that a lid would prevent me from observing when the barley was done. To this she made no comment but flitted off on her way, having made her point.

Ever since this encounter, I actually find myself using lids more often, turning the flame down and checking the food from time to time. This makes me feel in sync with the universe and reminds me that you can teach a middle-aged dog new tricks.

Salad of Chervil, Apples, Walnuts, Quinoa, and Onion

I make this sort of salad whenever I have leftover grains. I rarely cook grains just to make a salad. But most often they end up tasting better in a salad than in the dish I originally made them for! As a substitute for the chervil I'd suggest using a quarter cup of another anise-flavored herb like tarragon or anise hyssop, or the full quantity of sorrel or arugula. I made a version of this salad that included locally grown Asian pears, and it was dy-no-mite!

You can prepare this salad up to twenty-four hours in advance, but don't toss in the chervil until just before serving.

1. Bring at least 6 cups water to a boil in a medium saucepan. Add the quinoa and let simmer until it is tender, about 10 minutes. Drain the quinoa in a fine-meshed strainer, and rinse it with very cold water. Let it sit in the strainer for 5 minutes to make sure that it drains well.
2. Combine the quinoa with the chervil, apples, onion, walnuts, vinegar, and olive oil in a large bowl. Season with salt and freshly cracked black pepper to taste.

Note: To toast the walnuts, roast in a 350-degree oven on a rimmed baking sheet for about 5 minutes, until they are golden brown.

MAKES 4 SERVINGS

- ⅔ cup quinoa, preferably red or black quinoa
- 3 cups loosely packed chopped chervil (hard stems removed)
- 2 apples (preferably a locally grown tart variety, like Rhode Island Greening) or 2 Asian pears, with peel, chopped into ¼-inch pieces
- ½ small red onion, chopped
- ½ cup walnut pieces, toasted
- 1½ tablespoons good-quality balsamic vinegar
- 4 tablespoons good-quality extra-virgin olive oil
- Salt and freshly cracked black pepper

MUSHROOMING WITH THE BOEGEHOLDS

Julie and Alan Boegehold, Eva's friends of forty years, ate their first wild mushrooms while living in Europe. In the summer of '69 the family moved from Greece into a Victorian house a mile away from Eva's farm. During that summer Julie and Alan took care of a bulging houseful of extended family and friends. For practically three full months it rained. The walls grew mildew and mushrooms began to pop up in moist spots of the house. Once everyone had tired of board games and the latest Beatles album, they ventured out in the rain to confront the advancing mushroom host, which in this case was an army of puffballs on their front lawn. These are the easiest of mushrooms to identify, and Julie knew enough from her time in Europe to know that they were not only safe to eat but tasty.

After eating most of the puffballs, Julie and Alan bought one good book (by Dr. Orson K. Miller Jr.) and began to very carefully hunt down mushrooms in the woods near their home. They became enthusiastic mushroom eaters and foragers, to the delight and terror of their family and friends.

Recently their son David, who is now a grown adult, was driving down the highway one gray day and spotted a monster oyster mushroom cascade surging down a tree. In the overcast conditions the mushrooms were easily visible, and he determined to return the next day to forage them. It was quite sunny and bright the next day, though, and as David drove the stretch of highway where he'd first spotted the mushrooms, he couldn't find them. Undeterred, he turned around at the nearest exit and headed back until he thought he was close. He parked and bushwhacked his way to the treasure trove. There were even more oyster mushrooms than he had spotted from the road. His bag filled quickly, so he made multiple trips and kept unloading mushrooms into his backseat. In total that one foraging stop amassed more than 20 pounds of mushrooms.

One more intriguing wild mushroom story I have heard is from Beau Vestal, the chef of New Rivers in Providence. He once found some chanterelle mushrooms (very pricey) in the woods and dug up part of fruiting body, including a few inches of the earth it grew on. And here is the cool part: he pureed the whole of it in batches in his food processor, adding water to make a slurry. Then he poured the slop onto a wooded area in his own yard. The next year he had a bevy of chanterelles! I can't promise that this will work for you, but it certainly worked for him!

There is one personality trait you do not want if you decide to forage for mushrooms: overconfidence. Never eat any mushroom without 100 percent positive identification! If you aren't "knowledge-able" and haven't foraged much, get an expert to identify your find.

To educate yourself further, buy at least two different field guides, as sometimes mushrooms differ in appearance within the same species, and having multiple photographs is very useful. If you live near a university, you might want to try the biology department; there may be a mycologist in residence willing to help. Or join a mycological group or society if there is one nearby.

A couple of helpful hints if you try to forage mushrooms:

- Usually the best time to go mushroom hunting is after a rain. Don't go during a drought.

- Mushroom season, at least in the Northeast, is July through November.
- Search near oak and pine trees or near manure or compost piles. For honey mushrooms, look near tree stumps or where stumps have been pulled. But though there certainly are sweet spots for foraging, wild mushrooms have been known to bust through cement.

Cook mushrooms simply in butter or olive oil with a bit of garlic, salt, and cracked pepper. If you add herbs, be sparing; my favorites to use are savory, thyme, and calaminth.

Chickweed

"A bane to the unenlightened gardener but a boon to the rest of us."

—Bruce Burnett, author

If you have ever spent hours pulling chickweed out of your garden, you might be surprised to hear that Eva sells it to chefs. But she does. She also chooses to call chickweed by its Latin name, "stellaria," because this means "little star," referring to the white star-shaped flower chickweed bears when mature. But Eva also likes to call the plant stellaria because, in her eyes, chickweed is a "star," in much the same way Meryl Streep and Michael Jordan are timeless stars for the rest of us. (Other common names for the plant include starweed, winterweed, and satinflower.)

Chickweed's etymology is not hard to break down—it is a weed that chickens love to eat. It forms an invasive low, sprawling, tangled mat of spindly stems and spade-shaped green leaves that spreads rapidly in many a garden, taking advantage of fertile soil. As many gardeners know, if neglected, it can spread as fast and as far as gossip. In other words, chickweed is unstoppable, enduring harsh sleet and severe snowstorms during the winter months and continually seeding all summer long. Having chickweed around is like owning a Steinway piano—it will probably be with you the rest of your life.

Chickweed may not be the most delicate-tasting green Eva grows, but she eats more of it than any other because of its unending supply and its health value, and also because her taste buds have grown to crave it. Chickweed takes up a prominent place in her revenues as well, and she educates chefs on its versatility. Her chickweed tends to taste far better than the chickweed I find around my neighborhood, undoubtedly because of her rich organic soil. Chickweed is sweetest in cool weather, not in the heat of summer when the plant flowers and the stems become spindly.

CULINARY USES

For a long time I avoided chickweed. It tasted like dirt the first time I tried it—organic dirt, but still. . . . Yet Eva kept praising its virtues year after year, and so, in a moment of weakness, I added it to our dinner salad one evening. Upon eating it, I learned that, dressed with a decent vinaigrette and mixed with another green or two, it really tastes pretty good.

This weed is now a welcome addition to my salads. I love it along with any collection of greens, especially greens that have a vivid personality like arugula, baby kale, or baby mustard. And it doesn't hurt to add a bit of sweetness to it, like raisins or sliced apples with the greens, or honey in the dressing.

Some people think chickweed is good sautéed like spinach, but Eva disagrees: "It is so good raw, I can not bring myself to cook it. The bounce, the fluff, the crunch . . . all would be mush. It does not have a strong flavor. The rewards are in texture." Gaining momentum she declares, "There are no benefits to cooking it, only drawbacks."

Continuing, Eva says, "Like pea greens, chickweed makes a great nest for hot food. The hot food wilts it rather than cooks it, and it leaves a lively raw wreath around." And this is how we often eat it—under seared fish or meat, or even at the bottom of a bowl of soup or stew.

HEALTH VIRTUES

Chickweed may be a small, spindly weed, but it is a nutritional superstar, and perhaps one of the healthiest foods on our planet. It is loaded with iron, antioxidants, omega-3 and omega-6 fatty acids, minerals, vitamins A, B, and C, and a host of other potent nutrients. It also contains steroidal saponins, which may increase our ability to absorb nutrients by increasing the permeability of mucous membranes in the digestive tract. So good-bye Wheaties, hello weedies.

FORAGING AND STORING

More people try to eradicate chickweed than grow it. You probably have chickweed growing very close to you, unless you live in Manhattan in a posh penthouse. But then you'd have plenty growing around your summer home in the Hamptons!

There is an old saying, "Chickweed tastes best when the trees have no leaves." The plant prefers cool temperatures, so to find top-notch specimens, look in untreated lawns or other unpolluted green spaces in spring and fall. In the summer heat, when blossoms appear, chickweed can be tough and stringy. You can identify chickweed by its long, thin flower stalk with paired leaves and singular green buds forming on top. Use scissors to harvest, and kindly leave enough growth behind for the plant to regenerate and reseed. If you really grow to love chickweed, like Eva, you can even cultivate a chickweed patch in your garden.

Store chickweed in a plastic bag in the fridge, where it will keep for about a week.

Freshness Tidbit ~ Cranberries

Just-picked cranberries sold loose have a sensational crunch—well, actually, it's more of a pop. The thing that makes one berry taste better than another is mainly the age factor. They are milder and less bitter when fresh. Besides tasting the berry, the best way to see whether a cranberry is old or bruised is to bounce it on the ground. If it doesn't bounce up a foot, it's probably either a dud or too old.

You can find fresh loose cranberries in late fall at farmers' markets, especially in eastern states. Cranberries sold in bags in the fall should also be fairly fresh: gently squeeze and pinch a berry or two inside the bag to see if they are hard; there should be no give.

Eva has friends who own a dune shack in Provincetown, at the tip of Cape Cod. Every year either they send her a big bag of cranberries or she picks them herself. When they are this fresh, they are very tasty eaten raw.

My favorite way to eat fresh cranberries is whole with granola and milk. I also make a killer salsa in the food processor with cranberries, cilantro, apple, green pepper, onion, a canned or dried chipotle pepper, lime juice, and olive oil. Eat this with just about everything! If you'd like more specific quantities, follow the Home Fries and Cranberry Salsa recipe on page 33. I also like the salsa on top of hot barley or millet as a lunch or snack, and certainly a taco or burrito would welcome it as well.

Chickweed Cheddar Grilled Cheese Sandwich

MAKES 1 SANDWICH

1 tablespoon butter or extra-virgin olive oil

2 slices whole wheat bread

2 ounces cheddar cheese, sliced

½ tart apple, with peel, thinly sliced

1 handful chickweed, enough to stuff into a sandwich

This is a good way to get chickweed into kids (and timid adults). Alfalfa sprouts are a good substitute if you can't find chickweed.

1. Melt the butter in a heavy-bottomed cast-iron pan over low heat. Set both slices of bread in the pan. Layer the cheese on one slice of bread, and set the apple slices in the empty spaces in the pan. Let the apples cook and the bread toast.

2. After a few minutes, set the warm apples on the cheese. Set the plain slice of bread on top of the apples. Flip the sandwich and cook until the underside is browned, about 3 minutes. Then pry open the bread and add the chickweed. Serve the sandwich warm from the pan.

Chickweed Apple Slaw with Ginger Dressing

MAKES 6 TO 8 SERVINGS

3 tablespoons freshly grated ginger

4 tablespoons apple cider vinegar

2 tablespoons extra-virgin olive oil

1 tablespoon honey

2 tart apples, with peel, finely chopped

3 cups shredded green cabbage (1/4 of a medium head)

3 cups loosely packed chickweed

½ onion, thinly sliced

½ cup toasted sunflower seeds (optional)

Salt and freshly cracked black pepper

Whenever chickweed is in season and available, which is about eight months of the year in New England, this is a great way to enjoy it. If you like, you can substitute grated carrots, julienned kale, or even purslane for the chickweed.

1. Combine the ginger, vinegar, olive oil, and honey with a fork in a large bowl. Toss the apples into the vinaigrette. The dish can be prepared up to this point a day before serving; just cover and refrigerate it.

2. Just before serving, toss the cabbage, chickweed, onion, and sunflower seeds with the apples and vinaigrette. Season with salt and freshly cracked black pepper to taste.

Laryngitis Tea

Chickweed purportedly helps reduce swelling in the throat. Ginger, thyme, and rosemary helps make it taste good. Add honey to your cup of tea if you like.

Combine the chickweed, thyme, rosemary, ginger, and lemon in a pot with 8 cups water. Bring to a boil, then cover, remove from the heat, and let steep for 30 minutes. Strain and serve as tea.

MAKES 6 SERVINGS

6 cups loosely packed chickweed

1 bunch thyme (optional)

4 or 5 sprigs rosemary

4-inch piece ginger root, thinly sliced

1 lemon, cut into 6 slices

Claytonia

Claytonia perfoliata · PERENNIAL

Claytonia is worth growing if for no other reason than to admire it. The plant is only half a foot tall, and each heart-shaped leaf holds one diminutive white flower, like a micro bouquet. I can see Martha Stewart selecting claytonia for Barbie to carry down the aisle when she finally marries Ken. But if the rumor is true about Ken and his proclivity, he might prefer to forgo the wedding and enjoy the claytonia as an indoor arrangement on his coffee table, accented with some bronze fennel. However, despite its beauty, claytonia is not an ornamental plant. It's a wild edible with considerable culinary virtue. It grows wild in the mountainous West, though not in New England; Eva plants it from seed in her greenhouse, which offers enough protection that it survives the winter.

Culinary Uses

Claytonia tastes a bit like spinach. Its flavor never wowed me, but I finally realized that its juicy crunch provides relief from the intensity of Eva's other greens like arugula, mustard, and sorrel. Some describe claytonia's flavor as a cross between butterhead lettuce and spinach. But its visual beauty surpasses either of those two greens in a salad.

Matt Jennings, the chef-owner of Farmstead in Providence, Rhode Island, is filled with ideas for claytonia: "One stem can make a lovely garnish floating in a bowl of a chilled late summer soup or early fall consommé. Claytonia makes a gorgeous 'nest' for a freshly poached egg—gently drizzled with an impeccable olive oil and tart, electric vinegar. The ideal edible garnish!" He continues, "Folded into garden-fresh salad mixes, claytonia adds a fresh, vegetal quality that I liken to sorrel, and, if you happen to find older and slightly more fibrous claytonia, blend it into a soup and watch the soup thicken before your eyes."

Health Virtues

Claytonia is sold at many farmers' markets under the name "miner's lettuce," a moniker that comes from the time when miners of the California Gold Rush sought it out as a fresh source of vitamin C to prevent scurvy. Like its cousin purslane, claytonia is unusually high in omega-3 fatty acids and many dietary minerals.

Foraging and Storing

Eva cultivates claytonia, though it grows wild in many western states and north into Canada. It commonly appears in May and June, when conditions are still slightly cool and damp, often in sunlit areas after the first heavy rains. But the best-tasting patches are found in shaded areas, especially in the uplands, into the early summer. As the days get hotter, the leaves turn a deep red color as they dry out. As a blogger in Mendocino County, California, points out, "It seems I seldom see [claytonia] growing wild, except along urban margins, and even then only in forgotten spots where someone hasn't 'cleaned up the weeds.'" These spots may include crop fields, orchards, vineyards, gardens, yards, and any other site where the soil has been disturbed.

Once you have clipped your claytonia, store it in the refrigerator in a plastic bag for up to a week (but, to fully enjoy its fresh flavor and crisp stems, it is best to eat it right away).

GROWING CLAYTONIA

Sow seed just beneath the surface of the soil in late fall for winter growth, or outdoors in early spring. Thin seedlings to 4 to 6 inches apart, and keep the soil moist. To harvest, clip the stems when small flowers begin to form, but before the plant goes to seed. Determined to reproduce, your claytonia plant will send up a second set of leaves, which you may mercilessly clip again and enjoy with your dinner.

Eva cultivates claytonia in her unheated greenhouses, where it grows throughout the cold, dark winter months and into the spring.

End-of-Harvest Salad

MAKES 4 SERVINGS

4 medium thin-skinned potatoes (about 1½ pounds), cut into 1-inch cubes

1 garlic clove, minced

¼ cup extra-virgin olive oil

2 tablespoons lemon juice (about ½ juicy lemon)

2 teaspoons Dijon mustard

Salt and freshly cracked black pepper

4 loosely packed cups herbs and greens (any mixture will do: arugula, baby Red Russian kale, chervil, chickweed, claytonia, parsley, pea greens, sorrel, spinach)

1 cup homegrown lentil sprouts (see page 42) or store-bought sprouts of your choice

¼–½ cup fromage blanc, creamy goat cheese, or a high-quality ricotta or cottage cheese

Some summer herbs and greens are resilient enough to grow outside in November and December in southern New England, making it past the first few frosts. It's fun to snip the last of the die-hards and bid farewell to the end of the outdoor greens with a celebratory salad. The potatoes and the creamy cheese make this salad into a real meal.

1. Bring a large pot of salted water to a boil. Add the potatoes and cook until tender, about 10 to 15 minutes. Drain the potatoes, rinse them with cool water, and set them aside.

2. Whisk together the garlic, olive oil, lemon juice, and mustard. Season the dressing with salt and freshly cracked black pepper to taste.

3. Combine the herbs and greens, sprouts, and cooked potatoes in a large bowl, and pour the vinaigrette over the vegetables. Toss the salad well and then add the cheese, tossing just a bit to distribute, and making sure the cheese doesn't clump. Season with additional salt and freshly cracked black pepper and serve.

Kale

Brassica oleracea, Acephala Group · ANNUAL

My first passionate moment with kale came eight years ago, when Tuscan kale was breaking onto the local food scene. I loved its intriguing deep pine color and lizardlike texture, and how its leaves were manageably flat and shaped into elegant long lobes. It was tasty, too, more tender than any other kale I knew. Then I had an even better interlude with Red Russian kale. My first time with it I went overboard, consuming the leaves like potato chips while picking one day in a big field of it. Impressed and a bit frightened with my consumption, I immediately realized that, fresh out of the dirt, kale is dramatically sweet and nutty. I now buy my kale as fresh as possible, from our town co-op or farmers' markets, especially in the fall when it is local and super-sweet.

CULINARY USES

Like spinach, fresh kale is a versatile green. My favorite cooking method is braising. First rough-chop the kale, and then fry it over medium-high heat with olive oil and minced garlic. After a minute or two, add ½ cup or so of water to the frying pan, along with salt and pepper. This braises and tames the texture of the kale. (You won't need much, if any, water if you're using spanking-fresh kale.) Cook the kale until all the water evaporates, about 5 minutes. You can make a tasty kale and egg dinner by dropping a couple of eggs into the pan once the water has evaporated (adding a bit more oil if your pan likes to stick). Fry the eggs sunny-side up, then season the eggs and kale and serve over toast.

Chef Patrick Connolly at Bobo in Manhattan makes orbs from kale. He blanches the kale then shapes one or two leaves into a packed ball, puts a few on a plate, then drizzles them with good-quality olive oil and sprinkles salt and cracked pepper over all. He calls them "Polina." I haven't tried my hand at these yet but I love to add braised kale to mac and cheese, pastas, burritos, and frittatas. I also like to eat it braised with kimchi on sticky rice. In soups and stews kale adds a wonderful dimension. The timeless Portuguese *caldo verde*, a soup made with kale, potato, onion, olive oil, and *chourico*, is served at weddings and other celebrations.

However, just eating braised kale, straight up, is cause for celebration in and of itself.

Eva mainly harvests kale at the baby stage, incorporating it into her vibrant salad mix as if it were a common green. The leaves of Red Russian kale are particularly useful for salads—noncurled, tooth-edged, and with attractive fuchsia-colored veins. If you can get kale at a farmers' market or buy it really fresh elsewhere, try Peter's Kale Salad (page 248). Or make a raw kale Caesar salad. Preserved lemons seem to have an affinity with greens. They can be added to many raw kale salads as well as braised kale with great success.

HEALTH VIRTUES

This cruciferous vegetable offers more nutrition for fewer calories than just about any other food out there. It is full of cancer-fighting phytonutrients, and 1 cup provides 100 percent of your daily requirement of vitamins A and K, along with 88 percent of your daily requirement of vitamin C. Kale also contains isothiocyanates, which help with the body's detoxification process.

BUYING, STORING, AND PREPPING

You'll probably be able to find kale in the supermarket year-round, but if you want to try kale at its finest, buy it direct from a farm (or farmers' market) in the fall after a few frosts have sweetened the leaves. Buy kale by the bunch, not already washed and cut. Look for lively green leaves that are not dreary, limp, or yellowing. Store kale in a plastic bag in the refrigerator for up to a week. Like most dark leafy greens, it freezes well once it has been cooked.

To prepare, strip the leaves from the stems. Chop the stems as finely as you can. Chop the leaves as thin or wide as you'd like.

GROWING KALE

Kale is a delight to grow—each plant can be continuously harvested throughout the grow-

ing season, and if you aren't in love with kale by the fall you will be forced to admire the plant in the winter when freezing temperatures have wiped out all other signs of life in the garden. According to Eva, Red Russian kale can survive all winter long and provides the sweetest imaginable early-spring leaves, buds, and then flowers.

After the final frost date in the spring, sow kale seed directly into the garden in full sun, thinning the plants to 16 inches apart, and keep the soil moist. If you live in a milder climate, kale can be planted in early fall and grown through the winter. To harvest, cut the larger outer leaves, leaving the small tender leaves forming at the center of the stalk to grow.

Kale with Apples, Raisins, Feta, and Walnuts

I like this best served over a grain like quinoa or as a bed for pork chops. The apples and onions break down, moisten, and sweeten the dish. Tuscan kale (also called lacinato or dinosaur kale) is my favorite variety for this recipe, because regular curly kale's center rib is a bit too crunchy. What is most important is freshness. You can make the recipe using collard greens too.

1. Heat the olive oil in a wide, heavy-bottomed saucepan over medium-high heat. Add the onions and cook, stirring every few minutes, for 10 minutes. Reduce the heat to low and add the chopped apple. The onions will start sticking to the pan; let them stick a little and brown, but then stir them before they burn. The trick is to leave them alone long enough to brown, but not so long so that they burn. Cook until the onions are quite brown, about 10 minutes.

2. Add the kale, raisins, garlic, and ¾ cup water. Turn the heat to high and cook for 10 minutes, stirring frequently.

3. Add the vinegar and continue to cook, stirring periodically, until all the liquid is gone, about 5 minutes. Add the walnuts, feta, and smoked paprika, stirring well, then season with salt and freshly cracked black pepper to taste.

Note: To toast the nuts, roast in a 350-degree oven on a rimmed baking sheet for 7 to 8 minutes, until golden brown.

MAKES 3 SERVINGS

- 1–2 tablespoons extra-virgin olive oil
- 1 onion, thinly sliced
- 1 large tart apple, skin-on and diced
- 1 bunch kale, thinly sliced (about 8 cups)
- ¼ cup raisins or currants
- 3 garlic cloves, minced
- 1½ tablespoons balsamic vinegar
- ¼ cup chopped walnuts or pecans, toasted
- 2–3 tablespoons crumbled feta
- ½ teaspoon smoked paprika or 1 teaspoon adobo sauce from canned chipotles (optional)
- Salt and freshly cracked black pepper

Peter's Kale Salad

MAKES 4 SERVINGS

1 bunch kale, thinly sliced (about 8 cups)

2 medium carrots, cut into matchstick pieces

½ cup raisins or dried cranberries

2 large garlic cloves, minced

1 teaspoon ground cumin

Pinch chile flakes

¼ cup lemon juice (about 1 lemon)

3 tablespoons extra-virgin olive oil

1 tablespoon shoyu

Peter, Eva's head farmer, has one of the most discriminating palates I know. He got the idea of a raw kale salad from Debra's Natural Gourmet shop in Concord, Massachusetts. Peter likes this with any kind of kale, as long as it's spanking fresh. It's important to use a good-quality shoyu. The kind Peter uses (Ohsawa Nama Shoyu) smells almost like beer, and when you open it, it fizzes like a soda.

Combine the kale, carrots, raisins, garlic, cumin, chile flakes, lemon juice, olive oil, and soy sauce in a large bowl, and mix well. Squeeze the leaves with the dressing to break down the fibrous nature of the kale. Let the salad sit for 30 minutes, then toss well. Serve immediately, or cover and store in the fridge, where it will keep for 2 to 3 days.

Linguine with Kale, Lemon, and Brown Butter

This recipe is great when you don't have a lot of time. Included is a secret recipe for quick-and-dirty preserved lemons. If you want, add a few spoonfuls of capers and a squeeze of lemon instead of the preserved lemon. This is equally good with broccoli or rapini instead of kale. You can also add a chopped tomato.

MAKES 3 OR 4 SERVINGS

18 sun-dried tomatoes

8 tablespoons (1 stick) butter

1 onion, thinly sliced

4 garlic cloves, minced

3–4 tablespoons preserved lemons (page 126) or 1 heaping tablespoon capers plus the juice of 1 lemon

½ teaspoon red chile flakes, or more to taste

1 pound whole-grain linguine or spaghetti

1 bunch kale, thinly sliced (about 8 cups)

Salt and freshly cracked black pepper

⅓ cup grated Parmesan

1. Bring a large pot of salted water to a boil for cooking the pasta. Reduce the heat to low, cover, and keep at a low simmer.
2. Bring 1 cup water to a boil in a small saucepan, then remove from the heat. Place the dried tomatoes in the boiling water and let soak until they are soft, about 15 minutes. Remove them from the water and slice thinly.
3. Melt the butter in a medium skillet over low heat. Stir with a wooden spoon until the butter begins to brown in spots, about 5 minutes. Once it seems uniformly golden, remove it from the heat, add the onion and garlic, and stir. Stir in the tomatoes, preserved lemons, and chile flakes. Set aside.
4. Bring the pasta water back to a rolling boil. Add the pasta and boil for 6 minutes. Add the kale and boil another 3 minutes. Drain, but do not rinse. Return the hot pasta and kale to the pot.
5. Add the tomato mixture to the pasta. Season with salt and freshly cracked black pepper to taste and more chile flakes if you'd like more heat.
6. Plate the pasta and serve with grated Parmesan.

Quick-and-Dirty Preserved Lemons

MAKES ABOUT 1 CUP

2 lemons, halved, then
  thinly sliced

1 teaspoon salt

1 teaspoon sugar

1 tablespoon cider vinegar

My old roommate Mo is a chef and hails from Morocco. He made these quick-and-dirty preserved lemons once while in a hurry for a catering gig. I think they're terrific. You can also make these with already juiced lemons if you don't want to throw out the rinds (if you do throw out your lemon rinds, don't let Eva see you!). Just slice the rind and what's left of the flesh and proceed with the recipe.

Combine the lemons, salt, sugar, and cider vinegar with 4 tablespoons water in a small saucepan. Bring the mixture to a boil, then reduce the heat and let simmer for 5 minutes. Remove from the heat, cover, and let steep for 10 minutes. Remove the lemons and let cool. Store in the fridge, where they'll keep for at least 3 weeks.

Creamed Kale

MAKES 4 OR 5 SERVINGS

3 tablespoons butter

1 tablespoon extra-virgin
  olive oil

3 garlic cloves, minced

2 tablespoons flour

1½ cups milk or
  half-and-half

1 large bunch kale, thinly
  sliced (8 to 10 cups)

Salt and freshly cracked
  black pepper

I devised this recipe to entice my extended family to partake in eating kale on Thanksgiving Day—and it worked. Everyone loved it. Any variety of kale will work as long as it is very fresh. If you want this dish to resemble creamed spinach, remove the central ribs from the kale and compost the stems. I usually just finely chop the stems and add them separately.

1. Heat the butter and olive oil in a small stockpot over medium heat. Add the garlic, stir, and then, after a minute, add the flour. Whisk for a minute. Gradually add the milk, and whisk well for a minute, until the sauce is boiling. Put the whisk aside.

2. Add the chopped kale and cook, stirring, for 2 to 3 minutes. Reduce the heat to low, cover, and let simmer for 8 to 10 minutes, stirring every 2 to 3 minutes, adding a spoonful of water if it is sticking to the pan. The kale should soften up quite a bit. Season with salt and freshly cracked black pepper and serve.

Leeks

Allium ampeloprasum var. *porrum* · BIENNIAL

Even in the midst of a blizzard, Eva will venture out into her garden to dig leeks. The vibrant green spires stand tall against the whipping wind, undaunted, like brave soldiers awaiting their rescue. Normally leeks can be pulled by hand, but if the ground is partially frozen, a long, thin shovel must be used to dig deep and uproot the leek. I think Eva enjoys digging in semi-frozen soil during a January blizzard because it brings her back to her childhood in Wisconsin, when she would get a thrill from letting her rubber boots flood with icy water while walking through a swampy field.

Leeks are long, slim, and glamorous—the ultimate in the "layered" look (a term popularized by the movie *Annie Hall*). Cut straight through a leek and you can see the layers of white and green rings, like concentric growth rings of a baby sapling. Leeks are a pet vegetable of Eva's. She quips, "I don't mean to disrespect the onion, but leeks are far better. They are sweeter, milder, prettier." I don't disagree, but I feel that leeks and onions have different features. Onions caramelize beautifully, but they can also melt into the woodwork. A bright green leek, on the other hand, doesn't caramelize so well, but its appearance and texture are rarely overlooked.

CULINARY USES

"Few people think beyond soups with leeks," Eva opines. She likes to add chopped leeks to soups and stews as well, but only at the last minute to preserve their brilliant green color and crunch. I often sear them quickly and use them for the finishing touch on a soup, stew, or seafood dish.

Leeks have a special affinity for fish and wine—try deep-fried julienned leeks as a garnish for fish. Leeks also do well in pickles and kimchi. Many chefs halve leeks lengthwise and grill them. I like to chop them and cook them in butter for a quiche or omelet filling.

One of Eva's favorite clients, Patrick Connolly of Bobo restaurant in Manhattan, has many inventive ideas for leeks. His signature burger sits on pickled leeks and is topped with Gruyère and then fried leeks. He also makes a dish called "Bacon, Eggs, and Cereal," which is a leek fondue (leeks poached in butter and pureed, simulating a hot cereal) topped with farro, bacon, and a poached egg.

A typically French method of preparing leeks is to simmer them whole until tender, about twenty minutes, then slit them in half, chill, and place them on a plate, cut side up. Drizzle with a mustard vinaigrette and top with a grated hard-boiled egg. In cooking school we simmered leeks in the same manner for terrines but left them whole. We placed two or three down the length of a terrine loaded with other blanched vegetables (like peas, green beans, and carrots), ladling gelatinous aspic into the terrine to bind it all together. The terrine was encased in blanched Swiss chard leaves and was weighted down for a few days. Once the terrine was cold, inverted, and sliced, the leeks resembled planets amid a constellation of vegetables. In France we also made our bouquet garni (an herb bundle for flavoring stocks) using the tough outer leaves of leeks to enclose thyme, parsley, and other herbs. The folded leek leaves are tied like a present with string.

A lot of people instruct you to discard the upper green leaf sheaths. Eva says these pale green inner leaves are the hidden treasure of the leek. I find the green part of a leek to be milder and sweeter than the white part, although some leaves may need to be discarded if they are worn or stressed. If your leek is fresh, certainly you can use the green part; chopped, it shines in salads, salsas, and more. Eva treats the dark green outer leaf sheaths like broccoli stems: slicing them thinly breaks down any toughness, and they become very palatable. "Even the rootlets of leeks are edible!" says Eva.

HEALTH VIRTUES

Like other members of the allium family, leeks are high in antioxidants. They are also high in vitamin B_6, vitamin C, folate, iron, and manganese and pack a lot of flavor with few calories.

BUYING, STORING, AND PREPPING

Buy leeks that have firm, hydrated skin. The white portion should be shiny and smooth

to the touch, and the greens should stand at attention for the most part. Fresh leeks should be stored unwashed and untrimmed in a sealed bag in the refrigerator, where they will keep for up to one month. Cooked leeks are highly perishable and will keep for only about two days in the refrigerator.

To clean and prepare a leek for cooking, trim off the rootlets (unless, like some chefs, you choose to cook them), any portion of the green tops that is withered and worn, and any tough outer layers. A leek's many layers inevitably trap dirt. To get rid of it, make a lengthwise incision down the middle of the shaft all the way through the leek, from the point where the white part meets the green part to the end of the green leaves. Holding the leek by the root end, plunge the top end gently into a tub of lukewarm water to dislodge the dirt. Let it sit for a few minutes to allow the dirt to settle. If your recipe calls for cross sections, first cut the leek into the desired pieces, then place the slices in a colander and run them under cool water.

GROWING LEEKS

Eva advises, "Start leeks from seed in February indoors and they will hold as babies until the ground is ready for planting—they can hang out up to 2 months or more in their trays before they are planted." Transplant into your garden up to two weeks before the last frost, burying seedlings up to the first leaf notch and spacing them 4 to 6 inches apart. Leeks need full sun, good soil, and lots of water. If you wish, you may mound soil around the leek as it grows to blanch the stalk.

Leeks are relatively cooperative and will survive almost all winter long in good condition if heeled into the dirt in a root cellar or transplanted from the field into an unheated hoop house.

Cod Potato Leek Gratin

My mom urged me to include this recipe because she feels everyone needs a good storehouse of simple recipes. I made it for my
parents a few days after their house burned down (after they had
lived there for fifty-two years). The only thing I could really offer,
since my sisters were on top of everything else, was to take the
three-hour drive and feed them some good food cooked with love
while they were dealing with the crisis and its many problems (the
worst of which was the loss of their dog Jamie). One of the few
things that did survive was my father's garden. It was November,
and the leeks were thriving, so I pulled three or four and featured
them in this gratin. The meal, along with red wine, had a healing
effect on us all.

MAKES 6 SERVINGS

2 tablespoons butter

3 leeks, chopped

6 garlic cloves, minced

**2 pounds potatoes,
scrubbed and thinly
sliced**

2½ cups half-and-half

½ teaspoon salt

**1½ pounds fresh cod or any
white-fleshed fish, cut
into 2-inch pieces**

**Half a loaf good hearty
bread, sliced thick**

1. Preheat the oven to 400 degrees F.
2. In a large stovetop casserole dish (at least 12 inches in diameter),
   melt the butter over medium heat. Add the leeks and sauté, stirring, until they are soft and slightly browned, about 5 minutes.
   Add the garlic and cook 1 minute. Add the potatoes and half-and-
   half, and season with the salt and freshly cracked black pepper.
   Bring to a boil, then reduce the heat to low and simmer, covered,
   for 5 minutes.
3. Stir in the cod, then set the casserole in the oven and bake, uncovered, for 25 to 30 minutes, or until the potatoes are tender.
4. Arrange the bread slices so that they hang half in and half out of
   wide soup bowls. Spoon the gratin into the bowls, partially on top
   of the bread. Ladle in the cream that remains at the bottom. Serve
   immediately.

Leek Miso Soup

MAKES 4 SERVINGS

1 tablespoon extra-virgin olive oil

2 medium leeks, chopped into ½-inch pieces, green and white parts separated

2 garlic cloves, minced

1 cup yellow split peas

2 teaspoons freshly minced ginger

½ teaspoon ground cumin

Pinch ground cloves

1 cup chopped carrots, in ¼-inch coins

2 heaping teaspoons *mugi* or soybean miso

Freshly cracked black pepper

4 handfuls chopped greens or herbs (such as arugula, chickweed, cilantro, mustard, or sprouts) or 1 tablespoon chopped rosemary (optional)

This soup calls for yellow split peas, which do not have the pasty texture of green split peas. You could substitute brown lentils or even white rice without changing the recipe. Feel free to add some chopped rosemary at the end if you like.

Most people think of miso as the soup they get before eating sushi in Japanese restaurants. Miso is actually a fermented soybean paste often mixed with barley, rice, and other grains. I recommend the darker kinds of miso for this soup, such as *mugi* (soy and barley) or soybean miso. The darker the color, the stronger and smokier the miso will taste.

1. Heat the olive oil in a soup pot over medium heat. Add the white part of the leeks and the garlic, and cook until the leeks soften, about 5 minutes.

2. Add the yellow split peas, ginger, cumin, cloves, and 5½ cups water. Bring to a boil, then reduce the heat and let simmer, uncovered, for 25 minutes. The split peas should still have some crunch.

3. Add the carrots and simmer another 3 minutes.

4. Add ½ cup or so more water if the soup has become terribly thick. Dissolve the miso in 1 tablespoon water and stir it into the soup, along with the the green parts of the leeks. Then remove from the heat. Whisk in more miso and freshly cracked pepper to taste. (Do not boil the miso; it will lose its health benefits.)

5. Serve the soup in big bowls, topped with chopped greens or herbs.

Leek Pie with a Millet Crust

This is a simple pie that satisfies both kids and adults. It's also sumptious the next day, served hot or cold. You need a 10-inch cast-iron skillet to make this recipe, or at least a 8 by 8-inch Pyrex pan. You could add blanched vegetables to the pie, such as broccoli or asparagus.

1. To make the crust, preheat the oven to 400 degrees F.
2. Bring 3 cups water to a boil, then add the millet. Simmer for 15 minutes, covered, and then remove from the heat. Stir in the butter, and let rest for at least 5 minutes, uncovered.
3. Grease a cast-iron skillet with some butter. Place the millet in the skillet and, using the back of a large spoon, press it down to form a uniform layer, bringing it up the sides as much as possible.
4. Bake the millet crust for 25 minutes, or until a light brown crust develops at the edges. Remove from the oven. Turn the oven temperature down to 350 degrees F.
5. To make the filling, melt the butter in a skillet over medium heat. Add the leeks and sauté for 6 to 8 minutes, stirring occasionally. Add the garlic and cook 1 to 2 minutes.
6. Whisk together the eggs, egg yolks, and milk. Season generously with salt and freshly cracked black pepper.
7. Spread the leeks over the millet crust. Top with the mozzarella and then the egg mixture.
8. Bake the pie for 30 minutes, or until the custard is set.

MAKES 4 TO 6 SERVINGS

The Crust:
1½ cups uncooked millet
1 tablespoon butter

The Filling:
2 leeks, chopped into ½-inch pieces
2 tablespoons butter plus a bit more for greasing
1 garlic clove, minced
3 large eggs
2 large egg yolks
1½ cups whole milk or half-and-half
Salt and freshly cracked black pepper
1 cup grated mozzarella

Smashed Leeky Potatoes

MAKES 2 OR 3 SERVINGS

3 Yukon Gold potatoes (1½ pounds), with peel, cut into 1-inch pieces

1 large leek, cut into ¼-inch pieces

1 garlic clove, minced

3 tablespoons butter

½ cup milk or light cream

Salt and freshly cracked black pepper

These are certainly first-rate as is, eaten perhaps alongside garlicky greens and/or roast chicken. If you have it on hand, add a handful of chickweed or chopped sorrel toward the end of the leeks' cooking time. You can make a vegan version by using a good olive oil and soy milk instead of the butter and milk.

1. Bring a large pot of salted water to a boil. Add the potatoes, reduce the heat, and simmer, covered, until the potatoes are tender, 10 to 15 minutes. Drain the potatoes, rinse them with cold water to cool, and set aside.

2. While the potatoes are cooking, melt 2 tablespoons of the butter in a large skillet over medium heat. Add the garlic and leek and cook, stirring, until the leeks are softened, about 8 to 10 minutes. Remove from the heat.

3. Mash the potatoes in a large bowl with a masher. Add the remaining 1 tablespoon butter, the leeks and garlic, and the milk. Mash some more, adding salt and freshly cracked black pepper to taste.

Preserving the Scorned

All Eva had for garlic was one head that had green sprouts erupting from the top, looking like evil green cat's claws. Any good cook or cookbook will tell you to remove the bitter green stem from each clove, which is what I proceeded to do when preparing dinner one night. But Eva will stand behind—or in front of—anything that is headed for the trash or compost. She explained to me that people often simply do as they are told, and that myths abound in this world. As she left the kitchen, she finished her rant by asking, "Has anyone ever really *tried* eating the green blade?" I was annoyed. Myths don't abound all that much, and wasn't I the chef between the two of us anyhow? Then I wondered: she referred to it as a blade; I call it a green stem. But wasn't it also a shoot or a sprout?

At this point I was sufficiently curious to jump in and work with these cat claws. So I decided to create a pesto using just the green stems of garlic. I used Eva's basil, almonds, and some olive oil and was pleasantly surprised by how good it was—not really bitter after all. I later read that the compounds responsible for garlic's pungency seep into the green stem as the garlic ages, leaving the bulb itself diminished in flavor. Hmmm, sounds a lot like when an herb goes to seed and its leaves turn bitter. I didn't find anything totally conclusive on its nomenclature, but it seems that while the culinary world refers to it as the bitter green stem, shoot, or sprout, it is, as Eva noted, botanically referred to as the blade.

Now I don't remove the blade when it is there. I use the whole clove with the cat's claw intact.

Mustard Greens

Brassica juncea · ANNUAL

Among the many vegetal personalities to line Eva's fields, mustard is one of the most forceful. Just one leaf can clear the most stubborn of nasal blockages. But just for a few seconds, because unlike chile peppers, once mustard has set your nose on fire, the heat promptly vanishes without a trace. Mustard's flavor gets stronger as the leaves grow bigger. Thankfully, at Eva's, most of the mustard is harvested at the baby stage, so you get the sense for just a millisecond that your head will pop off. She sells baby mustard in her salad green mix, and it's one of the dazzlers.

Mustard has an uncanny ability to reseed itself. I find Eva's red mustard growing everywhere: in her gravel driveway, at my feet in her outdoor shower, and acting like a flitting socialite among the other herbs, arriving at the party without an invitation. When I was a garden guppy, knowing next to nothing, I commented on mustard's success to one of Eva's strapping young farmhands. He told me that these plants were volunteers, that is, the seeds had traveled and the plants were not intentionally planted. I was impressed with his creative language, furthering my admiration for Eva's staff, which mirrored how I felt about lifeguards at the beach when I was ten. Turns out, "volunteer" is a very old gardening term; still, my adoration for her brawny staff remains strong.

CULINARY USES

Eva grows most of her mustard just to the baby stage, so although there is a punch to the greens, they don't bowl you over. We like them in salads. They are best coupled with milder greens, like Bull's Blood beet greens, chickweed, and pea greens and dressed simply with olive oil and balsamic vinegar or preserved lemon bits. I chop mustard greens, add them to wheat berries or bulgur with chopped tomato, and toss with a lemon dressing for a spin on tabbouleh. Heat tames the greens' peppery quality; try adding baby mustard at the last moment to simmering soups, or make a nest on a plate of chopped young greens and top it with hot seared meat, fish, or even a veggie burger. I tried making a mustard green pesto, but pureeing the greens kills both the heat and the flavor. The yellow mustard flowers that appear at the end of summer are pretty and peppy in salads as well.

In most cuisines it's not economically advantageous to harvest the plants at such a young stage as Eva does. People in southern China eat mustard simply seared with oil and garlic. It becomes almost as mild as spinach when cooked like this (although little kids might disagree). Many Asians preserve the greens by salting them. These spicy pickles (spicy not so much from the mustard but because they add chiles) are paired with rich meats (like pork belly) or added to soups or stir-fries. In the Punjabi cuisine of northwest India mustard is stewed with ginger and spices and served with clarified butter (ghee) and a corn-flour flatbread. African Americans have long enjoyed mustard greens braised with ham hocks or smoked turkey.

If you are really adverse to heat, try mizuna greens. They are the "bunny trail" of mustards, as they have only a touch of heat.

HEALTH VIRTUES

If you aren't yet convinced that you should work mustard greens into your diet, perhaps its health virtues will push you over the edge.

Mustard greens are a good source of antioxidants and also contain vitamin E, which has been found to protect against the decline in memory and cognitive function that can occur with age.

Buying, Storing, and Prepping

When buying mustard greens, look for vibrant green leaves that have not begun to wilt. The stems should be stiff. Store mustard greens, unwashed, in a plastic bag in the refrigerator for up to a week, but try to use them soon after they are harvested.

Growing Mustard Greens

Eva usually grows three or four varieties of mustard. Some have more kick than others.

All are attractive; in particular I like Ruby Streaks and Red Giant.

Sow seeds ¼ inch deep in full sun and keep the soil moist. Harvest leaves as needed by pinching them off at the base; new leaves will keep sprouting until the plant is ready to go to seed.

Eva takes advantage of the plant's natural growth cycle by allowing the mustard to flower. Some flowers are able to go to seed before she cuts the plants back to sell the remaining flowers and cook the greens. If conditions are amenable the mustard will perpetually renew itself, producing more greens and flowers before seeding again (and again). The tenacity of mustard knows no bounds.

Mustard Green, Potato, and Corn Soup

MAKES 4 SERVINGS

1 tablespoon extra-virgin olive oil

2 cups chopped leeks or onion, in ½-inch pieces

2 carrots, peeled and chopped into ¼-inch pieces

5 garlic cloves, minced

1 large potato, scrubbed and chopped (about 2½ cups)

½ teaspoon salt

6 ounces smoked turkey necks or thinly sliced kielbasa (optional)

1 tablespoon chopped rosemary or sage

Kernels from 3 ears fresh corn

Freshly cracked black pepper

Extra-virgin olive oil for drizzling, if desired

5–6 cups chopped mustard greens (use full-grown, not baby, leaves)

This soup is luscious as long as the vegetables are fresh.

1. Heat the oil in a soup pot over medium heat. Add the leeks, carrots, and garlic and sauté for 5 minutes, stirring regularly. Add the potato, salt, meat (if using), and 6 cups of water. Bring the soup to a boil, then reduce the heat and let simmer until the potatoes are tender, about 25 minutes.

2. Remove the turkey necks (if you've used kielbasa, you can leave it in). Add the rosemary and corn kernels and let simmer another couple of minutes. Season to taste with additional salt and freshly cracked black pepper.

3. Ladle the soup into bowls, drizzle in a bit of extra-virgin olive oil, and top with chopped mustard greens to serve.

Pasta with Mustard Greens, Shredded Chicken, and Smoky Cream Sauce

This heartwarming (but spicy!) recipe is also nice with leftover shredded turkey or pork, preferably pasture-raised. Feel free to use kale, collards, or turnip greens if mustard greens aren't available, though if you're using kale and collards you should add them at the same time as the pasta.

MAKES 6 SERVINGS

- 1 or 2 dried chipotle peppers
- 3–4 tablespoons extra-virgin olive oil
- 2 large onions, thinly sliced
- 1–2 teaspoons balsamic vinegar
- 3 garlic cloves, minced
- ½ cup heavy cream
- 4 cups shredded cooked chicken (grilled if possible; thigh meat is good)
- 1 pound penne (or any petite pasta)
- 1 pound mustard greens, chopped into 1-inch pieces
- ½ teaspoon salt
- Freshly cracked black pepper

1. Bring 1 cup water to a boil. Pour the boiling water over the chipotles, cover, and let soak for 30 minutes. Remove the rehydrated chipotles from their liquid; remove the seeds and finely chop the peppers. (Reserve the soaking liquid.)

2. Bring a large pot of salted water to a boil for cooking the pasta. Reduce the heat to low, cover, and leave at a simmer.

3. Heat the oil in a large skillet over medium-high heat. Add the onions and cook, stirring every few minutes, for 10 minutes. Reduce the heat to low. The onions will start sticking to the pan; let them stick a little and brown, but then stir them before they burn. The trick is to leave them alone enough to brown, but not so long so that they burn. Cook until the onions are quite brown, about 15 to 20 minutes longer.

4. Once the onions are brown, add a teaspoon or two of balsamic vinegar. Add the garlic to the caramelized onions and cook for 1 minute, then add the cream, the chipotle soaking water, and the chopped chipotles. Boil the mixture for 5 minutes. Add the shredded chicken and set aside.

5. Bring the pasta water back to a rolling boil. Add the pasta and boil for 8 minutes, then stir in the mustard greens and boil for 1 minute. Drain the pasta and greens (saving the water for a future soup!), then return them to the hot pot.

6. Add the chicken mixture to the cooked pasta, and season with the salt and freshly cracked black pepper to taste.

Parsley

At many restaurant jobs I've held, parsley has been an herb to loathe. No machine could achieve what a knife and hand could. One "famous" chef I worked for wanted the parsley as fine as table salt. I would hammer away furiously with two big chef knives, one in each hand. I'd beat on the parsley for nearly half an hour, like a drum solo in a rock concert (but less fun), stopping only when the chef said I could. Before that I'd worked at a restaurant where we had to collect chopped parsley in a towel, which we'd form into a little sack, and run it under water until most of the chlorophyll had run out of the herb—when the water ran clear I knew I was done. Then I'd wring the life out of it, and voilà, the resulting parsley was like confetti—light, fluffy, and easy to shower on foods. Because it had been stripped of its oils, it had a great shelf life in the fridge. The only problem was its flavor; it tasted like sawdust.

The parsley you purchase at a supermarket has usually been out of the ground for a week or two, maybe even three, and has been grown in relatively unfertile soil. Collectively I know we'd have a different opinion of parsley if it were sold under more favorable circumstances. Eva's parsley, both curly and flat leaf, has a sweet, nutty celery flavor that can't compare to the parsley I knew B.E. (before Eva). I think what is crucial is that it tastes best when just snipped from nutrient-dense soil. (See the sidebar on nutrient density on page 75.) Eating fresh parsley makes me wonder why we all aren't growing it on windowsills, decks, and front stoops, and in our yards.

Parsley taken out of the soil has the ability to retain its youthful appearance, but its flavor wanes quickly as its volatile oils evaporate. Thin-leafed herbs like parsley (and basil, chervil, and cilantro, among others) are best either grown yourself or bought at a farmers' market.

Culinary Uses

There are two main types of parsley: curly and flat-leaf, also called Italian. Curly parsley is Eva's favorite. I feel strongly the other way; I think Italian parsley's flavor is deeper and sweeter, and it reigns supreme in my mind.

When Eva does use flat-leaf parsley, it's usually in slaws. She doesn't chop the leaves much and she adds copious amounts to cabbage, scallions, and lemon juice—a brilliant combo.

Chef Adam Halberg of Barcelona restaurants in Connecticut feels that parsley is the most underutilized herb around because most chefs write it off as a garnish. Halberg likes to use it in a mixed herb salad with chervil, chives, and dill, or chopped up in a bread salad. Other chefs use parsley in salsa verde or on beef cheeks. When it grows in profusion, which it can, I like to make parsley pesto.

Parsley, if fresh, needs to partake in the meal rather than just sit prettily next to the entrée. Chopped parsley, fine or coarse, can add a bright flavor to an endless array of dishes, whether it's a flurry or a blizzard (Eva will douse a soup or entrée with half a cup of chopped parsley!). Sprinkle some parsley on roast lemon chicken, shrimp and pasta, lamb tagine or osso buco, rice and other grain salads, stewed clams and fennel bulb, soups and chowders, and paella.

Be generous when adding chopped curly parsley to tabbouleh-style salads, and move beyond bulgur; use cooked millet, Kamut, wheat berries, barley—even couscous or lentils.

HEALTH VIRTUES

Parsley sprigs, in restaurants especially, are often thrown into the garbage (or compost, if they're lucky) after having posed as a garnish with our dinner, but if we only knew what we were missing out on, more of us might take to finishing them off after meals. Parsley is a storehouse of antioxidants and nutrients, most notably iron and calcium. It is a great source of vitamins A and C as well as the B-complex vitamins, especially folic acid. With its high chlorophyll content, parsley makes a good breath freshener. And it is often used as a substitute for salt in foods, for example in soups, stews, and sauces.

BUYING, STORING, AND PREPPING

You can find both curly and flat-leaf parsley in the produce section of your supermarket year-round, but the quality may be inferior (as discussed above). So it is best to source this herb from a reliable grower who is giving you the fresh stuff. Store parsley, unwashed, in a plastic bag in the fridge for up to one week. You can also try storing the parsley by putting its stems in a glass of water in the refrigerator, which some say keeps it fresher longer.

To prepare, pull the leaves from the stems and chop. Don't chop Italian parsley too finely, though, or it will lose its flavor. If the parsley is super-fresh, the stems can be finely chopped and added to foods as well. You can also freeze the stems, whole, in a ziplock bag for use in making stocks.

If you have a lot of parsley and want to freeze it, chop the leaves, puree them in a blender with a little olive oil or lemon juice, and freeze in ice cube trays. You can then plop a cube into your pots of soup (at the end of cooking) all winter long and relive that green summer taste of fresh parsley.

GROWING PARSLEY

Starting parsley from seed is a slow process, so start the seeds indoors at least eight weeks before the last frost, or buy seedlings in the spring. When all danger of frost has passed, transplant seedlings to your garden, spacing them 10 to 12 inches apart in rich soil with ample moisture and full sun. Water the plants deeply at least once a week, and don't let the soil dry out completely.

Harvest parsley throughout the season by clipping the outer stems about 1 inch above the soil surface every one to two weeks. New growth will continue to sprout from the center of the plant. Don't cut the youngest stalks until freezing temperatures threaten the plants in late fall or early winter. In areas with mild winters, you can harvest parsley year-round.

Green Tomatoes

Green tomatoes are usually plentiful in the fall, and I don't understand why they are so often left on the vine to rot. I know Southerners love them, either pickled or breaded and fried. For me, they come to the rescue when I'm cooking the same-old, same-old vegetables. Their acidic flavor is a welcome complement to the sweeter squashes and root vegetables. For example: Add some olive oil to a hot skillet over medium heat, and sauté some chopped green tomatoes (I find cutting them into wedges works best) with some cooked butternut squash. After a few minutes add a clove of minced garlic and cook, not stirring too often, letting the vegetables form a crust. Add salt and pepper to taste, and serve just as is or with fish, roast chicken, or a grain like rice or millet.

Fish with *Charmoula* Sauce

MAKES 6 SERVINGS

Charmoula Spice Mix:

1 tablespoon chile powder

1 tablespoon ground coriander

1 tablespoon ground cumin

1 tablespoon sweet paprika

½ teaspoon ground allspice

½ teaspoon ground cinnamon

½ teaspoon ground fennel seed

Charmoula Paste:

1 cup plus 2 tablespoons extra-virgin olive oil

2 garlic cloves, minced

1 shallot, minced

1 tablespoon *charmoula* spice mix

2 tablespoons chopped fresh cilantro

2 tablespoons chopped fresh mint

2 tablespoons chopped fresh flat-leaf parsley

2 tablespoons lemon juice (about 1 lemon)

Salt and freshly cracked black pepper

36 ounces (six 6-ounce filets) bluefish, salmon, or tuna; or 1 whole Boston mackerel (gutted); or 3 Portuguese sardines

Steve Johnson has been a customer and friend of Eva's for a long time. While sitting at his bar at Rendezvous in Cambridge, Massachusetts, I listened to him muse about Eva: "Americans collectively are just beginning to appreciate bitter flavors like Eva's greens and herbs, whereas other cultures revere bitter foods as much as they do sweets. Eva is changing our palates by blurring the boundaries between what is cultivated and what is wild."

I asked Steve for a recipe that includes parsley. He told me about his *charmoula* recipe and how he acquired it: "When I lived in Montpellier in the late '70s, it had the third-largest North African population of any French city. This is where I came in contact with a whole new set of flavors and aromas in cooking: whole neighborhoods where Arabic was the primary language, devoted to stores and restaurants, spice shops and open-air markets. I remember being amazed and inspired by the displays in the markets. One day when I tried to buy a bunch of flat-leaf parsley, the vendor explained to me that I had to buy equal amounts of mint and cilantro as well. This wasn't just an up-sell on his part; in fact, in much of North Africa, these three fresh herbs are used together and are inseparable. I dutifully followed his instructions, and have since come to refer to these herbs as 'the holy trinity' of North African cooking."

Charmoula is both a spice mix and a marinade, and in this recipe it is also used as a condiment. Steve says, "It is sort of like a North African version of chimichurri sauce. We use the sauce to season grilled fish, vegetables, or meats, as is the custom. We also use it to season the sauce that we use for final dishes, usually as a table condiment. It is best to make this sauce and use it the same day; overnight the lemon juice will 'cook' the herbs and they will lose their brilliant color."

Any extra *charmoula* spice mix can be stored in a tightly sealed container for up to one week in the fridge.

1. To prepare the spice mix, combine the chile powder, coriander, cumin, paprika, allspice, cinnamon, and fennel seed, and mix well.

2. To prepare the *charmoula* paste, heat 2 tablespoons of the olive oil in a small skillet over medium heat. Add the garlic and shallot and stir until they are just softened, about 5 minutes. Add the *charmoula* spice mix, and mix well. Remove the mixture immediately from the heat and let it cool to room temperature. Transfer to a bowl.

3. Add the chopped cilantro, mint, and parsley to the bowl with spice mix, along with the remaining cup of olive oil and the lemon juice. Season to taste with salt and freshly cracked black pepper. Refrigerate the spice paste until you're ready to use it (although it is best used the same day).

4. Marinate the fish in about half of the sauce for at least 2 hours in the fridge. The fish can then be grilled, broiled, or baked and is best served with rice. Serve the remaining *charmoula* as a table condiment or spooned onto the fish.

Victoria George's Tabbouleh

MAKES 4 TO 6 SERVINGS

1 cup very fine bulgur

3 or 4 tomatoes, chopped

¼ cup extra-virgin olive oil

½ teaspoon salt or more to taste

8 cups loosely packed chopped parsley (about 4 bunches)

½ cup chopped mint leaves

3–4 bunches scallions, green and white parts, chopped

Juice of 3½ lemons (about ¾ cup plus 2 tablespoons lemon juice)

Freshly cracked black pepper

When I heard that chef Dan George soaks his bulgur in the juice of tomatoes rather than boiling water, I was intrigued. I couldn't really imagine it working out—how could tomato juice soften bulgur? Dan, who is 100 percent Lebanese, learned this method from his mom, Vicki. She was a brazen cook (no other women in the Lebanese community made their tabbouleh like this), and Dan remembers his mom receiving the ultimate compliment from a Lebanese friend one day: "Vicki sure knows how to use a lemon!" Lemon, as well as parsley, is at the nucleus of Lebanese cooking.

Now Dan's wife, Kris, who is not at all Lebanese, has taken over the tabbouleh production and makes it for gatherings, having also learned it from Vicki years ago. To make this tabbouleh, you need to buy very fine bulgur, available at Middle Eastern markets. But this recipe makes it worth seeking out.

1. Combine the bulgur, tomatoes, olive oil, and the salt in a large bowl and stir well. Let the bulgur sit for 45 minutes, stirring every now and then.

2. Add the parsley, mint, scallions, and lemon juice to the bulgur, and stir well. Season the salad with salt and freshly cracked black pepper. Serve.

Preserved Lemon Tabbouleh

This recipe is easiest to make if you grow mint, know someone who does, or can find big bunches at the farmers' market, as it calls for more than 2 cups of it. Parsley, on the other hand, is usually sold in big bunches. There are no tomatoes in the recipe, which is handy because local tomatoes aren't as readily available as these herbs are.

MAKES 4 TO 6 SERVINGS

1 cup very fine bulgur

½ teaspoon salt, plus a pinch or two for bulgur

2 cups chopped mint

2 cups chopped parsley

1½ cups chopped chives or garlic chives (or more if you have them)

2 tablespoons chopped preserved lemons (page 250)

3 tablespoons olive oil

Juice of ½ lemon

1. Place the bulgur in a large bowl with a pinch or two of the salt. Bring ⅔ cup water t a boil and pour over the bulgur. Stir, cover the bowl, and let sit for 5 minutes. Then remove the cover and let cool for 5 minutes.

2. Add the mint, parsley, chives, preserved lemon, olive oil, and lemon juice to the bulgur, and stir well. Season with the remaining ½ teaspoon salt and freshly cracked pepper to taste. Serve.

Make Your Own Cereal

It took me a while to take in the brilliance of Eva's breakfast. Every week she cooks a different grain, oftentimes with raisins—for example, oat groats, wheat berries, kasha, millet, barley. Then each morning, she spoons some into a bowl and eats it warm or cold with soy milk or raw milk and chopped apples, or maybe some frozen raspberries. She always offers some to me, but it never looks appetizing and, well, I usually opt for toast. However, one morning I agreed to eat some because there was no bread. She gave me some cold kasha (these are toasted buckwheat groats, which is pretty intense stuff), and she poured soy milk over it. I was daunted, not sure I could eat it. So I hunted through her fridge to try to improve the situation. There were some autumn olives, so I topped the kasha with that and drizzled in some maple syrup. Then I added a handful of a trail mix Eva had made with pumpkin seeds,

raisins, and walnuts. I tasted this mélange, and it was like some delicious cereal that no one had invented yet. Now I do this often at home. My favorite grains to use are quinoa, millet, and now even kasha.

Cooking whole grains is a commonsensical alternative to forking out four dollars for a box of cereal that contains about a quarter's worth of highly processed food—mostly grains and sugar.

Preserving Curly Parsley's Dignity

Eva is on the phone with yet another chef. She'd rather be in the garden, but no one can take her place selling. Talking with chefs requires patience, passion, relentless persistence, a steel will, and a solid knowledge of plants. And a little personality goes a long way. Eva specializes in *creative* selling. The chefs love her, and many close relationships develop from these phone calls.

She dials up Susie Regis, one of the head chefs at UpStairs on the Square, a hot spot in Cambridge, Massachusetts. Here is Eva's side of the conversation, typical of the kind of banter I hear whenever I visit.

"Susie! It's Eva! How are you?"

"I'm well, and so are my greens!"

"Today, I am trying to influence the fate of curly parsley!"

I've taken an informal poll asking chefs why they prefer flat Italian parsley to curly, and most chefs say it's because the flavor is better. But the truth is, curly parsley is just unbeatable when it comes to flavor. So I've devised a theory for this misconception. Curly parsley has been a ubiquitous garnish in the last century. The good and the bad news is that it can hold its curl and color for weeks, but it loses its flavor within days. So when people nibble on their garnish it is usually weeks old and tasteless. And this is how curly parsley got its bad rap.

Eva's sales pitch continues:

"Would you be willing to reconsider curly parsley? Its current social status has no bearing on reality. Fresh curly parsley is as delicious as Italian. And it's a better choice for Middle Eastern salads like tabbouleh. The curly parsley is more three-dimensional; it occupies space, even chopped, fluffing the salad, preventing it from clumping. Three pounds? And we have some superlative lemon basil . . ."

Sage

Sage's culinary reputation seems to be divided. Some chefs feel its flavor is harsh, while others revel in it. But the truth is, it is the application and amount that determine sage's harshness or appeal. One thing is for sure: it's hard to mistake its flavor, with its notes of black pepper, mint, and camphor, for that of another herb.

Culinary Uses

By using little more than shredded cabbage, lemon juice, lots of snipped sage, garlic, and salt, Eva made a slaw one day that blew conventional slaw out of its bland, creamy waters. What an odd combination, I thought; I would never have used sage in a slaw or salad, and I assumed lemon juice lacked sufficient punch for cabbage slaw. Sometimes foods unexpectedly electrify each other.

Sage pairs well with assertive herbs like thyme and rosemary. I like to chop up sage and garlic and stir them into soft goat cheese, along with good olive oil. You could also mix sage with marjoram or savory to season roasted mushrooms, winter squashes, and root vegetables. Sage can be added during the roasting, but if you want more flavor add it at the end, since it contains a high level of volatile oils. Curiously, if the sage is cooked while incorporated into a stuffing or bread, the flavor does not deteriorate much.

Sage truly shines with rich, fatty foods: cheese, pork, cream, bacon, and butter (as in butter browned with sage spooned over ricotta gnocchi, roasted pumpkin, and bits of a good smoked bacon). It's wonderful in a creamy pasta with pancetta, or any cured meat. Germans like it in sausage. It is delicious in stuffings. On a lighter note, Eva marinates venison in red wine and sage.

Deep-fried sage, though popular, is not my bag. Usually the deep-frying renders the sage insipid and excessively oily.

Eva grows four varieties of sage, but my favorite is purple sage. It is a beauty, contrasting green against purple.

Health Virtues

The Latin name for sage, *salvia*, means "to heal." Historically, the Romans didn't cook with sage but used it medicinally. Sage tea dries up mother's milk and can help relieve perimenopausal hot flashes. To prepare it as a tea, steep the leaves in just-boiled water for ten minutes. Studies have also shown sage to be effective in the management of mild to moderate Alzheimer's disease.

Buying, Storing, and Prepping

When buying sage, look for leaves that are fragrant and perky. Store fresh sage, unwashed, in a sealed bag in the refrigerator, where, thanks to its low moisture content, it will keep for up to three weeks.

To enjoy sage year-round, dry it by hanging it in small bunches or spreading the leaves out flat on a screen in a dry, well-ventilated room. At Eva's, sage is the last herb to die come winter, and it lives in her unheated greenhouse all winter long.

In general only the leaves are consumed. You can save the stems for flavoring stocks or broths.

Growing Sage

Sage grows very slowly from seed, so buying a seedling from a nursery is well worth the cost. It prefers full sun and it isn't picky about soil as long as it isn't overwatered. Space plants 3 to 5 feet apart so they have room to grow. The flavor of sage peaks just before it flowers, making this the optimal time for harvesting if you are going to use your entire crop at once or dry the leaves. Otherwise you can harvest individual leaves as needed. If your sage does flower, enjoy the edible blooms as a garnish.

At the end of the growing season it is best to prune your sage down to a compact bush. At the first sign of life in the spring, Eva likes to cut her sage plants down to the ground. She believes that the leafing is healthiest when it is from new wood.

Spaghetti Squash with Lentils and Sage

Here is a vegetarian meal where you won't miss the mighty carb. As for all of my recipes, improvise here if you want to. I've made this with parsley and it turned out great. If you don't have feta, use a soft goat cheese or a Pecorino. If you have extra energy, you could toast and salt the squash seeds for garnish. Also, this recipe and other spaghetti squash recipes I've had are effective served cold.

1. Preheat the oven to 325 degrees F.
2. Bake the squash whole on a baking sheet for 1½ hours.
3. Meanwhile, bring a medium saucepan with plenty of salted water to a boil. Add the lentils and cook until al dente, about 20 minutes. Rinse the lentils with cold water and drain them well.
4. Remove the softened squash from the oven and let it cool a bit. Then cut the squash in half and scoop out the seeds. Use a fork to pull the strands of squash out of the shell and into a bowl. You can use a spoon to get the last bits out. Set aside.
5. Heat 2 tablespoons of the olive oil in a large skillet over medium heat. Add the garlic and the lentils, frying them without stirring for about 3 minutes. Season generously with salt and freshly cracked black pepper, stir or toss, and fry for a few more minutes until they become a bit crispy. Transfer to a plate.
6. Add the remaining 3 tablespoons olive oil and squash to the pan, and reheat, stirring, for 2 to 3 minutes. Add the feta, sage, and salt and freshly cracked pepper to taste. Stir in the lemon juice. Spoon onto plates and top with lentils and serve.

MAKES 3 SERVINGS

1 spaghetti squash (about 3 pounds)

1¼ cups uncooked brown lentils or French lentils

5 tablespoons extra-virgin olive oil or butter

4 garlic cloves, minced

Salt and freshly cracked black pepper

2 tablespoons lemon juice (about ½ lemon)

4 ounces feta, cut into small pieces (my favorite is goat's-milk feta)

2–4 tablespoons chopped sage leaves

Eva's Remarkable Cabbage Slaw No. 2

MAKES 6 SERVINGS

1 medium head green cabbage (about 3 pounds), cored and thinly sliced

2 sweet crisp apples (such as Gala or Fuji), skin-on, cut into matchstick pieces

½ cup chopped fresh parsley (optional)

¼ cup chopped fresh sage

½ to 1 teaspoon salt

½ cup lemon juice (about 2 lemons)

Freshly cracked black pepper

3 tablespoons extra-virgin olive oil

Two factors make this slaw unusual. First, it's low-maintenance: no slicing onions or grating carrots; no fatty dressing to make. Second, it uses fresh sage. Sage can be harsh-tasting when raw, and I never imagined it in a salad or slaw. But little did I know how well it performs in this situation. It just goes to show, even herbs shouldn't be pigeonholed.

1. Combine the cabbage, apple, parsley (if using), sage, and salt in a large bowl. Toss the ingredients well, adding the additional salt and freshly cracked black pepper to taste. Add the olive oil and toss again.

2. Let the slaw sit for 10 minutes, and then toss it again. Serve immediately, or chill in the refrigerator and serve within 24 hours.

Grits with Sage and Cheddar

MAKES 4 SERVINGS

2 tablespoons butter

1 yellow onion, thinly sliced

1 garlic clove, minced

½ teaspoon salt, plus more for seasoning

1 cup hominy grits

1 tablespoon chopped sage

1 cup grated sharp cheddar cheese

Freshly cracked black pepper

A good-quality sharp cheddar makes a big difference here. These grits are great with eggs for breakfast or as a side dish for dinner. If you can only find instant grits, follow the recipe through step 1, then follow the directions on the package for cooking the quick grits. Add the butter and cheese when the grits are done.

1. Melt 1 tablespoon of the butter in a heavy-bottomed saucepan over medium heat. Add the onion and garlic and cook until the onions are golden, about 9 to 10 minutes.

2. Add 4 cups water and the salt. Bring to a boil. Add the grits, and stir until the mixture comes to a soft boil. Reduce the heat to very low, and cook the grits for 30 minutes, stirring often.

3. Add the sage and cook the grits for 10 minutes longer, then remove them from the heat. Add the cheddar cheese, and season with salt and freshly cracked black pepper to taste.

Café DiCocoa's Apricot Sage Cookies

My good friend Cathi di Cocco up in Maine has been making these southern Italian cornmeal cookies for years. The sweet dried apricots and savory sage mix well with the crunchy cornmeal to create this rustic yet refined cookie. It's the signature cookie at DiCocoa's Marketplace, her café in Bethel, Maine. This recipe makes a lot of cookies.

MAKES 30 COOKIES

½ pound (2 sticks) unsalted butter, softened

1¼ cups raw "turbinado" sugar or lightly packed brown sugar; or 1 cup granulated sugar

1 large egg

1¼ cups cornmeal (preferably stone-ground)

⅔ cup whole dried apricots

1 cup white flour

½ cup whole wheat flour

2–3 tablespoons chopped fresh sage or 1–2 tablespoons dried sage

1 teaspoon baking soda

1 teaspoon salt

1. Place butter in the bowl of electric mixer (or in a freestanding bowl, if you're using a handheld mixer). Beat, gradually adding the sugar, until all is incorporated. Beat in the egg. Set aside.

2. Combine half of the cornmeal and the whole dried apricots in a food processor, and pulse until eraser-size pieces appear. Add the cornmeal mixture to the butter mixture, along with the white flour, whole wheat flour, sage, baking soda, and salt. Mix on low speed until the mixture comes together. Refrigerate the dough for 30 minutes (or chill in the freezer for 15 minutes).

3. Preheat the oven to 350 degrees F.

4. Once the dough is chilled, form into 1-inch balls. Place the balls 2 inches apart on an ungreased baking sheet. With a bit of flour on your fingers, press down on the cookie to flatten it.

5. Bake for 10 to 15 minutes, until golden. Let cool on racks.

Sunchokes

Helianthus tuberosus · PERENNIAL

Looking more like a widget than a vegetable, this knobby tuber knows that it's the inside that counts. It's one of Eva's favorite plants to grow. She says, "It's wild, which is another way to say that it doesn't require much effort. Plus it's winter-hardy—you can harvest the chokes in the fall and if you haven't dug them all up, they'll hang in come spring."

Despite its name, this tuber is not related to the artichoke. Nor is it from Jerusalem, despite its other common name, Jerusalem artichoke. This plant originated in North America and in 1585, Sir Walter Raleigh found Native Americans in what is now Virginia, cultivating these tubers which they called "sunroots". The edible root belongs to a tall plant sporting big yellow flowers closely resembling those of its cousin, the sunflower. The Italians came over and they named it, logically, *girasola*, the Italian word for sunflower. At some point a settler was talking about this tuber, *girasole*, and whomever he was talking to misheard it as "Jerusalem." The name somehow stuck, so the poor plant's name got corrupted in a real-life version of the game "telephone." Then, in 1605, a French mariner, Samuel de Champlain, described eating "a Jerusalem" on Cape Cod. Champlain was an influential fellow, founding Quebec City and "discovering" a body of water (of course, the Indians had discovered it long before him) that he named, modestly, Lake Champlain. He savored this tuber and proclaimed that the Jerusalem had the taste of artichokes. So the two ideas—Jerusalem and artichoke—came together rather comically as Jerusalem artichoke in the 1600s. Many food buffs prefer to call these tubers sunchokes (as do many supermarkets), since this name is much less misleading. Maybe it would have

been wiser, food historian Elizabeth Schneider writes in *Uncommon Fruits and Vegetables* and *Vegetables from Amaranth to Zucchini*, if we had hadn't veered from the Native American name, sun root.

Culinary Uses

Sunchokes are a big favorite of mine. When they are roasted, an artichoke flavor comes forth, the interior becomes soft as pudding, and the exterior caramelizes and develops a sweet, nutty crunch. Just thinly slice them and toss with plenty of minced garlic, salt, pepper, and a splash of olive oil, and roast on a sheet pan until they are crunchy and caramelized on the outside and soft on the inside. Roasted sunchoke is a great side dish at Thanksgiving. Sunchokes also perform miracles in soups, veggie burgers, stews (like pork stew), and mashes with other tubers. Chef Denis Cotter (author of *Wild Garlic, Gooseberries . . . and Me*) makes a roasted sunchoke risotto with lemon thyme oil; he does so by peeling and braising the sunchokes, then pureeing them.

I have added chopped sunchokes to my own tomato sauce; with their earthy flavor, it's akin to adding mushrooms. Some people eat the sunchoke raw, like daikon radish or jicama, in salads or use it for making kimchi. The flavor and texture are similar to those of a water chestnut—there is a nice crunch, but the flavor in my opinion is bland. In terms of raw vegetables, I'd much rather stick with raw jicama or daikon—and I'll take my sunchokes roasted, thanks very much.

Health Virtues

One warning: sunchokes can cause flatulence, so it's best to send your friends right along home after dinner. The primary form of carbohydrate in sunchokes is inulin (not insulin), and we can't digest it, so therefore we need to release it. Some need to release it more than others. The upside is that sunchokes have significant health benefits, and they make a great potato substitute for diabetics because of their low impact on blood sugar.

Buying, Storing, and Prepping

Just-dug sunchokes are in a different league from supermarket sunchokes. Fresh chokes are juicier, nuttier, and just yummier. Besides, a good farmers' market will have plenty in the fall when they are in season; a supermarket may or may not have them at any given time.

Sunchokes can be stored for up to six weeks in the vegetable bin of your refrigerator, in a plastic bag. However, they store best in the ground. Dig a trench or hole, add the sunchokes, then cover with soil and a thick layer of mulch. You can dig them up as you need them. The

mulch should keep the ground insulated and unfrozen.

Chefs like to peel sunchokes for a smoother, silkier texture. My opinion is that no matter how you are using them, you don't need to take the skin off. The skin is as thin as that of red-skinned potatoes, and we could all use the extra fiber and vitamins. Just scrub lightly to get rid of any soil.

Growing Sunchokes

In the spring, plant fresh sunchokes 6 inches deep in loose, well-drained soil, spacing plants 18 inches apart, preferably in full sun to encourage well-developed tubers, But, as Eva warns, "you might regret it," since the sunchoke patch will spread over time. Definitely give them a dedicated area of the garden or border, since any small piece of tuber you leave behind (intentionally or not) will sprout a new plant the following year. It is almost impossible to overharvest sunchokes.

Come October, the tall stalks with their yellow flowers (which some people say have a light cocoa fragrance) will wither, and then you can start digging. Simply dig up the plant and collect the tubers with your hands. Or, depending on your climate, you can leave them in the ground through the winter, digging them up as you need them; cover the plant area with heavy mulch (like burlap bags, hay, or wood chips) to keep the ground from freezing solid.

Sunchokes in Chicken Broth

MAKES 4 SERVINGS

1–2 pounds cooked chicken bones

3 stalks celery, coarsely chopped

3 medium onions, coarsely chopped

1 carrot, coarsely chopped

1 head garlic, split crosswise like an English muffin

2 sprigs rosemary

3 cups thinly sliced sunchokes

1 cup greens or herbs (chervil, chickweed, cilantro, spinach, sprouts, or whatever you have)

Salt and freshly cracked black pepper

I happened to be teaching a group of sixteen-year-olds how to make chicken pot pie one day, and we roasted three chicken breasts on the bone. Afterward I brought the cooked bones home and made a little stock. Customarily stocks, as you may know, are made from raw bones. But this stock was rich and redolent. I recommend roasting the chicken a day or two before, so you have your bones to make broth.

1. Make a stock by combining the bones with 8 cups water and the celery, onions, carrot, garlic, and 1 sprig of the rosemary. Bring to a simmer and let simmer for at least 2 hours, adding more water as it cooks down.

2. Strain the bones and vegetables from the liquid. You should end up with about 6 cups stock.

3. Place the stock in a large soup pot and add the sunchokes. Bring to a simmer and let simmer for 8 minutes, then remove from the heat and let steep for 10 minutes. Bring the soup back to a simmer and add the greens and any chicken meat left on the cooked bones. Season the soup generously with salt and freshly cracked black pepper to taste and serve.

Conserving Energy

Eva revels in conserving fossil fuels. Her wood-stove gets a workout. She gets the wood from her own land. In cold months she capitalizes on the hot flat-top surface to heat water for tea, for cooking, and for washing dishes. She'll stack pots on top of pots, Asian-style, when steaming or reheating food, to reap the benefit of the emanating heat. She'll simmer stocks all night in a Dutch oven or pressure cooker on the flat top. She'll make toast or bake whole pota-toes on the flat top under an inverted stainless steel bowl. She puts a little rack inside the fire-box for grilling fish or meat.

She keeps her hot water tank set on vacation mode (around 100 degrees F) throughout the year and only turns it up for a shower. She uses a washing machine for clothes but always uses a cold-water cycle. And she hangs her clothes on a clothesline year-round.

Sunchoke Bisque

A velvety-smooth version of sunchoke soup. The recipe comes from Kristin Costa, Jim Mercer's sous chef at the Bay Club in Mattapoisett, Massachusetts, not far from Eva's farm. Jim is a good friend of Eva's and comes for dinner often with his boyfriend, John McCormack, who is an avid gardener. But this recipe is all Kristin's, he quips. She says, "It is a pretty simple recipe; there is a minimum of ingredients because I like to showcase Eva's beautiful fresh-dug sunchokes."

1. Heat the butter and oil in a heavy-bottomed pot over medium heat. Add the leeks and onion and sauté until slightly caramelized, about 15 minutes. Add the sunchokes, potatoes, and chicken stock. Season to taste with salt and freshly cracked black pepper. Bring to a simmer, and let simmer until the potatoes and sunchokes are soft, about 15 minutes. I skim off the foam that forms with a ladle.

2. Puree the soup in small batches in a blender until smooth. If you prefer a thicker soup, keep some of the liquid in the pot when you ladle the soup into the blender.

3. Strain the soup through a fine-mesh sieve to remove any fiber; you should get a silky-smooth bisque. Taste and adjust seasonings if necessary, and serve with caramelized chestnuts (if using) and a few drizzles of olive oil.

MAKES 10 SERVINGS

- 2 tablespoons butter
- 1 tablespoon canola oil
- 2 cups chopped leeks (whites only)
- 2 cups minced onion
- 3 pounds sunchokes, roughly chopped (I like to leave the skin on, but make sure you scrub well)
- 1 large russet potato, peeled and roughly chopped
- 7 cups fresh chicken stock
- Salt and freshly cracked black pepper
- Caramelized chestnuts (very optional, but nice)
- Extra-virgin olive oil for drizzling

Sunchoke Dumplings
with Swiss Chard and Walnuts

MAKES 3 OR 4 SERVINGS

1¼ pounds sunchokes

2 large eggs

½ teaspoon salt or more to taste

1¾ cups white whole wheat flour (or unbleached white flour)

4 tablespoons butter, softened

4 tablespoons chopped walnuts

1 leek, chopped into ½-inch pieces

1 large garlic clove, minced

1 bunch Swiss chard, chopped into 1-inch pieces

4 tablespoons grated blue cheese (Gorgonzola, Stilton, or any artisan blue)

Eva says this dish oozes *umami*, a Japanese word for a taste sensation of meaty or savory, produced by several amino acids typically found in meats, cheeses, broths, stocks, and other protein-heavy foods. It is not always easy for a vegetarian dish to achieve this satisfying meaty quality. I think it is the earthy flavor of the chokes and chard, as well as the rich texture of dumplings, that does it.

1. Scrub the sunchokes clean under warm running water. You may want to peel them if the skin is tough. Using a steamer, cook the sunchokes for about 20 minutes, until they are tender.

2. Mash the steamed sunchokes in a bowl with a fork. Add the eggs and salt and mix well. Incorporate the flour ½ cup at a time, mixing well after each addition. The mixture should be soft and sticky.

3. Bring a large pot of salted water to a boil.

4. Meanwhile, heat the butter in a large skillet over medium heat. Add the walnuts and cook, stirring regularly, until they are toasted, about 7 minutes. Remove the walnuts from the skillet with a slotted spoon, and set aside

5. Add the leeks and garlic to the skillet and cook for 4 minutes or so, stirring. Add the chard and cook, stirring, until the chard is wilted and cooked through, about 2 minutes. Remove the skillet from the heat.

6. With an oiled spoon and your finger, take spoonfuls of the sunchoke dough and drop them into the boiling water. Continue until all the dough is used. (If you have leftover batter, make it into pancakes the following morning, cooking them in butter.) As the dumplings rise to the surface, remove them from the boiling water with a slotted spoon and place them in the skillet with the chard mixture. Stir in the walnuts.

7. Heat the chard and dumplings to the desired temperature on the stovetop over medium heat. Spoon the mixture onto plates, then top with grated cheese.

Roasted Sunchokes

Try inserting these sweet sunchokes in a roasted vegetable sandwich with goat cheese and arugula or chickweed. You could also feature them in a pasta dish or serve them with roast chicken, pork, lamb, venison, duck, or beef.

MAKES 4 SERVINGS AS A SIDE DISH

3 cups thinly sliced sunchokes

2 garlic cloves, minced

1 tablespoon extra-virgin olive oil

Salt and freshly cracked black pepper

1. Preheat the oven to 400 degrees F. Scrub the sunchokes clean under warm running water.
2. Combine the sunchokes, garlic, and olive oil, garlic in a medium bowl. Season generously with salt and freshly cracked black pepper. Toss well.
3. Transfer the sunchokes to a baking sheet, using a plastic spatula to get all the garlic bits, and bake for approximately 25 minutes, or longer if you want them crispy. Let cool for 5 minutes, then serve.

Note: Once cooked, the sunchokes can be kept in cool spot in the kitchen for a few hours if need be. Reheat by placing them in a 400-degree oven for 5 minutes.

ADDITIONAL FALL RECIPES

Lesli's Sweet Corn Pudding

This revelatory dessert pudding comes from my good friend and talented pastry chef Lesli Turock. I highly recommend you make this recipe.

MAKES 6 SERVINGS

1 tablespoon plus 1½ teaspoons cornstarch

1¾ cups milk

Kernels from 3 or 4 large ears corn (about 2½ cups)

2–3 tablespoons sugar, agave syrup, honey, or maple syrup (more or less depending on how sweet the corn is)

½ vanilla bean

1/8 teaspoon salt

2 tablespoons heavy cream or unsalted butter

1. Make a slurry by mixing the cornstarch into ¼ cup of the milk, whisking until it is smooth. Set the slurry aside.

2. Combine the remaining 1½ cups milk with the corn, sugar, vanilla bean, salt, and cream (if using) in a medium saucepot over medium heat. Bring to a gentle simmer, and cook the mixture just until the corn is soft, about 10 to 12 minutes. Remove the vanilla bean and scrape any seeds out into the pudding.

3. Using an immersion bender, puree the corn mixture. If you want a really refined, smooth pudding, strain this mixture, pressing on the solids to extract as much liquid as possible.

4. Whisk the cornstarch slurry into the pudding. Bring the mixture to a simmer, while continuing to whisk, and cook until it thickens. If you are using butter instead of cream, whisk it in after pudding has thickened. Serve warm.

Chipotle Apple Butter

My old roommate Courtney makes a terrific apple butter and I've borrowed her secret: apple cider vinegar. Apple butter takes a couple of hours to cook and needs frequent stirring. Courtney would watch a movie on her laptop while stirring.

If you'd like to can your apple butter, you can find directions on the Internet. I usually don't do this. Instead I fill two large jars for myself, refrigerating them, and then I give the rest away, instructing people to refrigerate it. It lasts at least six months in the fridge. I love it with pasture-raised pork chops.

MAKES ROUGHLY 3 OR 4 PINT JARS

8 pounds apples, the tarter the better (such as Baldwin, Ida Red, Macoun, Newtown Pippin, and Northern Spy)

1²/₃ cups apple cider vinegar

4 cups sugar

½ teaspoon salt

½ cup chopped chipotles in adobo sauce or 1 tablespoon ground star anise

1. Cut the apples into quarters without peeling them or coring them. Much of the pectin is in the cores and peels of the apples, and the pectin will help thicken your butter.
2. Put the apples in a large pot with the vinegar and 3½ cups of water. Cover the pot and bring the contents to a boil. Boil for about 20 minutes, until the apples are soft.
3. Ladle the apple mixture into a conical strainer or food mill. Press the mixture through the strainer or food mill and into a bowl. Add the sugar, salt, and star anise (if using) and mix well.
4. Transfer the apple butter to a large, wide, heavy-bottomed pot and cook over medium-low heat, stirring almost constantly to prevent burning. Scrape the bottom of the pot while you stir to make sure a crust is not forming. Cook the apple butter for 1 to 2 hours, until it is thick and smooth. You'll need to stir every 3–4 minutes. Add the chipotles (if using) and stir well. Taste the apple butter, and if it doesn't seem spicy enough for you, you can just add more of the adobo sauce.
5. To test the butter for thickness, chill a metal spoon in a glass of ice water. Remove the spoon, scoop half a spoonful of the butter from the pot, and let it cool to room temperature. If it thickens up the way you like it, then you're done. If it is still too loose for your liking, continue to cook it.
6. When the consistency of the butter seems right to you, pour it into the jars using a ladle and a funnel. Let cool before securing the lid. This apple butter will last for 6 months in the fridge.

ADDITIONAL FALL RECIPES

Sweet Potato, Nut, and Fruit Biryani

MAKES 6 SERVINGS

1 cup red or green lentils

1 tablespoon vegetable oil

4 star anise pods, ground, or 1 teaspoon ground fennel seed

2-inch piece ginger root, peeled and minced

1 teaspoon ground cardamom

1 teaspoon ground cloves

1 teaspoon ground fenugreek seed (optional)

1 teaspoon ground turmeric

½ teaspoon ground cayenne pepper

½ teaspoon ground cinnamon

2 large tomatoes, cubed

1 cup coconut milk

1 cup soy milk

1 cup long-grain basmati rice

1 sweet potato or butternut squash, peeled and chopped

½ cup chopped cilantro (leaves and/or stems)

1 pound firm tofu, chopped

1 cup chopped raisins, dates, or apricots

½ cup almonds or peanuts, toasted

Salt and freshly cracked black pepper

Here is a sublime meatless meal. This biryani, a rice curry based loosely on one in Dave DeWitt's book *A World of Curries*, is from an area in Pakistan that borders Afghanistan. I've taken out the dairy, because it doesn't need it. The recipe looks lengthy, but it's pretty quick if you have the spices. I roast my own peanuts; they taste much better this way.

1. Bring 1½ cups water to a boil in a small saucepan. Add the lentils and boil until they're tender, about 10 minutes.

2. Heat the oil in a large skillet over medium heat. Add the star anise, ginger, cardamom, cloves, fenugreek, turmeric, cayenne, and cinnamon, along with the tomatoes. Cook the mixture, uncovered, until the tomatoes turn into a thick pulp, about 8 minutes.

3. Add the coconut milk, soy milk, rice, sweet potato, and cooked lentils with their water. Simmer the curry, covered, until the rice is tender, about 20 minutes.

4. Add the tofu, raisins, and nuts. Cook until all the vegetables are tender and the flavors have melded, about 5 minutes. Add the cilantro and season generously with salt and freshly cracked black pepper.

Note: To toast the nuts, roast in a 350-degree oven on a rimmed baking sheet for almonds about 8-10 minutes or for raw peanuts, about 30 minutes or until golden brown.

Intensely Pumpkin Bread Pudding

I've tripled the quantity of pumpkin from a similar recipe in my book *Vegetarian Planet*. It makes the pudding much creamier. If you don't have a small sugar pumpkin, feel free to use any winter squash or other type of pumpkin, but don't use canned pumpkin—it will bring the pudding down more than a notch. Serve warm with ice cream, or cold, like a flan.

MAKES 10 SERVINGS

- 1 (3-pound) Small Sugar pumpkin
- 4 large eggs
- 1 cup plus 3 tablespoons Sucanat or sugar
- 2 cups half-and-half
- 1 cup soy or cow's milk
- 2 pinches salt
- 1 teaspoon ground cinnamon
- 1 teaspoon grated nutmeg
- 4 cups cubed bread (I prefer a crusty white or wheat), in 1-inch cubes
- 3 tablespoons butter

1. Preheat the oven to 400 degrees F.
2. Cut the pumpkin in half, scoop out the seeds, and set on a baking sheet, flat side down. Roast for 40 to 45 minutes, until the flesh inside the pumpkin is completely tender. Remove the pumpkin from the oven and let cool.
3. Reduce the oven temperature to 325 degrees F. Liberally butter a 9 by 13-inch casserole or Pyrex pan.
4. When the pumpkin is cool enough to handle, scoop out the cooked pumpkin flesh. Measure out 3 cups; save the rest to eat it on the spot with a little butter and nutmeg!
5. Whisk together the eggs and 1 cup of the Sucanat in a large bowl. Add the half-and-half, milk, salt, cinnamon, and nutmeg, then stir in the 3 cups pumpkin.
6. Arrange the bread cubes in the casserole pan in a single layer. Pour the pumpkin mixture over the bread. Dot the bread pudding with the butter and sprinkle on the 3 tablespoons Sucanat evenly over all.
7. Bake the pudding, uncovered, for at least 1½ hours, or until it is mostly set. Let cool before serving.

ADDITIONAL FALL RECIPES

Sharon Kane's Fermented Butternut Squash

MAKES APPROXIMATELY 3 QUARTS

Pumpkin Pie Spice Mix:

12 whole allspice

3 cinnamon sticks

1 tablespoon whole cloves

½ nutmeg

Fermented Squash:

1 medium-large (3–4 pound) butternut squash

3 or 4 apples, not too sweet (Granny Smiths are good)

3–4 medium onions

3 bay leaves

About ½ cup sea salt

Sharon came to our nonprofit, Haley House Café, to teach a Slow Food class on fermenting vegetables. I was the supervisor for the event, and although I couldn't listen to every word of the lecture, she sounded well informed. However, being a teacher myself, I was surprised to see her present only one recipe for quite a long class. When I teach, I cram five or six recipes into two hours, so I kept wondering, how could she get away with just one recipe? As I observed her, Sharon was my polar opposite: technical, methodical, and calculating. What's more, her recipe asked to prep only two ingredients (apples and squash). I scratched my head over this, but I took some of this squash home in a jar and let it sit for the prescribed three weeks. This was the embodiment of Slow Food. In fact it was so slow (and dull looking) that I almost forgot about it. But when I finally tasted it, this squash was just about the most divine substance my tongue had come across in quite some time. The raw squash softens, and its sweetness balances the acidity of the ferment. Try using it as a condiment with roasted meats, in pasta dishes or stir-fries, or straight out of the jar. Sharon later told me that this recipe was adapted from *Making Sauerkraut and Pickled Vegetables at Home*, by Klaus Kaufmann and Annelies Schoneck.

You'll need three widemouthed quart jars, with lids, for fermenting the vegetables, as well as some rocks to press down the vegetables. All—jars, lids, and rocks—will need to be sterilized.

1. To prepare the pumpkin-pie spice mix, toss together the allspice, cinnamon sticks, cloves, and nutmeg. Set aside.

2. To make the fermented squash, peel the squash with a peeler or a knife. Cut the squash open and scoop out the seeds. Reserve the seeds and peels. Set the cut squash aside in a covered bowl.

3. To make the brine, combine the squash seeds and peels with 1 gallon water, the pumpkin-pie spice mix, and 8 tablespoons salt. (I wouldn't use this much salt normally, but since we're using apples, which are sweet, we need to make sure there is plenty of salt or the fermentation may not go properly.) Bring to a boil, and let boil for 30 minutes. Strain out the solids and let cool to room temperature.

4. Sterilize the jars, bands, lids, and rocks in a small saucepan by boiling them for 4 minutes. Drain the water and let them cool until they are needed.

5. Slice the squash very thinly, using the narrow slicing blade on a food processor or a very sharp knife. If the squash slices are thicker than ¼ inch they will be dense and challenging to chew.

6. When the brine has come to room temperature, coarsely chop the onions, and peel, core, and coarsely chop the apples.

7. Start filling the jars with sliced squash, alternating with small handfuls of onion and apple. Press down to compress the vegetables and eliminate any spaces between them (without mushing the apples).

8. Stop filling the jars when the vegetables are 2 to 3 inches from the top. Lay a few bay leaves on top of the vegetables. Lay one or two rocks on top of the leaves and ladle the brine in, leaving at least 2 inches of headspace between the top of the brine and the rim of the jar. Screw the lids on the jars.

9. Let the kimchi ferment, with the lid on, at room temperature for 3 days (it should bubble), then move it to the refrigerator where it will continue to ferment for about 2 weeks. After this, the fermentation slows down. It will keep for up to a year in the refrigerator.

ABOUT THE AUTHOR

Didi Emmons began cooking omelets when she was ten and had her own catering business by the age of fourteen. She earned a BS in food-service management at NYU and moved to Boston, working first for food writer Steven Raichlen in Boston. Emmons worked as a stagiaire to receive her Grande Diplôme from La Varenne (cooking school) in Paris and then returned to work in Boston kitchens. She opened and ran four successful restaurants over the next thirteen years.

She has written two cookbooks: Vegetarian Planet, which was nominated for a James Beard Award, and Entertaining for a Veggie Planet, which won an IACP Cookbook Award (formerly the Julia Child Cookbook Award) in the healthy-cooking category.

Emmons subsequently opened Haley House Bakery Café, a nonprofit café in Roxbury, whose staff are people transitioning from homelessness and incarceration. She has since begun a program at Haley House Bakery Café called "Take Back the Kitchen," teaching Roxbury and Dorchester residents how to eat and cook healthfully. Emmons also serves as a trans-fat consultant for the Boston Public Health Commission, as well as a food consultant for the Boston Public School food service.

ABOUT EVA

Forty-two years ago, in South Dartmouth, Massachusetts, **Eva Sommaripa** began growing herbs and greens for her family. A few years later her garden evolved into a bucolic 2-acre organic farm. With the help of a skilled crew, she grows over 200 varieties of herbs, greens, flowers, and wild edibles that are sought by Boston's top chefs. She now sells to restaurants around New England and New York, as well as Whole Foods. She is an authority on herbs and greens and is often quoted in newspapers and magazines.

INDEX